T0398596

Mallephana Rabba

Perspectives on Linguistics and Ancient Languages

15

Perspectives on Linguistics and Ancient Languages (PLAL) contains peer-reviewed essays, monographs, and reference works. It focuses on the theory and practice of ancient-language research and lexicography that is informed by modern linguistics.

Mallephana Rabba

Aramaic Studies in Honor of Edward M. Cook

Edited by

Stephen M. Coleman

Andrew D. Gross

Andrew W. Litke

2023

Gorgias Press LLC, 954 River Road, Piscataway, NJ, 08854, USA

www.gorgiaspress.com

2023

ISBN **ISSN 2165-2600**

Hardback 978-1-4632-4583-2
eBook 978-1-4632-4584-9

Cover: detail of British Library Add MS 26878, fol. 147r.
Used with permission of the British Library.

Library of Congress Cataloging-in-Publication Data

A Cataloging-in-Publication Record is available at the Library of Congress.

Printed in the United States of America

TABLE OF CONTENTS

Introduction

It is our joy to honor Edward M. Cook, Ordinary Professor of Semitic and Egyptian Languages and Literatures at The Catholic University of America with this Festschrift. Cook has been a leading figure in the field of Aramaic studies for decades, and the range of his interests is exemplified by the breadth and depth of this volume. It includes essays on dialects from the earliest inscriptions to the modern day, and it features lexical, linguistic, and literary analyses. Such is the vibrant and far-reaching field of Aramaic studies, and such are the contributions of our honoree.

The first section of the volume focuses on inscriptional and epigraphical material. William Fullilove explores the relationship between definiteness and grammatical state in the earliest Aramaic documents and demonstrates that they already show a correlation in these texts, and more specifically, the emphatic state of a noun in these texts indicates the identifiability of the noun. Andrew D. Gross utilizes conceptual metaphor theory to investigate the use of metaphors in Aramaic legal documents. He traces the persistence of certain metaphors of emotion and metaphors of cleaning from the Akkadian cuneiform record of the second millennium BCE to the Middle Ages. These metaphors show different degrees of continuity and change in the legal tradition, and they show how scribes understood legal concepts.

The second section of the volume contains studies on the biblical book of Daniel and texts from the Judean Desert. Daniel E. Carver addresses the visionary formula חזה הוית 'I was watching', categorizing it as a participial periphrastic construction whose situation aspect is an unbounded (without temporal boundaries), ongoing activity. When this construction is followed by עד and an adverbial clause, it becomes a bounded activity (with temporal boundaries), which impacts the temporal interpretation of the verbs. Tarsee Li refines and expands his earlier (2009) analysis of the prefix conjugation in Daniel by incorporating a more complete description of the conjugation's diachronic development and the grammaticalization of its functions. Stephen M. Coleman revisits the meaning of עדנא in Daniel 2.8, which is usually interpreted as an example of the metaphor TIME IS MONEY. Utilizing cognitive methodologies and a diachronic survey of the noun, Coleman argues that in the verse under consideration, עדנא should be understood as a discrete, bounded moment best translated as 'the time', which reflects the power dynamics between Nebuchadnezzar and his diviners.

Martin G. Abegg, Jr. analyzes a subset of reciprocal and distributive expressions in the Hebrew Qumran Scrolls. After surveying the attested expressions and their syntax, he applies his findings to a particularly difficult passage in 1QS 6.2 and notes that the distribution of these constructions evidences the communal focus of certain sectarian compositions. Aaron Koller envisages the possibility of reconstructing lost books from the Persian and Hellenistic periods that have not survived in the Bible or at Qumran. As a test case, he investigates stories that circulated following Nabonidus' desert sojourn. He unravels the many traditions, some of which survive in 4Q242 and Daniel 4, and traces their development. Peter Y. Lee surveys the interpretations of 4Q246, the so-called 'Son of God' text. He categorizes the interpretations as either negative or positive, and he notes potential areas of future research. Finally, Michael Owen Wise presents a new study of Mur 42, including a description of the papyrus, paleography, text, translation, and philological commentary.

The third section of the volume contains studies on Aramaic translations of scripture, both Jewish and Christian. Christian M. M. Brady discusses the image of God treading an enemy as one would tread grapes in a wine press in Lamentations 1.15, Isaiah 63.3, and Joel 3.13. Despite the related image, Brady argues that the targumists followed the contours of their sources, and that there is no discernible influence between them. Stephen A.

Kaufman presents select notes on *aleph* initial words as they are presented in the Comprehensive Aramaic Lexicon project, with particular attention to the targumic lexicon. Andrew W. Litke analyzes three features in Targum Song of Songs and other Late Jewish Literary Aramaic texts that have been referred to as archaisms, namely the *he-* preformative of the causative stem, historic שׂ, and the third feminine singular pronominal suffix *-ahā* on nouns. After a diachronic analysis, he argues that the first is a root-specific, occasional variant with ties to the Biblical Aramaic lexicon; the second follows Hebrew spelling conventions; and the third is a modeling and expansion of the same form in Onqelos and Jonathan.

Jerome A. Lund discusses translation features in the Harqlean version of 1 Peter. He analyzes the translation of Greek vocabulary, grammatical categories, and syntax, before closing with a discussion of the theological translation with ܡܠܬܐ 'word' when referring to Jesus. Lund concludes that this version of 1 Peter is a 'source-oriented translation', though it disallows certain Greek features and reflects the Syriac of its time. Alexandra Lupu analyzes the Syriac D stem in the Peshitta. She argues that the factitive and pluractional meanings of the Syriac D stem are semantically-conditioned manifestations of a single, overarching function, which is to raise the transitivity of the basic verb. Lupu then applies her findings to the G and D forms of the root *knš*, 'to gather'.

The fourth section contains studies of poetic and religious texts from three different religious traditions. Moshe J. Bernstein analyzes the Jewish piyyut *SYAP* #26 and argues that the poem's 'serial narrative' of challenges to Jews and their ancestors is held together by the careful use of doublets and the way the poem binds itself to the audience. Though the content of the poem is not focused on the Purim narrative, he offers three suggestions for locating the poem in a Purim liturgical context. Laura S. Lieber analyzes three Samaritan Aramaic poems from Late Antiquity: the piyyutim Amram Dare #21 and Marqe #17 and a poem from *Tibat Marqe* §71. Though the piyyutim and the poetry from *Tibat Marqe* have different forms and functions, she notes areas of poetic convergence in the Samaritan tradition and observes comparands with contemporaneous Jewish and Christian liturgical poetry. Matthew Morgenstern shows that many concepts in classical Mandaean literature are attested in much earlier epigraphic sources, and further, parts of the liturgy are paralleled by magical texts from the corpus. Morgenstern then analyzes CP 15 and its many parallels in the epigraphic magic corpus, and he argues that it is an apotropaic amulet formula incorporated into the liturgy as a prayer of protection prior to baptism.

We are pleased to close this Festschrift of studies on Aramaic language and literature with a new text written in Cook's honor, a poem by Shawqi N. Talia in his native Northeast Neo-Aramaic dialect of the Chaldean Catholic Christians of Tel Kape on the Plain of Nineveh. It is a fitting conclusion that celebrates Cook in his seventieth year, his contributions, and his character, while at the same time exhibiting the enduring and vibrant legacy of the Aramaic language.

Abbreviations

Bibliographical Abbreviations

AB — Anchor Bible

ADAB — Joseph Naveh and Shaul Shaked, *Aramaic Documents from Ancient Bactria (Fourth Century BCE)*, London, 2012

AfO — *Archiv für Orientforschung*

AfOB — Archiv für Orientforschung: Beiheft

AGJU — Arbeiten zur Geschichte des antiken Judentums und des Urchristentums

AHw — Wolfram von Soden, *Akkadisches Handwörterbuch*. 3 vols., Wiesbaden, 1965–1981

AIOA — Stephen A. Kaufman, *The Akkadian Influences on Aramaic*, Chicago, 1974

AION — *Annali dell'Istituto Orientale di Napoli*

AKM — Abhandlungen für die Kunde des Morgenlandes

AOAT — Alter Orient und Altes Testament

AOS — American Oriental Series

ArOr — *Archiv Orientální*

AS — *Aramaic Studies*

AS — Assyriological Studies

ATTM — Klaus Beyer, *Die aramäischen Texten vom Toten Meer*, Göttingen, 1984–2004

BarBahlul — Rubens Duval, *Lexicon Syriacum auctore Hassano bar Bahlule*, Paris, 1888–1901

BASOR — *Bulletin of the American Schools of Oriental Research*

BBR — *Bulletin for Biblical Research*

BDAG — Walter Bauer, Frederick W. Danker, William F. Arndt, and F. Wilbur Gingrich, *Greek-English Lexicon of the*

	New Testament and Other Early Christian Literature, 3rd edn. Chicago, 2000
Bib	*Biblica*
BibOr	Biblica et Orientalia
BJS	Brown Judaic Studies
BJSUCSD	Biblical and Judaic Studies from the University of California, San Diego
BR	*Bible Review*
BRLJ	Brill Reference Library of Judaism
CBQ	*Catholic Biblical Quarterly*
BZAW	Beihefte zur Zeitschrift für die alttestamentliche Wissenschaft
CAD	*The Assyrian Dictionary of the Oriental Institution of the University of Chicago*, 20 vols., Chicago, 1956–2010
CAL	Comprehensive Aramaic Lexicon, http://cal.huc.edu
CDOG	Colloquien der Deutschen Orient-Gesellschaft
CHANE	Culture and History of the Ancient Near East
Ch-W	Jacob Levy, *Chaldäisches Wörterbuch über die Targumim und einen grossen Theil des rabbinischen Schriftthums,* Leipzig, 1867–1867
CSG	Theodor Nöldeke, *Compendious Syriac Grammar,* trans. James A. Chrichton, London, 1904
DJA	Michael Sokoloff, *A Dictionary of Judean Aramaic*, Ramat-Gan, 2003
DJBA	Michael Sokoloff, *A Dictionary of Jewish Babylonian Aramaic,* Baltimore and Ramat-Gan, 2002
DJPA	Michael Sokoloff, *A Dictionary of Jewish Palestinian Aramaic,* 2nd edn., Baltimore and Ramat-Gan, 2002
DJD	Discoveries in the Judaean Desert
DQA	Edward M. Cook, *Dictionary of Qumran Aramaic*, Winona Lake, IN, 2014
DSA	Abraham Tal, *A Dictionary of Samaritan Aramaic*, 2 vols., Leiden, 2000
DSD	*Dead Sea Discoveries*
DSSDL	Dead Sea Scrolls Digital Library, http://www.deadseascrolls.org.il
FOTL	Forms of the Old Testament Literature
FT	Fragment Targum

FTP	Fragment Targum, Paris 110 manuscript
HALOT	Ludwig Koehler and Walter Baumgartner, *The Hebrew and Aramaic Lexicon of the Old Testament*, Leiden, 1994–2000
HAR	*Hebrew Annual Review*
HdO	Handbuch der Orientalistik
HSAO	Heidelberger Studien zum Alten Orient
HS	*Hebrew Studies*
HSS	Harvard Semitic Studies
JA	*Journal Asiatique*
JAJ	*Journal of Ancient Judaism*
JAJSup	Journal of Ancient Judaism Supplements
JANES	*Journal of the Ancient Near Eastern Society*
JAOS	*Journal of the American Oriental Society*
JBL	*Journal of Biblical Literature*
JBS	Jerusalem Biblical Studies
JCS	*Journal of Cuneiform Studies*
JDS	Judean Desert Studies
JHebS	*Journal of Hebrew Scriptures*
JJS	*Journal of Jewish Studies*
JNES	*Journal of Near Eastern Studies*
JQR	*Jewish Quarterly Review*
JSem	*Journal of Semitics*
JSJSup	Supplements to the Journal for the Study of Judaism
JSNT	*Journal for the Study of the New Testament*
JSNTSup	Journal for the Study of the New Testament. Supplement Series
JSOT	*Journal for the Study of the Old Testament*
JSOTSup	Journal for the Study of the Old Testament. Supplement Series
JSP	*Journal for the Study of the Pseudepigrapha*
JSPSup	Journal for the Study of the Pseudepigrapha. Supplement Series
JSS	*Journal of Semitic Studies*
KAI	Herbert Donner and Wolfgang Röllig, *Kanaanäische und aramäische Inschriften*, 5th edn., 2002

LBA	Ernst Vogt, *A Lexicon of Biblical Aramaic: Clarified by Ancient Documents*, trans. and rev. by Joseph A. Fitzmyer, Rome, 2011
LNTS	The Library of New Testament Studies
LSAWS	Linguistic Studies in Ancient West Semitic
MT	Masoretic Text
NEA	*Near Eastern Archaeology*
Neof	Neofiti
NTS	*New Testament Studies*
NTTS	New Testament Tools and Studies
Nvar	Neofiti variant
OLA	Orientalia Lovaniensia Analecta
Or	*Orientalia*
OTL	Old Testament Library
PAAJR	*Proceedings of the American Academy of Jewish Research*
PAM	Palestine Archaeological Museum
PEQ	*Palestine Exploration Quarterly*
PLO	Porta Linguarum Orientalium
PsJ	Targum Pseudo-Jonathan
PT	Palestinian Targum
PTSDSSP	Princeton Theological Seminary Dead Sea Scrolls Project
RB	*Revue biblique*
REJ	*Revue des études juives*
RevQ	*Revue de Qumran*
SAIS	Studies in the Aramaic Interpretation of Scripture
SBLMS	Society of Biblical Literature Monograph Series
SBS	Stuttgarter Bibelstudien
STAS	Supplements to Aramaic Studies
STDJ	Studies on the Texts of the Desert of Judah
SYAP	Joseph Yahalom and Michael Sokoloff, *Jewish Palestinian Aramaic Poetry from Late Antiquity* (in Hebrew), Jerusalem, 1999
TAD	Bezalel Porten and Ada Yardeni, *Textbook of Aramaic Documents from Ancient Egypt*, 4 vols., Jerusalem, 1986–1999
TBN	Themes in Biblical Narrative

TDOT	G. Johannes Botterweck, Helmer Ringgren, Heinz-Josef Fabry, *Theological Dictionary of the Old Testament*, trans. John T. Willis et al., 16 vols., Grand Rapids, 1974–2021
Tg	Targum
TgJon	Targum Jonathan
TgOnq	Targum Onqelos
TLZ	*Theologische Literaturzeitung*
TSAJ	Texts and Studies in Ancient Judaism
TSO	Texte und Studien zur Orientalistik
VAB	Vorderasiatische Bibliothek
VT	*Vetus Testamentum*
VTSup	Supplements to Vetus Testamentum
WAW	Writings from the Ancient World
WBC	Word Biblical Commentary
WUNT	Wissenschaftliche Untersuchungen zum Neuen Testament
ZRGG	*Zeitschrift für Religions- und Geistesgeschichte*

LANGUAGES AND DIALECTS

BA	Biblical Aramaic
BH	Biblical Hebrew
CPA	Christian Palestinian Aramaic
Gal	Galilean
Heb.	Hebrew
IA	Imperial Aramaic
JBA	Jewish Babylonian Aramaic
JBAg	Jewish Babylonian Aramaic gaonic period
JLA	Jewish Literary Aramaic
JLAtg	Jewish Literary Aramaic targum: i.e., Targums Onkelos and Jonathan
JPA	Jewish Palestinian Aramaic
JPAtg	Jewish Palestinian Aramaic targum
LJLA	Late Jewish Literary Aramaic
OA	Old Aramaic
QA	Qumran Aramaic
RH^2	Rabbinic Hebrew of the Amoraim
Syr	Syriac

OTHER ABBREVIATIONS AND SYMBOLS

abs.	absolute
adj.	adjective
adv.	adverb
CL	cognitive linguistics
col.	column
conj.	conjunction
div.	divinity
emph.	emphatic
f	feminine
inte.	interjection
m	masculine
mng.	meaning
mss.	manuscripts
n/N	noun
NP	noun phrase
obj.	object
p/pl.	plural
perf.	perfect
PP	prepositional phrase
pron.	pronoun
s	singular
s.v.	*sub verbum*
v.	verse
var.	variant
vb.	verb
v.n.C	verbal noun C-stem
†	*hapax legomenon*

EDWARD M. COOK: AN APPRECIATION

ANDREW W. LITKE

The title 'scholar' is not tied to a job or university appointment. Rather, it is tied to the ways that one masters the craft of their field, contributes to scholarship, and shapes the direction of the academic conversation. It is in these more significant ways that Ed Cook, the honoree of this Festschrift, has time and again proven himself to be a true scholar, though he was without a formal academic appointment for roughly twenty years. It is a testament to his resilience, his love of Aramaic and Hebrew, and his relentless drive to write 'just one more' piece that he continued to persevere, and much to all our benefit. Finally, in 2008 he received the well-deserved appointment as an Associate Professor in the Department of Semitic and Egyptian Languages and Literatures at The Catholic University of America, where he would eventually earn the title of Ordinary Professor. His expertise as an Aramaist and Hebraist was well-established by that point, but it was his exceptional teaching abilities along with his warmth, generosity of spirit, and good humor that endeared him to the students and faculty of the department.

Ed's contribution to the field of Aramaic studies is vast, where he has greatly impacted our understanding of different dialects and corpora through in-depth studies of language and texts, as well as his lexical works and many translations, where his careful attention to semantic and syntactic nuances coincide with a profound literary sensibility.

In the field of targum studies, Ed's dissertation under the direction of Stanislav Segert at UCLA, *Rewriting the Bible: The Text and Language of the Pseudo-Jonathan Targum* (1986), remains the definitive presentation of Pseudo-Jonathan's language. Since then, his conclusions have helped guide the conversation about the complicated linguistic makeup of all the late targumim. Thus began an enduring interest in the targumim that has resulted in numerous articles, *A Glossary of Targum Onkelos (*2008*),* and the first English translation of Targum Psalms (2001).

Shortly after finishing his doctorate, he moved to Cincinnati to work with the Comprehensive Aramaic Lexicon Project at the Hebrew Union College-Jewish Institute of Religion. While there, Ed had a front row seat to watch the tectonic plates of Biblical and Near Eastern studies shift when his friend and future collaborator, Martin G. Abegg, Jr., used his computer skills to stitch together the Dead Sea Scrolls texts from the official concordance. This 'liberation' of the Scrolls in 1991 turned what had been a trickle of publications on the scrolls into a firehose, and Ed quickly established himself as a leading expert on Qumran, the Scrolls, and their languages. He published an early, influential article on Qumran Aramaic that set it within its dialectal setting (1992) and followed this up with a more systematic presentation of the language (1998). Amidst many other studies, he collaborated with Abegg and Michael Owen Wise to publish an English translation of the Scrolls, *The Dead Sea Scrolls: A New Translation* (1996). This popular translation was itself translated into several other languages, and in 2005, it was significantly revised and expanded into a second edition and remains a standard translation of the Scrolls for students and scholars alike. Other significant achievements include another collaboration with Abegg (and James E. Bowley) on a multi-volume concordance of all the Scrolls (2003–2015) as well as Ed's *Dictionary of Qumran Aramaic* (2015). All these studies have a special place on the shelves of Aramaists and Qumran scholars.

While much of Ed's Aramaic scholarly output has focused on the targumim and the Dead Sea Scrolls, his interest and fluency in all things Aramaic is much broader than that. He has maintained an interest in inscriptions and Biblical Aramaic (with a grammar published in 2022), the Semitic background of the New Testament, Peshitta, incantation bowls, and he has recently turned his attention to the influence of Aramaic on Mishnaic Hebrew. Throughout all of this, he displays a deep love and concern for modern Aramaic and its speakers.

In addition to traditional scholarly outlets, Ed's career has spanned a unique time in developing technologies, from the growth of the internet to the development of biblical software programs. His contributions through these new technologies have not only informed us, but they have entertained us as well. The Comprehensive Aramaic Lexicon Project, where Ed spent a decade, is an online resource that has made tagged Aramaic texts and lexical analyses available to students and scholars around the world. His language work with Accordance Bible Software has likewise contributed to countless research projects. And then there is his blog, 'Ralph the Sacred River', which came with the rise of the biblioblogs. Through 'Ralph', Ed jotted down ideas, probed social and theological issues, dabbled in creative writing, surveyed popular culture, shared philological and linguistic insights on Hebrew and Aramaic, engaged with other scholars on the hottest issue of the day, and of course, discussed Bob Dylan. There is probably no other blog that can boast being referenced in *The New York Times* and *Revue de Qumran*. While his activity on the blog began to wane when he joined Catholic University, he is sure to make at least one appearance a year to hand out his 'Ralphie' awards to the best books, songs, albums, and more – many of which turn up in his classroom discussions in one way or another.

When thinking about the classroom experience with Ed, I am reminded that some people are able to learn how to be better teachers, and others have an innate ability to teach, explain, and guide with both deep understanding and good humor. Ed is the latter. In each class, he walks students through the inductive labyrinth of philological growth. Grounded in linguistic principles, he takes you through the intricacies and nuances of individual words and expands to set each one in their phrases and clauses, and all the while, he brings you to a more profound understanding of the text under discussion. Throughout each class, humor is never far from the surface, and he regularly introduces his students to bands, books, and movies that are auditioning for a 'Ralphie' at the end of the year. And at the end of the semester, more than one student has remarked that he has the unique ability to craft an assessment in which the students learn *while* taking the test.

Ed wrote an appreciation for the Festschrift of his own Doktorvater (1990), and in it he wrote these words:

> In person, Segert is the most modest of men. He is not capable of patting himself on the back or of stabbing anyone else in theirs. In class, he does not intimidate, does not criticize; he is able to turn even the most ill-conceived comment or question into an opportunity for learning.

Such words could just as appropriately be said about Ed. There is a depth of humanity and concern that he brings to his interactions with students and colleagues, and just as much as his scholarly acumen, these interactions have had an enduring significance. To give but one example, after my first year at Catholic University, a year in which I took five courses with Ed, I remember asking to have a meeting with him. Since he was well aware of my abilities at that point and the many gaps in my knowledge, I asked if he would mind letting me know what I should work on during the summer so that I would be better prepared for the next year. His response was something along the lines of, 'Take a break. Don't overdo it or burn out. You're doing okay'. Of course, there were plenty of things that I could have worked on during that summer, but Ed knew what this fearful student brimming with imposter syndrome sitting in front of him needed to hear: that his advisor believed in him and that he was doing okay. It meant even more knowing that it came from a man who had lived the life and understood the struggles of the world of academia.

As we celebrate the life and work of Ed Cook with this Festschrift and look forward to what he has in store for us in the future, I close with one of his translations, a selection from the 'Testament of Qohath' (2005):

> [May you receive the blessing of] the greatest of all gods forever, and may he shine his light upon you, and tell you his great name so that you may truly know him. For he is the God

of the ages, and Lord of everything that is done, and ruler of all people, doing with them whatever he pleases. May he give you happiness, and to your descendants joy, in the generations of truth forever.

PUBLICATIONS OF EDWARD M. COOK

BOOKS

Biblical Aramaic and Related Dialects: An Introduction (Cambridge, UK: Cambridge University Press, 2022).

Co-author with Martin G. Abegg, Jr. and James E. Bowley, *The Dead Sea Scrolls Concordance*, (3 vols, Leiden/Boston: Brill, 2003–2016).

Dictionary of Qumran Aramaic (Winona Lake, IN: Eisenbrauns, 2015).

Numbers: The Syriac Peshitta Bible with English Translation (Antioch Bible, 4, Piscataway, NJ: Gorgias, 2015).

A Glossary of Targum Onkelos (SAIS, 6, Leiden: Brill, 2008).

Co-Author: with Michael O. Wise and Martin G. Abegg, Jr., *The Dead Sea Scrolls: A New Translation* (revised, expanded second edition, New York: Harper Collins San Francisco; Canada: Hodder & Stoughton, 2005) [First edition, 1996].

- French Translation: Michael Wise, Martin Abegg, Jr., et Edward Cook, *Les manuscrits de la mer morte*. Traduit par Fortunato Israel (Paris: Plon, 2001).
- German Translation: Michael Wise, Martin Abegg, Jr., und Edward Cook, *Die Schriftrollen von Qumran: Übersetzung und Kommentar mit bisher unveröffentlichten Texte* (with revisions and additional material, Munich: Pattloch, 1997).

The Psalms Targum: A New Translation. The Newsletter for Targumic and Cognate Studies, The University of Wyoming/The International Organization for Targum Study. (http://targum.info/targumic-texts/targum-psalms/) [Web publication, 2001].

Solving the Mysteries of the Dead Sea Scrolls: New Light on the Bible (Grand Rapids, MI: Zondervan Books; UK: Paternoster Books, 1994).

Editor: *Sopher Mahir: Northwest Semitic Studies Presented to Stanislav Segert* (Winona Lake, IN: Eisenbrauns, 1990). [Includes 'Stanislav Segert: An Appreciation', pp. 7–10; this Festschrift was also published as *Maarav* 5/6 (1990)].

Word Order in the Aramaic of Daniel (Afroasiatic Linguistics, 9/3, Malibu: Undena, 1986).

Rewriting the Bible: The Text and Language of the Pseudo-Jonathan Targum (PhD Diss., University of California, Los Angeles, 1986).

Books (collaborator)

'Key-Word in Context Concordance to Targum Sheni to the Book of Esther', in Bernard Grossfeld, *The Targum Sheni to the Book of Esther: A Critical Edition Based on Ms. Sassoon 282 with Critical Apparatus* (New York: Sepher-Hermon Press, 1994) pp. 119–195.

A Key-Word-in-Context Concordance to Targum Neofiti: A Guide to the Complete Palestinian Aramaic Text of the Torah, by Stephen A. Kaufman and Michael Sokoloff, with the assistance of Edward M. Cook (Baltimore: Johns Hopkins, 1993).

An Aramaic Bibliography, Part I: *Old, Official, and Biblical Aramaic*, by Joseph A. Fitzmyer and Stephen A. Kaufman, with the collaboration of Stephan F. Bennett and Edward M. Cook (Baltimore: Johns Hopkins Univ. Press, 1991).

Articles and Book Chapters

'Alternating Constructions with Biblical Hebrew שָׁרַץ "to swarm"', for memorial volume for Michael Patrick O'Connor (ed. John Huehnergard, Mark Leson, and Edward Greenstein; Eisenbrauns, accepted for publication).

'Another Look at the Curse in Sefire I A 24', *AS* 20 (2022), pp. 3–8.

'The Aramaic Influence on Mishnaic Hebrew: Borrowing or Interference?', in Steven E. Fassberg (ed.), *Hebrew Texts and Language of the Second Temple Period: Proceedings of an Eighth*

Symposium on the Hebrew of the Dead Sea Scrolls and Ben Sira (STDJ, 134, Leiden: Brill, 2021), pp. 25–36.

With Daniel E. Carver, 'Situation Aspect, (Un)boundedness and the Participial Periphrastic Construction in Biblical Hebrew', *JSS* 66 (2021), pp. 1–15.

'On Some Supposed Archaisms in Mishnaic Hebrew', *Maarav* 22 (2018), pp. 11–20.

Language Contact and the Genesis of Mishnaic Hebrew (The Edward Ullendorff Lectures in Semitic Philology, Fourth Lecture, DOI 10.17863/CAM.9630) [https://doi.org/10.17863/CAM.9630].

'Qumran Aramaic, Corpus Linguistics, and Aramaic Retroversion', *DSD* 21 (2014), pp. 356–384.

'The Balaam Text from Tell Deir ʿAllā: A New Translation and Introduction', in Richard Bauckham, James R. Davila, and Alexander Panayatov (eds.), *Old Testament Pseudepigrapha: More Noncanonical Scriptures* (Grand Rapids, MI: Eerdmans, 2013) pp. 236–243.

'4Q541 Fragment 24 Revisited', in Marilyn J. Lundberg, Steven Fine, and Wayne T. Pitard (eds.), *Puzzling Out the Past: Studies in Northwest Semitic Languages and Literatures in Honor of Bruce Zuckerman* (CHANE, 55, Leiden: Brill, 2012) pp. 13–17.

'The Interpretation of the Bible in the Targums', in Matthias Henze (ed.), *A Companion to Biblical Interpretation in Early Judaism* (Grand Rapids, MI: Eerdmans, 2012) pp. 92–117.

'The Causative Internal Passive in Qumran Aramaic', *AS* 8 (2010), pp. 5–12.

'The "Kaufman Effect" in the Pseudo-Jonathan Targum', *AS* 4 (2006), pp. 123–132.

'The Forgery Indictments and BAR: Learning from Hindsight', *NEA* 68. 1–2 (2006), pp. 73–75.

Texts and translations for *The Dead Sea Scrolls Reader*, Volume 6: *Additional Genres and Unclassified Texts* (Leiden: Brill, 2005): '4QPrEsther ar' (pp. 6–12), 'New Jerusalem' (38–59), 'Symbolic Apocalypses' (75–81), 'Words of Michael' (131), 'Revelatory Texts' (136–153), '4QpapApocryphon ar' (329),

'4QDanSuz ar' (334), '4QProverbs ar' (334), 'XQOffering ar' (347).

'Stanislav Segert (1921–2005): In memoriam', SBL Forum, [http://www.sbl-site.org/Article.aspx?ArticleId=448]. [Web publication, October 2005].

'Covenantal Nomism in the Psalms Targum', in Stanley E. Porter and Jacqueline C.R. de Roo (eds.), *The Concept of the Covenant in the Second Temple Period* (JSJSup, 71, Leiden: Brill, 2003) pp. 203–220.

'Remarks on the Aramaic of the James Ossuary', *The Bible and Interpretation* [https://bibleinterp.arizona.edu/articles/Cook_remarks]. [Web publication, 2003].

'The Psalms Targum: Introduction to a New Translation, with Sample Texts', in Paul V.M. Flesher (ed.), *Targum and Scripture: Studies in Aramaic Translations and Interpretation in Memory of Ernest G. Clarke* (SAIS, 2, Leiden: Brill, 2002) pp. 185–201.

'What Did the Jews of Qumran Know about God and How Did They Know It? Revelation and God in the Dead Sea Scrolls', in Alan J. Avery-Peck, Jacob Neusner, and Bruce Chilton (eds.), *Judaism in Late Antiquity 5. The Judaism of Qumran: A Systemic Reading of the Dead Sea Scrolls*. Volume Two: *World View, Comparing Judaisms* (HdO Section 1 The Near and Middle East, 57, Leiden: Brill, 2001) pp. 3–22.

'The Aramaic of the Dead Sea Scrolls', in James C. VanderKam and Peter W. Flint (eds.), *The Dead Sea Scrolls After Fifty Years: A Comprehensive Assessment* (Leiden: Brill, 1998) pp. 1.359-378.

'A Thanksgiving for God's Help (4Q434 II–III)', in Mark Kiley et al. (eds.), *Prayer from Alexander to Constantine: A Critical Anthology* (London: Routledge, 1998) pp. 14–17.

'Our Translated Tobit', in Kevin J. Cathcart and Michael Maher (eds.), *Targumic and Cognate Studies: Essays in Honour of Martin McNamara* (JSOTSup, 230, Sheffield: Sheffield Academic Press, 1996) pp. 153–162.

'What Was Qumran? A Ritual Purification Center', *BARev* 22.6 (November/December 1996), pp. 39, 48–51, 73–75.

'4Q246', *BBR* 5 (1995), pp. 43–66.

'On the Linguistic Dating of the Phoenician Ahiram Inscription (KAI 1)', *JNES* 53 (1994), pp. 33–36.

'A New Perspective on the Language of Onqelos and Jonathan', in Derek R.G. Beattie and Martin J. McNamara (eds.), *The Aramaic Bible: Targums in their Historical Context* (JSOTSup, 166, Sheffield: JSOT Press, 1994) pp. 142–156.

'1 Samuel xx 26–xxi 5 According to 4QSam^{b}', *VT* 44 (1994), pp. 442–454.

'Remarks on the Testament of Kohath from Qumran Cave 4', *JJS* 44 (1993), pp. 204–219.

'The Latest on MMT: Strugnell vs. Qimron' [Report on Notre Dame Dead Sea Scroll Symposium], *BARev* 19.4 (July/August 1993), pp. 68–69.

'An Aramaic Incantation Bowl from Khafaje', *BASOR* 285 (1992), pp. 79-81.

'Qumran Aramaic and Aramaic Dialectology', in Takamitsu Muraoka (ed.), *Studies in Qumran Aramaic* (Abr-Nahrain Supplement, 3, Louvain: Peeters, 1992) pp. 1–21.

'The Orthography of Final Unstressed Long Vowels in Old and Imperial Aramaic', in Edward M. Cook (ed.), *Sopher Mahir: Northwest Semitic Studies Presented to Stanislav Segert* (= *Maarav* 5/6; Winona Lake, IN: Eisenbrauns, 1990) pp. 53–67.

'"In the Plain of the Wall" (Dan. 3:1)', *JBL* 108 (1989), pp. 115–116.

'Response to Dr Chaney', in *American Missions in Bicentennial Perspective* (South Pasadena, CA: William Carey Library, 1977), pp. 35–39.

ENCYCLOPEDIA ARTICLES

'God. V. Judaism. B. Hellenistic Judaism' and 'God, Names and Epithets. III. Judaism. A. Second Temple and Hellenistic Judaism', in *Encyclopedia of the Bible and Its Reception* (Berlin: De Gruyter, 2009-), cols. 10:398–399, 446–447.

'Hebraisms in the Targumim', in Geoffrey Khan (ed.), *Encyclopedia of Hebrew Language and Linguistics* (4 vols, Leiden; Boston: Brill, 2013) pp. 2:202–204.

'Aramaic', in John J. Collins and Daniel C. Harlow (eds.), *The Eerdmans Dictionary of Early Judaism* (Grand Rapids, MI: Eerdmans, 2010) pp. 360-364.

'Ahikar, Ahiqar' and 'Nabonidus, Prayer of', in Katharine D. Sakenfeld (ed.), *The New Interpreter's Dictionary of the Bible* (5 vols, Nashville, TN: Abingdon, 2006–2009) pp. 1:86–87 and 4:203–204.

'Aramaic Language and Literature', in Eric M. Meyers et al. (eds.), *The Oxford Encyclopedia of Archaeology in the Near East* (Oxford: Oxford University Press, 1997) pp. 1:178–184.

'Kue', 'Nezib', 'Nibshan', 'Nod', 'Ophir', 'Weights and Measures', in Geoffrey W. Bromiley (ed.), *The International Standard Bible Encyclopedia* (4 vols, Grand Rapids, MI: Eerdmans, 1979-1988) pp. 3:52, 532, 546, 607–608, and 4:1046–1055.

Book Reviews

Review of Frederick Mario Fales and Giulia Francesca Grassi, *L' aramaico antico: Storia, grammatica, testi commentati, con un'appendice paleografica di Ezio Attardo*, in *JSS* 64 (2019), pp. 297–300.

Review of Tarsee Li, *The Verbal System of the Aramaic of Daniel: An Explanation in the Context of Grammaticalization*, in *JSS* 57 (2012), pp. 424–426.

Review of Søren Holst, *Verbs and War Scroll: Studies in the Hebrew Verbal System & the Qumran War Scroll*, in *CBQ* 71 (2009), pp. 861–863.

Review of Ursula Schattner-Rieser, *L'araméen des manuscrits de la Mer Morte*: I. *Grammaire*, in *JSJ* 37 (2006), pp. 491–494.

Review of Michael Sokoloff, *A Dictionary of Judean Aramaic*, in *Maarav* 11 (2004), pp. 95–101.

Review of Peter W. Flint (ed.), *The Bible at Qumran: Text, Shape, and Interpretation*, in *CBQ* 64 (2002), pp. 190-191.

Review of Takamitsu Muraoka and John F. Elwolde (eds.), *Diggers at the Well: Proceedings of a Third International Symposium on the Hebrew of the Dead Sea Scrolls and Ben Sira*, in *CBQ* 64 (2002), pp. 196–197.

Review of Robert A. Kugler and Eileen M. Schuller (eds.), *The Dead Sea Scrolls at Fifty: Proceedings of the 1997 Society of*

Biblical Literature Qumran Section Meetings, in *CBQ* 63 (2001), pp. 175–177.

Review of Stanley E. Porter and Craig A. Evans (eds.), *The Scrolls and the Scriptures: Qumran Fifty Years After*, in *CBQ* 61 (1999), pp. 201–203.

Review of Loren T. Stuckenbruck, *The Book of Giants*, in *JAOS* 119 (1999), pp. 511–512.

Review of Yeshayahu Maori, תרגום הפשיטתא לתורה והפרשנות היהודית הקדומה [The Peshitta Version of the Pentateuch and Early Jewish Exegesis], in *HS* 40 (1999), pp. 298–300.

Review of Johann Maier, *Die Qumran-Essener: die Texte vom Toten Meer*, Band 1: *Die Texte der Höhlen 1–3 und 5–11*, in *CBQ* 60 (1998), pp. 124–125.

Review of Florentino García Martínez and Julio Trebolle Barrera, *People of the Dead Sea Scroll: Their Writings, Beliefs and Practices*, in *BARev* 23.2 (1997), pp. 62–63.

Review of John J. Collins, *The Scepter and the Star: The Messiahs of the Dead Sea Scrolls and other Ancient Literature*, in *CBQ* 58 (1996), pp. 506–508.

Review of Hartmut Stegemann, *Die Essener, Qumran, Johannes der Täufer, und Jesus*, in *DSD* 2 (1995), pp. 114–118.

Review of James C. VanderKam, *The Dead Sea Scrolls Today*, in *CBQ* 57 (1995), pp. 377–378.

Review of Elisha Qimron, ארמית מקראית, in *CBQ* 57 (1995), pp. 158–159.

Review of Steven E. Fassberg, *A Grammar of the Palestinian Targum Fragments from the Cairo Genizah*, in *CBQ* 55 (1993), pp. 755–756.

Review of Bruce K. Waltke and Michael O'Connor, *An Introduction to Biblical Hebrew Syntax*, in *CBQ* 54 (1992), pp. 338–339.

Review of Bernard Grossfeld, *The Aramaic Bible*, Vols. 6–9, in *CBQ* 53 (1991), pp. 102–105.

Review of Choon-Leong Seow, *A Grammar of Biblical Hebrew*, in *JAOS* 110 (1990), pp. 337–338.

Review of various authors, *The Aramaic Bible*, vols. 10-13, in *Critical Review of Books in Religion* 1990, pp. 3:343–348.

Review of Klaus Beyer, *The Aramaic Language: Its Distribution and Subdivisions*, in *JBL* 107 (1988), pp. 314–315.

Review of Omar Carena, *Il resto di Israele: Studio storico-comparativo delle iscrizioni reali assire e dei testi profetici sul tema del resto*, in *JBL* 107 (1988), pp. 121–122.

Review of David M. Golomb, *A Grammar of Targum Neofiti*, in *Maarav* 4 (1987), pp. 93–100.

'Maximally Conservative', review of Kenneth A. Kitchen, *The Bible in its World: The Bible and Archaeology Today*, in *Reformed Journal* 30.1 (January 1979), pp. 29-30.

'The Way Home', review of Richard J. Neuhaus, *Christian Faith and Public Policy: Thinking and Acting in the Courage of Uncertainty*, in *Reformed Journal* 28.1 (January 1978), pp. 28–29.

'The Gnostic Question', review of John Dart, *The Laughing Savior: The Discovery and Significance of the Nag Hammadi Gnostic Library*, in *Reformed Journal* 27.6 (June 1977), pp. 20-21.

Inscriptions and Epigraphic Material

THE ADVENT OF DEFINITENESS MARKING IN ARAMAIC

WILLIAM FULLILOVE

1. INTRODUCTION

Most interpreters have only an impressionistic approach to how the Aramaic language encodes the definiteness or indefiniteness of a noun phrase, an impression that can be refined with data. In 2014 work done under Dr. Cook's direction, I established that definiteness and state are categorically related in Qumran Aramaic (QA).[1] Even with the limited corpus that QA represents, one can conclude that the emphatic form[2] of the noun was used to indicate the definiteness of a noun phrase. Further, it is generally agreed that such a correlation existed in Imperial Aramaic (IA), which raises the question whether this connection was true from the earliest dialects of Aramaic (and only disappeared in Eastern dialects) or whether it was something peculiar to certain dialects such as QA. An analysis of Old Aramaic (OA) answers the question: the evidence available indicates that grammatical state and definiteness correlate in a statistically significant way in OA. More specifically, the emphatic

[1] William Fullilove, *Definiteness in Qumran Aramaic* (PhD Diss., The Catholic University of America, 2014).

[2] The term 'emphatic form' is used simply to avoid prejudging the analysis via the other common term 'determined state'.

state of the noun indicates the identifiability of that noun, a subset of the overall concept of definiteness. [3]

This analysis includes the following OA texts: the Asshur Ostracon,[4] the Bar-Rakib inscriptions from Zincirli,[5] the Kuttamuwa inscription from Zincirli,[6] the Tel Fakhariyeh bilingual inscription,[7] the Zakkur stele,[8] the Bukân stele,[9] the Sefire treaty texts,[10] and the Tel Dan inscription.[11] Unless otherwise noted, the text follows that of the Comprehensive Aramaic Lexicon, though other studies have been consulted as indicated.[12] All these texts

---

[3] Peter Bekins' excellent introductory handbook *Inscriptions from the World of the Bible: A Reader and Introduction to Old Northwest Semitic* (Peabody, MA: Hendrickson Academic, 2020) only came across my desk after the manuscript for this chapter had been submitted. Bekins has paid careful attention to issues of definiteness in other work, and he several times mentions observations about some of these texts that accord with the conclusions reached in this study.

[4] *KAI* 233; Herbert Donner and Wolfgang Röllig, *Kanaanäische und aramäische Inschriften* (Wiesbaden: Harrassowitz, 2002). *Editio princeps*: Mark Lidzbarski, *Altaramäische Urkunden aus Assur* (Wissenschaftliche Veröffentlichung der deutschen Orient-Gesellschaft, 38, Leipzig: Hinrichs, 1921) pp. 5–15.

[5] The individual inscriptions that were initially published separately are collected in *KAI* 216–221.

[6] Dennis Pardee, 'A New Aramaic Inscription from Zincirli', *BASOR* 356 (2009), pp. 51–71.

[7] Ali Abou-Assaf, Pierre Bordreuil, and Alan R. Millard, *La statue de Tell Fekherye et son inscription bilingue assyro-araméenne* (Paris: A.D.P.F, 1982).

[8] *KAI* 202. *Editio princeps*: H. Pognon, *Inscriptions sémitiques de la Syrie, de la Mésopotamie et de la région de Mossoul* (Paris: Imprimerie nationale, 1907) pp. 156–178, plates 9–10, 35–36.

[9] A. Lemaire, 'Une Inscription Araméenne du VIIIe S. av. J.-C. trouvée à Bukân (Azerbaïdjan Iranien)', *Studia Iranica* 27 (1998), pp. 15–30.

[10] *KAI* 222–224. *Editio princeps*: André Dupont-Sommer and Jean Starcky, 'Les inscriptions araméennes de Sfiré (stèles I et II)', in *Mémoires présentés par divers savants à l'Académie des Inscriptions et Belles-Lettres de l'Institut de France*, tome 11, première partie (Paris: Imprimerie nationale, 1958) pp. 197–348.

[11] Avraham Biran and Joseph Naveh, 'The Tel Dan Inscription: A New Fragment', *IEJ* 45 (1995), pp. 1–21.

[12] Stephen A. Kaufman (Gen. Ed.), *The Comprehensive Aramaic Lexicon* (http://cal.huc.edu/). Accessed between 11/1/2019 and 8/15/2020.

clearly belong to OA and employ the emphatic state as a grammatical option. Deir ʿAlla is therefore excluded as not being clearly OA,[13] and Samalian is likewise excluded since it does not employ the emphatic state.[14] Texts must be long enough and sufficiently well-preserved to allow for semantic analysis. Shorter and more broken texts, like the Melqart stele, have therefore been excluded. This study takes a conservative approach to the dataset, only including noun phrases if they are clear and have the necessary context to make a judgment on their semantic definiteness. If the ending of the noun is restored, even with high confidence – for example: [א]נצב in line 1 of the Bukân Stele is almost certainly in the emphatic state – it is excluded from the data set because the ending is restored. Similarly, חרן (Sefire 2.B.12) [15] is almost certainly the first mention of this noun in the text, which would typically make it semantically indefinite; however, it is the only word on the line, depriving the reader of sufficient context to make a semantic judgment of its definiteness, and is therefore excluded from the data set.

Grammatical state in Aramaic is a morphological category, encoded in the language and typically evident in the writing system. Gzella notes that the OA noun can be characterized

---

[13] Deir ʿAlla is debatably Aramaic, Aramaic with Canaanite forms, or some other dialect or language. Given the contention over this issue, it is excluded from this data set.

[14] As is widely noted, Samalian does not have any emphatic ending, even in clear semantic definites. Its dialectal relationship with Kuttamuwa will be discussed below. Kuttamuwa matches Samalian in this isogloss (see Pardee, 'A New Aramaic Inscription from Zincirli', pp. 52–53.), but this isogloss only impacts Samalian and Kuttamuwa. Should Kuttamuwa be excluded from the data set on those grounds, the conclusions reached here would only be incrementally stronger. On the question of multiple OA dialects, see Jonas C. Greenfield, 'The Dialects of Early Aramaic', *JNES* 37 (1978), pp. 93–99.

[15] References here and in later lists indicate the line number of the inscription in which the noun is used. A simple number is used in a single column inscription. Multiple inscriptions are indicated by an initial Roman number, and faces or columns are indicated by a letter. So, for instance, Sefire 1.C.19 is the first Sefire inscription, side C, line 19.

clearly as being in the absolute, construct, or emphatic state via its ending consonants:[16]

Singular Forms	Masculine	Feminine
Absolute	---	-ה
Construct	---	-ת
Emphatic	-א	-תא
Plural Forms	Masculine	Feminine
Absolute	-ן	-ן
Construct	-י	-ת
Emphatic	-יא	-תא

The state of any given noun can thus be determined easily, so long as the text is legibly preserved.

Definiteness, on the other hand, is a semantic category. Linguists have long debated the nature of definiteness, and this study will adopt Christopher Lyons' summary approach that defines a noun phrase as definite if it is either identifiable or unique, two categories that overlap but which are not identical.[17]

This approach provides clarity but runs the risk of oversimplification, as semantic definiteness is complex. For this reason, semantic definiteness is not usually considered to be binary, but instead is a scalar phenomenon, meaning that at the semantic level one may discern degrees of definiteness.[18] An illustrative definiteness hierarchy would include the following:[19]

Most Definite – Demonstratives
Proper Nouns
Anaphoric References

---

[16] Holger Gzella, 'Language and Script', in Herbert Niehr (ed.), *The Aramaeans in Ancient Syria* (HdO, 106, Leiden: Brill, 2014) pp. 71–107 (88).

[17] Christopher Lyons, *Definiteness* (Cambridge Textbooks in Linguistics, Cambridge [England]: Cambridge University Press, 1999) p. 260.

[18] Andrew Chesterman, *On Definiteness: A Study with Special Reference to English and Finnish* (Cambridge Studies in Linguistics, 56, Cambridge: Cambridge University Press, 1991) p. 6.

[19] Chesterman, *On Definiteness*, pp. 189–190.

Cataphoric References
Inclusive Sets
Abstract Concepts
Possessive Forms
Least Definite – Indefinites

Such definiteness hierarchies complicate the picture of semantic definiteness, as they do not linearly correlate with Lyons' summary definition of definiteness as a noun phrase that is identifiable or unique. For instance, both demonstratives and possessives are typically considered definite because of their identifiability, while inclusive sets are definite as a unique referent. Accordingly, many linguists return to consider definiteness to be a semantic phenomenon that includes a cluster of noun phrase types with multiple distinctions. It is precisely these complexities that commend Lyons' general approach. Though not perfect, it accurately encapsulates how most speakers of a language innately know whether something is clearly definite or indefinite.

2. SIMPLE NOUN PHRASES

In the simple noun phrase,[20] the OA corpus studied shows a strikingly strong connection between the emphatic state and semantic definiteness. The forms included in the data set are as follows:

	Semantically Definite	Semantically Indefinite
Absolute	31	87
Emphatic	18	0

[20] This analysis distinguishes simple noun phrases (a bare noun or a noun plus attributive modifiers) from complex noun phrases. Complex noun phrases include those with specific types of attributive modifiers (such as possessives and demonstratives which may have their own unique behavior) and more complex noun phrases (such as construct phrases, etc.). Such phrases should therefore initially be studied separately, not assumed to follow the same behavior.

These data indicate a clear statistical categorical dependence between state and definiteness, not an accidental connection between the two features.[21]

Initially notable is the relatively small number of emphatic forms, only eighteen. The inscriptional nature of the available corpus explains some of that paucity, as there are numerous semantically indefinite forms in curse formulae (e.g., ושבע שאן יהינקן אמר 'and if seven ewes suckle a lamb' – Sefire 1.A.23). Noticeably, none of these emphatic forms are used for a semantic indefinite. The complete list is as follows:

Asshur Ostracon

כלביא the auxiliary troops (7) – mutually identifiable to the writer and original (though not necessarily modern) reader as a familiar type of troop or unit of troops[22]

מלכא the king (4x: 6, 7, 8, 17) – identifiable in context as there is one king as ruler over the writer

מדברא the desert (5) – identifiable to the original reader given the itinerary that is laid out in this line

Bar-Rakib

מלכיא[23] the kings (1.14–15) – identifiable, appositionally defined as 'my brothers'

---

[21] A chi-square test of independence gives a p value < .00001 (versus a typical view that the data are statistically significant at p < .05), indicating that these two features are clearly connected. x^2 (1, $N=137$) = 33.3905, p < .00001

[22] Frederick Mario Fales, 'Aramaic Letters and Neo-Assyrian Letters: Philological and Methodological Notes', *JAOS* 107 (1987), pp. 451–469 (468). See also: Fales, 'New Light on Assyro-Aramaic Interference: The Asshur Ostracon', in Frederick Mario Fales and Giulia Francesca Grassi (eds.), *Proceedings of the 13th Italian Meeting of Afro-Asiatic Linguistics* (*History of the Ancient Near East / Monographs*, 10, Padova: S.A.R.G.O.N. Editrice e Liberia, 2010) pp. 189–204 (196).

[23] Note that the *aleph* is on line 15.

Fakhariyeh

קלקלתא the garbage heaps (22) – identifiable because garbage heaps would be expected in a settlement[24]

Sefire

ארחא the road (3.9) – identifiable because of its relationship to the kings involved

טבתא the good (1.C.19) – identifiable as the good relations enshrined by the treaty

טבתא the goodness (2.B.2) – identifiable because of a following relative clause

מליא the words (3.2) – identifiable as an anaphoric reference

ספר[י]א the inscriptions (2x: 2.C.4, 2.C.6–7) – in the context of the quotation, these refer to the inscription itself, therefore identifiable to the hypothetical speaker

קשתא the bow (1.A.38) – identifiable as a specific bow in context, especially given its use in parallel with a following demonstrative form (חציא אלן)

עדיא the treaty (2.B.2) – identifiable as the current treaty

שמשא the sun (1.C.5) – identifiable as a unique entity

Zakkur

[נ]צבא the stele (A.1) – identifiable as a cataphoric reference because of the following relative clause

Equally noticeable, absolute forms can be used for nouns which are arguably semantically definite or are at least 'more definite' in a scalar concept of definiteness. These especially include generic nouns, class nouns, and abstract concepts:

Asshur Ostracon

שלם peace (1) – identifiable as an abstract concept

---

[24] This is a first use of the noun in the text, which would typically therefore be semantically indefinite. This form, however, is semantically definite due to the expectation that any human settlement would have garbage heaps, meaning the city should be expected to have one. (For example, compare the English clauses: 'I went to a restaurant. The dumpster smelled'.)

Bukân

אלהן the gods (3, 4) – inclusive as the entire set

Fakhariyeh

אלה (oh) god (5) – identifiable as a vocative form
מרא (oh) lord (6) – identifiable as a vocative form

Kuttamuwa

נצב stele (1) – identifiable as the current stele[25]

Sefire

אלהן the gods (1.A.30, 1.B.31, 1.C.15, 21; 2.B.2; 3.24) – inclusive as the entire set
ארבה the locust (1.A.27) – inclusive of the species
ארנב the hare (1.A.33) – inclusive of the species
ארק earth (1.A.26) – identifiable as a unique referent
חרב the sword (3.13, 14) – identifiable as a concept
יום day (1.A.12) – identifiable as a concept
לילה night (1.A.12) – identifiable as a concept
מעינן fountains (1.A.12) – identifiable (most likely) as the name of a god
ערק the magpie? (1.A.33) – inclusive of the species
צבי the gazelle (1.A.33) – inclusive of the species
צדה the owl (1.A.33) – inclusive of the species
שלם peace (3.8) – identifiable as an abstract concept
שמין heaven (1.A.26; 1.B.7, 1.B.23) – identifiable as a unique referent
שעל the fox (1.A.33) – inclusive of the species
שרן the cat (1.A.33) – inclusive of the species
תולעה the worm (1.A.27) – inclusive of the species

The remainder of the absolute forms are semantically indefinite:

---

[25] Note that this form is likely not actually an absolute form, as demonstrative noun phrases in Kuttamuwa are also not in the emphatic form (see below), most likely indicating a dialectal relationship with Samalian. It is most likely that Kuttamuwa did not have the emphatic form available as a grammatical state.

Asshur Ostracon

אשה	fire (17) – first mention and unidentifiable
עבדן	slaves (13) – descriptive predicate in a verbless clause
שׂנה	year (16, 20) – indeterminate which year (only relatively identified)
שבי	captive(s) (15) – not identifiable

Bar-Rakib

בי טב	a good house (1.16) – first mention

Bukân

לחמה	war (2) – no specific or identifiable referent
שלם	peace (2) – no specific or identifiable referent

Fakhariyeh

אדקור	a water vessel (3) – first mention
אכלו	eating (22) – not identifiable
אלהן	gods (14) – not an inclusive set
אמר	a lamb (20) – first mention
אנשן	men (14) – not an inclusive set
משקי	watering (place) (3) – first mention[26]
לחם	bread (22) – first mention
מותן	pestilence (23) – first mention
מרק	sickness (9)– first mention
עגל	a calf (21) – first mention
עלים	a boy (21) – first mention
פריס	a paris (19) – first mention
רעי	pasture (2) – first mention
שלה	watering (3) – first mention
שערן	barley (22) – not inclusive
תנור	an oven (22) – first mention

Kuttamuwa

יבל	a ram (3, 4 [2x], 5 [2x]) – all first mentions, as in each case it is a different ram

[26] Stephen A. Kaufman ('Reflections on the Assyrian-Aramaic Bilingual from Tell Fakhariyeh', *MAARAV* 3 (1982), pp. 137–175 [164]) argues this and רעי below are feminine absolute forms because masculine singular nouns ending in *-y* are 'almost unknown in Aramaic'.

יומן year (10 [2x]) – indeterminate
שא a ewe (9) – first mention
שור a bull (3) – first mention
שק a leg (13) – first mention

Sefire

אלהן gods (1.B.6) – not a categorical reference
אמר a lamb (1.A.23) – first mention
אשם a guilt offering (1.C.25) – first mention
המל a fracas (1.A.29) – first mention
זכרן a remembrance (1.C.2–3) – first mention
חוה a snake (1.A.31) – first mention (possibly to be restored as part of a construct phrase)
חצר grass (1.A.28) – indeterminate amount
יד a hand (1.B.25, 1.B.34) – both first mentions
יום a day (1.B.31, 1.C.20) – first mention (line 31) and modified by a descriptive, not identifying, clause (line 20)
יללה lamentation (1.A.30) – first mention
ירק vegetation (1.A.28) – first mention
לחית bad (1.C.20) – general term, not inclusive
לחם bread/food (1.A.24, 1.B.38, 1.B.39; 3.5, 3.7) – first mentions, not inclusive
מלח salt (1.A.36) – indeterminate amount
מלך רב a great king (1.B.7) – descriptive
מרק sickness (1.A.29) – first mention
סס a moth (1.A.31) – first mention
עגל a calf (1.A.23) – first mention
עדן חי[ן] a living treaty (1.B41–42) – descriptive
על a foal (1.A.22) – first mention
עלים a young boy (1.A.22) – first mention
עמל labor/toil (1.A.26) – category, but not an inclusive set
פגר corpse (1.B.30 [2x]; 2.B.11 [2x]) – first mention, unidentifiable
קמל a louse (1.A.31) – first mention
קקבתן jackal howls? (1.A.31) – first mention
שהדן witnesses (1.A.12) – not an inclusive set
שחלין weeds (1.A.36) – indeterminate amount
שט a large oven? (1.A.24) – first mention

תל	a ruin (1.A.32) – first mention
גבר	a man (2.B.19) – unidentifiable
גדה	a kid (2.A.2) – first mention
שית	thorns (2.A.5) – unidentifiable
לשן	a tongue (3.21) – first mention, possibly also a fixed phrase
מלך	a king (3.28) – first mention
מלן	words (3.2) – first mention
מרמת	treachery (3.22) – first mention
קריה	a city (3.12) – first mention
קרק	a fugitive (3.4) – first mention

Tel Dan

מצר	siege (13) – first mention

Zakkur

חרץ	a ditch (A.10) – first mention
מצר	a seige (A.9) – first mention
שר	a wall (A.10) – first mention

The formulaic nature of curses provides a high proportion of first mention uses of nouns. While this may in some sense bias the data in comparison to natural speech, those first mentions, which are semantically indefinite, are consistently in the absolute form.

Notably, certain noun phrases, especially some that indicate a genus, species, or abstract concept, often use the absolute form. Such forms are typically considered to be semantically definite either due to their identifiability, e.g., שלם 'peace' (Sefire 3.8), or their inclusiveness, e.g., ארבה 'the locust' (Sefire 1.A.27). Nonetheless, other quite similar uses of the terms such as לחמה and שלם in Bukân are arguably semantically indefinite because they cannot be identified. The difficulty in classification arises because such genericity is often ambiguously encoded in a language. As Krifka et al. state:

> If we look at the linguistic realization of kind-referring NPs and characterizing sentences, we find that they seldom are encoded in an unambiguous way. Not only are there many linguistically distinct ways to state a particular generic

> sentence, but also it often happens that a given sentence can have both a particular and a characterizing reading.[27]

The scalar nature of definiteness helps explain this difficulty, as such forms convey an intermediate definiteness. In OA, such forms are consistently encoded with the absolute form.

If abstract concepts and inclusive sets such as a genus or species are considered separately, the distribution of the emphatic form is more regular:

	Semantically Definite		Semantically Indefinite
	By Identifiability	By Inclusivity	
Absolute	8	23	87
Emphatic	18	0	0

The identifiable absolute forms are:

- two vocatives (אלה and מרא in Fakhariyeh 5 and 6)
- two unique referents (four occurrences) in Sefire ארק (1.A.26) and שמין (1.A.26; 1.B.7, 1.B.23)
- מעינן in Sefire (1.A.12), which is most likely the name of a god
- נצב in Kuttamuwa (1), which, given its dialectal relationship with Samalian, likely had no emphatic option

Many languages do not mark definiteness on obviously definite forms – e.g., the lack of the definite article on English proper nouns – which could explain the lack of the emphatic state for clearly identifiable vocatives, unique referents, and the proper noun.[28] The lack of an emphatic option in Kuttamuwa relates to the question of dialectal differences in OA, as the absence of the

---

[27] Manfred Krifka et al., 'Genericity: An Introduction', in Gregory N. Carlson and Francis Jeffry Pelletier (eds.), *Generic Book* (Chicago: University of Chicago Press, 1995) pp. 1–124 (5).

[28] Some amount of variation must also be noted at this early stage of definiteness marking in Aramaic. For instance, Sefire 1.C.5 reads שמשא ('the sun') for an equally identifiable referent. Such inconsistent use of the emphatic state would accord with a developing feature in the language, as the use of the emphatic state is here argued to be.

emphatic state is one of the clear isoglosses separating Samalian from the remainder of OA.

In summary, one can state with a high level of confidence that morphological state and semantic definiteness are statistically categorically related in the simple noun phrase, with the emphatic state indicating a semantically definite noun phrase. The emphatic state does not mark all definite noun phrases, consistent with conceiving of it as an incipient feature in Aramaic. In counterpoint, the OA absolute form is used for both indefinites and various definites, indicating that the emphatic is the marked and more limited form. Further, the subset of definiteness the emphatic state encodes is that of identifiability. Degen simply indicates that the emphatic state is used when the noun is supposed to be definite.[29] Kaufman accurately notes that the emphatic in OA has not developed into a truly determined state in a comprehensive way.[30] More precisely, my analysis indicates the emphatic state is used regularly to indicate definiteness via identifiability. Only a few obviously identifiable nouns such as vocatives and unique referents break this pattern.

3. COMPLEX NOUN PHRASES

Complex noun phrases may be negatively defined as those which contain more than a bare noun or a noun plus modifiers.[31] Complex noun phrases in the corpus include demonstratives, possessives, quantified forms, and construct phrases. Because the possessive suffix attaches to the construct form of the noun, possessive noun phrases do not show state and therefore do not give useful data for this study, but the other three forms can be analyzed.

---

[29] Rainer Degen, *Altaramäische Grammatik der Inschriften des 10.-8. Jahrhunderts V. Chr.* (AKM, 38, 3, Wiesbaden: Harrassowitz Verlag, 1969) p. 84.

[30] Kaufman, 'Reflections on the Assyrian-Aramaic Bilingual from Tell Fakhariyeh', p. 148.

[31] Lyons, *Definiteness*, p. 2.

3.1. Demonstratives

As deictic words, demonstrative noun phrases are among the most definite phrases in a scalar conception of definiteness, and they are consistently presented in the emphatic state whenever it is available as an option. Only Kuttamuwa presents demonstratives in the absolute state:

חיל כרם זנן	the best of this vineyard (9)
סיד זנן	this chamber (2–3, 8)
נצב זן	this stele (5)

These morphologically absolute state demonstratives are likely explained by Kuttamuwa's dialectal relationship with Samalian.[32] All other demonstratives in the corpus are in the emphatic form:

Asshur

מליא אלה	these words (12)

Bar-Rakib

ביתא זנה	this house (1.20)

Bukân

מלכא הא	that king (10)
מלכא הוא	that king (3–4)
נצבא זנה	this stele (11, 13)

Fakhariyeh

דמותא זאת	this likeness (15)

Sefire

חציא אלן	these arrows (1.A.38)
נצבא זנה	this stele (1.C.17)
ספרא זנה	this inscription (1.B.8–9, 1.B.28, 1.B.33; 2.C.13–14; 3.4, 3.14, 3.17, 3.23)
[ספ]ריא אלן	these writings (2.C.2, 2.C.9)
עגלא זנה	this calf (1.A.40)

[32] Pardee, 'A New Aramaic Inscription from Zincirli', p. 53.

עדיא אלן	these stipulations (1.A.7 [2x], 1.B.11–12, 1.B.24, 1.B.38; 3.7, 3.9, 3.19, 3.20-21, 3.27)
שעותא זא	this wax (1.A.35, 1.A.37)[33]

Zakkur

מלכיא אל	these kings (A.9, A.16)
נצבא זנה	this stele (B.14, B.18, B.19)
שורא זנה	this wall (A.17)

The correlation between the emphatic state and semantic definiteness is buttressed by these forms. Further, demonstratives are necessarily identifiable, showing that the use of the emphatic state for identifiability is consistent with that of the simple noun phrase.

3.2 Quantified Forms

Quantified forms can be, depending on the context, either semantically definite or indefinite. The corpus shows twenty-three quantified forms, all of which are contextually indefinite, most as first mentions in curse formulae, and all of which are in the absolute state:

Bar-Rakib

בית חד מלכן רברבן	the house of one of the powerful kings (1.13) – first mention

Bukân

עגל חד	one calf (6)
שבע נשן	seven women (6–7)
שבע שורה	seven cows (5)
שבע שנן	seven years (12)
תנר חד	one oven (7)

Fakhariyeh

אלף שערין	1000 (measures of) barley (19)

[33] Likely a wax figurine that would have accompanied the curse formula. See Scott Layton and Dennis Pardee, 'Literary Sources for the History of Palestine and Syria: Old Aramaic Inscriptions', *The Biblical Archaeologist* 51 (1988), pp. 172–189 (179).

מאה נשון	100 women (21, 22)
מאה סאון	100 ewes (20)
מאה סור	100 cattle (20)

Sefire

חד מלכן	one king (1.B.26, 1.B.28)
שבע שנן	seven years (1.A.27 [2x]; 2.A.5, 2.A.6)
שבע בנתה	seven daughters (1.A.24)
שבע שאן	seven ewes (1.A.23)
[שבע] שורה	seven cows (1.A.22–23)
שבע ססיה	seven mares (1.A.22)

Tel Dan

אלפי פרש	thousands of horsemen (7)

Zakkur

ש[בעת] עשר מלכן	seventeen kings (A.5)

Forms with כל typically indicate an inclusive set and are therefore semantically definite. Noun phrases with כל occur in both the absolute and emphatic forms:

Absolute:

אלהין כלם	all the gods (Fakhariyeh 4)
כל גבר	any man (Sefire 3.1–2)
כל מה אכל	every sort of devourer (Sefire 1.A.30)
כל מה מלך זי [יסק וימלך] באשרה	any king who [will arise and rule] after him (Sefire 1.B.2)
מת כלן	all lands (Fakhariyeh 4–5, 5)
נהר כלם	all rivers (Fakhariyeh 4)

Emphatic:

כל אלהי עדיא	all the gods of the treaty (Sefire 1.B.23; 2.B.18, 2.C.13; 3.4, 3.14, 3.23)
כל ארקא	all the land (Bukân 3)
כל לוץ נצ̇[ב]א זנה	all the curse of this stele (Bukân 13)
כל מלכיא אל	all these kings (Zakkur A.9, A.16)
כל מלכיא זי ימלכן בארפד	all the kings who will rule in Arpad (Sefire 1.B.22)
כל מלכיא זי סחרתי	all the kings of my surroundings (Sefire 3.8)

With only twenty data points, caution is in order when trying to discern a trend. Nonetheless, it is notable that, although כל makes a noun phrase inclusive and therefore semantically definite, the state of the noun in the phrase follows a pattern. All the nouns which would have been semantically definite without כל as a modifier are identifiable and in the emphatic state. All the noun phrases which only become semantically definite because their modification by כל makes them inclusive sets show the noun in the absolute state. For example, כל גבר ('any man' – Sefire 3.1–2) is only semantically definite as a noun phrase because the quantifier כל makes the set inclusive of every man who might act in such a way (consider even the typical translation as 'any man' which is clearly not an identifiable referent).

3.3. Construct Phrases

The corpus contains 150 construct phrases which can be categorized for semantic definiteness. Of those, ninety-seven have a *nomen rectum* that is either a possessive form or a proper noun, leaving fifty-three that can be analyzed for state. Of those, all the construct phrases with an emphatic *nomen rectum* are definite, and those with an absolute *nomen rectum* are more often indefinite:

	Semantically Definite	Semantically Indefinite
Absolute	8	22
Emphatic	21	0

The emphatic forms are all semantically definite because they are identifiable:

Asshur

לבת אלהא the wrath of the god (19) – followed by an identifying clause

Bar-Rakib

בית שתוא the winter house (1.18) – identifiable
בית כיצא the summer house (1.19) – identifiable

מרא רבעי ארקא	the lord of the four (corners) of the earth (1.3–4) – unique referent[34]

Bukân

כל לוץ נצ̇[ב]א זנה	all the curse of this stele (13) – demonstrative
[מ]ת מלכא הוא	the country of that king (3–4) – demonstrative

Sefire

אלהי עדיא	the gods of the treaty (1.B.23, 1.B.33; 2.B.18, 2.C.13; 3.4, 3.14, 3.17. 3.23) – anaphoric reference
בתי [א]להיא	the houses of the gods (2.C.2–3, 2.C.7, 2.C.9-10) – first mention is identified by a following relative clause; others are anaphoric references
גבר שעותא	the man of wax (1.A.39) – identifiable as a specific figure used in the treaty ceremony
מלי ספרא	the words of the writing (1.C.17) – followed by an identifying clause
מלי ספרא זנ[ה]	the words of thi[s] writing (1.B.8–9) – demonstrative

Zakkur

כל מלכיא אל all these kings (A.9, A.16) – anaphoric reference

The absolute definites are definite either as unique referents, because of quantification by כל, or they occur in Kuttamuwa:

Fakhariyeh

גוגל נהר כלם	canal inspector of all rivers (4) – unique referent
גוגל שמין וארק	canal inspector of heaven and earth (2) – unique referent[35]

34 Layton and Pardee ('Literary Sources', p. 193) note this as a calque on the Akkadian title for the Assyrian ruler, so its value for the analysis of OA may be diminished.

35 The phrase describes Hadad Sikanu, delineating his specific role, and is therefore presumably unique.

מהנחת עסר	the one who brings down prosperity (2) – unique referent[36]
מעדן מת כלן	the one who makes fertile all lands (4–5) – unique referent

Kuttamuwa

חיל כרם זנן	the best of this vineyard (9) – demonstrative

Sefire

בית מלך	the house of the king (1.A.6) – unique referent
כל מה אכל	every sort of devourer (1.A.30) – definite only because of כל
עקר כל מה מלך זי [יסק וימלך] באשרה	the offspring of any king who [will arise and rule] after him (1.B.2) – definite only because of כל

The indefinites are not identifiable:

Bar-Rakib

בית חד מלכן רברבן	the house of one of the powerful kings (1.13)
בעלי זהב	lords of gold (1.11)
בעלי כסף	lords of silver (1.10-11)
מצעת מלכן רברבן	the midst of powerful kings (1.9-10)

Bukân

פרע ראש	poison weeds (10)
קל רחין	the sound of millstones (8–9)[37]
תנן אשה	the smoke of fire (8)[38]

Kuttamuwa

[36] As with the preceding phrase, this phrase describes Hadad Sikanu, delineating his specific role, and is therefore presumably unique.

[37] This renders into English as 'the sound of millstones' because millstones make a sound and the English genitive phrase can take an article on each noun. The construct phrase as a whole is a first mention and therefore indefinite.

[38] This renders into English as 'the smoke of a fire' because fires have smoke and the English genitive phrase can take an article on each noun. The construct phrase as a whole is a first mention and therefore indefinite.

בני אש	sons of a man (7)

Sefire

גבר עדן	a man of treaty (1.B.24)[39]
עדי אלהן	a treaty of gods (1.B.6)[40]
פם נמל̇ה	the mouth of an ant (1.A.31)
פם דב{ה}<ר>ה	the mouth of a bee (1.A.31)
פם עקרב	the mouth of a scorpion (1.A.31)
קל כנר	a sound of a lyre (1.A.29)
מלכת חלם	a kingdom of a dream (1.A.25)
פם נמר	the mouth of a panther (2.A.9)
פם [זא]ב̇	the mouth of a wolf (2.A.9)
פם אריה	the mouth of a lion (2.A.9)[41]
בר אנש	a person (3.16)

Zakkur

יד עדדן	the hand of diviners (A.12)[42]
יד חזין	the hand of seers (A.12)[29]

3.4. Analytic Genitives

There are five analytic genitives in the corpus:

כל מלכיא זי סחרתי	all the kings of my surroundings (Sefire 3.8) – identifiable
[מ]לכן [זי סחר]תי	kings of my surrounding (Sefire 3.19) – identifiable

---

[39] This is the predicate of a verbless clause and descriptive and therefore indefinite.

[40] As the predicate of a verbless clause, the definiteness of this form is debatable depending on whether one considers it an identifying or descriptive clause.

[41] This is a first mention and therefore indefinite.

[42] This is a first mention and therefore indefinite. The typical translation 'the hand of…' is due to the differing treatment of the genitive in English versus the Aramaic construct phrase. A seer or diviner would be understood, as a human, to have hands, so English says 'the hand of a seer' or 'the hand of seers' due to the fact that both elements of the genitive phrase in English can bear an article.

דמותא זי הדיסעי	the likeness of Hadad-Yithʿi (Fakhariyeh 1) – identifiable[43]
מאניא זי בת הדד	the vessels of the temple of Hadad (Fakhariyeh 16–17) – identifiable set
שבט זי נירגל	the rod of Nergal (Fakhariyeh 23) – identifiable as a unique referent

The alternation in what seems to be a similar phrase in Sefire is surprising, though the restoration of the middle of the phrase gives pause to drawing a firm conclusion. The phrase שבט זי נירגל may be a unique referent.[44]

Complex noun phrases, then, show a strikingly similar pattern regarding the emphatic state. Identifiable noun phrases are typically in the emphatic state. Semantic definites that indicate a unique referent or that are quantified by כל are in the absolute state.

4. CONCLUSIONS

Because of the limited sources available, any statements about the grammar of OA must be provisional. Nonetheless, there are enough data points to conclude a statistical analysis: at a high confidence level, we can conclude that morphological state (indicated by the use of the emphatic form) and semantic definiteness are connected in OA. The phenomenon of IA that continued in QA – the use of the emphatic state to indicate definiteness – stretches back into OA and can be observed with a clear statistical significance.

Maurice Casey argues that the earliest Aramaic evidenced an alternation between the emphatic and absolute states for generic terms.[45] Casey bases this conclusion on the Aramaic letter from King Adon and the story of Ahiqar preserved in the Elephantine

---

[43] Though there would have doubtless been multiple statues that bore this image, this is an identifiable phrase, as there would be a single likeness of this king, even if chiseled into multiple stelae.

[44] Kaufman ('Reflections on the Assyrian-Aramaic Bilingual from Tell Fakhariyeh', p. 148) treats this as definite, but he allows that he finds its 'self-determining element…less convincing'.

[45] Maurice Casey, 'Aramaic Idiom and the Son of Man Problem: A Response to Owen and Shepherd', *JSNT* 25 (2002), pp. 3–32 (12).

documents.[46] Joseph Fitzmyer dates the former to the seventh century,[47] and the latter is generally agreed to date to approximately the fifth century. Casey's contention about early Aramaic is therefore invalidated by the evidence adduced from this study. Instead, the earliest Aramaic had, from what the data show, a regular feature with a clear distinction.

Given the regular correlations observed in the corpus, the emphatic state in OA should not be considered a marker of definiteness more broadly but instead a marker of identifiability, a subset of the overall definiteness spectrum. The absolute state can be used for semantic definites in certain cases such as a unique referent or an abstract concept, but the emphatic state is only used in OA for identifiable noun phrases. The absolute state, then, is the unmarked form, while the emphatic state is marked for identifiability.

---

[46] Casey, 'Aramaic Idiom', p. 13. See André Dupont-Sommer, 'Un papyrus araméen d'époque saïte découvert à Saqqarah', *Semitica* 1 (1948), pp. 43–68; Casey works from the edition of Ahiqar in James Miller Lindenberger, *The Aramaic Proverbs of Ahiqar* (PhD Diss., Johns Hopkins University, 1974).

[47] Joseph A. Fitzmyer, 'The Aramaic Letter of King Adon to the Egyptian Pharaoh', *Biblica* 46 (1965), pp. 41–55 (43).

LEGAL METAPHORS IN ARAMAIC*

ANDREW D. GROSS

Metaphors are very persistent in the Aramaic legal tradition. This persistence may be understood in the context of conceptual metaphor theory, an approach to metaphors stemming from George Lakoff and Mark Johnson's seminal work *Metaphors We Live By*.[1] They take a cognitive linguistic approach and argue that metaphors are not merely literary devices, but reflect how the mind processes information. In their view, 'the essence of metaphor is understanding and experiencing one kind of thing in terms of another'.[2] For example, in the metaphor LOVE IS A JOURNEY, love is the target domain onto which the source domain, journey, is mapped. Thus, love can be at a 'crossroads' or 'not going anywhere'. Different types of journeys may be reflected in the metaphor. When love is described as 'a long, bumpy road' or 'a dead-end street', it is compared to a car trip, and when it is

---

* I am proud to honor my friend, colleague, and longtime office suitemate Ed Cook. In addition to helping shape my career in many positive ways, our morning chats have made my life immeasurably more enjoyable.

[1] George Lakoff and Mark Johnson, *Metaphors We Live By* (Chicago and London: The University of Chicago Press, 1980). For a convenient overview of conceptual metaphor theory and the subsequent developments and critiques since the seminal works by Lakoff and Johnson, see Johan de Joode, *Metaphorical Landscapes and the Theology of the Book of Job: An Analysis of Job's Spatial Metaphors* (VTSup, 179, Leiden: Brill, 2018) pp. 12–45.

[2] Lakoff and Johnson, *Metaphors We Live By*, p. 5.

described as 'on the rocks' or 'foundering', it is compared to a sea voyage.[3]

Analyzing metaphors in Aramaic legal documents is not the same as with literary works or everyday language. Its standardized formularies use language very economically and efficiently, leaving little room for extended metaphors. That being said, conceptual metaphor theory can help elucidate why these legal metaphors are so persistent. What is so striking about these metaphors is how they remain consistent over centuries, if not longer. This is not merely due to the conservative nature of legal terminology, as the terminology itself varies over time. What remains consistent is the metaphor in place. These metaphors do not simply persist within the Aramaic tradition but stretch back well into the cuneiform record.

Within the cuneiform record, these metaphors occur in what can be called 'upstream' traditions. Cuneiform legal traditions can roughly be divided into 'downstream' traditions, those of southern Mesopotamia, and 'upstream' traditions which are attested in northern Mesopotamia, Syria, Anatolia, and Elam.[4] Chronologically, these metaphors are attested as far back as the early second millennium BCE and persist through the Aramaic tradition well into the Middle Ages. Thus, the distribution of these metaphors is quite broad chronologically and geographically. Their persistence can be attributed to how the scribal tradition conceived of the concepts embedded within these formularies.

1. METAPHORS OF EMOTION

One general characteristic of the aforementioned stream of tradition is the dynamic way it describes transactions. This dynamism manifests itself in a number of details that, for example, convey a party's disposition or reaction to a certain aspect of the transaction. These details are expressed through metaphors of emotion, and I will consider four examples of such metaphors.

---

[3] See Lakoff and Johnson, *Metaphors We Live By*, pp. 44–45.

[4] Sometimes these are referred to as 'core' and 'peripheral' traditions.

1.1 VOLITION IS JOY

The metaphor VOLITION IS JOY has no direct reflexes in the Aramaic tradition, but it is worth exploring here to establish context. In the context of property conveyances, volition refers to the fact that the ceder of this property undertook this transaction free-willingly, rather than, say, under economic duress. Volition is important in this context because its presence or absence in such transactions can have material legal consequences. To express this volition, deeds recording property conveyances often use emotional terminology. Yochanan Muffs traces the development of these terms of volition (both nominal and verbal) in Akkadian contracts, drawing particular attention to two expressing emotions of joy: *ḫadû* and *ṭâbu'*.[5] Muffs cites a number of examples from across different time periods and regions in a variety of forms, and the following brief sampling of those will illustrate the forms that these expressions take.

CT 8 49a, an Old Babylonian adoption contract from Sippar, describes the adoption of a young woman by another woman.[6] After detailing everything in the older woman's estate that the younger woman stands to inherit, the contract then describes an additional gift of several slaves that the adoptee's father provides to her and her adoptive mother:

> [25]*i-nu-ma* PN [26]*a-na ma-ar-ti-ša iš-ṭu-ru(!)* [27]PN$_2$ *iḫ-du-ma* … [35]*a-na* PN [36]*ù* PN$_3$ [37]PN$_2$ *i-di-in*

> When PN recorded (PN$_3$) as her daughter, PN$_2$ voluntarily gave [SEVERAL SLAVES LISTED] to PN and PN$_3$. (*CT* 8 49a.25–37)

---

[5] Muffs, *Studies on the Aramaic Legal Papyri from Elephantine* (Leiden: Brill, 1969) pp. 128–141. See also idem, *Love and Joy: Law, Language and Religion in Ancient Israel* (New York and Jerusalem: The Jewish Theological Seminary of America, 1992) pp. 144–145, 148–149.

[6] For an edition and translation of this text, see Moses Schorr, *Urkunden des altbabylonischen Zivil- und Prozessrechts* (VAB, 5, Leipzig: J.C. Hinrichs, 1913) pp. 29–30. See also the Cuneiform Digital Library Initiative (CDLI) edition at: https://cdli.ucla.edu/P365213 (Accessed: June 9, 2023).

The verbs *iḫdû-ma* and *iddin* can literally be translated as 'he rejoiced ... and gave', but we have followed *CAD* in rendering them above as a hendiadys.[7]

Middle Assyrian Law A §55 deals with the consequences of the rape of an unbetrothed virgin. Similar to Deut. 22.28–29, the father may force the rapist to marry her without the possibility of divorce. As detailed in the following excerpt, however, he may choose a different option:

> *šum-ma a-bu la-a ḫa-a-di* KU$_3$.BABBAR *3–a-te ša* ^{f}*ba-tul-te i-ma-ḫar* DUMU.MUNUS-*su a-na ša ḫa-di-ú-ni i-id-dan*
>
> If the father does not desire it so, he shall receive 'triple' silver for the maiden, and he shall give his daughter in marriage to whomever he chooses.[8] (MAL A §55)

According to this excerpt from the end of the law, the father may decide to accept a financial payment and marry his daughter to whomever he desires, with this volition on the part of the father being expressed twice by forms of the verb *ḫadû*.

Finally, for the verbal root *ḫadû*, we should mention the phrase *ina ḫūd libbišu nadānum* 'he gave in the joy of his heart (= freewillingly)'. This phrase uses the nominal form *ḫūdu* and is quite old,[9] though it is most common in Neo-Babylonian documents.[10]

Moving on to *ṭâbu* as a term of volition, we should first consider its usage as a term of emotion in its source domain. This term does not seem to be primarily a description of an emotional state. As an adjective (*ṭābu*), *CAD* includes among its general glosses 'good', 'sweet', 'of good quality', 'favorable', and 'pleasing'.[11] It glosses the verbal form *ṭâbu* as 'to become good,

---

[7] *CAD* Ḫ, p. 27.

[8] Translation from Martha T. Roth, *Law Collections from Mesopotamia and Asia Minor* (2nd edn., SBL Writings from the Ancient World, 6, Atlanta: Scholars Press, 1997) p. 175.

[9] It is attested in at least one Akkadian text from Ugarit, RS 8.333.

[10] For examples, see *CAD* Ḫ, p. 223 s.v. *ḫudû* mng b and p. 224 s.v. *ḫūdu* mng b.

[11] *CAD* Ṭ, p. 19.

pleasant, sound, sweet'.[12] In finding an emotional nuance in this verbal root, Muffs begs the question somewhat when he glosses the verbal form as 'to be sweet/to be happy'.[13] That all being said, it does express emotional nuance when used within specific locutions such as when the subject is *libbu* 'heart' or *kabattu* 'mind'.[14] In another common locution, it combines with the preposition *eli* 'upon' to indicate the person being gladdened.[15]

As an example of this latter locution, let us consider Laws of Hammurabi §179, which deals with questions of discretion in alienating property:

> *šum-ma* NIN.DINGIR LUKUR *ù lu* ^{mí}ZI.IK.RU.UM *ša a-bu-ša še-ri-ik-tam iš-ru-ku-ši-im ku-nu-kam iš-ṭú-ru-ši-im i-na ṭup-pí-im ša iš-ṭú-ru-ši-im wa-ar-ka-sà e-ma e-li-ša ṭa-bu na-da-nam iš-ṭur-ši-im-ma ma-la li-ib-bi-ša uš-tam-ṣí-ši wa-ar-ka a-bu-um a-na ši-im-tim it-ta-al-ku wa-ar-ka-sà e-ma e-li-ša ṭa-bu i-na-ad-di-in aḫ-ḫu-ša ú-ul i-pa-aq-qá-ru-ši*
>
> If there is an *ugbabtu*, a *nadītu*, or a *sekretu* whose father awards to her a dowry and records it for her in a sealed document, and in the tablet that he records for her he grants her written authority to give her estate to whomever she pleases and gives her full discretion—after the father goes to his fate, she shall give her estate to whomever she pleases; her brothers will not raise a claim against her.[16] (LH §179)

The phrase *ēma elīša ṭābu nadānam*, which could literally be rendered, 'wherever it is favorable upon her to give' occurs twice in this law and expresses the woman's rights of property disposition.

---

[12] *CAD* Ṭ, p. 34.

[13] Muffs, *Studies*, p. 136. On p. 129, he defines it merely as 'to be happy'.

[14] For examples, see *CAD* Ṭ, pp. 35–36 s.v. *ṭâbu* mng 1a and pp. 118–120 s.v. *ṭūbu* mng g.

[15] For examples, see *CAD* Ṭ, p. 31 s.v. *ṭābu* mng s2´.

[16] For all citations from the Laws of Hammurabi, transliterations are adapted from the CDLI edition: https://cdli.ucla.edu/P464358 (Accessed: June 23, 2023), and translations are taken from Roth, *Law Collections from Mesopotamia*.

CT 6 47a, an Old Babylonian court record from Sippar, expresses volition with a slightly different version of this locution.[17] The text concerns five siblings who agree not to sue their sister over inheritance rights, and at the end, it declares that the sister has the right to dispose of her inheritance as she sees fit using the following language:

> [15]*a-ša-ar ṭà-bu-ši-im* [16]*ap-lu-sà i-na-di-in*
>
> She may dispose of her inheritance as she sees fit (*CT* 6 47a.15–16)

The phrase *ašar ṭābūšim* can be rendered literally, 'the place that is favorable to her'. Where LH §179's *ēma elīša ṭābu* uses a prepositional phrase headed by *elī*, this text uses a dative suffix.[18]

Finally, we should also mention the phrase *ina ṭūb libbišu*, a phrase of volition synonymous with the abovementioned *ina ḫūd libbišu* that is well-attested in the Old Babylonian period.[19]

1.2 VOLITION IS LOVE

Just as in the metaphor VOLITION IS JOY, where we see verbs of joyfulness expressing volition, in the metaphor VOLITION IS LOVE we see the Akkadian verb *râmu* 'to love' and the related Aramaic verb רחם expressing volition as well.[20] As an example, let us consider this excerpt from the Laws of Hammurabi:

---

[17] For an edition and translation of this text, see Schorr, *Urkunden*, pp. 413–414. See also Luc Dekiere, *Old Babylonian Real Estate Documents from Sippar in the British Museum*: Part I: *Pre-Hammurabi Documents* (Mesopotamian History and Environment, Series III, Texts, 2, Ghent: University of Ghent, 1994) pp. 79–81 (text 44). For the CDLI edition, see: https://cdli.ucla.edu/P365161 (Accessed: June 9, 2023).

[18] For examples, see *CAD* Ṭ, p. 32 s.v. *ṭābu* mng. s4´.

[19] For examples, see *CAD* Ṭ, pp. 117–118 s.v. *ṭūbu* mng f.

[20] Establishing the etymology for this particular term within this metaphor has proven to be a bit complicated. CAL glosses רחם as 'to love' (accessed May 2022). Akkadian has two verbs, *râmu* 'to love' and *rêmu* 'to show mercy', and Muffs suggests that this metaphor of volition belongs to the latter one. *CAD*, however, has a more complicated presentation of the evidence. This example and similar ones are listed under *râmu* A mng 1f, which is glossed 'to have a preference for'. *CAD*

> *šum-ma a-wi-lum a-na aš-ša-ti-šu* A.ŠÀ ^{GIŠ}KIRI$_6$ É *ù bi-ša-am iš-ru-uk-šim ku-nu-uk-kam i-zi-ib-ši-im wa-ar-ki mu-ti-ša* DUMU.MEŠ-*ša ú-ul i-ba-qá-ru-ši um-mu-um wa-ar-ka-sà a-na* DUMU-*ša ša i-ra-am-mu i-na-ad-di-in a-na a-ḫi-im ú-ul i-na-ad-di-in*
>
> If a man awards to his wife a field, orchard, house, or movable property, and makes out a sealed document for her, after her husband's death her children will not bring a claim against her; the mother shall give her estate to whichever of her children she loves, but she will not give it to an outsider. (LH §150)

This law establishes a woman's ownership rights over a part of the paternal estate that has been deeded to her by her husband. While she does not have discretion to alienate this property outside of the family, she does have the right to show preferential treatment among her children in disposing of this property.

Similar language may be found in a testament from Nuzi, HSS 13 366. In this document, a husband bequeaths property to his wife.[21] After describing the property, it includes a clause similar to the above-cited excerpt from the Laws of Hammurabi:

> ^{21}*ma-an-nu-ma i-na* ŠÀ DUMU-*ia* ^{22}*i-ra-am ù šu-nu li-id-dì-in* ^{23}*a-na* LÚ *na-ka$_4$-ri la i-na-an-din*
>
> Whomever among my sons she loves, she shall give them (the property). To an outsider, she shall not give (it). (HSS 13 366.21–23)

Again, this is not merely an expression of maternal affection, but a legal term of art whereby she shows a preference in the disposal of her property. These examples could be multiplied and continue well into the first millennium.[22]

Turning to the Aramaic evidence, this metaphor of VOLITION IS LOVE turns up in the Elephantine papyri in two forms. The first

---

also includes a separate *râmu* B, which it glosses as 'to present, to grant, to deed an estate', all attestations of which are post-Old Babylonian.

[21] For an edition and translation of this text, see Jonathan Solomon Paradise, *Nuzi Inheritance Practices* (PhD Diss., University of Pennsylvania, 1972) pp. 165–168. For the CDLI edition, see: https://cdli.ucla.edu/P408540 (Accessed: June 9, 2023).

[22] For more examples, see *CAD* R, p. 145 s.v. *râmu* mng 1f.

is the phrase ברחמן 'in affection'. This phrase is used in transactions in which no consideration is involved, such as deeds of gift, and it is important in these cases to establish that the transaction is being undertaken free-willingly. At Elephantine, the phrase ברחמן is attested in three deeds of gift involving both real estate and moveable property (*TAD* B3.5, B3.10, and B5.5). As an example, let us consider *TAD* B3.5, in which a husband gives an apartment to his wife. After establishing the parties to the transaction and describing the property in question, the husband declares his intention to convey the property using the locution יהב ... ברחמן:

[4] ... אנה ענניה יהבתה לכי ברחמן

I, PN, have given it to you in affection. (*TAD* B3.5.4)

The same locution can be found in *TAD* B3.10, in which a father grants a house to his daughter. The phrase יהב ... ברחמן occurs three times in this document, though the following example will suffice:

[11]... ביתא זנה זי משחתה[12]ותחומוהי כתבן בספרא זנה אנה ענני
בר עזריה יהבתה לך ברחמן

This house whose measurements and boundaries are written in this document—I, PN son of PN_2, have given it to you in affection. (*TAD* B3.10.11–12)

The phrase also occurs in *TAD* B5.5 wherein one sister gives another sister a gift of six shekels. The phrase יהב ... ברחמן was also standard in dowry descriptions.[23] Specifically, it was used in a 'waiver of reclamation' clause in which the father (or whoever was giving the dowry) could not try to reclaim any items given as part of the dowry by asserting that they were merely given 'in affection' (ברחמן). This further confirms that the phrase was restricted to transactions not involving consideration.

H. Z. Szubin and Bezalel Porten argue that the phrase ברחמן does have literal connotations of affection because it occurs in

[23] For examples, see *TAD* B3.8.40–41, B3.1.9–10, B6.4.7.

transfers of property that are *inter familia*.[24] While we cannot entirely rule this out, substantial gifts of property, not to mention dowries, of the kind attested in the evidence available to us would likely only be between family members. The only other attestation of this phrase in the Elephantine corpus occurs in *TAD* B2.10, a ספר מרחק or document of withdrawal, a type of document in which one party relinquishes a claim or right. In this document, the principal party renounces all ownership claims to a house and any right to bring suit over this property. The document contains two no-contest clauses in which the principal party relinquishes the right to bring suit over the property against its present owners or against any future owners of the property. The clauses take care to specify that the renouncement of these rights apply whether those future owners acquired the property through sale or through a gift:

> [10] ... אף לא נכהל נרשה לבר וברה לכם [11]אח ואחה אנתה ואיש
> לכם או גבר זי תזבנון לה ביתא זך או זי ברחמן תנתנון לה

> Moreover, we shall not be able to bring (suit) against son or daughter of yours, brother or sister, woman or man of yours, or a person to whom you sell that house or to whom you give (it) in affection. (*TAD* B2.10.10-11)

In the other attestations listed above, the parties to the transactions were always family members. This clause, which clearly distinguishes between sales and gifts, refers to future contingencies and does not make clear whether it only contemplates transfers of ownership between familial relations.

The second form of the metaphor VOLITION IS LOVE uses the verb רחם 'to love' to refer to the discretion a property owner has in the disposition of property, which is closer to what we see in the Akkadian examples cited above.[25] In the Elephantine papyri, it occurs in the so-called investiture clause, a clause unique to Aramaic deeds of conveyance. In this clause, the conveyer of the property (be it a seller or one bestowing a gift) invests its new

---

[24] H. Z. Szubin and Bezalel Porten, 'Testamentary Succession at Elephantine', *BASOR* 252 (1983), pp. 35–46 (36).

[25] For Egyptian examples of this metaphor, see Szubin and Porten, 'Testamentary Succession at Elephantine', p. 38.

owner with all the rights of ownership. One of the most important of these rights—a true test of good title—is the ability to convey property ownership to another party. Among the Elephantine papyri, this delineation of rights is phrased in the attested versions of the investiture clauses in one of the following two ways:

> [9]אנתי שליטה בה מן יומא זנה ועד עלם ובניכי אחריכי למן זי
> [10]רחמתי תנתנן
>
> You are empowered regarding it from this day and forever and (so are) your children after you. To whomever you love you may give (it). (*TAD* B2.3.9-10)

> [11]... אנת ענניה בר עזריה שליט [12]בביתא זך ובניך מן אחריך ולמן די
> צבית למנתן
>
> You, PN, are empowered with regard to this house and (so are) your children after you, and to whomever you desire to give (it). (*TAD* B3.4.11–12)

The key term here comes at the end of the clause, expressing the new owner's right to alienate title. Some instances of the investiture clause use the verb רחם,[26] whereas others use the verb צבי, 'to desire'. Porten and Szubin argue that the terms have distinctive legal nuances, specifically that the former term is more restrictive, limiting alienation to heirs and descendants, whereas the latter term allows alienation to any party.[27] This explanation is quite attractive, though there are a couple cases for which it fails to account, such as *TAD* B2.7, which seemingly uses both verbs interchangeably. Assuming Porten and Szubin are correct, perhaps one could dispute whether רחם is in fact a metaphor as it refers specifically to family members, people for whom the property owner presumably had a distinctive emotional affection. That being said, there may be an analogous distinction in LH §§150 and 179 cited above, as the latter uses *ṭābu* to indicate that

---

[26] For other examples in the Elephantine papyri, see *TAD* B2.7.8, B2.10.9, B3.10.21, and B3.12.23, 26, 31.

[27] Szubin and Porten, 'Testamentary Succession at Elephantine', p. 38.

the woman may dispose of her property to whomever she wants, whereas the former uses *râmu* to indicate that she may only grant the estate within her family. If so, perhaps we can further map our source domain to our target domain with the metaphor the FAVORED HEIR IS BELOVED.

1.3 SATISFACTION IS JOY

Our third example of a metaphor of affection is the well-known satisfaction clause, which has deep roots in the cuneiform tradition and occurs in a variety of contract types. Unlike the VOLITION IS JOY metaphor which lasted well into the first millennium BCE, the satisfaction clause disappears by the latter part of the second millennium only to reemerge in the Aramaic materials from Elephantine. Muffs devoted the bulk of his monograph to this clause, concluding that it served as a quitclaim whereby one party acknowledges that the other has satisfactorily performed some legal obligation. Thus, satisfaction is a legal term of art rather than an emotion. There are, however, instances of this clause in the Elephantine papyri that Muffs regards as atypical and cannot be explained according to his analysis of the clause as a quitclaim. Before assessing these issues, let us first consider some of the evidence. In Emar 144, a deed of sale for a building, we see a typical usage of this clause in Akkadian.[28] The contract begins by describing the property being sold, and then at the end of the operative section it specifies the parties to the transaction and the sale price being exchanged:

> ^{14}KI ^{d}*Nin-urta ù* LÚ.MEŠ *ši-bu-ut* ^{uru}*E-*[*mar*^{ki}] ^{15}*be-lu-ú* É *tu-ug-gu*$_{8}$-*ru* ^{16m}*be-li-ia* ^{17}DUMU *Ḫi-in-nu-*^{d}*Da-gan* ^{18}*a-na 5 me-at* KÙ.BABBAR ^{19}ŠÁM.TIL.LA ^{20}[É *tu-ug-g*]*u*$_{8}$*-rù i-ša-am* ^{21}K[Ù.BABBAR *maḫ-*]*rù* ŠÀ-*šu-nu ṭà-a-ab*
>
> From Ninurta and the elders of E[mar], owners of a *tugguru* house, PN son of PN$_{2}$ for 500 (shekels of) silver, the full price,

[28] For an edition of this text, see Daniel Arnaud, *Recherches au pays d'Aštata. Emar VI.3: Textes sumériens et accadiens* (Synthèse, 18, Paris: Éditions Recherche sur les civilisations, 1986) pp. 156–158.

> purchased a *tugg[uru* house]. They are in rec[eipt of the silver]. Their heart is satisfied. (Emar 144.14–21)

There are three key elements here that signify the successful completion of this transaction. First, it notes that the buyer gave the full sale price rather than a reduced one that resulted from economic duress; second, it acknowledges that the sellers are in receipt of the sale price; third, it expresses the sellers' satisfaction with what they have received. This last element, the satisfaction clause, uses an emotional metaphor, *libbašunu ṭāb* 'their heart is satisfied'.

In the following paragraph from the Laws of Hammurabi, we have an atypical usage of this idiom. It deals with the wages of a shepherd and the consequences for any losses to his flock that occur:

> *šum-ma* SIPA *ša* ÁB.GU$_4$.ḪÁ *ù lu* U$_8$.UDU.ḪÁ *a-na re-im in-na-ad-nu-šum* Á-*šu ga-am-ra-tim ma-ḫi-ir li-ib-ba-šu ṭa-ab* ÁB.GU$_4$.ḪÁ *uṣ-ṣa-aḫ-ḫi-ir* U$_8$.UDU.ḪÁ *uṣ-ṣa-aḫ-ḫi-ir ta-li-it-tam um-ta-ṭi a-na* KA *ri-ik-sa-ti-šu ta-li-it-tam ù bi-il-tam i-na-ad-di-in*
>
> If a shepherd, to whom cattle or sheep and goats were given for shepherding, is in receipt of his complete hire to his satisfaction, then allows the number of cattle to decrease, or the number of sheep and goats to decrease, or the number of offspring to diminish, he shall give for the (loss of) offspring and by-products in accordance with the terms of his contract. (LH §264)

As noted above, in Muffs' analysis, the satisfaction clause in deeds of sale indicates that the buyer has completed his or her legal obligation, prompting the seller to relinquish his or her rights to the property being sold. In LH §264, however, the shepherd has no rights to relinquish, and so the nuance of the clause would seem to be somewhat different. Muffs accounts for this by arguing that the clause indicates the triggering of an obligation. The shepherd was not obligated to cover any losses from his wages until having received his wages in full, but once he had, he was so obligated.[29]

---

[29] Muffs, *Studies*, pp. 87–90.

In the Aramaic evidence, we also have usages of the satisfaction clause that Muffs regarded as both typical and atypical. An example of typical usage can be found in *TAD* B3.4, the real estate sale contract cited above. After identifying the principal parties and then describing the property's boundaries and contents, we have the declaration of sale clause, in which the sellers declare the following:

> [5] ... אנחן זבנהי לך ויהבת [6]לן דמוהי כסף כרש 1 שקלן 4 באבני
> מלכא כסף זוז לכרש 1 וטיב לבבן [7]בדמיא זי יהבת לן

> We have sold it to you, and you have given us its payment, silver, 1 karsh and 4 shekels, 4 in the stones of the king, silver zuz to 1 karsh, and our heart was satisfied with the payment that you gave us. (*TAD* B3.4.5–7)

In this case, the sellers report their satisfaction with the buyer's performance of his obligations, namely providing the sale price, using an emotional metaphor to acknowledge receipt of the sale price in full and their readiness to transfer ownership of the property to the buyer.

Another typical usage occurs in *TAD* B2.2, a ספר מרחק in which the principal party relinquishes his claim regarding a boundary dispute on a specific piece of real estate. In the course of the litigation that had led up to this settlement, the judges had required the other party to affirm these boundaries through an oath. In response to this oath, the principal party states:

> [11] ... ימאת לי ביהו והוטבת [12]לבבי על ארקא זך

> You swore to me by DN and satisfied my heart about that land. (*TAD* B2.2.11–12)

In this case, the root יטב appears in a verbal form rather than as an adjective, but once again, the satisfaction clause appears to be acting as a form of quitclaim.

Muffs describes *TAD* B4.4, a fragmentary bill of lading, as an atypical usage of the satisfaction clause. In this document, some barley is consigned to two men for delivery, and when they receive the barley, the text says that their heart is satisfied with it. In Muffs' view, this is atypical because with the deed of sale, it is important for the buyer to be satisfied with receiving the sale price as he or she is relinquishing rights to property. The delivery agents, however, are not relinquishing any rights, and so it is hard to describe the satisfaction clause as a quitclaim. Muffs explains this as an extended usage in which the receipt of the barley generates an obligation on the part of the delivery agents.[30]

Raymond Westbrook disputes Muffs' analysis that the satisfaction clause encompassed such divergent uses.[31] He argued that it was unlikely to have served as a quitclaim, because the other adjacent clauses easily served that function as did the existence of the contract itself. He alternatively explained the clause as a 'conclusive evidence clause'. In his view, the common thread uniting all the attestations of the satisfaction clause was the affirmation that certain specified quantities and measures had been rendered accurately.[32] Assuming Westbrook's analysis to be correct, we can then tie all of the Akkadian and Aramaic evidence together into a single persisting metaphor.

1.4 DIVORCE IS HATRED

One last metaphor of emotion is DIVORCE IS HATRED or perhaps DISSOLUTION OF A RELATIONSHIP IS HATRED. Beginning with the Akkadian evidence, the normal verb for divorce is *ezēbu* 'to leave, abandon', but the verb *zêru* 'to hate' also arises on occasion in matters of divorce. For example, consider the following excerpt from *CT* 6 26a, an Old Babylonian marriage contract:[33]

> [6]*sú-ka-lí-ia* [7]*i-zi-ib-ši-ma* [8]*1* MA.NA KÙ.BABBAR Ì.LÁ.E [9]*aḫ-ḫu-a-ia-bi* [10]*i-ze-er-šu-ma* [11]*iš-tu di-im-tim* [12]*i-na-du-ni-iš-ši*
>
> If PN divorces her, he shall pay 1 mina of silver. If PN_2 'hates' him, they will throw her from a tower. (*CT* 6 26a.6–12)

---

[30] Muffs, *Studies*, pp. 88–90.
[31] Westbrook, 'The Phrase "His Heart Is Satisfied" in Ancient Near Eastern Legal Sources', *JAOS* 111 (1991), pp. 219–224.
[32] Westbrook, 'The Phrase "His Heart Is Satisfied"', p. 222.
[33] For an edition and translation of this text, see Raymond Westbrook, *Old Babylonian Marriage Law* (PhD Diss., Yale, 1982) pp. 1.111–112. For the CDLI edition, see: https://cdli.ucla.edu/P365140 (Accessed: June 9, 2023).

These clauses use *ezēbu* for when the man initiates divorce, but for the woman, the verb is *zêru*. This verb is also used in other contexts when talking about the dissolution of a relationship, such as this adoption contract from Ugarit:

> ^{7}*ur-ra-am še-ra-am* ^{8}*šum-ma* ^{I}*ar-*^{d}IŠKUR *i-zi-ir* ^{9I}DINGIR-^{d}MAŠ.MAŠ ^{10}ŠEŠ-*šu* ^{UZU}GEŠTU.MEŠ-*šu* ^{11}*i-ṣa-bat ù i-páṭ-ṭar* ^{12}*ù šum-ma* ^{I}DINGIR-^{d}MAŠ.MAŠ ^{13}*i-zi-ir* ^{I}*ar-*^{d}IŠKUR ŠEŠ-*šu* ^{14}1 *li-im* KÙ.BABBAR *i-na-din* ^{15}*a-na* ŠU.MEŠ ^{I}*ar-*^{d}IŠKUR *ù* ŠU.MEŠ DUMU.MEŠ-*šu* ^{16}*ù i-páṭ-ṭar* ^{I}*ar-*^{d}IŠKUR
>
> In the future, if PN 'hates' PN$_2$, his brother, he will seize his ears[34] and depart. And if PN$_2$ 'hates' PN, his brother, 1000 (shekels of) silver he will give into the hands of PN and the hands of his sons and PN will depart. (RS 16.344.7–16)

In this contract describing an adoption into brotherhood (between PN and PN$_2$), the decision to dissolve the relationship being formed here is expressed with the same 'hatred' terminology.

In his discussion of Old Babylonian marriage law, Westbrook considers this usage of *zêru* to be an abbreviation of a longer protasis. As evidence he cites the following three uses of *zêru* in the Laws of Hammurabi: LH §136, in which a man abandons his city, LH §142, in which a woman repudiates her husband, and LH §193, when an adopted son abandons his adoptive parents to live with his biological father:[35]

> … *aš-šum* URU-*šu i-ze-ru-ma in-na-bi-tu* …
>
> … because he hated his city and fled … (LH §136)

> *šum-ma* MUNUS *mu-sà i-ze-er-ma ú-ul ta-aḫ-ḫa-za-an-ni iq-ta-bi* …
>
> If a woman hates her husband and says, 'You shall not take me…' (LH §142)

---

[34] On this expression, see Meir Malul, *Studies in Mesopotamian Legal Symbolism* (AOAT, 221, Neukirchener-Vluyn: Neukirchener Verlag, 1988) pp. 100–101.

[35] Raymond Westbrook, *Old Babylonian Marriage Law* (AfOB, 23, Horn, Austria: Berger & Söhne, 1988) p. 22.

> *šum-ma ...* É *a-bi-šu ú-we-ed-di-ma a-ab-am mu-ra-bi-šu ù um-ma-am mu-ra-ab-bi-sú i-zé-er-ma a-na* É *a-bi-šu it-ta-la-ak*
>
> If (he) ... finds out the house of his father and hates his foster-father and mother and goes to the house of his father ... (LH §193)

In each case, the 'hating' is followed by a specific action, which leads Westbrook to argue that the 'hatred' here establishes the person's *mens rea.*[36] In other words, it conveys the subjective motive behind the action rather than referring to the action itself.

In marriage contracts from Elephantine, the verb שנא 'to hate' is not paired with any action and has become synonymous with 'divorce'.[37] As an example, let us consider the divorce clauses from the marriage contract *TAD* B3.3:[38]

> [7]... מחר או יום אחרן יקום ענני בעדה ויאמר שנאת לתמת אנתתי
> [8]כסף שנא בראשה ינתן לתמת כסף תקלן 1-3-3 ר 2 וכל זי הנעלת
> בידה תהנפק מן חם [9]עד חוט
>
> Tomorrow or (the) next day, should PN stand up in an assembly and say, 'I hate PN_2 my wife', silver of hatred is on his head. He shall give PN_2 silver, 7 shekels 2 q(uarters) and all that she brought in in her hand she shall take out, from straw to string.

> [9]... מחר או יום אחרן תקם תמת ותאמר שנאת לבעלי ענני כסף
> ש<נ>אה בראשה [10]תנתן לענני כסף שקלן 1-3-3 ר 2 וכל זי הנעלת
> בידה תהנפק מן חם עד חוט

---

[36] Westbrook, *Old Babylonian Marriage Law*, p. 81.

[37] Szubin and Porten argue that the verb שנא in these Elephantine marriage contracts refers not to divorce but to a wife's demotion in status, which may ultimately lead to divorce. For a reassessment of this position, see Alejandro F. Botta, 'Hated by the Gods and Your Spouse: Legal Use of שנא in Elephantine and Its Ancient Near Eastern Context', in Anselm C. Hagedorn and Reinhard G. Kratz (eds.), *Law & Religion in the Eastern Mediterranean: From Antiquity to Early Islam* (Oxford: Oxford University Press, 2013) pp. 105–128.

[38] For further examples, see *TAD* B2.4.8–9; B2.6.22–26; and B3.8.21–24, 24–28.

> Tomorrow or (the) next day, should PN$_2$ stand up in an assembly and say, 'I hate PN my husband', silver of hatred is on her head. She shall give PN silver, 7 shekels 2 q(uarters) and all that she brought in in her hand she shall take out, from straw to string.

The divorce is effectuated by the spouse uttering specific *verba solemnia* in a public or judicial setting, and the 'hatred' here does not merely represent the spouse's emotional disposition, but the actual act of divorce itself.

2. METAPHORS OF CLEANING

From metaphors of emotion, let us move to a totally different category, metaphors of cleaning. In English, we use metaphors of cleanliness in different sorts of legal contexts, such as CORRUPT IS DIRTY. Those who have criminal liability or ethical lapses can be described as 'dirty' as opposed to those who do not and are thus 'clean'. In the federal legislative process in the United States, one can refer to a 'clean bill' using the metaphor UNCONTENTIOUS IS CLEAN. In such cases, one produces a 'clean' bill by stripping out any parts of the legislation or amendments that are contentious so that they may be considered separately, thereby allowing the remaining 'clean' part of the bill to move forward more easily.

In ancient Near Eastern documents, the metaphor we see most commonly in legal contexts is FREE OF CLAIMS IS CLEAN. The item being declared clean can either be a piece of property subject to adverse claims or a person with some sort of financial obligation.[39] When referring to property, it often appears in the warranty clauses of sales transactions (this is quite common in the Aramaic tradition). According to the warranty clause, the seller is obligated to protect the buyer against any adverse claims to his or her newly acquired property. When such claims arose, the seller was to appear in court and 'clean' the property of any such

---

[39] This latter sense is attested among Old Assyrian texts and in the Old Babylonian texts from Mari. For examples, see *CAD* E, pp. 6–7 s.v. *ebēbu* mng 2c3´. Slave manumission texts refer to cleaning the slave's forehead, using the verbs *ebēbu and elēlu*. This, however, was likely an actual ritual act of legal symbolism rather than just a metaphor.

adverse claims, and this usually would mean paying off liens. In Akkadian, the warranty clauses of Old Assyrian texts from Anatolia and Old Babylonian texts from Susa use the verb *ubbubu* (D-stem of *ebēbu*), whose basic meaning is 'to clean'.[40] In later corpora of the second millennium BCE, this verb gets replaced with *zakû*, another verb whose basic meaning is 'to clean', but is subsequently borrowed into the same legal contexts as *ebēbu*.[41]

In the first half of the first millennium BCE, this metaphor of FREE OF CLAIMS IS CLEAN disappears from the warranty clause (as did the warranty clause itself in certain corpora) until the Persian Period. It resurfaces with the verb *murruqu*, which in this context appears to be an Aramaic loan into Akkadian.[42] Akkadian does have a verb *marāqu* that means 'to crush, grind',[43] but the sense of scouring and cleaning can more clearly be found in Hebrew and Aramaic מרק.[44] *CAD* even lists the attestations of *murruqu* as a legal term, which only occur in the Persian Period and later, as a completely separate verb.[45]

The metaphor FREE OF CLAIMS IS CLEAN attested in the cuneiform record continues into the Aramaic tradition. In warranty clauses, sometimes referred to as defension clauses, we find verbs of cleaning being used in the same manner as in the examples listed above. Let us first begin with *TAD* B1.1, which dates to the late 6th century BCE and so is slightly older than the Elephantine papyri and comes from a site further north in Egypt. Some of the content of this Aramaic contract is lost due to its fragmentary state of preservation, but it appears to be a joint venture involving a land lease. Fortunately for us, its warranty

---

[40] For examples, see *CAD* E, pp. 6, 7 s.v. *ebēbu* mngs 2c1´ and 2c4´. Old Assyrian texts sometimes also use forms of the verb *šaḫātu*.

[41] For more details, see Andrew D. Gross, *Continuity and Innovation in the Aramaic Legal Tradition* (JSJSup, 128, Leiden: Brill, 2008) pp. 157–160.

[42] See W. von Soden, 'Aramäische Wörter in neuassyrischen und neu- und spätbabylonischen Texten. Ein Vorbericht. I (*agâ* -**mūš*)', *Orientalia* N.S. 35 (1966), pp. 1–20 (18).

[43] *CAD* M/I, pp. 266–267.

[44] For Biblical Hebrew, see *HALOT*, p. 638a. For Aramaic, see CAL.

[45] *CAD* M/II, pp. 222–223.

clause is well-preserved, wherein the land owner promises the following:

> [10]אקנס אקם ואנקה ואנתן ל[ך ו]הן לא קמת [11]ונקת ונתנת לך
> אתננהי לך מ[ן]חלקי למלך

> I swear to stand up and cleanse and give (it) to [you. And] if I do not stand up and cleanse and give (it) to you, I shall give it to you fr[om] my portion from the king. (*TAD* B1.1.10-11)

As we will see in warranty clauses throughout the Aramaic tradition, it consists of three elements in which the seller promises (1) to 'arise' or 'stand up', meaning to appear in court or some analogous legal setting, (2) to 'cleanse' the property of any claims, and (3) to return it to the buyer's possession. The second element uses the verb נקי, 'to cleanse', a verb whose basic meaning is well-established in Aramaic and in other Semitic languages.

The evidence from the Elephantine papyri is somewhat spotty as only two well-preserved deeds of sale have been found among this corpus. In conveyances of property, warranty clauses only appear in deeds of sale, because in deeds of gift, the party conveying the property does not have the same obligations to deal with adverse claims. Furthermore, in one of the two deeds of sale, *TAD* B3.12, the seller possesses the deed of sale through which he had acquired the property and thereby can establish the pedigree of ownership through documentation. This documentation obviates the need for the warranty clause as the seller simply provides this older document to the buyer in order to establish his good title. With that in mind, let us consider the warranty clause from the other real estate sale discovered at Elephantine, *TAD* B3.4:

> [19]... והן גבר אחרן יגרנך ויגרה [20]לבר וברה לך אנחן נקום ונפצל
> וננתן לך בין יומן 30

> And if another person institute (suit) against you or institute (suit) against son or daughter of yours, we shall stand up and 'cleanse' (it) and give (it) to you within 30 days. (*TAD* B3.4.19-20)

Here, we see all of the same elements as the clause given above. The one key philological sticking point is the verb פצל, translated here as ‘to cleanse’. While its general meaning is not in dispute, its etymology remains obscure, and so it is not clear whether we have a verb whose basic meaning is ‘to clean’.

The only other place where this verb is attested is *TAD* B3.2, a document of withdrawal (ספר מרחק), which has a clause very similar to the warranty clause.[46]

8... הן גרך אח ואחה 9קרב ור<ח>ק בשם הירא זנה אנה אפצל ואנתן לך

If brother or sister, near or f<a>r raise a suit against you because of this *hyrʾ*, I will ‘cleanse’ it and give it to you. (*TAD* B3.2.8–9)

The verb פצל may be related etymologically to the Akkadian verb *peṣû*, another verb meaning ‘to clean’. Various philological suggestions have been proposed to account for the presence of the *lamed*. E. Y. Kutscher suggested that it was some sort of ‘metanalysis’ resulting from פצי being joined to the accusative *lamed*.[47]

Later in the Aramaic tradition, the metaphor FREE OF CLAIMS IS CLEAN persists in the warranty clause attested in the fourth century BCE deeds of sale from the Wadi ed-Daliyeh Samaritan papyri. Because of the highly fragmentary nature of this corpus, the warranty clause only appears in full in the following example:[48]

5... הן גׄ[בר] אׄחרןׄ דינן יעבד עם יהוׄפדיני 6[ועם בנוהי מן אחרוהי]
יקׄים הו[ ]ימרק ינתן ליהו[פׄ]דיני

[46] The inclusion of a warranty clause in a document of withdrawal is rather unusual. For further discussion, see H. Z. Szubin and Bezalel Porten, ‘Litigation concerning Abandoned Property at Elephantine (Kraeling 1)’, *JNES* 42 (1983), pp. 279–284.

[47] E. Y. Kutscher, ‘New Aramaic Texts’, *JAOS* 74 (1954), pp. 233–248 (240). J. J. Rabinowitz suggests that it resulted from some sort of ‘amalgamation’ between the verbs פצי and נצל (*Jewish Law: Its Influence on the Development of Legal Institutions* [New York: Bloch Publishing Company, 1956] p. 148).

[48] A fragmentary attestation appears in WDSP 18.4.

> If so[meone] else enters into litigation with PN, [or with his sons after him,] PN_2, he will clear (him and) give (him back) to PN. (WDSP 3.5–6)

This sale formulary uses a different verb of cleaning, מרק, the same one that finds its way into the Neo-Babylonian sale formulary.

In the sale formulary attested in the Judaean Desert documents dating to the first and second centuries CE, the warranty clause is formulated somewhat differently, resembling the pledging clause, a clause known from contemporaneous marriage contracts in which the husband pledges all of his property as a guarantee for his wife's dowry.[49] Even so, the metaphor FREE OF CLAIMS IS CLEAN persists, also using the verb מרק. As an example, let us consider P. Hever 50 + P. Mur 26, a real estate sale contract from Wadi Murabbaʿat:

> [13]... ואנה [14]או...ס מזבנה וכל די איתי לי ודי אקנה אחראין ו[ערבין]
> [15]למרקא ולקימא זבנה דך קדמ[כן] וקדם ירתכן]

> And I, PN, the seller, and all that I own and whatever I will acquire, are responsible and [guarantors] for cleansing and establishing that sale before [you] and before your heirs (P. Hever 50 + P. Mur 26.13–15)

Instead of מרק, this corpus sometimes uses the verb שפי in this clause, such as in P. Hever 9:

> [... [8]ואנה יעקוב ודי אי]תי לי א[חר]אין וערב[י]ן למשפיה למקימה
> אתרה קדמך ו[קד]ם [9]ירת[י]ך מ[ן יומה דנן ולעלם מן]כל חרר ותגר
> נזקן ובטלה ד[י יתנך]על אתרה[דנן] [10]פטר.. [.. פר]ען תשלמתה
> מן נכ[סי ודי אק]נה לקבלדך

> [And I, PN, and (all) that] I [ow]n, are re[spon]sible and a guaran[t]ee for cleansing and establishing the place before you and be[fo]re your he[i]rs, f[rom this day and forever, from] any dispute and challenge, damage and annulment

[49] For more on this clause, see Andrew D. Gross, 'The Aramaic Law of Sale Considered from the Papyrological and Rabbinic Evidence', in Anselm C. Hagedorn and Reinhard G. Kratz (eds.), *Law & Religion in the Eastern Mediterranean: From Antiquity to Early Islam* (Oxford: Oxford University Press, 2013) pp. 129–164 (152–153).

> th[at may come upon you] regarding [this] place … [the fulfill]ment of the payment (will be) from my pro[perty and (from) whatever I will acq]uire accordingly. (P. Hever 9.8–10)

The basic meaning of the verb שפי is 'to smooth, burnish', and so it has a semantic range similar to that of מרק.

P. Dura 28, a Syriac slave sale from 243 CE, shows an interesting development in its warranty clause by using two verbs to express the metaphor FREE OF CLAIMS IS CLEAN:[50]

> ܘܐܢ ܐܢܫ ܢܕܘܢ ܐܘ ܢܬܗܓܐ ܥܡ ܬܝܪܘ ܙܒܘܢܐ ܐܘ ܥܡ ܝܪ̈ܬܘܗܝ ܥܠ
> ܫܒܩ ܐܡܬܐ ܗܕܐ ܕܙܒܢܬ ܠܗ ܐܘܣܡ ܐܢܐ ܡܬܬܪܥܬܐ ܡܙܒܢܢܝܬܐ
> ܘܝܪ̈ܬܝ ܘܐܕܘܢ ܘܐܡܪܘܩ ܘܐܕܟܐ ܘܐܩܝܡܝܗ̇ ܒܐܝܕܗ ܕܬܝܪܘ ܙܒܘܢܐ

> And if anyone shall bring suit or conspire against PN, the buyer, or against his heirs concerning this slave that I have sold him, I, PN_2, the seller, and my heirs shall rise and defend and clean and clear (her with respect to her title) and place her in PN the buyer's possession. (P. Dura 28.12–15)

In each element of the clause, the number of verbs has multiplied, a process known to happen in legal formulations to ensure that all facets in a given situation are covered (cf. 'cease and desist' in English). Thus, in addition to the verb *mrq*, the clause also lists another verb among the seller's obligations, *dky*. In this case again, we have a verb whose basic meaning is 'to clean' being used in this metaphorical sense.

When we jump forward a few centuries, we see the same FREE OF CLAIMS IS CLEAN metaphor persist into Jewish Babylonian Aramaic. In addition, the multiplication of terminology also continues apace. In a discussion about creditors and improved land, the Babylonian Talmud quotes a warranty clause from a deed of sale:

> אנא איקום ואשפי ואדכי ואמריק זביני אילין אינין ועמליהון
> ושבחיהון ואקים קדמך

[50] For an edition of this text, see John F. Healey, *Aramaic Inscriptions and Documents of the Roman Period: Textbook of Syrian Semitic Inscriptions, Volume IV* (Oxford: Oxford University Press, 2009) pp. 264–275.

> I shall arise, and satisfy, cleanse, and clear these purchases—them and their labor costs and their improvements, and I will substantiate (them) before you. (B. B. Meṣ. 15a)

Here we have three verbs referring to the satisfying of adverse claims, all of which we have seen before, and each of which has the basic meaning 'to clean' or something closely related.

Our final example also comes from Jewish Babylonian Aramaic, though several centuries after the compilation of the Babylonian Talmud. In the 10th century CE, Rav Hai Gaon compiled a handbook of formularies to serve as a model for drafting standard types of contracts. The formulary for the sale of a house includes the following warranty clause: [51]

> ואינש לא ימחא בידיה ולא ביד ירתיה בתריה מן יומא דנן ולעלם
> ואחראיות שטר זביני אילין עלאי אנא פל' בר פל' ועל ירתאי בתראי
> ודכל מאן דייתי ויטעון ויערער על פל' דנן או על ירתיה בתריה בזביני
> אילין איקום אנא פל' בר פל' וירתאי בתראי ונפצי ונברי ונדכי
> ונמריק ונשיזיב ונציל ית זביני אילין וית שבחיהון ונוקים יתהון ביד
> פל' דנן וביד ירתיה בתריה לעלם ונשלים להון כל זיאנא וחוסראנא
> דימטי להון מתחות זביני אילין לעלם

> And let no person protest or his heirs after him from this day and forever, and the responsibility of the deed of these purchases is upon me, I, so-and-so son of so-and-so, and upon my heirs after me, and should anyone come and sue and bring legal action against this very so-and-so or against his heirs after him regarding these purchases, I, so-and-so son of so-and-so and my heirs after me will arise and clear, quit the claim, cleanse, clear, indemnify, and make clear these purchases and their improvements, and we will substantiate them in the hand of this so-and-so and in the hand of his heirs after him forever. And we will recompense for them any loss or damages that may come regarding these purchases forever. (Rav Hai Gaon, 6a.16–21 in ספר שטרות)

[51] For an edition of this text, see Simcha Assaf, *The Book of Shetaroth (Formulary) of R. Hai Gaon* [Hebrew] (Supplement to *Tarbiz*, I, 3, Jerusalem: Azriel Press, 1930) pp. 24–26.

Here the number of verbs has multiplied to six, although not all of them mean 'to clean', as some of them mean 'to save'. Still, the verbs מרק and דכי have persisted into this formulary.

3. The Lifespan of an Aramaic Legal Metaphor

Let us conclude by looking at the respective lifespans of these metaphors (to use another metaphor). The use of these metaphors, or the lack thereof, reflects the continuity and change within these broader traditions. The two types of metaphors described here are not equally distributed throughout the Aramaic tradition. Some of the metaphors of emotion I have discussed above, such as VOLITION IS LOVE and SATISFACTION IS JOY, have a long history in the cuneiform record and find robust expression among the Elephantine papyri. In later Aramaic corpora, however, these metaphors are not present. While the Elephantine papyri use the phrase ברחמן to express a party's full willingness to relinquish ownership of a piece of real estate, in later Aramaic conveyances, this disposition was expressed through the decidedly non-metaphorical phrase מן רעותי 'from my own will' (or variations thereof). In addition, this latter phrase was incorporated into sale formularies, not only deeds of gift. The metaphor the FAVORED HEIR IS BELOVED, which specifies legal heirs as those 'whom you love', is also unknown in later Aramaic corpora. Instead, the investiture clause grants the new owner the right to convey the property to whomever he or she desires. This may reflect a substantive change in the law as much as in style, but we cannot be entirely sure due to the relative paucity of evidence.

These later Aramaic conveyances also do not make use of the satisfaction clause and its metaphor SATISFACTION IS JOY. Rather, to indicate full payment in sales transactions, they include another non-metaphorical phrase, דמין גמירין 'the full price', when specifying how much the buyer had paid. This phrase also has a long history in the cuneiform record. Conversely, the warranty clause's metaphor FREE OF CLAIMS IS CLEAN remained part of the Aramaic legal tradition well into the Middle Ages.

The distribution of these metaphors reflects the variegated influences on the Aramaic tradition as a whole. While some elements—and we are not speaking merely about the use of metaphors here—are ubiquitous in this tradition, others are not. The cuneiform record was obviously quite diverse and influenced the Aramaic traditions in different ways at different points, leaving one sort of imprint on some Aramaic corpora and leaving other types of imprints on other Aramaic corpora. The full price element I just mentioned is an interesting example. This seems to have come into Aramaic from cuneiform traditions, but only at a relatively late date. The persistence of these metaphors over time demonstrates the degree to which they were—to use one last metaphor—baked into how the scribes understood these legal concepts.

Daniel and Texts from the Judean Desert

THE SEMANTICS AND FUNCTIONS OF A VISIONARY FORMULAIC CONSTRUCTION IN BIBLICAL AND QUMRAN ARAMAIC*

DANIEL E. CARVER

1. INTRODUCTION

In the Aramaic portions of Daniel and the Aramaic texts from the Judean Desert, a seer's experience of a vision is frequently highlighted by a periphrastic participial construction that occurs mostly in the first person, חָזֵה הֲוֵית, 'I was watching', (e.g., Dan. 4.7; 7.4) but does appear twice in the second person, חָזֵה הֲוַיְתָ, 'you were watching', when Daniel described Nebuchadnezzar's dream to the king (Dan. 2.31, 34). This formulaic construction makes each of these vision reports 'as much a story about a man who saw a vision and its interpretation, as a report of the vision and the interpretation given'.[1] It is widely recognized that the

---

* It is with a profound sense of appreciation and gratitude that I offer this study in honor of an excellent scholar, teacher, and friend. I can only hope to pass on to my students the same love and enthusiasm for Hebrew and Aramaic that he daily demonstrated to me.

[1] T. J. Meadowcroft, *Aramaic Daniel and Greek Daniel: A Literary Comparison* (JSOTSup, 198, Sheffield: Sheffield Academic Press, 1995) p. 210; cf. René Péter-Contesse and John Ellington, *A Handbook on the Book of Daniel* (UBS Handbook Series, New York: United Bible Societies, 1993)

construction has literary significance,[2] introducing new scenes in the visions.[3] However, the uses of the construction have significance for more than highlighting the seer's experience of the vision and the structure of the vision reports.[4]

Sometimes the formulaic construction (חזה הוית) is accompanied by a prepositional phrase that locates the activity in a vision[5] (such as, בחזוי ראשי על משכבי, Dan. 4.10)[6] or a presentative particle that draws attention to an object or situation in the vision (אלו/ארו or הא, Dan. 2.31; 4.7; 7.6; 4Q206 4 i 16),[7] and in one instance there is no accompanying phrase or particle (Dan. 7.21). But not infrequently the formulaic construction is followed by the subordinating conjunction עד and a relative clause that functions adverbially, 'until (the time) that…' (Dan. 2.34; 7.4, 9, 11; 1QapGen 13.11; 2Q24 4 17; 4Q206 4 i 18; and the partially broken but probable occurrences in 2Q24 4 14–15; 4Q530 6.9). Since these constructions often occur multiple times in close proximity, the non-initial instances have largely been interpreted

p. 181; Carol A. Newsom, *Daniel: A Commentary* (OTL, Louisville: Westminster John Knox Press, 2014) p. 231.

[2] M. Delcor, 'Les sources du chapitre VII de Daniel', *VT* 18 (1968), pp. 290–312 (290); Paul R. Raabe, 'Daniel 7: Its Structure and Role in the Book', *HAR* 9 (1985), pp. 267–275 (269–270); John E. Goldingay, *Daniel* (WBC, 30, Dallas: Word Books, 1989) p. 154; John J. Collins, *Daniel: A Commentary on the Book of Daniel* (Hermeneia – A Critical and Historical Commentary on the Bible, Minneapolis: Fortress Press, 1993) p. 277; Newsom, *Daniel*, p. 220.

[3] It has also been observed that the phrase is accompanied by a prepositional phrase that lengthens it at key junctions of Daniel 7: חזה הוית בחזוי [עם] ליליא וארו, 'I was watching in the visions of the night, and behold', appears at the beginning (Dan. 7.2) and at the introduction of the fourth beast (7.7); see Goldingay, *Daniel* 154; Ernest C. Lucas, *Daniel* (Apollos Old Testament Commentary, Downers Grove: InterVarsity Press, 2002) p. 166.

[4] See John J. Collins, *Daniel: With an Introduction to Apocalyptic Literature* (FOTL, 20, Grand Rapids: Eerdmans, 1984) pp. 76–77; cf. Collins, *Daniel*, pp. 277–279.

[5] See Edward M. Cook, *Biblical Aramaic and Related Dialects: An Introduction* (Cambridge: Cambridge University Press, 2022) p. 236.

[6] Similar prepositional phrases occur after חזה הוית in Dan. 7.2, 7, 13.

[7] On occasion, the phrase is followed by a prepositional phrase and then a presentative particle (Dan. 4.10; 7.2, 7, 13).

as repetitive or resumptive of the first instance, so that each occurrence of the construction functions essentially the same as the others.[8]

In contrast to that perspective, I argue in this study that there is a significant semantic and functional difference between the instances of the formulaic construction followed by the conjunction עד and an adverbial clause, and those that are not. Linguistically, the difference is one of (un)boundedness. The (un)boundedness of these constructions affects the temporal interpretation of the vision report. In the following sections, I describe the semantics of חזה הוית from the vantage points of the verbal construction (as a participial periphrastic construction) and situation aspect. Then I explain the category of (un)boundedness and how the semantics of the formulaic construction are affected by the addition of the subordinating conjunction עד and an adverbial clause. Ultimately, it is argued that the temporal interpretation of the vision is significantly impacted by the (un)boundedness of the construction and that there is a functional privative opposition between the bounded and unbounded constructions.

2. VERBAL SEMANTICS AND (UN)BOUNDEDNESS

The formulaic construction חָזֵה הֲוֵית (here in the first person)[9] is a participial periphrastic construction consisting of an active participle used verbally (חזה) with a suffix conjugation of √הוי. The finite verb signals past time reference and the participle signals duration for the situation. Although the participial construction is used to express other kinds of situations (e.g., habitual), the formulaic construction always expresses an ongoing situation.[10]

---

[8] E.g., Tarsee Li, *The Verbal System of the Aramaic of Daniel: An Explanation in the Context of Grammaticalization* (SAIS, 8, Leiden: Brill, 2009) pp. 86–88; cf. Péter-Contesse and Ellington, *A Handbook on the Book of Daniel*, p. 181.

[9] For convenience, when discussing the construction, I will use its more common form with the first person singular and with the orthographic and spelling practices found in Biblical Aramaic.

[10] Hans Bauer and Pontus Leander, *Grammatik des Biblisch-Aramäischen* (Halle: Max Niemeyer Verlag, 1927) pp. 293–294; Stanislav Segert,

In terms of situation aspect, the past, ongoing situation expressed by חזה הוית is an *activity*. There are four canonical situation types,[11] distinguished by two properties: *stages* and *telicity* (see Table 1).[12]

Situation type	[± *stages*]	[± *telic*]	English example
State	–	–	Lemuel is happy
Activity	+	–	Boaz is reading
Achievement	–	+	Ezra won the race
Accomplishment	+	+	Zimri built a house

A situation that is [+*stages*] can be analyzed 'as progressing or developing',[13] while (a)telicity is determined by whether the situation has a natural or intended endpoint.[14] The situation expressed by חזה הוית is an activity in that it has stages or sub-events (such as *began watching*, *kept watching*, and so on) but is atelic because it has no inherent endpoint. Situation aspect is affected by various features of a clause, such as the verb forms as well as the presence and type of complements or adjuncts, including noun phrases and prepositional phrases.[15] In Dan. 7.1, חֵ֫לֶם חֲזָה, 'he saw a dream', the verb form is a perfect and the situation expressed is an *accomplishment*, meaning the situation is [+*stages*] and [+*telic*]. In this case, the perfect verb form and the nature of the object require that the situation has an inherent

---

Altaramäische Grammatik: mit Bibliographie, Chrestomathie und Glossar (Leipzig: VEB Verlag Enzyklopädie, 1975) p. 386; Holger Gzella, *Tempus, Aspekt, und Modalität im Reichsaramäischen* (Veröffentlichungen der Orientalischen Kommission, 48, Wiesbaden: Harrassowitz, 2004) p. 308; Li, *The Verbal System of the Aramaic of Daniel*, p. 89.

[11] Zeno Vendler, 'Verbs and Times', *Philosophical Review* 66/2 (1957), pp. 143–160.

[12] Susan Rothstein, *Structuring Events: A Study in the Semantics of Lexical Aspect* (Explorations in Semantics, Oxford: Blackwell, 2004) pp. 6–35; table adapted from p. 12.

[13] Rothstein, *Structuring Events*, p. 7.

[14] Carlota S. Smith, 'Activities: States or Events?', *Linguistics and Philosophy* 22 (1999), pp. 479–508 (480).

[15] Ilse Depraetere, 'On the Necessity of Distinguishing between (Un)-Boundedness and (A)Telicity', *Linguistics and Philosophy* 18 (1995), pp. 1–19 (4, 9–13); Rothstein, *Structuring Events*, p. 4.

endpoint, meaning it is [+*telic*], specifically when the dream was over. But in the formulaic construction חזה הוית, √חזי is a participle, and the construction expresses an ongoing *activity* in past time without a natural endpoint [-*telic*].[16]

An important semantic distinction must be recognized between telicity and 'actual temporal boundaries' which is best described in terms of *(un)boundedness.*[17] The situation *Boaz read a book* is an accomplishment, since there are stages that progressively work toward a natural or inherent endpoint (i.e., the book having been read by Boaz). The natural endpoint in this situation has been reached and so the situation is temporally *bounded.* However, in the sentence, *Boaz was reading a book*, the situation still has stages progressively leading to a natural or intended endpoint (i.e., it is still an accomplishment), but the natural endpoint has not been reached. This is even more clearly seen when *Boaz was reading a book* is followed by *when his friends came over to play.* The arrival of his friends prevented the situation from meeting its natural or intended endpoint. Therefore, the situation, *Boaz was reading a book*, is temporally *unbounded* because the temporal boundary provided by the natural endpoint is not met.

Like situation aspect, (un)boundedness is affected by verb forms and the presence and type of complements and adjuncts.[18] Especially significant are adverbials, because they can add temporal boundaries to situations that do not have such boundaries otherwise. For example, *Ezra read the book* is an accomplishment, but changing the object to an indefinite plural, *Ezra read books*, changes the situation to an activity because there is no longer a

---

[16] Some vision descriptions are introduced with √חזי in the perfect (e.g., חזית TAD D7.17; 4Q206 fg. 1, 6.5; 4Q213a 2 16). The perfect is also capable of expressing a situation that temporally overlaps with other situations, but it does so without making the event explicitly ongoing. To such perfects, one might compare the Biblical Hebrew *wayyiqtol* (e.g., Isa. 6.1) and perfect (e.g., Jer. 4.23–26) as well as the aorist in New Testament Greek (e.g., Rev. 4.1; 5.1; passim).

[17] Depraetere, 'On the Necessity of Distinguishing between (Un)-Boundedness and (A)Telicity', pp. 1–6, quote 2.

[18] Depraetere, 'On the Necessity of Distinguishing between (Un)-Boundedness and (A)Telicity', pp. 3–4, 9–13.

natural or inherent endpoint. But this activity can be temporally bounded by an adverbial, as in *Ezra read books for three hours* or *Ezra read books until the length of time required by his mother was met.* It should also be noted that while telicity only concerns a natural or intended endpoint, temporal boundaries may be indicated for the beginning or the endpoint of a situation.[19] In the sentence *Ezra read books from 8 a.m. till noon*, the adverbial *from 8 a.m. till noon* puts left (starting point) and right (endpoint) temporal boundaries on the activity.

In terms of situation aspect and (un)boundedness, the formulaic construction חזה הוית expresses an unbounded, ongoing activity ('I was watching'). However, when חזה הוית is followed by the conjunction עד ('until') and an adverbial clause, a right temporal boundary is added to the situation, making it a bounded activity. Though the difference may seem subtle, it is very important because, along with tense, viewpoint aspect, mood, and situation aspect, noting the (un)boundedness of a situation is critical for the correct temporal interpretation of verbs and verb forms.[20]

3. עד ADVERBIALS

Before discussing the occurrences of the construction חזה הוית, it is first necessary to discuss temporal adverbials with עד. Some scholars have mistakenly interpreted עד די in a handful of passages (such as Dan. 2.34; 6.25; 7.4, 9) as 'a marker of attendant circumstance'[21] and translated the conjunction and

---

[19] Depraetere, 'On the Necessity of Distinguishing between (Un)-Boundedness and (A)Telicity', p. 3.

[20] Depraetere, 'On the Necessity of Distinguishing between (Un)Boundedness and (A)Telicity', p. 18. It should also be noted that (un)boundedness is an important semantic feature to recognize when making foreground and background distinctions. Nevertheless, other features and factors must be taken into consideration; see John A. Cook, *Time and the Biblical Hebrew Verb: The Expression of Tense, Aspect, and Modality in Biblical Hebrew* (LSAWS, 7, Winona Lake: Eisenbrauns, 2012) pp. 287–288.

[21] James Swanson, *Dictionary of Biblical Languages with Semantic Domains: Aramaic (Old Testament)* (Oak Harbor: Logos Research Systems, Inc., 1997).

relative word 'as' or 'while'.[22] According to this interpretation, the main clause is co-temporal with the following clause(s) and there is no right temporal boundary. But does עד or עד די function in that way in Biblical or Qumran Aramaic? It is true that עד followed by a relative clause is used to express co-temporal situations without a right temporal boundary in later dialects of Aramaic, but none earlier than the Late Aramaic period (c. 3rd-13th centuries CE).[23] This use occurs, for example, in Targum Pseudo-Jonathan and it is translated 'while still'.[24]

ואמר משה יאות מלילתא

אנא עד דהוינא יתיב במדין

יתאמר לי במימר מן קדם ייי

> And Moses said, 'You have said (what is) proper. **While** I was **still** dwelling in Midian, it was said[25] to me by the word from before the Lord…' (TgPsJ Exod. 10.29)

In this example, 'while I was still dwelling in Midian' is clearly cotemporaneous with the situation of the main clause ('it was said') and there is no right temporal boundary. The situation is unbounded and is part of the discourse background. However, to my knowledge, neither עד nor עד די function in this way in the dialects of the Old, Imperial, or Middle Aramaic periods. In the dialects of these periods, every occurrence of עד that has temporal

---

[22] E.g., Louis F. Hartman and Alexander A. Di Lella, *The Book of Daniel* (AB, 23, Garden City: Doubleday, 1978) pp. 202–204; Goldingay, *Daniel*, pp. 142–154; Lucas, *Daniel*, pp. 158–160, 164–165; Li, *The Verbal System of the Aramaic of Daniel*, pp. 86–88.

[23] Although Fitzmyer's original articulation of the periodization of Aramaic limits the Late Aramaic period to the 3rd-7th centuries (Joseph A. Fitzmyer, 'The Phases of the Aramaic Language' in *A Wandering Aramean: Collected Aramaic Essays* [SBLMS, 25, Chicago: Scholars Press, 1979] pp. 57–84 [61–63]), it is now recognized that the time of Late Aramaic should be extended to the 13th century; see Andrew W. Litke, *Targum Song of Songs and Late Jewish Literary Aramaic: Language, Lexicon, Text, and Translation* (STAS, 15, Leiden: Brill, 2019) pp. 16–17.

[24] CAL (accessed April 2022); this use is also attested in earlier Targums, e.g., TgJon 1 Kgs 18.12; 20.40; 2 Kgs 2.11.

[25] Contextually, יתאמר must refer to a past situation; the morphology is not readily explained.

significance marks a right temporal boundary, just as the examples below from Biblical and Qumran Aramaic do.[26] It seems to me that this is a case of wrongfully reading the function of a word in later dialects of Aramaic back into the earlier texts.

Properly understanding the temporal uses of עד, with or without an accompanying relative clause, is critical for interpreting the passages in which the formulaic construction occurs. In Biblical and Qumran Aramaic, עד functions as a preposition ('up to', 'as far as', 'until') with spatial or temporal significance and as a subordinating conjunction ('until').[27] As a preposition, עד forms an adverbial phrase that marks a right temporal boundary. Consider the adverbial phrases in the following examples:

> אֱדַיִן שֵׁשְׁבַּצַּר דֵּךְ אֲתָא יְהַב אֻשַּׁיָּא דִּי־בֵית אֱלָהָא דִּי בִירוּשְׁלֶם וּמִן־אֱדַיִן וְעַד־כְּעַן מִתְבְּנֵא וְלָא שְׁלִם׃
>
> Then, this Sheshbazzar came (and) laid the foundations of the house of God which is in Jerusalem. And **from then until now**, it has been (in the process of) being built but is not completed. (Ezra 5.16)
>
> אִתְיָעַטוּ כֹּל סָרְכֵי מַלְכוּתָא סִגְנַיָּא וַאֲחַשְׁדַּרְפְּנַיָּא הַדָּבְרַיָּא וּפַחֲוָתָא לְקַיָּמָה קְיָם מַלְכָּא וּלְתַקָּפָה אֱסָר דִּי כָל־דִּי־יִבְעֵה בָעוּ מִן־כָּל־אֱלָהּ וֶאֱנָשׁ עַד־יוֹמִין תְּלָתִין לָהֵן מִנָּךְ מַלְכָּא יִתְרְמֵא לְגֹב אַרְיָוָתָא׃
>
> All the chief ministers of the kingdom, the prefects, the satraps, the advisers, and the governors have taken counsel together to establish a royal edict and to make firm a prohibition that anyone who seeks a request from any god or man **for thirty days** except from you, O king, should be thrown to the den of lions.[28] (Dan. 6.8 [cf. 6.13])

---

[26] Exceptions include idiomatic phrases such as עד עלמא 'until eternity (=forever)' which is ubiquitous in the texts of the Imperial and Middle Aramaic periods and is already attested in the Old Aramaic period in the Sefire inscriptions (e.g., *KAI* 224.25).

[27] *HALOT*; *LBA*; *DQA*.

[28] *HALOT* glosses the occurrence of the preposition in this verse with 'during, within'.

In the first example, the עד adverbial phrase sets the right temporal boundary while another adverbial phrase (מן אדין, 'from then') sets the left temporal boundary. These phrases put temporal boundaries on the expressed, progressive situation. The adverbial phrase in Dan. 6.8 (and 6.13) indicates not only the duration (thirty days) but also marks the end of the prohibition, specifically when the thirty days were complete.

As a conjunction, עד subordinates a clause, or clauses, that functions adverbially, marking the right temporal boundary.

וּבְטַל שְׁמַיָּא יִצְטַבַּע וְעִם־חֵיוַת בָּרָא חֲלָקֵהּ עַד דִּי־שִׁבְעָה עִדָּנִין יַחְלְפוּן עֲלוֹהִי

And with the dew of heaven let him become wet, and (let) his portion be with the beasts of the field **until seven times shall pass over him.** (Dan. 4.20)

וְשִׁבְעָה עִדָּנִין יַחְלְפוּן עֲלָיךְ עַד דִּי־תִנְדַּע דִּי־שַׁלִּיט עִלָּיאָ בְּמַלְכוּת אֲנָשָׁא

And seven times shall pass over you, **until (the time) that you know that the Most High has authority over the kingdom of man.** (Dan. 4.22)

וּלְגֹב אַרְיָוָתָא רְמוֹ אִנּוּן בְּנֵיהוֹן וּנְשֵׁיהוֹן וְלָא־מְטוֹ לְאַרְעִית גֻּבָּא עַד דִּי־שְׁלִטוּ בְהוֹן אַרְיָוָתָא

And to the den of lions they threw them, their children, and their wives. And they had not reached the bottom of the den **before the lions had power over them.**[29] (Dan. 6.25)

עם לעם ידוש ומדינה למדינה עד יקום עם אל

People shall trample people and nation (shall trample) nation **until the people of God shall arise.** (4Q246 1 ii 3–4)[30]

In Dan. 4.20, the king's portion will be with animals until a specific time that marks the right temporal boundary, i.e., once

[29] Cf. Li, *The Verbal System of the Aramaic of Daniel*, p. 86.

[30] Text according to Edward M. Cook, '4Q246', *BBR* 5 (1995), pp. 43–66 (45).

seven times have passed over (cf. Dan. 2.9; 7.12, 25).[31] The right temporal boundary is marked by a state in Dan. 4.22, the state-of-knowing that the Most High has authority over the kingdom of man (also 4.29; 5.21). The adverbial clause in Dan. 6.25 marks the right temporal boundary as the time when the lions had power over Daniel's slanderers. In 4Q246, the fighting between peoples and nations will come to an end when the people of God arise, and the following lines describe that blessed time to follow. In each of these examples, the discourse is advanced, and a time reference is set by the right temporal boundary.

It is very important to note that, when עד functions as a conjunction, the right temporal boundary is often set by the last of two or more situations. In the following example, the conjunction עד subordinates two clauses, the final one setting the temporal boundary.

> וְעֵין אֱלָהֲהֹם הֲוָת עַל־שָׂבֵי יְהוּדָיֵא וְלָא־בַטִּלוּ הִמּוֹ עַד־טַעְמָא
> לְדָרְיָוֶשׁ יְהָךְ וֶאֱדַיִן יְתִיבוּן נִשְׁתְּוָנָא עַל־דְּנָה׃
>
> But the eye of their God was on the elders of the Jews, and they did not stop them **until the report should go to Darius and then a letter be returned about this**. (Ezra 5.5)

The elders did not stop the rebuilding of the temple when Tattenai inquired by what authority they were doing these things, nor did they stop when a letter was sent to king Darius. Rather, the right temporal boundary is set by the arrival of the king's response, which of course assumes that a report would have already been sent to him at that time. Once the king's letter arrived, they acted in accordance with the king's decree (Ezra 6.13–15).

Particularly interesting examples come from Dan. 6.15 and 1QapGen 20.34–21.1 which, like the formulaic construction חזה הוית, have participial periphrastic constructions.

[31] Similarly, in Dan. 4.30, the right temporal boundary is once Nebuchadnezzar's hair and nails had grown out.

וְעַל דָּנִיֵּאל שָׂם בָּל לְשֵׁיזָבוּתֵהּ וְעַד מֶעָלֵי שִׁמְשָׁא הֲוָא מִשְׁתַּדַּר לְהַצָּלוּתֵהּ

And concerning Daniel, he set (his) mind to save him, and **until** the setting of the sun, he was striving to deliver him. (Dan. 6.15)

והוית שרא [עמה ב]כל אתר משריאתי עד די דבקת לבית אל

And I would camp [with him in] every place of my (prior) encampments **until (the time) that** I arrived at Bethel. (1QapGen 20.34–21.1)[32]

In Dan. 6.15, the adverbial phrase 'until the setting of the sun' puts a right temporal boundary on the otherwise unbounded accomplishment, 'he was striving to deliver him'. The participial periphrastic construction indicates that the situation was ongoing from the time that Darius set his mind to save Daniel until sunset. But at sunset, Darius' striving ceased. In the Genesis Apocryphon, Abram describes his return journey from Egypt to Bethel. Over an unspecified period of time, Abram traveled with Lot, habitually camping at the same sites they had camped before, until their arrival at Bethel. At that time, the situation (i.e., camping in all the places they had before) ceased, and he rebuilt the altar that he had built there before. In each of these two examples, the situation expressed by the participial periphrastic construction is bounded by the adverbial with a right temporal boundary. These participial periphrastic constructions, the first being progressive and the second habitual, would have been unbounded but for the adverbials. As a result, they are bounded and each advances the reference time of the narrative.

4. THE חזה הוית CONSTRUCTIONS

To this point, I have described the formulaic construction חזה הוית regarding the semantics of the participial periphrastic construction, situation aspect, and (un)boundedness. In the following sections, it will be shown that attention to each of these is

[32] Text according to Joseph A. Fitzmyer, *The Genesis Apocryphon of Qumran Cave 1 (1Q20): A Commentary* (BibOr, 18/B, 3rd edn., Rome: Biblical Institute Press, 2004) pp. 102–104.

necessary for correctly identifying the temporal interpretation of חזה הוית with and without an עד adverbial clause.

4.1 Unbounded

In Biblical Aramaic, חזה הוית occurs without an עד adverbial clause nine times (Dan. 2.31; 4.7, 10; 7.2, 6, 7, 11, 13, 21)[33] and in Qumran Aramaic only four times (1QapGen 13.9, 10; 4Q206 4 i 16 [partially broken]; 4Q530 6.6 [context broken]). Each of these expresses a progressive, unbounded situation ('watching') that temporally overlaps with the situations in the clauses that follow, such as those describing the large image (2.31), the tree (4.7), the four winds (7.2), and the chopping and taking (1QapGen 13.9-10).[34] In nine of the thirteen unbounded constructions, the vision descriptions begin with a presentative particle (ארו/אלו or הא).[35] With a presentative particle, the unbounded construction highlights the activity of watching while introducing new elements into the vision. In Daniel 7, it is used for introducing the wind stirring the sea from which the four beasts come (7.2), the third beast (7.6), the fourth beast (7.7), and the 'son of man' (7.13) (cf. 4Q206 4 i 16–17).[36] Without a presentative particle, the unbounded construction is used to re-

---

[33] חזה הוית occurs twice in Dan. 7.11a-bα: חָזֵה הֲוֵית בֵּאדַיִן מִן־קָל מִלַּיָּא רַבְרְבָתָא דִּי קַרְנָא מְמַלֱּלָה חָזֵה הֲוֵית עַד דִּי קְטִילַת חֵיוְתָא. 'I was watching – then, because of the sound of the great words that the horn was saying. I was watching until the beast was killed…' Some scholars prefer to delete one or the other (Collins, *Daniel: With an Introduction to Apocalyptic Literature*, p. 76; Collins, *Daniel*, p. 279; Newsom, *Daniel*, p. 231), though not all do, as other scholars find special literary significance in the formulaic construction occurring twice in this verse (Goldingay, *Daniel*, p. 154; Lucas, *Daniel*, p. 167). Although a decision would affect one's analysis of Daniel 7, this matter of possible textual corruption is immaterial to the argument at hand. In this study, I deal with the text as it stands.

[34] The surrounding context of 4Q530 6.6 is too broken for meaningful analysis.

[35] The exceptions are found in Dan. 7.11, 21; 1QapGen 13.9–10 (2x).

[36] Compare the semantically and functionally similar construction משׂתכל הוית ('I was considering') and a presentative particle (ואלו) in Dan. 7.8, which introduces the horn that rose up among the ten.

introduce the horn in two sub-units that elaborate on it (7.11a, 21).

The unbounded construction expresses a situation that temporally overlaps with ongoing situations, expressed with participles (Dan. 4.10; 7.2, 21; 4Q206 44 i 16) and participial periphrastic constructions (Dan. 7.13; 1QapGen 13.9, 10), though it can also temporally overlap with stative situations, expressed through copular clauses (Dan. 2.31; 4.7; 7.6, 7) or passive states with a *peal* passive (Gp) in the perfect (Dan. 7.5, 6; 4Q206 4 i 16–17).

אַנְתְּה מַלְכָּא חָזֵה הֲוַיְתָ וַאֲלוּ צְלֵם חַד

You, O king, **were watching**, and behold, a singular image! (Dan. 2.31)

וְחֶזְוֵי רֵאשִׁי עַל־מִשְׁכְּבִי חָזֵה הֲוֵית וַאֲלוּ אִילָן בְּגוֹא אַרְעָא וְרוּמֵהּ שַׂגִּיא

And the visions of my head upon my bed: **I was watching** and behold, a tree in the midst of the land and its height was great! (Dan. 4.7)

עָנֵה דָנִיֵּאל וְאָמַר חָזֵה הֲוֵית בְּחֶזְוִי עִם־לֵילְיָא וַאֲרוּ אַרְבַּע רוּחֵי שְׁמַיָּא
מְגִיחָן לְיַמָּא רַבָּא׃

And Daniel responded and said, '**I was watching**, in my vision of the night, and behold, the four winds of heaven were stirring up the great sea!' (Dan. 7.2)

אבניא וחספיא הווא קצין ונסבין להון מנה חזה הוית לדהביא
ולכס[פי]א [...] פרזלא ולאילניא כולהון קצין ונסבין להון מנה חזה
הוית לשמשא ולשהרא ולכוכביא קצין ונסבין להון מנה

[...] stones and ceramic pots they were breaking and taking from it for themselves. **I was watching** those of gold and silver, the [... of] iron; and they were chopping all the trees and taking from it for themselves. **I was watching** the sun, the moon, and the stars; they were chopping and taking from it for themselves. (1QapGen 13.9-10)[37]

[37] Text according to Fitzmyer, *The Genesis Apocryphon*, p. 88.

[והוית] חזה והא מרזבין שבעה שפכין [על ארעא מין שגיאין]

[And **I was**] **watching** and behold, seven sluices pouring out [much water on the earth!] (4Q206 4 i 16–17)[38]

[ב]חלמי הוית חזא בליליא דן [...]

[In] my dream, **I was watching** on this night [...] (4Q530 6.6)[39]

It should be noted, however, that the unbounded construction may express a situation that temporally overlaps with a situation that inherently has a right temporal boundary, as it does in Dan. 7.6. There, the activity of watching overlaps with three copular clauses describing the third beast and also a verbal situation, ושלטן יהיב לה 'and authority was given to it'. All of that is perceived before the seer turns to the fourth beast in the following verse.[40]

4.2 Bounded

The construction חזה הוית is followed by the conjunction עד and an adverbial clause (or clauses) four times in Biblical Aramaic (Dan. 2.34; 7.4, 9, 11) and five times in Qumran Aramaic, though two of these are partially broken (1Q20 13.11; 2Q24 4 17; 4Q206 4 i 18; partially broken in 2Q24 4 14–15; 4Q530 6.9). Each of these expresses an ongoing *activity* of 'watching' that is bounded by an adverbial. The seer's watching continues as one or several situations are described, and the right temporal boundary is set by the final situation (see above, Ezra 5.5). The reference time of the vision report is therefore advanced to the time of the right temporal boundary. Accordingly, the clauses that follow חזה הוית and the conjunction עד have perfects expressing either a complete situation or a passive state.[41] This is a significant point of contrast

---

[38] Text according to J. T. Milik, *The Books of Enoch: Aramaic Fragments of Qumran Cave 4* (Oxford: Clarendon, 1976) p. 238.

[39] Text according to Milik, *The Books of Enoch*, p. 304.

[40] The description of the second beast in 7.5, introduced by a presentative particle, also has a right temporal boundary implicitly set by the conclusion speech קומי אכלי בשׂר שׂגיא 'rise, eat much flesh'.

[41] Frequently, the passive state, expressed by a perfect in the G passive (Gp) stem, implies a passive process that leads to that state; see Daniel

with the unbounded constructions of the previous section, which are followed by clauses with stative situations or ongoing situations expressed by participles and participial periphrastic constructions. Stative situations can follow the unbounded construction (e.g., Dan. 7.5) and can also occur in an adverbial clause setting a temporal boundary (e.g., Dan. 7.4), but the progressive semantics of the active participle are incompatible with an adverbial clause that sets a right temporal boundary.

The bounded construction is used to draw attention to certain figures or situations of great importance in the vision. In Daniel 2.34 and 7.4b (below), the figures are, respectively, the stone that was 'cut without hands', representing the kingdom of God and his people, and the first beast, which, representing Babylon, is of some significance given the literary setting of Babylon (Dan. 7.1). The literary spotlight remains on these figures as several situations take place in the clauses following, and the seer watches them through to completion.

חָזֵה הֲוַיְתָ עַד דִּי הִתְגְּזֶרֶת אֶבֶן דִּי־לָא בִידַיִן וּמְחָת לְצַלְמָא עַל־רַגְלוֹהִי
דִּי פַרְזְלָא וְחַסְפָּא וְהַדֵּקֶת הִמּוֹן׃

> You were watching until a stone was cut without hands, and it struck the image on its feet of iron and clay, and it crushed them. (Dan. 2.34)

חָזֵה הֲוֵית עַד דִּי־מְּרִיטוּ גַפַּיהּ וּנְטִילַת מִן־אַרְעָא וְעַל־רַגְלַיִן כֶּאֱנָשׁ
הֳקִימַת וּלְבַב אֱנָשׁ יְהִיב לַהּ׃

> I was watching until its wings were plucked, and it was lifted up from the earth, and it was set up on feet like a man, and a human heart was given to it. (Dan. 7.4b)

The other instances draw attention to critical situations, such as the courtroom of the Ancient of Days being set up, the destruction of the fourth beast, the flood, and priestly rites. Each of these bounded constructions draws attention to the seer watching these situations until their completion.

E. Carver, 'The Use of the Perfect in Daniel 7:27', *JBL* 138 (2019), pp. 325–344 (334–342).

חָזֵה הֲוֵית עַד דִּי כָרְסָוָן רְמִיו וְעַתִּיק יוֹמִין יְתִב

I was watching until (the) thrones were set and the Ancient of Days sat down. (Dan. 7.9a)

חָזֵה הֲוֵית עַד דִּי קְטִילַת חֵיוְתָא וְהוּבַד גִּשְׁמַהּ וִיהִיבַת לִיקֵדַת אֶשָּׁא:

I was watching until the beast was killed, and its body destroyed, and it was given to the burning fire. (Dan. 7.11b)

חזה הוית עד די אסיפוהי שרץ ארעא ושרץ מיא וסף מיא וסף

I was watching until the swarming creatures of the earth and the swarming creatures of the waters destroyed it, and the waters were finished, and it was finished.[42] (1QapGen 13.11–12)[43]

[חזי] הוית עד חדא מן תרתי לחמא יהיבת [ל]כ[הן ראשא]

I was [watching] until one of the two (loaves) of bread was given to the [high p]ri[est…] (2Q24 4 14–15) [44]

---

[42] The text וסף מיא is ungrammatical. The expected form of the verb (ספו [מיא]) occurs in 4Q206 4 ii 3; Milik, *The Books of Enoch*, p. 240.

[43] Text according to Daniel Machiela, *The Dead Sea Genesis Apocryphon: A New Text and Translation with Introduction and Special Treatment of Columns 13–17* (STDJ, 79, Leiden: Brill, 2009) 58; see also Florentino García Martínez and Eibert J. C. Tigchelaar, *The Dead Sea Scrolls Study Edition* (2 Vols., Leiden: Brill, 1997–1998) Vol. 1, p. 36; *DQA* (n. שרץ). The reading שרין ארעא ושרין מיא is found in some editions (e.g., Fitzmyer, *The Genesis Apocryphon*, p. 88; Matthew Morgenstern, Elisha Qimron, and D. Sivan, 'The Hitherto Unpublished Columns of the Genesis Apocryphon', *Abr-Nahrain* 33 (1995), pp. 30–54 [46]), but it is nonsensical. Compare the comments of Fitzmyer (*The Genesis Apocryphon*, p. 164) and the ellipses where translation should have appeared in Morgenstern, Qimron, and Sivan ('The Hitherto Unpublished Columns', p. 47).

[44] Text according to M. Baillet, J. T. Milik, and R. de Vaux, *Les 'petites grottes' de Qumran* (DJD, 3, Oxford: Clarendon, 1962) p. 86.

חזי הוית עד די יהיב לכ[ול כהניא]

> I was watching until it was given to a[ll the priests...] (2Q24 4 17)[45]

[ו]אנה הוית חזה עד ארעא חפית מין

> [And] I was watching until the earth was covered with water. (4Q206 4 i 18)[46]

However, the texts surrounding the partially broken instance in 4Q530 are too fragmentary for analysis as the formulaic construction and the finite verb are partially or wholly reconstructed.

[חזא] הוית עד די לשנין די נור מן

[שמין נחתו חזא הוית עד די אתכסי עפ]רא בבכל מיא ונורא דלק בכל [...]

> I was [watching] until tongues of fire [came down] from [heaven.] I was [watching] until the [ear]th was cov[ered] with all the waters, and fire burned in every [...] (4Q530 6.9-10)[47]

The reconstructed instances in 4Q530 aside, the activity of 'watching' goes all the way to the right temporal boundary in each of the examples, which advances the reference time in the vision reports. Once meeting the boundary, however, semantically the activity ends. That might initially seem problematic because these right temporal boundaries do not mark the end of the vision and the vision continues in the text that follows. However, in each passage, the text continues in a way that signals the continuation

---

[45] Text according to Baillet, Milik, and De Vaux, *Les 'petites grottes' de Qumran*, p. 87.

[46] Text according to Milik, *The Books of Enoch*, p. 238.

[47] Text according to Émile Puech, *Qumran Cave 4. XXII: Textes araméens, première partie: 4Q529–549* (DJD, 31, Oxford: Clarendon, 2001) p. 28. The underlined portion is reconstructed based on 6Q8 ii 2, [...] הוית עד די אתכ[...] and is accepted in CAL but not in García-Martínez and Tigchelaar, *The Dead Sea Scrolls Study Edition*, p. 1062. Although the reconstruction is persuasive, it is inappropriate to include it as an instance of the formulaic construction.

of the visionary experience. On four occasions, the text immediately following the adverbial continues the vision with another explicit reference to watching,[48] while in other instances the vision descriptions are resumed after a temporal conjunction (באדין, 'and then' Dan. 2.35) or presentative particle (וארו, 'behold' Dan. 7.5) introducing a new element into the vision. On at least one occasion, the seer begins to describe the foreground but then quickly moves to the description of the background (Dan. 7.9, and possibly in the fragmentary 4Q206 4, i 19).[49] But importantly, even when the text does quickly move to background, it assumes the reference time that was advanced by the right temporal boundary of the preceding adverbial. Thus, in Dan. 7.9, the background material describing the Ancient of Days depicts the scene after the courtroom had been set up (vv. 9b–10a). This is affirmed by Dan. 7.10b which returns to the time reference set by the bounded construction in 7.9 as it re-establishes the foreground.

5. CONCLUSIONS

The formulaic construction חזה הוית ('I was watching') occurs frequently in the Aramaic visions of the Bible and the Dead Sea Scrolls. It repeatedly draws the activity of the seer into the narrative, highlighting the seer's experience of seeing the vision thereby drawing the reader into the vision and inviting the reader to imagine what he saw and heard. In this study, I have argued that the presence (or absence) of the subordinating conjunction עד and an adverbial clause(s) makes a significant impact on the temporal interpretation of the vision reports with the formulaic construction חזה הוית. The formulaic construction חזה הוית is a participial periphrastic construction expressing a *past, ongoing* situation ('I was watching') that is, with regard to situation aspect, an *activity*. The expressed situation is *unbounded* in that it has no actual temporal boundaries. The situation is co-temporal

---

[48] E.g., חזה הוית, 'I was watching' Dan. 7.13; ואתפנית למחזה, 'and I turned to see' 1Q20 13.13; חזה הוית עד, 'I was watching until' 2Q24 4 17.

[49] In these cases, the situations are stative. The clauses following the relevant constructions are missing or too broken in 2Q24 4 17–18 and 4Q530 6.10.

with other situations, which are either stative or ongoing (expressed by active participles or active participial periphrastic constructions).

However, other features of a clause can affect the (un)boundedness of a situation, especially adverbial phrases and clauses which can put temporal boundaries on a situation. When חזה הוית is followed by the conjunction עד and an adverbial clause, the adverbial puts a right temporal boundary on the activity in the main clause making it temporally *bounded*. The situations that set the temporal boundary in the adverbial clause(s) are expressed with the perfect conjugation (either complete situations or passive states). As a result, the activity of watching overlaps with those situations in the subordinate clauses, the last of which advances the time reference of the narrative. After reaching the right temporal boundary set by the adverbial, the narrative continues from that reference time.

I conclude that, functionally, there is a privative opposition between the unbounded and bounded constructions. The unbounded construction may or may not overlap with situations that have a right temporal boundary, but the bounded construction always overlaps with a situation(s) that sets a right temporal boundary. In other words, the bounded construction is marked for setting a right temporal boundary, while the unbounded construction is unmarked. The unbounded construction is often used, especially with a presentative particle, to introduce a new element into the vision report. The bounded construction is capable of doing the same (e.g., Dan. 2.34), but it is specifically crafted to draw attention to a series of situations that the seer watches through to completion. That point of completion then sets the time reference of the narrative.

THE PREFIX CONJUGATION IN DANIEL REVISITED*

TARSEE LI

1. INTRODUCTION

The present study is an attempt to refine and expand an earlier description of the prefix conjugation in the Aramaic of Daniel, which is found in my monograph.[1] There, the view was presented that the prefix conjugation was a general imperfective in the process of becoming a future. The present study presents a more complete description of its diachronic development and the grammaticalization of its functions.[2] Although it is necessary to

* It is a great pleasure to join other scholars in this volume in honoring Edward Cook. I treasure his friendship and admire his scholarship.
An earlier version of this study was presented during an Alumnus in Residence session at Hebrew Union College–Jewish Institute of Religion, Cincinnati, March 11, 2019. I wish to express my gratitude to those who were present for all their questions and comments. This research also benefitted from a series of email exchanges with Andrew Daniel. Any errors or shortcomings are my responsibility.

[1] Tarsee Li, *The Verbal System of the Aramaic of Daniel: An Explanation in the Context of Grammaticalization* (SAIS, 8, Leiden: Brill, 2009) pp. 98–128.

[2] The discussion of diachronic development, both in my earlier monograph and in this present study, relies to a large extent (though not completely) on grammaticalization. Grammaticalization refers to a set of phenomena that involve words with lexical meaning becoming words that denote grammatical functions and grammatical items further developing new grammatical functions. For a brief summary of relevant

categorize the various functions of the prefix conjugation, and this will involve some overlap with the monograph, this study will attempt to keep repetition to a minimum. A fuller discussion of many of the instances can be found in the monograph, though my interpretation of a few instances has changed. Similarly, I will here dispense with a full discussion of the secondary literature, which can be found in the monograph.

The starting point for a discussion must be the fact that in early West Semitic there were at least three prefix conjugations: *yaqtulu*, *yaqtula*, and *yaqtul*. Additionally, the label '*yaqtul*' can denote two distinct conjugations, the preterit *yaqtul* and the jussive *yaqtul*. The preterit *yaqtul* is attested in the Akkadian *iprus*, as well as in West Semitic, as exemplified in, inter alia, Ugaritic,[3] Old Aramaic, and Biblical Hebrew (*wayyiqtol*).[4] It was eventually replaced by the suffix conjugation in the West Semitic languages as part of the process of renewal.[5] Alternatively, one can also consider *yaqtul* a single conjugation with two functions, narrative and jussive.[6] The narrative/preterit function was replaced by the suffix conjugation, but not the jussive function. A full discussion of the nature and function of the preterit *yaqtul* is beyond the

---

grammaticalization phenomena, see Li, *The Verbal System of the Aramaic of Daniel*, pp. 2–7. For a fuller treatment of grammaticalization, see Paul J. Hopper and Elizabeth Closs Traugott, *Grammaticalization* (Cambridge Textbooks in Linguistics, Cambridge: Cambridge University Press, 2nd edn., 2003).

[3] For a summary of the debate concerning the existence of a *yaqtul* preterit in Ugaritic and a defense of its attestation, see Alexander Andrason and Juan-Pablo Vita, 'The YQTL-Ø "Preterite" in Ugaritic Epic Poetry', *ArOr* 85 (2017), pp. 345–387.

[4] For some recent discussions on the functions of the Biblical Hebrew *wayyiqtol*, see Alexander Andrason, 'Biblical Hebrew *Wayyiqtol*: A Dynamic Definition', *JHebS* 11.8 (2011), pp. 1–58; Tarsee Li, '*Wayyiqtol* (The Narrative Preterite)', in H. Dallaire, B. J. Noonan, and J. E. Noonan (eds.), *'Where Shall Wisdom Be Found?' A Grammatical Tribute to Professor Stephen A. Kaufman* (Winona Lake: Eisenbrauns, 2017) pp. 213–243.

[5] Renewal refers to the process by which a word or expression acquires the meaning expressed by another. For a more detailed explanation, see Hopper and Traugott, *Grammaticalization*, pp. 122–124.

[6] E.g., Burkhart Kienast, *Historische Semitische Sprachwissenschaft* (Wiesbaden: Harrassowitz Verlag, 2001) pp. 275–277.

scope of this study. Instead, this study will focus primarily on the remaining forms and their relationship with the prefix conjugation in Aramaic.

The existence of *yaqtulu*, *yaqtula*, and *yaqtul* as separate conjugations is attested in both Ugaritic and classical Arabic, as well as in the mixed dialect of El Amarna Akkadian. In later ancient Aramaic (e.g., Syriac) there was only one prefix conjugation, as these all coalesced into one prefix conjugation form. This process of merging began with a historical phenomenon that occurred in the phonology of the Northwest Semitic languages, i.e., the loss of final short vowels, resulting in many forms becoming homophones.

In Biblical Hebrew, *yaqtula* is attested in the cohortative, which is mostly restricted to first person forms, and *yaqtul* is attested in the jussive, which is mostly restricted to second and third person forms. However, there are a few rare occurrences of second and third person cohortatives (Deut. 33.16; Isa. 5.19; Job 11.17; Ps. 20.4) and first person jussives (Deut. 18.16; 1 Sam. 14.36; Isa. 41.23, 28; Ezek. 5.16; Hos. 9.15; 11.4; Zeph. 1.2, 3 [2x]; Job 23.9, 11; Neh. 1.4). Further, due to the loss of final short vowels, the original *yaqtulu* and *yaqtula* are in many instances morphologically indistinguishable, and are usually analyzed simply as the long imperfect.[7] The same is true of *yaqtul* forms, since the long imperfect and the jussive are identical in most forms, except for some weak verbs. Hence, the *yaqtulu* form is attested in the long imperfect, which, however, is also often indistinguishable from instances of *yaqtul* and *yaqtula*.

In the Aramaic of Daniel, the occurrences of the long prefix conjugation or 'imperfect' comprise both *yaqtulu* and *yaqtula*, as well as some instances of *yaqtul*. The short prefix conjugation *yaqtul*, or 'jussive', is in many cases indistinguishable from the long prefix conjugation, but its existence is attested in a few distinguishable forms (2.24; 4.16; 5.10 [2x], 12). Clear instances of the long prefix conjugation *yaqtulu* occur in 3mp and 2mp

---

[7] Hélène Dallaire, *The Syntax of Volitives in Biblical Hebrew and Amarna Canaanite Prose* (LSAWS, 9, Winona Lake: Eisenbrauns, 2014) pp. 121–141 and passim.

forms that end with *nun*, as well as in instances where the pronominal suffixes are preceded by the letter *nun* (-*n*- or -*nn*-).[8] As for *yaqtula*, there are no instances attested.[9] Presumably, the coalescing of *yaqtulu* and *yaqtula* into one single grammatical form was more advanced than that of *yaqtulu* and *yaqtul*. It is possible that the process had not yet reached full completion, in which case the morphological distinctions between *yaqtulu* and *yaqtul* also apply to *yaqtula*, since the latter is similar to *yaqtul* in having short endings. However, since no clear instances of *yaqtula* are attested in the Aramaic of Daniel, this study will provisionally assume that the merging of *yaqtulu* and *yaqtula* was a completed process, though occasional instances might merit further discussion.

Based on evidence from West Semitic languages where the distinctive conjugations are attested, the *yaqtulu* form was a general imperfective, whereas the *yaqtula* form was a modal. In classical Arabic, *yaqtulu* corresponds to the imperfect indicative, and *yaqtula* corresponds to the subjunctive. The former functions as a general imperfective, and has been described as expressing 'a begun, incomplete, enduring existence, either in present, past, or

[8] The attested forms of 3mp that end in *nun* are: 2.5c, 18, 30a, 43a, 43b; 3.28a, 28b; 4.13a, 13b, 14a, 20b, 22b, 22c, 29a, 29b, 33c; 5.2, 15, 21a; 6.2, 3a, 27a; 7.10b, 14a, 17, 18a, 18b, 24a, 25d, 26b, 27a, 27b, 28b. The attested forms of 2mp that end in *nun* are: 2.5b, 6a, 6b; 3.5a, 5b, 5c, 15a, 15b, 15c, 15d, 15e. In addition, forms of 2fs that end in *nun* would also qualify, but there are no instances attested. The *nun* at the end of the 3fp (e.g., לֶהֶוְיָן in 5.17a) is not significant. Attested forms that include a *nun* before a pronominal suffix include: 3ms + suff (3.15f; 4.2a, 14c, 22f, 29e; 5.7b; 6.17; 7.16b); 3fs + suff (2.11; 7.23d, 23e); 1cs + suff (5.17c); 3mp + suff (4.2b, 3, 16; 5.6; 7.10a, 15, 28a); and 2mp + suff (2.5a, 9a, 9b). For a discussion of the *nun* before the pronominal suffix and its possible relationship with ventive and/or energic forms in other Semitic languages, see Rebecca Hasselbach, 'The Ventive/Energic in Semitic – A Morphological Study', *ZDMG* 156 (2006), pp. 309–328.

[9] On the possible but uncertain existence of the cohortative in Old Aramaic, see Stanislav Segert, *Altaramäische Grammatik: mit Bibliographie, Chrestomathie und Glossar* (Leipzig: Verlag Enzyklopädie, 4th edn., 1990) p. 253.

future time'.[10] The latter is used in subordinate modal contexts. In Ugaritic, *yaqtulu* can also be explained as a general imperfective,[11] though some prefer to classify it as a present tense[12] or as expressing both present and future.[13] The *yaqtula* form occurs mostly in the 1st person, as in Hebrew, and serves as a volitive.[14] Topper calls it an expanded short prefix conjugation ('die erweiterte Kurzform') or an emphatic jussive ('der emphatische Jussiv'). Bordreuil and Pardee argue that the 2nd and 3rd person forms were probably still 'in use in the poetic language'. However, they translate the example they cite, *ymẓa* (KTU 1.12.i.37), as 'that he might find' (cf. Tropper's translation, 'auf daß er finde'), which is not volitive, but better matches the modal/subjunctive function of *yaqtula* in Arabic. Hence, it is possible that *yaqtula* in Ugaritic was originally a modal/subjunctive whose 1st person volitive function was due to analogy with the jussive.[15] The same process may have occurred in Hebrew.[16]

---

[10] Carl Paul Caspari, *A Grammar of the Arabic Language* (transl. and ed. William Wright; 3rd edn. revised by W. Robertson Smith and M. J. de Goeje; 2 vols.; Cambridge: Cambridge University Press, 1896–1898) vol. 2, p. 18.

[11] Pierre Bordreuil and Dennis Pardee, *A Manual of Ugaritic* (LSAWS, 3, Winona Lake: Eisenbrauns, 2009) pp. 46–47; John Huehnergard, *An Introduction to Ugaritic* (Peabody: Hendrickson Publishers, 2012) p. 55.

[12] Josef Tropper, *Ugaritische Grammatik* (AOAT, 273, Münster: Ugarit Verlag, 2nd edn., 2012) p. 457.

[13] Stanislav Segert, *A Basic Grammar of the Ugaritic Language: with Selected Texts and Glossary* (Berkeley: University of California Press, 1984) p. 90.

[14] Bordreuil and Pardee, *A Manual of Ugaritic*, p. 49; Tropper, *Ugaritische Grammatik*, pp. 455–457.

[15] Analogy is defined as, 'a process whereby one form of a language becomes more like another with which it is somehow associated'; Anthony Arlotto, *Introduction to Historical Linguistics* (Lanham: University Press of America, 1972) p. 130.

[16] For a discussion of the various functions of the Hebrew cohortative, see Jan Joosten, *The Verbal System of Biblical Hebrew: A New Synthesis Elaborated on the Basis of Classical Prose* (JBS, 10, Jerusalem: Simor Ltd., 2012) pp. 319–326; John A. Cook *Time and the Biblical Hebrew Verb: The Expression of Tense, Aspect, and Modality in Biblical Hebrew* (LSAWS, 7, Winona Lake: Eisenbrauns, 2012) pp. 237–244; Hélène Dallaire, *The Syntax of Volitives*, pp. 111–116. Joosten summarized well the function

Clues for their distinctive functions may also be found in the development of Aramaic. In later ancient Aramaic (e.g., Syriac), the primary temporal distinction is between the past (i.e., the suffix conjugation) and the present-future (i.e., the participle). Although the prefix conjugation may occasionally express the future, it is generally a modal form, since the simple future function of the prefix conjugation was eventually replaced by the participle.[17] Further, the prefix conjugation no longer expresses the past frequentative in later Aramaic, since past imperfective functions were taken over by participial expressions with הוה. Therefore, as the prefix conjugation lost the imperfective functions that originated from *yaqtulu*, it became restricted to the expression of modal functions, which originated from *yaqtula*.

2. PREFIX CONJUGATION FUNCTIONS

Excluding instances of clear jussives, instances of the prefix conjugation of הוה functioning as an auxiliary in participial expressions, and instances of the verb phrase עֲתִיד דִּי + prefix conjugation, there are 177 instances of the prefix conjugation in the Aramaic of Daniel.[18] For the sake of simplicity, in the remainder of this study, unless otherwise stated, these 177 instances will be referred to as 'prefix conjugation' forms, and the label 'long prefix conjugation' will be reserved for occasions where it is necessary for clarity.[19]

---

of the Hebrew cohortative as expressing intention to act when the speaker is able but a request for permission when he is not; *The Verbal System of Biblical Hebrew*, p. 121.

[17] Jan Joosten, *The Syriac Language of the Peshitta and Old Syriac Versions of Matthew: Syntactic Structure, Inner-Syriac Developments and Translation Technique* (Studies in Semitic Languages and Linguistics, 22, Leiden: Brill, 1996) pp. 113–114.

[18] The jussive forms occur in 2.24; 4.16; 5.10a, 10b, 12 (on the instance in 5.12, see Franz Rosenthal, *A Grammar of Biblical Aramaic* (PLO, Wiesbaden: Harrassowitz Verlag, 1961) p. 52). The prefix conjugation of הוה functioning as an auxiliary in participial expressions occurs in 2.43a, 43b; 6.3a, 3b, 27. The phrase עֲתִיד דִּי + prefix conjugation occurs in 3.5b, 5c.

[19] In passing, it may be of significance that several instances of the prefix conjugation occur in poetic contexts. Poetry occurs in at least the following passages: 2.20–23; 3.31–33; 4.7–13(14?), 31–32; 6.27–28;

2.1 Functions Derived from yaqtulu

Instances of the prefix conjugation that arose from the imperfective *yaqtulu* occur in past, present, and future contexts.

2.1.1 Past Imperfective

In past time contexts the prefix conjugation can be either imperfective or modal. The imperfective instances trace their origin to the earlier *yaqtulu* form. As Comrie explained, imperfective aspect views a situation from within, making explicit reference to its internal temporal structure.[20] Many languages have specific grammatical constructions for various subcategories of imperfectivity, such as progressive/durative (e.g., English, 'he was doing') or habitual/frequentative ('he used to do'). A few languages also have imperfective expressions, which can express all or most categories of imperfectivity. The fact that the Aramaic prefix conjugation can express both progressive and habitual/iterative/customary functions suggests that it inherited the broad imperfective function of its *yaqtulu* precursor.

2.1.1.1 Past Progressive

All attested instances of the prefix conjugation with a past time imperfective function occur in main clauses. That is, they occur in clauses that are not introduced by an explicit subordinating

---

7.9–10, 13–14, 23–27. It is possible that other passages may also be poetic. Determining its function in such contexts may be more challenging due to poetic style. However, poetic style does not abrogate a form's normal grammatical functions, but may employ additional functions that are less common and found in less usual settings. One important significance of the poetic contexts is that, as in Ugaritic, poetic contexts often employ grammatical forms in archaic functions. Thus, there may be some distinctions between the functions in poetic and prose contexts that are due to poetic archaisms. However, it is unclear whether diachronic conclusions based on poetic style are possible in this corpus, given the small size of the corpus and the uncertainty concerning the exact boundaries of some poetic sections.

[20] Bernard Comrie, *Aspect* (Cambridge Textbooks in Linguistics, Cambridge: Cambridge University Press, 1976) p. 24.

conjunction.[21] The majority of these can be analyzed as progressive in function. Most of these occur in circumstantial clauses, especially in connection with a suffix conjugation verb (4.8, 16, 17, 31, 33a, 33b, 33c; 5.6; 6.20; 7.15). Some instances occur in descriptive contexts, where the progressive sense is not circumstantial but part of the descriptive context (7.10a, 10b, 28a, 28b). In a few instances, the prefix conjugation could be alternatively analyzed as modal in unmarked purpose clauses (5.2; 7.14a, 16a, 16b) or unmarked result clauses (4.2a, 2b).

אֱדַ֫יִן מַלְכָּא זִיוֺ֫הִי שְׁנ֫וֺהִי וְרַעְיֹנֹ֫הִי יְבַהֲלוּנֵּ֫הּ

Then as for the king, his face changed [suffix conjugation], as his thoughts *were troubling him*. (Dan. 5.6)

נְהַ֣ר דִּי־נ֗וּר נָגֵ֤ד וְנָפֵק֙ מִן־קֳדָמ֔וֹהִי אֶ֤לֶף אַלְפִין֙ יְשַׁמְּשׁוּנֵּ֔הּ וְרִבּ֥וֹ רִבְוָ֖ן קֳדָמ֣וֹהִי יְקוּמ֑וּן

A river of fire was flowing [participle] and coming out [participle] before him, a thousand thousands *were serving him*, and a myriad of myriads *were standing* before him. (Dan. 7.10)

The above examples illustrate prefix conjugation verbs with a past progressive function. The instance in the first example (5.6) can be analyzed as occurring in a circumstantial clause, providing background information for the clause with the suffix conjugation. However, the instances in the second example (7.10) are not circumstantial, but part of a descriptive context (vv. 9–10), where the Ancient of Days and the judgment court are described.

2.1.1.2 Past Habitual

The label 'habitual' is here used as an umbrella term for habitual, iterative, frequentative, and customary functions. There are nine instances of the prefix conjugation with a habitual function (4.9a,

[21] For the purpose of this study, clauses are defined as independent or subordinate based on form rather than function. That is, the presence or absence of an explicit subordinating conjunction determines the classification of the form, regardless of the function.

9b, 9c, 18a, 18b, 30a, 30b; 5.21a, 21b).[22] The past habitual can also be considered a type of modality,[23] but it is 'less commonly' expressed by modal forms, since different languages can express the past habitual with either the realis or the irrealis mood.[24] Since imperfective expressions encompass both progressive and habitual expressions, one can conclude that the past habitual function of the prefix conjugation derives from its imperfective *yaqtulu* origin.

> תְּחֹתוֹהִי תַּטְלֵל ׀ חֵיוַת בָּרָא וּבְעַנְפּוֹהִי יְדֻרוּן צִפְּרֵי שְׁמַיָּא וּמִנֵּהּ יִתְּזִין כָּל־בִּשְׂרָא
>
> Under it, the wild animals *used to seek shade*, in its branches the birds of the sky *used to nest*, and from it all creatures *used to feed themselves*. (Dan. 4.9)

In the above example, the prefix conjugation verbs describe the habitual action of various creatures under the tree in the king's dream.

2.1.2 General Present

In present time contexts, there is a distinction between actual and general presents. Actual presents describe events in progress in the present, whereas general presents describe events that may not be in progress but occur habitually or customarily, which, in turn, could also be viewed as a-temporal. Hence, the distinction between actual and general presents can be viewed as the present time equivalent to past time progressives and habituals respectively.

There are no instances of the prefix conjugation as an actual present in the Aramaic of Daniel. Attested instances function rather as general presents. Most, if not all, instances occur in subordinate clauses. That is, they occur in either a clause introduced by a subordinating conjunction or one that continues a subordinate clause. There are at least three instances that occur

[22] The instances in 4.18 are a loose quotation of 4.9, and those in 5.21 are a loose quotation of 4.30.

[23] F. R. Palmer, *Mood and Modality* (Cambridge Textbooks in Linguistics, Cambridge: Cambridge University Press, 2nd edn., 2001) p. 179.

[24] Palmer, *Mood and Modality*, pp. 22, 55, 158, 159.

in relative clauses (2.10; 3.29d; 6.16) and perhaps seven instances in complement clauses (3.18b; 4.14c, 14d, 22f, 29e; 5.16a, 21d).[25]

> עַד דִּֽי־יְדַע דִּֽי־שַׁלִּיט אֱלָהָא עִלָּיָא בְּמַלְכוּת אֲנָשָׁא וּלְמַן־דִּי יִצְבֵּה יְהָקֵים עֲלַֽיהּ׃
>
> ... until he understood that the Most High God is ruler over the human kingdom, and (that) *he sets up* over it whomever he wishes. (Dan. 5.21)

In the above example the prefix conjugation verb יְהָקֵים occurs in the second of a series of complement clauses, and it continues the a-temporal sense of the preceding nominal sentence. It expresses not an ongoing action, but a habitual one. Hence, it is a general present, not an actual present.

The fact that the present time function of the prefix conjugation is only attested in the expression of the general present in subordinate clauses may be due to the grammaticalization of the active participle. In contrast to the prefix conjugation, the participle is employed in the expression of both the actual and the general presents. Hence, although the participle may not yet be a full-fledged present tense since its function is not limited to the present temporal sphere,[26] it is quite advanced in that process.

2.2 Functions Derived from yaqtulu and/or yaqtula

2.2.1 Simple Future

The future refers to a situation at a time subsequent to the present moment. There is some disagreement concerning whether the future is a tense or a modality. It can be considered a modality because what occurs in the future is not yet a reality.[27] Also,

---

[25] Some of these are loose citations/repetitions of earlier instances (e.g., 4.14 is repeated in vv. 22 and 29).

[26] Li, *The Verbal System of the Aramaic of Daniel*, pp. 39–57.

[27] Palmer, *Mood and Modality*, pp. 104–106, 124–125, 168–170; Mario Squartini, 'Interactions between Modality and Other Semantic Categories', in Jan Nuyts and Johan van der Auwera (eds.), *The Oxford Handbook of Modality and Mood* (Oxford: Oxford University Press, 2016) pp. 50–67 (53–54).

various modalities often grammaticalize into futures.[28] However, Dahl defends the traditional view of the future as a tense rather than a modality, because in future grammatical expressions the future time reference is a constant element, whereas the modal features may or may not be present.[29] Comrie also defends the notion of future as tense, because in languages that distinguish degrees of remoteness in the future the said forms have no modal uses without future time reference.[30] Nevertheless, it is beyond the scope of this study to settle the linguistic debate on the nature of the future. Rather, it is more important to recognize that it is common for languages to have more than one grammatical construction that expresses the future (cf. the English sentences, '*I will speak* with him', '*I am going to speak* with him', and '*I am speaking* with him tomorrow'). Therefore, although notionally the future can be explained as a category of modality, it can also be expressed, inter alia, by a general imperfective in future context. Hence, it is possible that both the general imperfective *yaqtulu* and the modal *yaqtula* overlapped in the expression of future time, perhaps with different nuances. If so, it is futile to attempt to distinguish the source of each instance of the prefix conjugation with future function. The label 'simple future' is used here to distinguish it from future predictions that are accompanied by an additional modal nuance.

The simple future function is the most frequently attested function of the prefix conjugation in the Aramaic of Daniel. There are forty-one instances in main clauses and nine instances in

---

[28] Östen Dahl, *Tense and Aspect Systems* (Oxford: Basil Blackwell, 1985) pp. 103–112; Bernard Comrie, *Tense* (Cambridge Textbooks in Linguistics, Cambridge: Cambridge University Press, 1985) pp. 43–48; Joan Bybee and Östen Dahl, 'The Creation of Tense and Aspect Systems in the Languages of the World', *Studies in Language* 13 (1989), pp. 51–103 (90–94); Joan Bybee, Revere Perkins, and William Pagliuca, *The Evolution of Grammar: Tense, Aspect, and Modality in the Languages of the World* (Chicago: University of Chicago Press, 1994) pp. 243–280; Palmer, *Mood and Modality*, pp. 104–106, 124–125, 168–170.

[29] Dahl, *Tense and Aspect Systems*, pp. 23, 106–107.

[30] Comrie, *Tense*, p. 46.

relative clauses.[31] There are also some ambiguous instances that could be analyzed either as simple future or modal in unmarked purpose clauses (2.4, 7b, 9c, 24).[32]

In the instances that occur in prophetic contexts, which constitute the majority of instances, it is possible to argue that these are not simple futures but they involve some type of modality because there may be an assertion of the certainty of the predicted future events. However, though possible, that is not necessarily so. In order to establish the presence of a modality in prophetic predictions, one must demonstrate that predictions in non-prophetic contexts employ a different grammatical expression. Such evidence does not occur in the corpus. Further, the fact that sometimes both the participle and the prefix conjugation occur in the same prophetic context also suggests that these instances express the simple future with no additional modal nuances. Therefore, these instances are provisionally included in the list of simple futures.

וְלָךְ טָרְדִין מִן־אֲנָשָׁא וְעִם־חֵיוַת בָּרָא לֶהֱוֵה מְדֹרָךְ וְעִשְׂבָּא כְתוֹרִין׀ לָךְ
יְטַעֲמוּן וּמִטַּל שְׁמַיָּא לָךְ מְצַבְּעִין וְשִׁבְעָה עִדָּנִין יַחְלְפוּן עֲלָיךְ

You will be driven away [participle] from people, and your dwelling *will be* with wild animals. *You will be fed* grass like oxen, and you will be drenched [participle] with the dew of heaven. Seven times *will pass* over you. (Dan. 4.22)

In the above example, the prefix conjugation follows a participle (4.22a), precedes a participle (4.22b), and occurs without a parallel participial construction (4.22c). There is no detectable difference in function between the participles and the prefix conjugation verbs in this context.

[31] Instances in main clauses consist of: 2.39a, 40a, 40b, 40c, 41a, 41b, 42a, 42b, 44a, 44b, 44c, 44d, 44e, 44f, 45; 4.22a, 22b, 22c, 29a, 29b; 5.17b, 17c; 7.17, 18a, 18b, 23a, 23c, 23d, 23e, 24a, 24b, 24c, 24d, 25a, 25b, 25c, 25d, 26a, 26b, 27a, 27b. Instances in relative clauses consist of: 2.9b, 28, 29a, 29b, 39b; 6.27; 7.14b, 14c, 23b.

[32] Other interpretations are also possible for 2.7b.

2.2.2 Functions Potentially Derived from the Simple Future

There are a number of functions that may be derived from either the simple future or from various other modal functions. These functions are discussed under the following section for the sake of clarity, since these other modal functions are discussed there. Discussing all of these functions in the next section also helps to avoid repetition.

2.3 Functions Derived from yaqtula

Since the West Semitic *yaqtula* conjugation was most likely a modal conjugation, it is also the source of most of the modal functions of the prefix conjugation.

There is no consensus on the definition of modality. One explanation of modality is that it is the expression of 'the speaker's cognitive, emotive, or volitive attitude toward a state of affairs'.[33] To the extent that it allows for more than one possible course of events, 'the essence of modality consists in the relative-zation of the validity of sentence meanings to a set of possible worlds'.[34] Alternatively, since the expression of modality varies greatly across languages, some prefer to explain modality simply as a set of diachronically related functions.[35]

There is also no consensus on how modal categories should be distinguished or classified. Palmer divides modality into two types, propositional and event modality.[36] Propositional modality is subdivided into epistemic and evidential, while event modality is subdivided into deontic and dynamic. That is, 'epistemic and

---

[33] Ferenc Kiefer, 'Modality', in R. E. Asher and J. M. Y. Simpson (eds.), *The Encyclopedia of Language and Linguistics* (Oxford: Pergamon Press, 1994) p. 2516a.

[34] Ferenc Kiefer, 'On Defining Modality', *Folia Linguistica* 21 (1987), pp. 67–94 (90).

[35] Joan L. Bybee, *Morphology: A Study of the Relation between Meaning and Form* (Typological Studies in Language, 9, Amsterdam: John Benjamins Publishing Company, 1985) pp. 191–196. For a brief history of the development of views on mood and modality, see Johan van der Auwera and Alfonso Zamorano Aguilar, 'The History of Modality and Mood', in Jan Nuyts and Johan van der Auwera (eds.), *The Oxford Handbook of Modality and Mood* (Oxford: Oxford University Press, 2016) pp. 9–27.

[36] Palmer, *Mood and Modality*, passim.

evidential modality are concerned with the speaker's attitude to the truth-value or factual status of the proposition', whereas 'deontic and dynamic modality refer to events that are not actualized, events that have not taken place but are merely potential'.[37] However, some scholars contend that not all evidential expressions are modal, and either subsume the ones that are modal under epistemic modality[38] or treat evidentiality as a separate category from tense, aspect, and modality.[39] On the other hand, Bybee, Perkins, and Pagliuca divide modality into agent-oriented, speaker-oriented, epistemic, and subordinate.[40] Agent-oriented modalities report the existence of conditions (internal or external) on an agent with respect to an action (e.g., obligation: 'I should go home now, because it's late'; ability: 'I can walk home, now that my legs are healed'). Speaker-oriented modalities consist of speech acts whereby a speaker imposes such conditions on an addressee (e.g., imperative: 'Go home!'; optative: 'Have a good trip!'). Epistemic modalities express the extent to which the speaker is committed to the factualness of a proposition (e.g., 'She might have come home already'). Under subordinate modalities Bybee, Perkins, and Pagliuca discuss finite verb forms that are restricted mostly to subordinate contexts (e.g., the subjunctive mood).

It is beyond the scope of this study to settle the linguistic debate concerning the nature of modality and its classifications. However, the classification of Bybee, Perkins, and Pagliuca is provisionally adopted here, because its description of the diachronic development of various modalities is relevant to this study. That is, there is a wide range of modalities expressed by the prefix conjugation, and the best way to account for this is to trace the diachronic relationships among the various functions.

---

[37] Palmer, *Mood and Modality*, p. 8.

[38] See Squartini, 'Interactions between Modality and Other Semantic Categories', pp. 61–64.

[39] Östen Dahl, 'Tense, Aspect, Mood and Evidentiality', in James D. Wright (ed.), *International Encyclopedia of the Social and Behavioral Sciences* (Oxford: Elsevier, 2nd edn., 2015) pp. 210, 213.

[40] Bybee, Perkins, and Pagliuca, *The Evolution of Grammar*, pp. 176–242.

2.3.1 Agent-Oriented Modalities

Agent-oriented modalities report the existence of conditions (internal or external) on an agent with respect to an action. These modalities include obligation, necessity, desire, ability, etc. Agent-oriented modalities are usually the earliest stages in the grammaticalization of modalities. Other modalities often arise out of agent-oriented senses (e.g., obligation, 'She must do so' may grammaticalize into epistemic probability, 'She must have done it by now').

2.3.1.1 Ability

Ability refers to the existence of internal conditions or factors that enable an individual to perform an action. Bybee, Perkins, and Pagliuca classify ability as a type of agent-oriented modality, whereas Palmer classifies it as a dynamic modality, which is one of the subdivisions of event modality.[41] Although their classification models differ, there is no disagreement on the nature of this modality.

Prefix conjugation verbs expressing ability consist of at least four instances in relative clauses (2.11, 25; 4.32a, 32b; possibly also 3.15f), one instance in a complement clause (2.9d), and possibly two instances in main clauses (3.17; 6.6). Some of these instances could be otherwise interpreted.[42]

הַשְׁכַּחַת גְּבַר מִן־בְּנֵי גָלוּתָא דִּי יְהוּד דִּי פִשְׁרָא לְמַלְכָּא יְהוֹדַע

I have found a man from the captives of Judah who *can make known* the interpretation to the king. (Dan. 2.25)

The above example occurs in a context where the ability of the wise men to interpret dreams is called into question (2.10–11), the king begins his dialogue with Daniel by asking him if he is 'able' (כהל) to interpret his dream (v. 26), and the chapter concludes with the king's acknowledgement that Daniel was 'able'

[41] Bybee, Perkins, and Pagliuca, *The Evolution of Grammar*, p. 177; Palmer, *Mood and Modality*, pp. 9–10, 76–80.

[42] The instance in 3.15f could be alternatively analyzed as expressing root possibility, the instance in 6.6 as expressing epistemic possibility, and the instance in 3.17 as expressing epistemic certainty or a simple future.

(יכל) to reveal the mystery (v. 47). Therefore, this instance more likely denotes ability rather than epistemic modality, since the question of whether or not Daniel has the ability to interpret dreams is more central to the context than the question of whether or not someone thinks that he does.

It may be useful to cite here the other instance in the same chapter that also expresses ability.

> וּמִלְּתָא דִֽי־מַלְכָּ֣ה שָׁאֵ֗ל יַקִּירָ֔ה וְאָחֳרָן֙ לָ֣א אִיתַ֔י דִּ֥י יְחַוִּנַּ֖הּ קֳדָ֣ם מַלְכָּ֑א לָהֵ֣ן
> אֱלָהִ֔ין דִּ֚י מְדָ֣רְה֔וֹן עִם־בִּשְׂרָ֖א לָ֥א אִיתֽוֹהִי
>
> The matter which the king asks is difficult. There is no one else who *can show it* before the king, except the gods whose dwelling is not with flesh. (Dan. 2.11)

In the above example, the wise men employ the prefix conjugation to say that only the gods are able to reveal the king's dream.

2.3.1.2 Root Possibility

Root possibility is an extension of ability. Whereas ability reports enabling conditions that exist in the agent himself/herself, root possibility describes more general conditions that can reside both inside and outside the agent (such as social or physical conditions). Hence, it is common for expressions of ability to grammaticalize into expressions of root possibility and then epistemic possibility.[43] Also, there is a distinction between root possibility and epistemic possibility. The former reports the existence of enabling conditions, whereas the latter expresses the speaker's assertion that a proposition is possibly true. There is at least one possible instance of the prefix conjugation expressing root possibility in the corpus (3.15f).

> וּמַן־ה֣וּא אֱלָ֔הּ דִּ֥י יְשֵׁיזְבִנְכ֖וֹן מִן־יְדָֽי
>
> Who is the God/a god who *could rescue you* from my hand? (Dan. 3.15)

The above is most likely a question about the possibility of a divine rescue rather than of God's ability to do so. Nevertheless,

---

[43] Bybee, Perkins, and Pagliuca, *The Evolution of Grammar*, pp. 194–199.

it could be interpreted either way. The ambiguity between ability and root possibility is most likely due to the diachronic relationship between ability and root possibility.

2.3.1.3 Intention

Intention is an agent-oriented modality that can develop from either obligation, desire, or ability. Since the modality of ability is attested for the prefix conjugation, the relevant path of grammaticalization consists of the development from ability to root possibility and then to intention.[44] There is at least one possible instance of the prefix conjugation expressing intention in a complement clause (3.18b). However, since 'intention is not a very frequent' development from root possibility, it is possible that the sole instance should be otherwise interpreted.[45]

וְהֵ֣ן לָ֔א יְדִ֥יעַ לֶֽהֱוֵא־לָ֖ךְ מַלְכָּ֑א דִּ֤י לֵֽאלָהָיךְ֙ לָֽא־אִיתַ֣ינָא פָֽלְחִ֔ין וּלְצֶ֧לֶם
דַּהֲבָ֛א דִּ֥י הֲקֵ֖ימְתָּ לָ֥א נִסְגֻּֽד׃

> If not, let it be known to you, O king, that we will not serve your gods and *we will not* [*/we do not intend to*] *worship* the statue of gold that you set up. (Dan. 3.18)

In the above example, the verb סגד occurs in the prefix conjugation. The words פלח and סגד are coupled together in four instances in the chapter. Other than in v. 18, they occur in the same conjugation, both either as participles (3.12, 14) or as prefix conjugation forms (v. 28). The verb סגד is also coupled with נפל in this chapter, both occurring in the same conjugation, either as prefix conjugation forms (3.5, 6, 10, 11, 15) or as participles (3.7). Hence, it is curious that there is a morphological distinction between פלח and סגד in v. 18. It is at least possible that the employment of a prefix conjugation form of סגד in this verse indicates a distinction in nuance, and that it expresses intention. However, it is equally possible that it expresses a simple future along with the preceding participle.

In passing, it is worth mentioning the two instances of the expression עֲתִיד דִּי + prefix conjugation (3.15b, 15c). It is possible

---

[44] Bybee, Perkins, and Pagliuca, *The Evolution of Grammar*, p. 266.

[45] Bybee, Perkins, and Pagliuca, *The Evolution of Grammar*, p. 266.

to analyze the prefix conjugation verb in this phrase as a complement clause of עֲתִיד introduced by the conjunction דִּי. However, the whole phrase also constitutes a distinct grammatical expression.

כְּעַ֞ן הֵ֣ן אִֽיתֵיכ֣וֹן עֲתִידִ֗ין דִּ֣י בְעִדָּנָ֡א דִּֽי־תִשְׁמְע֡וּן קָ֣ל קַרְנָ֣א מַשְׁרוֹקִיתָ֣א קַיתְרֹ֣ס שַׂבְּכָ֡א פְּסַנְתֵּרִין֩ וְסוּמְפֹּ֨נְיָ֜ה וְכֹ֣ל׀ זְנֵ֣י זְמָרָ֗א תִּפְּל֣וּן וְתִסְגְּדוּן֮ לְצַלְמָ֣א דִֽי־עַבְדֵת֒

Now, if *you are ready to fall down and worship* the image that I made when you hear the sound of ... (Dan. 3.15)

In the above example, the verb phrase עֲתִיד דִּי + prefix conjugation expresses either willingness or intention. Since the semantic meaning of this expression derives from the word עֲתִיד, it has a different grammaticalization path from the prefix conjugation. That is, עֲתִיד is an example of a word with lexical meaning ('ready, prepared') that grammaticalized into an auxiliary in a verb phrase ('be willing/intend to ...'). Grammatical expressions of desire or willingness can develop into the expression of intention and then of the future.[46] This path of development accounts for the fact that in later ancient Aramaic this verb phrase became an alternative expression for the future.

2.3.2 Epistemic Modalities

Epistemic modality expresses the speaker's judgment concerning the factual status of a proposition. According to Bybee, Perkins, and Pagliuca, 'epistemic senses develop later than, and out of, the agent-oriented senses', such as obligation or ability.[47] For example, expressions that denote ability can develop into expressions of possibility.

In passing, it should be noted that there is a difference of opinion on whether deontic modalities can become epistemic

[46] Bybee, Perkins, and Pagliuca, *The Evolution of Grammar*, pp. 254–257; Bernd Heine and Tania Kuteva, *World Lexicon of Grammaticalization* (Cambridge: Cambridge University Press, 2002) p. 310.

[47] Bybee, Perkins, and Pagliuca, *The Evolution of Grammar*, p. 195.

modalities.[48] However, deontic modality is an umbrella term for various types of modalities. According to Palmer, deontic refers to 'obligation or permission'.[49] Bybee, Perkins, and Pagliuca distinguish obligations and commands, grouping the former with agent-oriented modality, and the latter with speaker-oriented modality.[50] Obligation reports 'the existence of external, social conditions compelling an agent' to an action, whereas directives, or commands, consist of a speaker imposing a condition on an addressee.[51] While it is common for obligation to evolve into epistemic modalities, the same is not true of expressions of command or permission.

2.3.2.1 Epistemic Possibility

Epistemic possibility expresses the speaker's assertion that a proposition is possibly true. This is to be distinguished from root possibility, which reports the existence of general internal or external enabling conditions. Although notionally different, it is common for these functions to overlap in actual usage. Therefore, it is common for expressions of ability to grammaticalize into expressions of root possibility and then epistemic possibility.[52] In fact, grammatical expressions for epistemic possibility do not usually arise in other grammaticalization paths.[53] That is, expressions of obligation or desire do not usually develop into expressions of epistemic possibility. There is one possible instance in a main clause (6.6) and fourteen instances in relative clauses, including clauses introduced by כָּל־דִּי (6.8a), כָּל־אֱנָשׁ דִּי (3.10a; 5.7a, 7b; 6.13a), מַן־דִּי (3.6a, 6b, 11a, 11b; 4.14b, 22e, 29d; 5.21c), or a variation of these expressions (3.29a).[54]

---

[48] Debra P. Ziegeler, 'Diachrony of Modality and Mood', in Jan Nuyts and Johan van der Auwera (eds.), *The Oxford Handbook of Modality and Mood* (Oxford: Oxford University Press, 2016) pp. 387–405 (392–397).

[49] Palmer, *Mood and Modality*, p. 9.

[50] Bybee, Perkins, and Pagliuca, *The Evolution of Grammar*, pp. 177–179.

[51] Bybee, Perkins, and Pagliuca, *The Evolution of Grammar*, pp. 177, 179.

[52] Bybee, Perkins, and Pagliuca, *The Evolution of Grammar*, pp. 194–199.

[53] Bybee, Perkins, and Pagliuca, *The Evolution of Grammar*, p. 266.

[54] The instances in 3.11 and 6.13 are repetitions of 3.6 and 6.8 respectively.

כָּל־דִּֽי־יִבְעֵ֣ה בָ֠עוּ מִן־כָּל־אֱלָ֨הּ וֶֽאֱנָ֜שׁ עַד־יוֹמִ֣ין תְּלָתִ֗ין לָהֵן֙ מִנָּ֣ךְ מַלְכָּ֔א

> Whoever *might make a petition* to any god or man for thirty days, except you, O king, … (Dan. 6.8)

The prefix conjugation verb in the above example denotes neither present nor future events, but only potential ones. Thus, it expresses the speaker's assessment that it is possible.

2.3.2.2 Certainty

Normally, the employment of epistemic modality expresses less certainty, whereas the employment of a non-modal form expresses total certainty. However, a modal form may also be employed to emphasize the speaker's certainty. There are two instances that possibly express certainty or confidence (3.17; 6.17). However, it is more likely that these instances express other modalities, such as ability (3.17) or optative (6.17), or even a simple future (3.17).

אֱלָהָ֗ךְ דִּ֣י אַ֤נְתְּה פָּֽלַֽח־לֵהּ֙ בִּתְדִירָ֔א ה֖וּא יְשֵׁיזְבִנָּֽךְ

> Your God, whom you serve continually, *he will (certainly) deliver you*! (Dan. 6.17)
>
> Your God, whom you serve continually, *may he deliver you*! (Dan. 6.17)

The above example can easily be read as a statement of confidence in God. Some see it as 'a rather firm affirmation of faith'.[55] However, the context seems to contradict the reading of the above example as a statement of confidence. The king spent a sleepless night fasting (v. 19), and then asked in the morning with a troubled/sorrowful (עֲצִיב) voice whether Daniel's God had been able to deliver him (v. 21). Clearly, the king was not certain that God would deliver Daniel.

Similarly, the instance in 3.17 can be variously interpreted, due to the syntactic uncertainties of the context.

---

[55] René Péter-Contesse and John Ellington, *A Handbook on the Book of Daniel* (UBS Handbook Series, New York: United Bible Societies, 1993) p. 168.

הֵן אִיתַי אֱלָהַנָא דִּי־אֲנַחְנָא פָּלְחִין יָכִל לְשֵׁיזָבוּתַנָא מִן־אַתּוּן נוּרָא
יָקִדְתָּא וּמִן־יְדָךְ מַלְכָּא יְשֵׁיזִב

> If it is so, our God, whom we serve, is able to deliver us. *He will (certainly) deliver us*, O king, from the furnace of burning fire and from your hand. (Dan. 3.17)
>
> If our God, whom we serve, is able to deliver us, *he will deliver us* [future], O king, from the furnace of burning fire and from your hand. (Dan. 3.17)
>
> If it is so, our God, whom we serve, is able to deliver us. *He can deliver us* [ability], O king, from the furnace of burning fire and from your hand. (Dan. 3.17)
>
> We do not need to answer you ..., if our God, whom we serve is able to deliver us and *(if) he delivers us* [conditional] ... (Dan. 3.17)

It is not clear how far the conditional protasis continues in the above passage, making the exact interpretation difficult.[56] However, although the chapter highlights the faithfulness of the three captives, v. 18 ('but if not') suggests that they were not certain that God would deliver them, but only that he could. Hence, it is better to interpret the prefix conjugation verb in v. 17 in one of the other possible functions. Since God's ability to deliver is so prominent in the context, the present writer favors viewing it as an expression of ability.

Cross-linguistic considerations are also relevant. Palmer points out that expressions of confidence usually involve more than just a morphological form. They often employ an adverb that expresses confidence along with a grammatical form expressing inference, which would otherwise express evidential rather than epistemic modality.[57] Palmer distinguishes epistemic and evidential modalities, the former indicating the speaker's confidence in the factualness of a proposition and the latter indicating the

---

[56] Li, *The Verbal System of the Aramaic of Daniel*, pp. 85, 118.

[57] Palmer, *Mood and Modality*, pp. 34–35. Also, categorical assertions can be part of the discourse system rather than inherent in the morphological form (pp. 59–60).

speaker's evidence for it.[58] In contrast, Bybee, Perkins, and Pagliuca do not distinguish epistemic and evidential, but simply call this function 'inferred certainty'.[59] However, they point out that the expression of inferred certainty generally grammaticalizes from the expression of strong obligation.[60] That is, the type of epistemic modality expressed by a grammatical construction is related to the agent-oriented modality from which it derived. Hence, ability grammaticalizes into epistemic possibility (e.g., 'the letter *may* have come yesterday'), weak obligation into epistemic probability (e.g., 'the letter *should* have come yesterday'), and strong obligation into epistemic certainty (e.g., 'the letter *must* already be here'). Since the prefix conjugation is not attested with a strong obligation function, the possible instances of the expression of certainty may be better alternatively analyzed.[61]

Moreover, since there are no unequivocal instances of the prefix conjugation expressing epistemic certainty in the corpus, the dearth of such instances may serve as further evidence for interpreting the instances in prophetic contexts as simple futures rather than futures expressing epistemic certainty.

2.3.2.3 Simple Future

The term 'simple future' is used here to distinguish it from future predictions that are accompanied by other types of modality. As mentioned earlier, since predictions are statements of what is not yet a reality, some consider the simple future to be a type of epistemic modality.[62] Hence, its mention here.

There are many possible paths of development that lead to the expression of the future. Especially common is the

---

[58] Palmer, *Mood and Modality*, p. 8.

[59] Bybee, Perkins, and Pagliuca, *The Evolution of Grammar*, p. 180.

[60] Bybee, Perkins, and Pagliuca, *The Evolution of Grammar*, p. 195.

[61] The modality of obligation is to be distinguished from the modality of a directive or command. Whereas an obligation expresses the existence of external conditions compelling an action, a directive imposes such a condition.

[62] Squartini, 'Interactions between Modality and Other Semantic Categories', pp. 53–54.

development from intention to prediction, though there are various paths that evolve into intention.[63] That is, although expressions that denote the agent-oriented modalities of obligation, desire, and ability can each develop into intention and later the future, they consist of different grammaticalization pathways. Thus, for example, the pathway from obligation to future is different from the pathway from desire to future.[64] Since the modality of ability is attested for the prefix conjugation, the relevant pathway would be: ability > root possibility > intention > future. However, such futures are not common, since there is a 'scarcity of futures derived from ability'.[65] While this fact does not preclude the possibility that the future function of the prefix conjugation partially derives from the earlier *yaqtula* modal, it does reinforce the likelihood that the future function developed, at least partially if not wholly, from the employment of the *yaqtulu* imperfective in future contexts.

Instances of the prefix conjugation expressing the simple future were discussed earlier in section 2.2.1, and there is no need to repeat the discussion here.

2.3.3 Speaker-Oriented Modalities

Speaker-oriented modalities consist of speech acts whereby the speaker imposes or proposes an action or behavior on someone. As mentioned earlier in this study, a distinction exists between speaker-oriented modality and deontic modality. Deontic modality includes both obligation and command/permission, whereas speaker-oriented modality includes only the latter. Obligation is an agent-oriented modality that reports the existence of external conditions compelling an action, whereas speaker-oriented modalities (e.g., command or permission) impose such a condition. While it is common for agent-oriented

---

[63] Bybee, Perkins, and Pagliuca, *The Evolution of Grammar*, pp. 287–288.

[64] Bybee, Perkins, and Pagliuca, *The Evolution of Grammar*, p. 257.

[65] Bybee, Perkins, and Pagliuca, *The Evolution of Grammar*, p. 266. Grammatical expressions 'marking one or more of the meanings of ability, root possibility, permission, and epistemic possibility are quite common, but their development into future markers is apparently not common' (p. 266).

modalities, such as obligation, to develop into speaker-oriented modalities, the reverse is not true.

2.3.3.1 Affirmative Directive

There are many possible paths by which grammatical constructions develop the function of expressing commands.[66] A common source of affirmative commands is the future.[67] Though the imperative/command function can develop out of the future, the reverse does not occur.[68] Alternatively, there is also a path of development from imperfective aspect to imperative/command modality,[69] which may be pertinent, since the prefix conjugation partially arose from an earlier *yaqtulu* imperfective.

In addition, since most forms of the jussive and the long prefix conjugation are indistinguishable, it is possible that some of the instances listed here are actually jussives. Further, the merging of the jussive and the long prefix conjugation, a process which was not completed until later ancient Aramaic, may have resulted in some conflation of their functions. However, since it is common for the future and other non-modal constructions to develop a directive function, there is no reason why the expression of command or exhortation must be restricted to jussives. Besides, the occurrence of the long forms with final *nuns* in some contexts (e.g., 2.5b, 5c, 6b) demonstrates that at least those forms are not jussives.

There are different views on how the prefix conjugation functions in commands.[70] Since it is not always easy to distinguish between direct commands, indirect/polite commands, and

---

[66] For a full account, see Caterina Mauri and Andrea Sansò, 'How Directive Constructions Emerge: Grammaticalization, Cooptation, Constructionalization', *Journal of Pragmatics* 43 (2011), pp. 3489–3521.
[67] Bybee and Dahl, 'The Creation of Tense and Aspect Systems', p. 93.
[68] Bybee, Perkins, and Pagliuca, *The Evolution of Grammar*, p. 273.
[69] Bybee, Perkins, and Pagliuca, *The Evolution of Grammar*, p. 212. 'Forms and constructions variously labelled as imperfective, perfective, present or past are indeed frequently used across languages as a strategy to convey orders'; Mauri and Sansò, 'How Directive Constructions Emerge', p. 3508.
[70] For a detailed discussion, see Li, *The Verbal System of the Aramaic of Daniel*, pp. 112–115.

requests, the more general umbrella term ‘directive’ is employed in this study. Nevertheless, that these functions include direct commands is evident from the fact that many of the instances occur in royal commands (2.5b, 5c, 6b; 3.5b, 5c, 6c, 15e; 5.7c, 7d, 16c, 16d) and divine/angelic decrees (4.11, 12, 13a, 13b, 13c, 20a).

Due to the nature of directives, they generally occur in main clauses. There are twenty-four clear instances of prefix conjugation affirmative directives in main clauses (2.5b, 5c, 6b, 7a; 3.5b, 5c, 6c, 15e, 18a; 4.11, 12, 13a, 13b, 13c, 20a, 24a; 5.7c, 7d, 12, 16c, 16d, 17a; 6.9a, 9b). Further, eight additional instances occur in complement clauses that cite royal commands (3.10b, 10c, 11c, 29b, 29c; 5.29; 6.8b, 13b).

> בְּעִדָּנָא דִּֽי־תִשְׁמְעוּן קָל קַרְנָא מַשְׁרוֹקִיתָא קַיתְרוֹס סַבְּכָא פְּסַנְתֵּרִין סוּמְפֹּנְיָה וְכֹל זְנֵי זְמָרָא תִּפְּלוּן וְתִסְגְּדוּן לְצֶלֶם דַּהֲבָא דִּי הֲקֵים נְבוּכַדְנֶצַּר מַלְכָּא׃
>
> When you hear the sound of the horn, flute, lyre, trigon, harp, accompaniment, and all kinds of music, *you are to fall down and worship* the image of gold that Nebuchadnezzar the king set up. (Dan. 3.5)

In the above example, the prefix conjugation verb occurs as part of a royal decree. The fact that the prefix conjugation can express an affirmative directive is further supported by its occurrence in parallel with the imperative.

> מַתְּנָתָךְ לָךְ לֶהֶוְיָן וּנְבָזְבְּיָתָךְ לְאָחֳרָן הַב
>
> *Keep* your gifts for yourself, or give [imperative] your presents to someone else. (Dan. 5.17)

In the above example, the prefix conjugation verb occurs together with an imperative (5.17), with no apparent distinction in function. Both express either a polite directive addressed to a superior or a hortative (literally, ‘*Let* your gifts *be* yours’).

2.3.3.2 Prohibition

Prohibition can be an umbrella term for all types of negative deontic expressions. However, ancient Aramaic, as other ancient Semitic languages, distinguished between negative commands and prohibitions. The former expressed the negative equivalent of an affirmative command (e.g., 'Don't go there!'), whereas the latter expressed the negative equivalent of an affirmative permission (e.g., 'You may not go there', 'You are not allowed to go there'). The former employed the jussive preceded by אַל־, whereas the latter employed the long prefix conjugation preceded by לָא.

Parallel to the path of grammaticalization from root possibility to epistemic possibility, root possibility can also develop into permission. In fact, permission can be viewed as a specialized form of root possibility, since, whereas the latter reports the existence of general enabling conditions, permission reports the presence of social enabling conditions.[71] Inasmuch as in Aramaic a prohibition can be considered a negative permission, the prefix conjugation's function in the expression of ability and root possibility may be considered the source for the expression of both permission and prohibition.

In the Aramaic of Daniel, negative commands are not expressed by the long prefix conjugation but by the jussive (see the discussion on the jussive in section 3 below). However, there are possibly two instances, both in subordinate relative clauses, of the long prefix conjugation preceded by לָא expressing prohibition (6.9c, 13c).[72]

כְּעַ֣ן מַלְכָּ֔א תְּקִ֣ים אֱסָרָ֔א וְתִרְשֻׁ֖ם כְּתָבָ֑א דִּ֣י לָ֧א לְהַשְׁנָיָ֛ה כְּדָת־מָדַ֥י וּפָרַ֖ס
דִּי־לָ֥א תֶעְדֵּֽא

Now, O king, issue the interdiction and write the document so that it may not be changed, according to the law of the Medes and Persians, which *may not pass away*. (Dan. 6.9)

The context of the prefix conjugation verb in the above example is neither a statement of fact nor an assessment of its (im)possibility. This is supported by the parallel between the prefix conjugation and the infinitive in this chapter. That is, the prohibition occurs both in the form of the prefix conjugation of

[71] Bybee, Perkins, and Pagliuca, *The Evolution of Grammar*, pp. 191–194.
[72] Compare the use of the prefix conjugation in 6.9, 13 with the infinitive in 6.16.

the verb עדה (vv. 9, 13) and the *Haphel* infinitive of the verb שׁנה (vv. 9, 16). Further, the fact that the king tried to find a way to rescue Daniel (v. 15) shows that the statement is not simply a statement of fact, but a statement of what is not allowed. Also, in v. 18 the king sealed the opening of the den with his ring with the purpose 'that it may not be changed/violated' (prefix conjugation of שׁנה), implying that it was not impossible to change/violate the king's degree, but simply prohibited.

2.3.3.3 Optative

Sometimes, the labels 'optative' and 'volitive' are used with overlapping meaning. However, volitive or volitional is an umbrella term for more than one modality. Volitive can include such modalities as willingness, intention, hortative, and optative.

Optative modality denotes the expression of wishes or hopes. According to Nikolaeva, optatives can be realizable or non-realizable.[73] An optative expression assumes that the situation wished for does not exist, at least not yet, and 'the state of affairs wished for is typically outside of the sphere of influence of the speaker'.[74] Thus, an optative expression can wish for the unrealizable, e.g., something that is unachievable or even in the past. In contrast, a hortative expression exhorts someone concerning something that is presumed to be achievable. Optatives often develop 'from markers of ability and possibility',[75] more specifically, root possibility.[76]

Instances of the prefix conjugation with an optative function include two instances in a greeting formula (3.31; 6.26), one instance in an exclamation of praise (2.20), and two other possible instances that could be alternatively explained (4.24b and 6.17, the latter of which was discussed earlier in this study).

שְׁלָמְכוֹן יִשְׂגֵּא

[73] Irina Nikolaeva, 'Analyses of the Semantics of Mood', in Jan Nuyts and Johan van der Auwera (eds.), *The Oxford Handbook of Modality and Mood* (Oxford: Oxford University Press, 2016) pp. 77–79.

[74] Nikolaeva, 'Analyses of the Semantics of Mood', p. 77.

[75] Bybee, *Morphology*, p. 194.

[76] Bybee, Perkins, and Pagliuca, *The Evolution of Grammar*, p. 205.

May your peace *increase*! (Dan. 3.31)

Although the above example is uttered by a king, the greeting formula could be used by a wide variety of individuals. The prefix conjugation verb expresses a wish/hope for the existence of a situation whose achievement is outside the sphere of influence of the speaker, i.e., it is optative.

The instance in 4.24b deserves an additional comment. Since it is introduced by the conditional conjunction הֵן, it could be interpreted as a conditional protasis. However, as Palmer points out, wishes can have the same form as conditionals in some languages.[77] Hence, the instance in 4.24b could also be interpreted as an optative.

הֵן תֶּהֱוֵא אַרְכָה לִשְׁלֵוְתָךְ

If only there may be a lengthening of your prosperity! (Dan. 4.24)

In the above example, the clause introduced by הֵן most likely expresses a wish. There is a Biblical Hebrew parallel in the optative use of the conjunction אִם (e.g., Ps. 81.9; 1 Chron. 4.10).

2.3.4 Subordinate Clauses

For the purpose of this study, a clause is considered subordinate if it is introduced by a subordinating conjunction or if it continues the subordinate sense of a preceding subordinate clause. That is, since a subordinating conjunction may introduce a series of clauses, all the clauses in the series are considered subordinate. Clauses that are not introduced by a subordinating conjunction are provisionally considered main clauses, even if their translation requires an English subordinate clause.

Since the category of subordinate refers to verbal forms that are to a large extent restricted to subordinate contexts, it is a mood rather than a modality (e.g., the subjunctive mood).[78] Hence, not all instances that occur in subordinate contexts actually express modality. However, the restriction of a

[77] Palmer, *Mood and Modality*, p. 132.

[78] Modality refers to the notions expressed, whereas mood refers to a morphosyntactic category.

grammatical construction to subordinate contexts is part of a typical diachronic development, usually occurring toward the end of its path of grammaticalization. In the process of grammaticalization, grammatical forms acquire new meanings in main clauses. As they replace older forms in main clauses, the older forms become restricted to subordinate contexts, a development that shows up 'very late on the grammaticalization paths'.[79] The specific subordinate functions of verbal expressions originate with some correspondence between their functions in main clauses and in subordinate clauses (mostly their epistemic or speaker-oriented functions), though they can later develop other meanings. Once grammatical forms become restricted to subordinate contexts, their only further development 'is their gradual loss from the language'.[80]

The prefix conjugation in the Aramaic of Daniel is not yet a subordinate mood. This label may be more appropriate in some forms of later ancient Aramaic, where it is more restricted to subordinate functions. However, the large number of instances that occur in subordinate clauses in Daniel demonstrates that it is developing in that direction.[81] Below is a discussion of the various types of subordinate clauses in which the prefix conjugation occurs.

2.3.4.1 Purpose Clause

Subordinate clauses that express purpose can have various sources. One of the most common precursors of the function of purpose is the future. Another common source is intention, which can develop into the expression of purpose either directly or by developing along the way as an expression of the future.[82]

---

[79] Bybee, Perkins, and Pagliuca, *The Evolution of Grammar*, p. 213.
[80] Bybee, Perkins, and Pagliuca, *The Evolution of Grammar*, p. 214.
[81] More than a third of the instances of prefix conjugation forms in Daniel occur in subordinate clauses (74 out of 179 instances). Considering only the instances expressing future and modality, about half occur in subordinate clauses (64 out of 125 or possibly out of 131). Of instances expressing modality aside from futures, the proportion is closer to two-thirds (56 out of 79, possibly out of 85).
[82] Bybee, Perkins, and Pagliuca, *The Evolution of Grammar*, pp. 228–230.

There are at least ten instances of the prefix conjugation in subordinate purpose clauses (2.18, 30a, 30b; 3.28a, 28b; 4.3, 14a; 5.15; 6.2, 18). In addition, there are also instances that could be analyzed either as expressing purpose in clauses without explicit subordinate markers or as expressing a past progressive (5.2; 7.14a, 16a, 16b) or a simple future function (2.4, 7b, 9c, 24).

עַל־דִּבְרַת דִּי פִשְׁרָא לְמַלְכָּא יְהוֹדְעוּן וְרַעְיוֹנֵי לִבְבָךְ תִּנְדַּע

> … so that *they may make known* the interpretation to the king and that *you may know* the thoughts of your heart. (Dan. 2.30)

בֵּלְשַׁאצַּר אֲמַר׀ בִּטְעֵם חַמְרָא לְהַיְתָיָה לְמָאנֵי דַּהֲבָא וְכַסְפָּא דִּי הַנְפֵּק
נְבוּכַדְנֶצַּר אֲבוּהִי מִן־הֵיכְלָא דִּי בִירוּשְׁלֶם וְיִשְׁתּוֹן בְּהוֹן מַלְכָּא וְרַבְרְבָנוֹהִי
שֵׁגְלָתֵהּ וּלְחֵנָתֵהּ

> Belshazzar commanded when drunk to bring the vessels of gold and silver which Nebuchadnezzar his father had brought out from the temple which was in Jerusalem, *so that* the king, his nobles, his concubines and maid servants *might drink* with them. (Dan. 5.2)

In the above examples, the prefix conjugation verbs occur in purpose clauses. Whereas in the first example (2.30) the clauses are introduced by a subordinating conjunction, in the second example (5.2) the prefix conjugation occurs without a subordinating conjunction.[83]

2.3.4.2 Result Clause

There is a close connection between purpose and result clauses. According to Palmer, the notional overlap between purpose, result, and indirect commands consists of the fact that these all express the effect or result of some cause.[84] That is, purpose and indirect commands express an intended effect, whereas result expresses an actual effect. On the other hand, it should be noted that purpose and result clauses can be compared both in terms of intention and result. Whereas a purpose clause does not assume

---

[83] For a more detailed discussion of the latter instance, see Li, *The Verbal System of the Aramaic of Daniel*, pp. 123–124.

[84] Palmer, *Mood and Modality*, pp. 83, 136.

the occurrence of the intended event (e.g., 'He was driving slowly, *so as to avoid* an accident, but to no avail'), a result clause assumes such an occurrence, though it does not assume an intention (e.g., 'He drove *so* fast *that he hit* another car'). However, in spite of this semantic distinction, there is enough overlap that the same grammatical construction can at times express both notions.

In the corpus, there are no prefix conjugation verbs in subordinate result clauses. That is, there are no instances expressing result in clauses with an explicitly subordinate marker. However, there are at least two instances where the prefix conjugation verb could possibly be understood as expressing result without a subordinate marker (4.2a, 2b).

חֵ֣לֶם חֲזֵ֔ית וִֽידַחֲלִנַּ֑נִי וְהַרְהֹרִין֙ עַֽל־מִשְׁכְּבִ֔י וְחֶזְוֵ֥י רֵאשִׁ֖י יְבַהֲלֻנַּֽנִי

I dreamed a dream, *so that it frightened me* and the imaginations on my bed and the visions of my head *scared me*. (Dan. 4.2)

The above examples have been variously interpreted. I suggest that one option is to understand them as expressing result in past time. Among the alternative possibilities, they could also be understood as expressing a past progressive function.

2.3.4.3 Conditional Protasis

According to Folmer, there was a diachronic development in Aramaic from the earlier use of the suffix conjugation in a conditional protasis to the more widespread use of the prefix conjugation.[85] The shift from suffix conjugation to prefix conjugation was probably due to the fact that the latter came to be more clearly associated with the expression of modality. More specifically, there is a path of development from epistemic

---

[85] Margaretha L. Folmer, 'Some Remarks on the Use of the Finite Verb Form in the Protasis of Conditional Sentences in Aramaic Texts from the Achaemenid Period', in K. Jongeling, H. L. Murre-van den Berg, and Lucas Van Rompay (eds.), *Studies in Hebrew and Aramaic Syntax: Presented to Professor J. Hoftijzer on the Occasion of His Sixty-Fifth Birthday* (Studies in Semitic Languages and Linguistics, 17, Leiden, New York, København, Köln: E.J. Brill, 1991) pp. 56–78.

possibility to conditional protasis.[86] Since 'an *if*-clause sets up a possible world',[87] it is reasonable that a grammatical construction expressing possibility can be employed in a conditional protasis. In such instances, conditionality is expressed by the conditional conjunction, while the verb itself is 'very generalized'[88] and often devoid of its regular non-protasis tense/aspect/modality functions.

There are six instances of the prefix conjugation introduced by the conditional conjunction הֵן. At least five of the instances are clearly conditional protases (2.5a, 6a, 9a; 3.15d; 5.16b). The remaining instance could be interpreted either as conditional or optative (4.24b, discussed above). The conjunction הֵן is not limited to only the prefix conjugation, since in three instances it does not introduce a prefix conjugation verb (3.15, 17, 18). Hence, the conditionality of the clause is expressed by the subordinating conjunction, but the fact that the prefix conjugation verb is devoid of its other tense/aspect/modality functions indicates that its employment in this context is part of its grammaticalization.

וְהֵן חֶלְמָא וּפִשְׁרֵהּ תְּהַחֲוֺן

If you make known the dream and its interpretation, ... (Dan. 2.6)

In the above example, the prefix conjugation verb occurs in a conditional protasis initiated by a conditional conjunction. It is devoid of its tense/aspect/modality functions other than to express a hypothetical condition.

2.3.4.4 Temporal Protasis

A temporal protasis that refers to a potential event is similar to a conditional protasis. Hence, they may share the same path of development. The markers of temporal clauses, however, have various sources, such as the word 'until'. What is significant here is that verbs used in subordinate environments, such as

---

[86] Bybee, Perkins, and Pagliuca, *The Evolution of Grammar*, pp. 208–210.
[87] Bybee, Perkins, and Pagliuca, *The Evolution of Grammar*, p. 208.
[88] Bybee, Perkins, and Pagliuca, *The Evolution of Grammar*, p. 209.

subjunctives, are 'semantically reduced'. That is, 'they are used more because they are strongly associated with the syntactic configuration than because of the semantic contribution they make'.[89] Thus, the prefix conjugation verb in a temporal protasis (as in a conditional protasis) is devoid of most of its other functions. That is, it does not express future time or other modal functions within a temporal or conditional protasis.[90] There are seven instances of the prefix conjugation in temporal clauses (2.9b; 3.5a, 15a; 4.20b, 22d, 23, 29c).

עַד דִּי עִדָּנָא יִשְׁתַּנֵּא

Until the time *changes*. (Dan. 2.9)

In the above example, the prefix conjugation verb occurs in a temporal clause initiated by a temporal conjunction. The temporal function of the clause derives primarily from the subordinating conjunction, while the verb is devoid of its other tense/aspect/modality functions.

However, a distinction must be made between a temporal protasis that refers to a potential event and a past time temporal expression. Past time temporal clauses employ suffix conjugation verbs (2.34; 4.30; 5.21; 6.25; 7.4, 9, 11, 22). A similar situation exists in English, where the future is not employed in a potential temporal clause ('Please, wait until I come', not *'... until I will come'), but the past tense is employed in a past time temporal clause ('You waited until I came').

2.3.4.5 Complement Clause

Deutscher defined finite complements as 'clauses which are arguments of predicates'.[91] That is, the complement clause is semantically, though not necessarily syntactically, dependent on/embedded within another clause.

Haspelmath noted that purpose markers tend to develop into markers of complements of various types of verbs, such as those

---

[89] Bybee, Perkins, and Pagliuca, *The Evolution of Grammar*, p. 236.
[90] Bybee, Perkins, and Pagliuca, *The Evolution of Grammar*, pp. 274, 209.
[91] Guy Deutscher, *Syntactic Change in Akkadian: The Evolution of Sentential Complementation* (Oxford: Oxford University Press, 2000) p. 9.

that express directives, potential, thinking, and cognition.[92] Further, according to Mauri and Sansò, it is common for subjunctive and infinitive forms to partially overlap in function.[93] This is true of both purpose and complement clauses. Therefore, it is relevant to mention the overlap between complement expressions with דִּי + prefix conjugation and those with the infinitive, as in the following example:

> וּמִנִּי שִׂים טְעֵם דִּי כָל־עַם אֻמָּה וְלִשָּׁן דִּי־יֵאמַר שָׁלָה עַל אֱלָהֲהוֹן דִּי־שַׁדְרַךְ מֵישַׁךְ וַעֲבֵד נְגוֹא הַדָּמִין יִתְעֲבֵד וּבַיְתֵהּ נְוָלִי יִשְׁתַּוֵּה
>
> A decree has been issued by me *that* any people, nation, or tongue that speaks amiss against the god of Shadrach, Meshach, and Abednego *shall be cut* into pieces, and his house *shall be turned into* a dunghill. (Dan. 3.29)

> וּמִנִּי שִׂים טְעֵם לְהַנְעָלָה קֳדָמַי לְכֹל חַכִּימֵי בָבֶל
>
> A decree was issued by me to bring up [infinitive] before me all the wise men of Babylon. (Dan. 4.3)

In both examples above the expression וּמִנִּי שִׂים טְעֵם is followed by a complement. The first example employs a prefix conjugation verb (3.29) and the second an infinitive (4.3). The complement of a royal command is very often expressed by an infinitive (2.12, 46; 3.2, 13, 19, 20; 4.23; 5.2, 7; 6.24), and the two grammatical constructions seem to overlap in function.

Bybee, Perkins, and Pagliuca likewise observed a strong tendency for verbal constructions expressing purpose to also function as complements of verbs of wanting and ordering.[94] However, they suggest that complements develop through a series of stages.[95] At first, grammatical constructions serve as complements to predicates that have harmonic functions. That is, the

---

[92] Martin Haspelmath, 'From Purposive to Infinitive', *Folia Linguistica Historica* 10 (1989), pp. 287–310.

[93] Caterina Mauri and Andrea Sansò, 'The Linguistic Marking of (Ir)realis and Subjunctive', in Jan Nuyts and Johan van der Auwera (eds.), *The Oxford Handbook of Modality and Mood* (Oxford: Oxford University Press, 2016) pp. 176–177.

[94] Bybee, Perkins, and Pagliuca, *The Evolution of Grammar*, p. 230.

[95] Bybee, Perkins, and Pagliuca, *The Evolution of Grammar*, pp. 214–218.

verb retains its normal semantic meaning and only occurs as a complement of predicates whose meaning is similar to or compatible with this meaning. Eventually, these grammatical constructions can develop as a 'concomitant of subordination', and serve as complements to predicates with non-harmonic functions. That is, the verb loses its normal semantic meaning in complement clauses and can occur as a complement of predicates with various other meanings. At this latter stage, the complement verb will occur in both harmonic and non-harmonic contexts.[96]

There are at least nineteen instances of the prefix conjugation in complement clauses. These complement clauses can be categorized based on the semantic meaning of the main clause predicate.[97] The instances attested in the corpus fall into two groups. One group consists of verbs of ordering and wanting, which are harmonic with either the modality of obligation or with verbs expressing future, imperative/command, or purpose. These instances include complements of requesting (2.16) and of royal commands (3.10b, 10c, 11c, 29b, 29c; 5.29; 6.8b, 13b; perhaps also 5.7c, 7d, though there the particle דִּי is better understood as a marker of direct speech).[98] Another group consists of verbs of thinking and hoping, i.e., epistemic verbs, which are harmonic with modalities expressing possibility or probability. These instances include complements of verbs of knowing (2.9d; 3.18b; 4.14c, 14d, 22f, 29e; 5.21d) and hearing (5.16a). The occurrence of the prefix conjugation in both groups of complement clauses

---

[96] Bybee, Perkins, and Pagliuca give the following examples involving the word 'should', which expresses weak obligation (words in brackets are added for clarification); *The Evolution of Grammar*, p. 215. Harmonic: 'I suggested [obligation] that they *should* [obligation] put (a)round each carriage door a piece of beading' (cited from Coates). Non-harmonic: 'The police are expecting [epistemic] that the Libyans *should* [not obligation/semantically empty] make the first move' (cited from British television).

[97] See Bybee, Perkins, and Pagliuca, *The Evolution of Grammar*, pp. 218–225.

[98] The list could possibly also include the instances of verbs in the phrase עֲתִיד דִּי + prefix conjugation (3.15b, 15c). However, this verb phrase is better analyzed as a distinct grammatical construction expressing willingness/intention. See the discussion of this phrase earlier in this study.

could suggest that it is at an advanced stage of its development in complement clauses. However, its wide attestation can also be explained as due to the dual source of the prefix conjugation (imperfective *yaqtulu* and modal *yaqtula*).[99]

The prefix conjugation verb in complement clauses can retain some of its other functions, such as general present (4.14c, 14d, 22f, 29e; 5.16a, 21d), ability (2.9d), or intention (3.18b). These various functions are discussed elsewhere in this study.

As for the conjunction דִּי, which occurs in all complement clauses with the prefix conjugation, one of its many functions is that of introducing direct speech. Therefore, its function in introducing the complement of verbs of saying, knowing, or hearing can be considered simply a natural extension of its other functions. Other verb forms besides the prefix conjugation also occur in complement clauses introduced by the conjunction דִּי. Compare the following two examples:

לָהֵן חֶלְמָא אֱמַרוּ לִי וְאִנְדַּע דִּי פִשְׁרֵהּ תְּהַחֲוֻנַּנִי

> Therefore, tell me the dream, so that I may know *that you can show me* its interpretation. (Dan. 2.9)

מִן־יַצִּיב יָדַע אֲנָה דִּי עִדָּנָא אַנְתּוּן זָבְנִין

> I know for sure that you are playing for [participle] time. (Dan. 2.8)

In the first example above (2.9) the complement clause contains a prefix conjugation verb, whereas in the second example (2.8) the verb is a participle. There are no instances of the prefix conjugation functioning as a complement without the subordinating conjunction דִּי.

2.3.4.6 Relative Clause

There are thirty-eight instances of the prefix conjugation in relative clauses. However, unlike the previously discussed subordinate clauses, its frequent occurrence in relative clauses

---

[99] As explained elsewhere in this study, the modality of possibility can be traced back to the *yaqtula* source, whereas future, directive, and purpose functions may have a more complicated history.

does not seem to be directly related to the grammaticalization of its functions. This is evident from the fact that the verbs in the relative clauses express the same functions that they would in main clauses. That is, the prefix conjugation is attested in relative clauses expressing the future (2.28, 29a, 29b, 39b; 6.27b; 7.14b, 14c, 23b), the general present (2.10; 3.29d; 6.16), and modalities such as ability (2.11, 25; 4.32a, 32b), root possibility (3.15f), epistemic possibility (3.6a, 6b, 10a, 11a, 11b, 29a; 4.14b, 22e, 29d; 5.7a, 7b, 21c; 6.8a, 13a), and prohibition (6.9c, 13c). These various functions have already been discussed elsewhere in this study. Further, other verb forms also occur in relative clauses, such as the suffix conjugation (e.g., 2.35) or the participle (e.g., 5.5), and they likewise express the same functions that they would in main clauses.

2.4 The Prefix Conjugation and the Grammaticalization of Its Modal Functions

The various modal functions of the prefix conjugation can be laid out in a coherent diachronic sequence. While a language may possess many grammatical constructions for modalities, any given construction will most likely conform to one specific path of grammaticalization, usually beginning with the expression of one agent-oriented modality.[100] It cannot be determined where along the path of grammaticalization the West Semitic modal *yaqtula* was when it coalesced with the imperfective *yaqtulu* to form the prefix conjugation. Nor can it be known whether *yaqtula* had an earlier non-modal function or what that might have been. Nevertheless, the most primitive attested function of the prefix conjugation is the expression of ability, which expanded into root possibility. Root possibility, in turn, developed into epistemic possibility, permission/prohibition, and optative, perhaps also intention. Epistemic possibility is also a precursor of conditional protasis. Although a few instances could be interpreted as expressing certainty, this is unlikely, because certainty develops out of the expression of strong obligation, which is not part of the grammaticalization path that starts with ability.

---

[100] Bybee, Perkins, and Pagliuca, *The Evolution of Grammar*, p. 256.

Several functions of the prefix conjugation may have had a more complicated history of development, to wit, the future, purpose, affirmative directives, and complement clauses. The future may have had a dual source. That is, the future consists of the employment of the imperfective *yaqtulu* in future time, but *yaqtula* may also have had a future function that developed from the expression of intention. The expression of purpose may have developed from the future. Intention is also a precursor of purpose, either directly or by first developing into a future. The future is also a very common source for the development of affirmative directives. Alternatively, there is also a possible path of development from imperfective aspect to imperative/command modality. In addition, since most forms of the jussive and the long prefix conjugation are indistinguishable, the merging of these conjugations, a process which was not completed until later ancient Aramaic, probably resulted in some conflation of their functions. As for the prefix conjugation in complement clauses, it complements a variety of main clause predicates, including both verbs of wanting and ordering and epistemic verbs. Its occurrence in a wide variety of complement clauses could be attributable to its dual source (i.e., imperfective *yaqtulu* and modal *yaqtula*).

Although the parallel is not exact, there are some similarities between the trajectory of the modal functions of the Aramaic prefix conjugation and the English modal word 'may' (past tense 'might'). The word 'may' comes from the Old English *mæg*, 'to be able', which can be traced back to the proto-Indo-European **magh-* 'to have power, be able'. This is also the root of nouns such as 'might', 'machine', 'magic', etc. In modern English, the word 'may' no longer expresses its original modality of ability, but the attested modalities reflect the expected grammaticalization path that originates in expressions of ability. Some of its attested functions are similar to the attested modal functions of the prefix conjugation: root possibility ('If so, it *may* be possible'), epistemic possibility ('I think that it *may* be true'), permission/prohibition ('You *may* do so'/'You *may* not do so'), optative ('*May* God be with you'), and purpose ('We will send you a letter, *so that* you *may* know what to expect').

In summary, many of the modal functions of the prefix conjugation can be traced back to the expression of ability. There are also some functions that may have resulted from the conflation of earlier West Semitic conjugations and their resulting functions. Finally, it should be mentioned that the prefix conjugation occurs in relative clauses, but does not of itself express relative subordination.

3. JUSSIVE

Since in many instances the form of the jussive and the long prefix conjugation are identical, it is possible that some of the instances listed above are actually jussive. There are only a few instances of clear jussives in the corpus, and these are too few to consider them representative of the full range of possible functions of the jussive. Nevertheless, the attested functions can be grouped under speaker-oriented modalities.

As mentioned earlier, the label '*yaqtul*' can denote either the preterit *yaqtul* or the jussive *yaqtul*. The two may be diachronically related. That is, the West Semitic jussive *yaqtul* conjugation can be considered to have originated as an extension of the preterit *yaqtul* in the expression of directives.[101] This is not unusual, since the development of a perfective or past tense into directive has been observed as a cross-linguistic phenomenon.[102] In Semitic, some examples include the Akkadian precative *liprus*, formed by the particle *lu/li-* combined with the preterit *iprus*, and the possible rare instances of the Biblical Hebrew precative perfect.[103] There is also the path from optative to directive.[104]

---

[101] For a detailed explanation of the diachronic development of *yaqtul*, see Alexander Andrason, 'The Dynamic Short Yiqtol', *JSem* 21 (2012), pp. 308–339.

[102] Mauri and Sansò, 'How Directive Constructions Emerge', pp. 3509–3510.

[103] Christo H. J. van der Merwe, Jacobus A. Naudé, and Jan H. Kroeze, *A Biblical Hebrew Reference Grammar* (London: Bloomsbury T&T Clark, 2nd edn., 2017) p. 169.

[104] Mauri and Sansò, 'How Directive Constructions Emerge', pp. 3504–3506.

That is, an expression of a wish can become a polite request and eventually a command.

3.1 Negative Directive

As in other Semitic languages, the jussive is employed as the negative counterpart of the imperative. Therefore, the jussive can express a wide range of negative directives including negative commands, negative requests (2.24), negative exhortations (4.16; 5.10a, 10b), etc.

In the Aramaic of Daniel, there are four instances of jussives preceded by אַל־ expressing negative directives (2.24; 4.16; 5.10a, 10b). Of these, three instances exhibit jussive morphology (4.16; 5.10a, 10b), and the remaining one can be reasonably analyzed as jussive because of the negative אַל־ (2.24).

לְחַכִּימֵי בָבֶל אַל־תְּהוֹבֵד

Do not *destroy* the wise men of Babylon! (Dan. 2.24)

מַלְכָּא לְעָלְמִין חֱיִי אַל־יְבַהֲלוּךְ רַעְיוֹנָךְ וְזִיוָיךְ אַל־יִשְׁתַּנּוֹ

O king, live forever! Do not *let* your thoughts *frighten you,* nor *let* your countenance *change*! (Dan. 5.10)

In the above examples, the jussive expresses a negative request (2.24) and negative exhortations (5.10). The latter is an example of hortative modality, albeit in negative sentences.

3.2 Affirmative Directive

As already mentioned, some of the instances of the prefix conjugation expressing affirmative directive modality listed above may actually be jussives. There is at least one instance that may be a clear jussive in an affirmative directive (5.12).

כְּעַן דָּנִיֵּאל יִתְקְרֵי וּפִשְׁרָה יְהַחֲוֵה

Now, *let* Daniel *be called,* and let him make known the interpretation. (Dan. 5.12)

In the above example, the jussive expresses a polite command. The polite nature of the command consists of its indirectness. That is, it is stated in the 3rd person and in a non-active voice (t-stem).[105] The spelling of יִתְקְרֵי with the letter *yod* instead of a *he* or *aleph* at the end may indicate that it is a jussive.[106]

4. CONCLUSION

In my earlier monograph, the view was presented that the long prefix conjugation in the Aramaic of Daniel was a general imperfective in the process of becoming a future.[107] However, upon further study I conclude instead that it consists of a form that coalesced from the merging of the earlier West Semitic *yaqtulu* and *yaqtula* conjugations, first as homophones due to the loss of final short vowels, and eventually into a single grammatical form.

Therefore, the functions of the long prefix conjugation must be described in light of the double source of this single form. The functions that derived from *yaqtulu* were those of a general imperfective, including at least past progressive, past habitual, and general present. The general imperfective function also included the future, though it is possible that both *yaqtulu* and *yaqtula* may have overlapped in the expression of the future. The functions that derived from *yaqtula* were the various modal functions that had their origin in the expression of ability. In the Aramaic of Daniel, the imperfective functions of the prefix conjugation were being taken over by the participle and participial expressions, which resulted in the prefix conjugation being gradually restricted to its modal functions.

As for the short prefix conjugation, or jussive, it developed from the West Semitic jussive *yaqtul* conjugation, which, in turn, probably developed as a result of the extension of the preterit *yaqtul* in the expression of directive modality.

In later Aramaic all three early West Semitic prefix conjugations, *yaqtulu*, *yaqtula*, and *yaqtul*, eventually coalesced into one prefix conjugation. Nevertheless, although this merged prefix conjugation retained the longer forms of *yaqtulu*, it did not

---

[105] See the discussion in Li, *The Verbal System of the Aramaic of Daniel*, pp. 113–114.

[106] Rosenthal, *A Grammar of Biblical Aramaic*, pp. 44, 52.

[107] Li, *The Verbal System of the Aramaic of Daniel*, pp. 98–128.

retain its imperfective functions. Instead, it retained the modal functions of *yaqtula* and *yaqtul*.

WHEN TIME IS NOT MONEY: A COGNITIVE-LINGUISTIC APPROACH TO עדנא IN DANIEL 2.8*

STEPHEN M. COLEMAN

In their book, *Metaphors We Live By*, George Lakoff and Mark Johnson offer the following expressions as evidence of the conventionality of the conceptual metaphor TIME IS MONEY in the English language:[1]

> You're *wasting* my time.
> This gadget will *save* you hours.
> I don't *have* the time to *give* you.
> How do you *spend* your time these days?
> That flat tire *cost* me an hour.

---

* It is with deep gratitude that I dedicate this essay to my Doktorvater, Ed Cook, whose instruction and guidance not only deepened my love for Aramaic but also instilled in me (and many others) an appreciation for cognitive linguistics and its seemingly countless applications to the study of Semitic languages. I also wish to thank Andrew Litke and Andrew Gross for their invaluable feedback on an early draft of this essay, and Michael Seufert, who initially suggested that this topic might be worth exploring.

[1] George Lakoff and Mark Johnson, *Metaphors We Live By* (Chicago: University of Chicago Press, 1980) pp. 7–8, emphasis original. This essay will follow the convention of distinguishing mental concepts from linguistic expressions by placing the former in capital letters and small font.

I've *invested* a lot of time in her.
I don't *have enough* time to *spare* for that.
You're *running out* of time.
You need to *budget* your time.

These examples, which could be multiplied many times over, demonstrate the pervasiveness of the metaphor TIME IS MONEY in both thought and expression. Time is often conceived and construed as a commodity which may be saved, spent, wasted, invested, budgeted, and so forth. Like money, time may be increased/gained or decreased/lost to one's advantage or disadvantage, respectively.

Given the entrenched and controlling character of the metaphor TIME IS MONEY, it is unsurprising that king Nebuchadnezzar's accusation עִדָּנָא אַנְתּוּן זָבְנִין (lit., 'you are buying *the*? time') in Daniel 2.8 is often interpreted as an allegation of stalling. The king, on this reading, accuses his diviners of manipulating the situation to 'gain time' to respond to the king's demand that they reveal his dream along with its interpretation (Dan. 2.5–6). To 'gain/buy time' is to accrue more of it, presumably to the benefit of the diviners. This interpretation of the expression עִדָּנָא אַנְתּוּן זָבְנִין is reflected in many modern translations. The NRSV, for instance, translates the expression, 'you are trying to gain time', and perhaps more colloquially, the JPS renders it, 'you are playing for time'.

Among commentators, the stalling interpretation, based as it is on the conceptual metaphor TIME IS MONEY, is likewise commonplace. William Nelson's remarks are representative: 'The king accuses them of *trying to gain time*, meaning they are stalling for time so that they can delay their execution. They are *hoping the situation will change*, meaning that it will become more favorable to them'.[2] Similarly, Norman Porteous says, 'Nebuchadnezzar is not deceived by the *appeal of the Chaldaeans for more time*... aware

---

[2] William Nelson, *Daniel* (Grand Rapids: Baker, 2012) pp. 81–82, emphasis original. So too John J. Collins, 'The Chaldeans here are merely stalling'. *Daniel* (Hermeneia, Minneapolis: Fortress, 1993) p. 157.

of their own inability, the *Chaldaeans play for time*'.[3] Louis Hartman and Alexander Di Lella write, 'The storyteller implies that, if the Chaldeans were given sufficient time to consult their dream books, they would naturally come up with a false interpretation'.[4] Though C. F. Keil came to the same conclusion as those already cited, his comments are notable for at least mentioning other interpretations: 'The words דִּי עִדָּנָא אַנְתּוּן זָבְנִין do not mean either "that ye wish to use or seize the favourable time" (Häv., Kran.), or "that ye wish to buy up the present perilous moment," i.e., bring it within your power, become masters of the time (Hitz.), but simply, *that ye buy*, that is *wish to gain time* (Ges. Maur., etc). זְבַן עִדָּן = *tempus emere* in Cicero'.[5]

This interpretation, however, is not without its difficulties, both narratological and grammatical. With respect to the narrative, it is unclear how knowledge of the king's dream (or perhaps the diviners' request to know it) amounts to a play for more time. As Carol Newsom and Brennan Breed keenly observe, 'Since the sages are willing to interpret the dream as soon as the king tells it to them, *their request can scarcely be interpreted as a stalling maneuver*'.[6] Furthermore, it is unclear how more time would be of help to the diviners, other than, perhaps, to allow the king time to change his mind. With respect to grammar, the use of the emphatic state (עִדָּנָא) suggests that 'time' is being conceived of and construed as a definite, identifiable, individuated reality which militates against the commodity sense of time (a point discussed in greater detail below).

Though the stalling interpretation is by far most common, there is a minority view. Commenting on this verse, John Goldingay notes, 'The meaning is less clear than the familiar English "buying time" suggests. Like BH עת, עדן denotes not time

---

[3] Norman Porteous, *Daniel: A Commentary* (OTL, Philadelphia: Westminster John Knox, 1965) p. 40, emphasis mine.
[4] Louis F. Hartman and Alexander Di Lella, *The Book of Daniel* (AB, 23, New York: Doubleday, 1978) p. 144.
[5] C. F. Keil and F. Delitzsch, *Ezekiel-Daniel* trans. James Martin and M. G. Easton (Peabody, MA: Hendrickson, 2001) p. 549.
[6] Carol Newsom with Brennan Breed, *Daniel: A Commentary* (Louisville: Westminster John Knox, 2014) p. 69, emphasis mine.

in general but a specific time during which to concoct an answer to the conundrum, or a specific time when they will come back with this answer'.[7] Building on Goldingay's observations, Newsom and Breed write:

> What the king accuses [the diviners] of is less clear than is often assumed. He claims certain knowledge that 'you are buying *'iddānā'*.' Most translators render this phrase as 'buying time,' but as Goldingay rightly observes, it is not the equivalent of the English idiom. The word *'iddānā'* does not refer to duration (*pace* BDB) but to a set time or defined period of time (so the CAL). In the phrase the word is also marked as definite ('the time').[8]

The goal of this essay is to revisit the meaning of עִדָּנָא in Daniel 2.8 from the perspective of cognitive linguistics, particularly cognitive linguistics' insights into how conceptualization of THINGS motivates syntactic encoding, and how the latter provides insight into the former. The argument, in sum, is that the common interpretation of עִדָּנָא in Daniel 2.8 as 'gaining time' imports a conceptual metaphor that is more at home in Western cultures than it was in the ancient Near Eastern world in which the Daniel narratives were written. The conventional use of עִדָּן to refer to a particular, discrete, bounded reality is underscored in Daniel 2.8 by the grammatical encoding of the noun in the emphatic state. Finally, it is argued that the understanding of עִדָּנָא as a definite, individuated reality – expressed in the English translation, 'the time' – offers a more accurate representation of the power dynamics operative in the dramatic action of the narrative than the traditional view.

---

[7] John Goldingay, *Daniel* (WBC, 30, Dallas: Word Books, 1989) p. 33.

[8] Carol Newsom with Brennan Breed, *Daniel: A Commentary*, p. 69. Though Newsom and Breed cite CAL in support of their rendering of עִדָּנָא as a 'set or defined period of time' the most recent version of CAL (cal.huc.edu, accessed 8/6/2021) lists Daniel 2.8 under the third heading, 'time, as passing', with a translation that adopts the durative sense, 'I know you are buying time'.

1. COGNITIVE FOUNDATIONS FOR TIME IS MONEY METAPHOR

1.1 Count Nouns and Mass Nouns

Vyvyan Evans summarizes one of the core commitments of Cognitive Linguistics (hereafter CL) when he writes that, 'linguistic organization and structure reflects, at least partially, the nature and structure of thought, as it must if we are to be able to employ language in order to facilitate the expression of our thoughts'.[9] Basic to the 'nature and structure of thought' are the concepts THING and RELATION which correspond to the grammatical categories noun and verb respectively. Fundamental to the former is the distinction between count nouns and mass nouns which, according to Ronald Langacker, 'correspond to the conceptual archetypes object and substance'.[10] Count nouns, as their name implies, refer to things which are enumerable (e.g., *cup, tree, pen, dog, house*); mass nouns designate things which are not (e.g., *air, homework, oxygen, patience, wood, sugar*).

At the conceptual level, the principal distinction between mass and count nouns regards the conceptualization of an entity's boundedness.[11] Leonard Talmy describes boundedness as follows:

> When a quantity is understood as *unbounded*, it is conceived as continuing on indefinitely with no necessary characteristic of finiteness intrinsic to it. When a quantity is understood as *bounded*, it is conceived to be demarcated as an individuated unit entity. Entailed by the boundedness category, but conceptually isolable from it, is the notion of a boundary. In the prototypical conceptualization, a boundary touches or

---

[9] Vyvyan Evans, 'How We Conceptualize Time: Language, Meaning and Temporal Cognition', in Vyvyan Evans, Benjamin Bergen, and Jörg Zinken (eds.), *The Cognitive Linguistics Reader* (Advances in Cognitive Linguistics, London: Equinox, 2007) pp. 733–765 (733).

[10] Ronald Langacker, *Cognitive Grammar: A Basic Introduction* (Oxford: Oxford University Press, 2008) p. 128. Langacker makes the important qualification that the 'descriptive labels that readily come to mind, object and substance, are straightforwardly applicable only to *prototypical* members, not to *all* members.' Ibid., p. 129, emphasis original.

[11] Leonard Talmy, *Toward a Cognitive Semantics*, Vol. 1 (Cambridge, MA: MIT, 2003) p. 51.

> constitutes the outermost portion of a bounded quantity, so that the boundary 'encloses' the bounded quantity, and the bounded quantity lies 'within' the boundary.[12]

Lexical concepts such as MEAT, WOOD, SKIN, ANGER, RIGHTEOUSNESS, WATER, and MOISTURE are conceived as unbounded and as a result typically function grammatically as mass nouns. The lexical concepts CLOUD, CAT, PENCIL, CAR, QUESTION, and COMPLAINING are conceived as bounded and thus typically function grammatically as count nouns.[13] The following grammatical reflexes exemplify the conceptual distinction between count nouns and mass nouns:[14]

- Only count nouns permit pluralization.

  *dog/dogs vs gold/*golds*[15]

- Only mass nouns may 'stand alone as a complete nominal expression'.[16]

  *They are looking for {*diamond/gold}*

- Only count nouns may take the indefinite article.

  *They are looking for {a diamond/*a gold}*

- Only mass nouns may take certain determiners, especially quantifiers (e.g., *most, all, a lot of*).

  *They have a lot of {*diamond/ gold}*

---

[12] Ibid., p. 50, emphasis original.

[13] What I describe here as the typical or conventional grammatical reflexes of count and mass nouns does not preclude certain exceptional morpho-syntactic constructions in which a typically mass noun may be used as a count noun and vice versa. In English, for example, a count noun may have a mass interpretation through the process called the 'universal grinder' in which the mass noun refers to the 'substance' which makes up the count noun (e.g., the count noun *a cat/the cat* used anarthrously in, *After the tragic accident, there was cat all over the road*). Such exceptional usages are typically triggered by specific morpho-syntactic realities.

[14] The following illustrations and explanations are adapted from Langacker, *Cognitive Grammar*, pp. 129–30.

[15] The 'kind interpretation' of mass nouns is an exception to this rule. E.g., *The golds of South America were compared to those of Africa.*

[16] Langacker, *Cognitive Grammar*, p. 129.

Many THINGS, however, may be conceived as either bounded or unbounded, and thus function grammatically as either a count noun or a mass noun, as, for example, *hair, life, belief,* and *paper.* Consider the following:

(1) Count: *They are looking for a paper/ papers.*
(2) Mass: *They are looking for paper.*
They have a lot of paper.

TIME, of course, is one of the most basic concepts in human cognition and at the same time arguably the most elusive. Naturally it lends itself to a variety of conceptualizations, one of which is the conceptualization of TIME as either a bounded or an unbounded reality. In English, *time* may be used as an unbounded, mass noun or a bounded, count noun as illustrated by the following:

(3) Mass: *Oliver needs more time to finish the paper.*
(4) Count: *Oliver mastered coding by the time he was six.*

(Un)boundedness is just one way in which TIME may be variously conceived and thus linguistically construed. Evans helpfully summarizes distinct senses of *time* with reference to boundedness (among other conceptual categories). He says, 'we can "count" moments of time, as when we count seconds or minutes, precisely because entities of this kind constitute discrete moments, duration cannot be enumerated in this way, and constitutes an internally un-analysable mass'.[17] Evans has identified eight distinct, but related, lexical concepts associated with the lexeme *time.*[18] Of particular interest for analyzing BA עִדָּנָא are the duration sense, moment sense, measurement-system sense, and the commodity sense, the last of which underwrites the conceptual metaphor TIME IS MONEY.

The duration sense construes TIME as an unbounded, undifferentiated whole, as in (5). As such, it resists being split up into discrete parts, parts which in principle could be enumerated.

---

[17] Evans, 'How we conceptualise time', p. 738.
[18] Ibid., p. 748.

(5) *The relationship lasted some time.*

The moment sense, by contrast, construes time as a 'discrete temporal' point and therefore is conceptually bounded and enumerable.[19]

(6) *The time for a decision is approaching.*

The measurement-system sense refers to the use of *time* to denote 'a system for measuring duration' and is, according to Evans, 'most saliently evidenced when dealing with time-reckoning'.[20] He notes that 'grammatically, the Measurement-system Sense is distinct in that it can take the form of a count noun, a mass noun, or a proper noun. No other sense associated with *time* appears to have such flexibility'.[21]

(7) Mass: *He worked overtime.*
Count: *They get paid double time on Christmas.*
Proper Noun: *Greenwich Mean Time is five hours ahead of EST.*

The saliant point of Evans' category 'commodity sense' is that it requires a conception of time as an unbounded reality, and thus it expresses TIME as a mass noun. In this respect it is similar to the duration sense. Regarding the conceptualization and construal of TIME as a commodity, Evans writes:

> In terms of grammatical encoding, the Commodity Sense… is a mass noun. Evidence for this comes from the fact that the Commodity Sense undergoes the operation of portion-excerpting, in which a mass noun can be bounded using a quantifier such as *some*. For instance, in sentences such as: *Can you spare me some time?* the Commodity Sense is preceded by the quantifier *some*.[22]

When one adds a handful of rice to a pile of rice, the resulting pile is still referred to simply as *rice*. Similarly, when one gains

---

[19] Ibid., p. 741.
[20] Vyvyan Evans, *The Structure of Time: Language, Meaning, and Temporal Cognition* (Amsterdam: John Benjamins, 2005) pp. 169, 171.
[21] Ibid., p. 173.
[22] Evans, 'How we Conceptualize Time', p. 747.

time or loses *time*, one does not have something more than, less than, or different than *time*. When used in the commodity sense, regardless of how much or how little one has, it is still conceived of and construed as *time*. The stalling interpretation of עִדָּנָא אַנְתּוּן זָבְנִין (translated along the lines of, 'you are buying time', or, 'you are gaining time') requires that עִדָּנָא be understood as a mass noun. The diviners, who in a sense have some time, would like more of it, presumably to concoct an answer or response.

1.2 Definiteness

The second feature relevant for our consideration of עִדָּנָא in Daniel 2.8 is the significance of the BA emphatic state. Though the function of the Aramaic emphatic state has been hotly disputed – largely in connection with the Aramaic background to the 'Son of Man' sayings of Jesus – its use as a marker of definiteness in QA (as well as OA) has recently been demonstrated by William Fullilove.[23] From the perspective of CL, definiteness brings into view two distinct but related conceptual realities, namely perceptions of identifiability and inclusiveness. According to Christopher Lyons, identifiability refers to the notion that, 'the definite article directs the hearer to the referent of the noun phrase by signalling that he is in a position to identify it… In such cases the hearer is invited to match the referent to the definite noun phrase with some real-world entity which he knows to exist because he can see it, has heard of it, or infers its existence from something else he has heard'.[24]

Particularly important for plural count nouns and mass nouns is the notion of inclusiveness which is the ability of the

---

[23] William Fullilove, *Definiteness in Qumran Aramaic* (PhD Diss., The Catholic University of America, 2014). It should be noted that Fullilove's work was conducted under the supervision of Ed Cook. Cf. Ibid., 'The Advent of Definiteness Marking in Aramaic', in the present volume, pp. 3–24; Peter Williams, 'Expressing Definiteness in Aramaic: A Response to Casey's Theory Concerning the Son of Man Sayings', in Larry W. Hurtado and Paul R. Owens (eds.), *Who is This Son of Man? The Latest Scholarship on a Puzzling Expression of the Historical Jesus* (LNTS, 390, London: T&T Clark, 2011) pp. 61–77.

[24] Christopher Lyons, *Definiteness* (Cambridge: CUP, 1999) p. 6.

definite noun to reference 'the totality of the objects or mass in the context which satisfy the description'.[25] Therefore, when used with plural count nouns or mass nouns, the definite marker essentially serves as a universal quantifier, much like the universal quantifier *all*.[26] This may be demonstrated by the fact that (9) can serve as a meaningful response to both (8a) and (8b).

(8) a. I sanded the wood.
b. I sanded all the wood.
(9) No you haven't, you only sanded some of it.

Interpreting BA עִדָּנָא as a mass noun – as the stalling interpretation requires – raises the question of the meaning and significance of the emphatic state of this noun in this context. Is 'the time' in some sense inclusive, perhaps with the sense of comprehending a period of time in its entirety? This does not appear meaningful in the context. Needless to say, it is difficult to account for the semantics of the emphatic state when עִדָּנָא is interpreted as a mass noun.

2. A Cognitive and Collocational Approach to עִדָּנָא

There is considerable consensus that BA עִדָּנָא is derived the common Semitic root **wʿd* meaning, 'to determine'.[27] The noun form is not attested in OA, but occurs frequently in IA, often in prepositional phrases with an adverbial function.[28] The following section will survey the attested usages of עִדָּן in IA, BA, and QA with a view toward establishing its range of meaning with reference to Evans' taxonomy of senses.

2.1 Imperial Aramaic

2.1.1 Moment Sense

אף איתי תבא שמה אמהם זי עלימיא אלה ולילו ברה זי לא עד נפלג
עלין כזי **עדן** יהוה נפלג המו עלין

[25] Ibid., p. 11.
[26] Ibid., p. 11. The examples in 8 and 9 are a modification of Lyons', Ibid.
[27] A. Gianto, *TDOT* 16, p. 554.
[28] Ibid., p. 554.

Moreover, there is Taba by name, the mother of these lads, and Lilu her son whom we shall not divide (between) us. **When it will be time**, we shall divide them (between) us.[29] (*TAD* B2.11 R.13)

ספינתא זי מהחסנן אנ̇חנה **עדן** הוה אופשרה למע]ב[ד

The boat which we hold in hereditary lease – **the time** has come to ma[ke] repairs[30]. (*TAD* A6.2.3[31])

אף קדמת זנה **בעדן** זי זא באישתא עביד לן

Moreover, before this – **at the time** that this evil was done to us (*TAD* A4.7.17[32])

[אף מ]ן זך **ע[ד]נא** ועד ז[נה יומא שנת

[Moreover **fr] om that t [i] me** and until t[his day, year...[33] (*TAD* A4.8.20)

אמרת קטלתה עד זי **לעד̇ן** [א]חרן

---

[29] Unless otherwise noted, texts and translations of Egyptian evidence are taken from Bezalel Porten and Ada Yardeni, *Textbook of Aramaic Documents from Ancient Egypt*, volumes 1, 2, and 4 (Winona Lake, IN: Eisenbrauns, 1986/1989/1999).

[30] 'Repairs' uncertain.

[31] The near identical expression with עדן is used later in the same letter (A6.2.9).

[32] Similarly: *TAD* A4.8.16.

[33] Though this usage of עדנא could potentially be regarded as duration, the reconstructed context suggests that it is referring to a specific, delimited period. *TAD* A4.8.18 reads: אף מן ירח תמוז ('Moreover, from the month of Tamuz...'). If this reconstruction is correct, then line 20 must be understood with the same sense; 'from that time' refers to the month of Tamuz, year fourteen of Darius, a delimited period of time. Interestingly, עדנא appears in the emphatic state probably because the referent ירח תמוז has already been mentioned. It is also possible that this is the measurement-system sense; however, if so, עדן is nevertheless a count noun.

I said, 'I killed him', until **at [an] other time...** (*TAD* C1.1.49)

בזך **עדנא** אשתמיע

At that time, it was reported... (*TAD* C1.1.70)

כען הלו חלם חזית ומן **עדנא** הו אנה חמם שגא תחזי

Now, behold, I have seen a dream, and **from that time on** I have been exceedingly feverish.[34] (*TAD* D7.17.3)

וכזי **עדן** יהוה אדין אגרא זך ופרכנא יעבדון

And when **the time** comes, then they will build that wall and ditch. (*ADAB* A.4.6)[35]

בזכ **עדנא**

At that **time**... (NSaqPap.79[36])

2.1.2 Ambiguous

אלהיא כל ישאלו שלמכי בכל **עדן**

May all the gods seek after your welfare **at all times (lit. in every time)**. (*TAD* A3.7.1[37])

(2x) [שלם מראן] אלה שמ[יא] ישאל בכל **עדן** לרחמן י[שי]מנ[ך
קדם ד]ריוהוש [מלכא... וחין] אריכן ינתן לך וחדה ושריר הוי בכל
עדן

May the God of Heav[en] seek after the welfare of our lord **at all times**, grant you favor [before King Da]rius.... give you

[34] Translation from Baruch Levine, 'Notes on an Aramaic Dream Text from Egypt', *JAOS* 84 (1964), pp. 18–22 (19).

[35] Joseph Naveh and Shaul Shaked, *Aramaic Documents from Ancient Bactria (Fourth Century BCE)* (London: The Khalili Family Trust, 2012) pp. 96–97.

[36] J. B. Segal, *Aramaic Texts from North Saqqâra* (London: Egypt Exploration Society, 1983) p. 98.

[37] Similarly: *TAD* A4.2.2; A4.4.1; D1.13.1: A3.6.1; D1.13.1 (fragmentary).

long [life], and may you be happy and strong **at all times**. (*TAD* A4.8.2–3[38])

ונצלה עליך בכל **עדן** אנחנה ונשין ובנין

And we will pray for you **at all times** – we and our wives and our children. (*TAD* A4.7.26)

שלם אחי אלהיא כ[ל]א ישאלו בכל **עדן**

May a[l]l the gods seek after the welfare of my brothers **at all times**. (*TAD* A3.10.1)

שלם מראן אלהיא [כלא ישאלו שגיא ב]כל **עדן**

May [all] the gods [abundantly seek after] the welfare of our lord **[at] all times**. (*TAD* A6.1.1–2[39])

In IA, עדן occurs roughly thirty-six times in the absolute state and four in the emphatic. Most, if not all, occurrences evidence a conceptualization of time as a bounded reality, instantiating the moment sense of עדן. Though the data is limited, the emphatic state seems to function either anaphorically (in combination with a demonstrative pronoun, e.g., *TAD* A4.8.20; *TAD* D7.17.3) or to profile the particularity of the moment in contradistinction to others (e.g., *TAD* C1.1.70). The conception of TIME underlying the use of עדן with בכל is, however, ambiguous. It is certainly possible that the expression reflects a conceptualization of עדן as a mass noun with a durative sense ('in all time'). Even if this is the case, however, the mass/durative sense of the expression may derive from the collocation of עדן with בכל and not so much from the basic specification עדן. Talmy notes that 'grammatical elements exist that can, in construction with a lexical item, shift its basic specification for state of boundedness to the opposite value'.[40] With regard to bounded nouns, בכל may have this 'debounding'

[38] Similarly: *TAD* A4.7.2–3; D7.56.4; D7.35.2; D7.57.3; and, though damaged, probably D1.15.1.

[39] Similarly: *TAD* A3.9.1.

[40] Talmy, *Toward a Cognitive Semantics*, p. 51. For example, the 'universal grinder' mentioned in n. 13 above.

function whereby 'the quantity formerly within bounds is now conceptualized in a form with indefinite extension'.[41]

However, it is also possible (and perhaps preferable) to interpret עדן in this expression as a bounded count noun instantiating the moment sense. Citing this expression בכל עדן in *TAD* A3.6.1, Takamitsu Muraoka and Bezalel Porten note that, 'כל in the sense of "every, each" is very often followed by a singular noun in the st.abs'.[42] In this case, when collocated with עדן, בכל may be understood as having a distributive sense (i.e., 'in each/every moment').

2.2 Biblical Aramaic

2.2.1 Moment sense

וּמִלָּה כִדְבָה וּשְׁחִיתָה הִזְדְּמִנְתּוּן לְמֵאמַר קָדָמַי עַד דִּי **עִדָּנָא** יִשְׁתַּנֵּא[43]

You have agreed to speak lying and deceitful words to me until **the time** changes. (Dan. 2.9)

בְּעִדָּנָא דִּי־תִשְׁמְעוּן קָל קַרְנָא

At the time you hear the sound of the horn... (Dan. 3.5[44])

2.2.2 Measurement-system sense

וְשִׁבְעָה **עִדָּנִין** יַחְלְפוּן עֲלוֹהִי׃

And seven **times** will pass over him. (Dan. 4.13[45])

וְהוּא מְהַשְׁנֵא **עִדָּנַיָּא**

---

[41] Ibid., p. 52.

[42] Takamitsu Muraoka and Bezalel Porten, *A Grammar of Egyptian Aramaic* (HdO, 32, Leiden: Brill, 1998) pp. 177–178. Similarly, Gianto, '*bkl ʿdn* "at any time," i.e., "ever."' *TDOT* 16, p. 554.

[43] Following the Qere of הִזַּמִּנְתּוּן

[44] Similarly: Dan. 3.14

[45] Similarly, Dan. 4.20, 22, 29. Many believe that עדן in these verses is employed with the sense of 'year' (e.g., Gianto, *TDOT* 16, p. 555).

He changes **the times.** (Dan. 2.21)

וְיִתְיַהֲבוּן בִּידֵהּ עַד־**עִדָּן וְעִדָּנִין** וּפְלַג **עִדָּן׃**

And they will be given into his hand **for a time, and times, and a half-time.** (Dan. 7.25)

וְאַרְכָה בְחַיִּין יְהִיבַת לְהוֹן עַד־זְמַן **וְעִדָּן׃**

But their lives were prolonged for a season **and a time.**[46] (Dan. 7.12)

Though the lexeme עִדָּן occurs only thirteen times in the Aramaic portions of the Hebrew Bible, and these only in Daniel, it nevertheless appears in a sufficient variety of forms and grammatical constructions as to provide visibility into the underlying conceptual structures which motivate its usage and determine its meaning. That BA עִדָּן is used to express a notion of time that is conceived as a bounded, quantifiable reality is clear from its function as a count noun. It appears as a plural noun in both states (e.g., abs. Dan. 4.13, emph. Dan. 2.21). BA עִדָּן is modified by the cardinal number שִׁבְעָה ('seven') (e.g., Dan. 4.13, 20, 22, 29). In Daniel 3.5, emphatic עִדָּנָא takes the preposition בְּ with the sense, 'at the time/moment when…'. Daniel 2.8 aside, there are no clear instances of BA עִדָּן in either the absolute or emphatic state being used as a mass noun in BA.

2.3 Qumran Aramaic

2.3.1 Moment sense

עדן מולדהי֯ן

[46] Contra BDB, p. 1105 which cites Daniel 7.12 along with 2.8 as having the sense of duration. Conceptually, the 'measurement-system sense' of time, like the 'moment sense', may refer in the real world to a long period of time. What distinguishes the measurement sense from the duration sense is that the former profiles boundaries, whereas the latter does not. BA עִדָּן in Daniel 7.12 is better understood as either the moment sense or the measurement-system (count noun) sense since 'a season and a time' both refer to a delimited, though perhaps long, period of time.

The time of their birth (11QtgJob 32.2)

עֹ֯ד֯ **עדן** ד֯י֯ [י]נדע

Until **a time** that he knows (4Q534 1 i 4–5)

בעד[נא דן]

At that **time**... (4Q196 4 1)

עדנא [די]

The **time** that... (4Q198 1 10)

לעדני[א] (fragmentary)

To/for times... (3Q14 4 4)

עד **עדן** די יתבו[........]

...until **a/the time** that they dwell. (2Q24 4 19)

דינין **בעדניהן**

Judgements **in their times** (4Q568 1 1)

2.3.2 Ambiguous

עדן רשיעין

The time of the wicked (4Q536 2 ii 13)

בעדן קץ

At **the time** of pruning/ the end (4Q558 26 1)

According to Agustinus Gianto, עדן appears nineteen times in Qumran Aramaic.[47] Though many instances of the lexeme appear in texts too fragmentary to understand, the use and distribution

[47] A. Gianto, *TDOT* 16, p. 555. The instances not cited here are too fragmentary to yield data relevant to the question under consideration.

patterns generally seem to follow that of IA and BA. In the absolute state, עדן typically functions as a count noun, referring to a specific, delimited period of time. It is possible that it could be used as a mass noun when combined with certain syntactic constructions, namely the construct state (4Q536 2 ii 13), and modified by the preposition ב (4Q558 26 1). What the combined evidence of IA, BA, and QA clearly suggests, however, is that עדן in the emphatic state is used exclusively as a count noun, manifesting the attributes bounded, quantifiable, and internally analyzable.

3. NARRATOLOGICAL IMPLICATIONS

The primary motivation driving the stalling interpretation of BA עִדָּנָא in Daniel 2.8 is likely the deep entrenchment of the cognitive metaphor TIME IS MONEY, especially in Western or Westernized cultures.[48] The collocation of עִדָּנָא with זָבְנִין naturally and understandably evokes this familiar conceptual metaphor. However, conceptual metaphors are, to a large extent, culturally conditioned, and therefore interpreters need to be careful about appealing to a conceptual metaphor that is foreign to the conceptual world of a text and the culture from which it emerged.[49] Lakoff and Johnson's suggestion that the conceptual metaphor TIME IS MONEY originated in Western and Westernized cultures largely as a result of industrialization has found significant, though not unambiguous, support in Simone Mueller's analysis of time metaphors across varieties of English.[50] Com-

[48] Lakoff and Johnson go so far as to say, 'the Westernization of cultures throughout the world is partly a matter of introducing the TIME IS MONEY metaphor into those cultures.' *Metaphors We Live By*, p. 145.

[49] Though he agrees with Lakoff and Johnson that the metaphor TIME IS MONEY is basically a Western concept, Zoltan Kövecses suggests that some conceptual metaphors may be universal or near universal, such as TIME IS SPACE; *Metaphor in Culture: Universality and Variation* (Cambridge: CUP, 2005) p. 47.

[50] Simone Mueller, 'Time is money – everywhere?: Analysing time metaphors across varieties of English', in Elisabetta Gola and Francesca Ervas (eds.), *Metaphor and Communication* (Amsterdam: John Benjamins, 2016) pp. 79–104. Lakoff and Johnson write, 'In our culture TIME IS MONEY in many ways: telephone message units, hourly wages, hotel room rates,

paring varieties of English in Western and non-Western corpora, Mueller remarks,

> The corpora from countries with a Western culture show high frequencies of realizations which express the TIME IS MONEY metaphor. In contrast, the corpora from countries with a non-Western culture, where English is only a second language and where the TIME IS MONEY metaphor might have been introduced with the English language (rather than being pre-existent), show lower frequencies of such realizations.[51]

Though I have argued that the TIME IS MONEY metaphor, at least as it is conventionally understood, is not operative in Daniel 2.8, TIME, nevertheless, is clearly construed within the narrative as something desirable. A distinction needs to be made between an instantiation of a conceptual metaphor (which, by definition, is a cognitively entrenched reality) and a figure of speech which, coincidentally, resembles it. The king's use of the verb זבן evokes the conceptual world of commerce and exchange, and, maybe more particularly, the world of the marketplace. BA זבן means simply 'to buy', and thus, given the context, is being used figuratively. Instead of an instantiation of the TIME IS MONEY

---

yearly budgets, interest on loans, and paying your debt to society by "serving time." These practices are relatively new in the history of the human race, and by no means do they exist in all cultures. They have arisen in modern industrialized societies and structure our basic everyday activities in a very profound way. ...TIME IS MONEY, TIME IS A LIMITED RESOURCE, and TIME IS A VALUABLE COMMODITY are all metaphorical concepts... This isn't a necessary way for human beings to conceptualize time; it is tied to our culture. There are cultures where time is none of these things'. Lakoff and Johnson, *Metaphors We Live By*, p. 8.

[51] Mueller, 'Time is money – everywhere?', p. 100. Mueller acknowledges that some of the data is ambiguous, notably the high prevalence of WASTE + time expressions in non-Westernized English-speaking countries. These, she suggests, are explained, 'not as indicators of a higher degree of Westernization but as due to the fact that these expressions are realizations of a conceptual metaphor that is more or less native to the country'; ibid., p. 102. Mueller believes this challenges Lakoff and Johnson's assumptions about how closely tied this cognitive metaphor is to Westernized cultures. That there is a general correlation between Westernization and the TIME IS MONEY metaphor is, however, borne out by Mueller's study as the quote above indicates.

conceptual metaphor, the sense of BA זבן here is not so much that of adding, increasing, or extending a reality ('time') that is already in one's possession, but rather that of acquiring or coming into possession of a reality which is not currently possessed. The king's accusation, therefore, is that the diviners are maneuvering, politicking, and attempting to acquire possession of a reality – namely 'the time' – that rightly belongs to him, or at least does not or should not belong to them.

A secondary motivation for the stalling interpretation is the fact that an interpretation of עִדָּנָא as a definite count noun is not self-evidently meaningful. What does it mean for Nebuchadnezzar to say, 'I know that you are buying *the time*' in the context of the narrative? To what specific 'time' is he referring? 'Time' has not been mentioned in the narrative previously, so the definite state is not functioning anaphorically. Time, as many have noted, serves as a *leitmotif* in both the narratives and visions of Daniel.[52] Nebuchadnezzar's humiliation is prophesied to last until 'seven times will pass over him' (וְשִׁבְעָה עִדָּנִין יַחְלְפוּן עֲלוֹהִי; Dan. 4.13). The arrogant and boastful 'horn', who will speak words against the Most High and who terrorize his people, will 'think to change the times and the law' (וְיִסְבַּר לְהַשְׁנָיָה זִמְנִין וְדָת, Dan. 7.25). These will come under his authority 'for a time, two times, and a half-time' (Dan. 7.25). The theme of time – or more specifically, the theme of who is sovereign over time(s) – is central to the narrative under consideration. Nebuchadnezzar's dream features a statue composed of different metals, each of which, as Daniel reveals, represent the times of successive empires. The two proposals below, therefore, attempt to interpret the emphatic noun עִדָּנָא in Daniel 2.8 as a count noun and with reference to this *leitmotif*.

One interpretation of 'the time' (BA עִדָּנָא) in Daniel 2.8 is as a metonym for the king's rule and sovereignty. Kings have times in the sense that their rule is necessarily delimited temporally by the span of their lives, spans often foreshortened due to machinations of those close to them. The close connection

---

[52] E.g., 'The visions and stories foreground motives of power, speech, and time' in Anathea E. Portier-Young, *Apocalypse Against Empire: Theologies of Resistance in Early Judaism* (Grand Rapids, MI: Eerdmans, 2011) p. 179.

between time and kingship is suggested in Daniel's blessing in Daniel 2.21a:

וְהוּא מְהַשְׁנֵא עִדָּנַיָּא וְזִמְנַיָּא מְהַעְדֵּה מַלְכִין וּמְהָקֵים מַלְכִין

He changes the times and the seasons,
He removes kings and he establishes kings.

This reading of Daniel 2.8 has the merit of being consistent with and anticipating a common interpretation of the same noun in the verse immediately following the one under consideration in which the king says, 'You have agreed to speak lying and deceitful words to me *until the time changes*' (עַד דִּי עִדָּנָא יִשְׁתַּנֵּא; Dan. 2.9). Many commentators have understood the reference of 'the time changing' in Daniel 2.9 to be a veiled reference to the king's demise, thus עִדָּנָא referring essentially to the king's reign.[53] Controlling the time of Nebuchadnezzar's kingship is to control him, and to control him is to control the time of his kingship.

A somewhat different but related interpretation is that 'the time' in Daniel 2.8 refers to the present moment or, perhaps, the present dangerous moment, which has just been created by the king with his ultimatum expressed in vv. 5–6. This is essentially the reading proposed by Ferdinand Hitzig over a century and a half ago:

> 'Die Zeit' ist die gegenwärtige, der jetzige gefährliche Augenblick *ἡμέρα πονηρά* (Eph. a. a. 0.); sie 'an' – oder 'aufkaugen' bedeutet: sie an sich, in seine Gewalt bringen, ihrer Meister werden. Sie wollen, wie Nebuk. meint, die Zeit, welche ernst drohend ihnen gegenübertritt, auf ihre Seite herüberbringen, sie unschädlich machen, also sich aus der Schlinge ziehen. Von einer 'Benutzung des glücklichen Zeitpunktes' kann allerdings hier nicht die Rede sein; aber die Deutung ihrerseits durch 'Aufschub suchen', 'Zeit gewinnen wollen' (z. B. v. Leng.) läuft jenem Sprachgebrauche des N.T. zuwider, und passt nicht zur richtig verstandenen 2. VH. Die Zeit kaufen können sie natürlich nicht mit ihrer Weigerung

[53] Cf. Portier-Young, *Apocalypse Against Empire*, p. 180, see discussion below.

> den Traum anzugeben, sondern nur durch ihre Bereitwilligkeit ihn zu deuten.[54]

The diviners, on this reading, are being accused of trying to 'buy the time' in the sense of acquiring or gaining control of the present moment. Knowledge of the king's dream would allow them to manipulate 'the time' to their advantage. This is related to the previous proposal in that the diviners' alleged attempt to gain control of 'the time' or 'the moment' may be an instantiation of what the king believes is a pattern of behavior which he characterizes as deception and lies (Dan. 2.9). Either interpretation – 'the time' as kingship or 'the time' as the present moment – construes TIME as a definite reality, perceived by the speaker as identifiable by his interlocutors. This set or fixed period of time is consistent with the usage of עִדָּנָא in earlier and later texts through the period of QA. Anathea Portier-Young's penetrating discussion of the role of 'the time' in the power struggle between king and diviners, as well as the part it plays in the characterization of Nebuchadnezzar is consistent with the interpretations proposed here and deserves to be quoted at length.

> The king's response evinces a view of time as commodity that can be bought or gained at will as an effort to control it. The following verse further links the king's anxiety concerning the dream and its interpretation – and his inability as king to command their revelation – with the theme of time. The king accuses the Chaldeans of conspiracy. 'You have conspired (הַזְמִנְתּוּן) to make false and lying speeches before me until the time changes (עַד דִּי עִדָּנָא יִשְׁתַּנֵּא)' (2:9). The king recognizes that time itself sets a limit on his word and authority. A wordplay reveals that time is at the very root of his anxiety, for the verb with which he expresses this accusation הַזְמִנְתּוּן ('you have conspired') is a denominative verb derived from the noun זמן, 'time'. His reference to time's changing fore–shadows the interpretation of his dream: with the passage of time God will bring change. Empire will succeed empire, until God effects the end of empire itself, shattering (2:44) the

[54] Ferdinand Hitzig, *Das Buch Daniel* (Leipzig: Weidmann'sche Buchhandlung, 1850) p. 23.

> destructive powers (2:40) and filling the earth (2:35) with a new kingdom (2:44).[55]

The portrayal of Nebuchadnezzar throughout the narratives is that of a suspicious, erratic, and paranoid figure. That the king would be deeply suspicious about his diviners, whose words and work so powerfully influences his decision-making, is consistent with his overall characterization. With his accusation, 'I know that you are buying the time', Nebuchadnezzar is accusing his diviners of trying to acquire or possess, and, by implication, to control 'the moment', which is either a metonym for his kingship or a reference to the present dangerous moment. The magicians speaking lying and corrupt words (Dan. 2.9) is a reference to their divinatory practices which Nebuchadnezzar suspects to be self-serving at best and dangerous for him at worst. Either way, Nebuchadnezzar sees the magicians' divination as the mechanism by which they can control the king, effectively using him as a proxy for their own rule and a means for furthering their own political ambitions.

4. CONCLUSION

Given the pervasiveness of the conceptual metaphor TIME IS MONEY in Westernized cultures, it is unsurprising that many interpreters assume that the metaphor is operative in Daniel 2.8. The diviners, on this reading, are 'buying time' in the sense of stalling in order to gain an advantage. However, the invocation of the TIME IS MONEY metaphor with its associated construal of time as an unbounded mass creates as many interpretive knots as it purports to untie. As Newsom and Breed have observed, should they be told its contents, the diviners seem ready, willing, and able to offer an interpretation of the king's dream, thus making 'more

[55] Portier-Young, *Apocalypse Against Empire*, p. 180. It should be noted that Portier-Young's expression 'time as commodity' does not seem to be identical to Evans' commodity sense of time which underwrites the 'stalling interpretation' of the expression. Her description of time as something 'that can be bought or gained at will *in an effort to control it*' (emphasis mine) suggests a view of 'time' in Daniel 2.8ff close to the one advanced here.

time' immaterial.[56] Further, the use of the word 'time' (עִדָּן) in the emphatic state (עִדָּנָא) construes the referent, 'time', as a definite reality, a feature that is rarely accounted for among translators and interpreters.

Recent treatments of the conceptualization of time have offered a nuanced taxonomy of various conceptions of time and the way such conceptions are encoded in language. TIME IS MONEY trades on a conceptualization of TIME as an unbounded mass which may be added to or taken from without changing its conceptualization and construal as 'time'. A survey of the uses of עִדָּן in IA, BA, and QA reveals that it is always (or almost always) employed as a count noun to refer to a set or fixed period of time. While these uses correspond to the moment or measurement-system (count noun) senses of time, both of which construe time as a bounded reality, they are incompatible with a duration and commodity sense of time, which construe time as an unbounded mass. The instances in which עִדָּן may be understood as a mass noun with a durative sense are ambiguous and possibly construction specific, and none of them employ the noun in the emphatic state. An interpretation of עִדָּנָא in Daniel 2.8 as a mass noun, therefore, would be highly idiosyncratic.

Understanding עִדָּנָא in Daniel 2.8 as a count noun referring to a bounded reality requires an adjustment to the conventional understanding of Nebuchadnezzar's accusation and the power dynamics involved in the scene. Instead of accusing them of stalling for time, the king is accusing his diviners of a power grab. 'The time', on this reading, stands either for the present moment or metonymically for the king's reign, perhaps both spatially (with reference to his kingdom) and temporally (with reference to his reign) considered. The diviners' knowledge of the contents of the dream, the king surmises, will allow them to manipulate him through their interpretation, in essence buying or acquiring 'the time' of his kingship for themselves. Though a minority interpretation, this reading is not essentially novel. What is, I hope, a genuine contribution, is the articulation of the cognitive and linguistic realities that support this minority view.

[56] Newsom and Breed, *Daniel: A Commentary*, p. 69.

REMARKS ON SOME RECIPROCAL AND DISTRIBUTIVE EXPRESSIONS IN THE SCROLLS FROM QUMRAN

MARTIN G. ABEGG, JR.

This study began as a discussion with University of Toronto professor, Robert Holmstedt, as we sought to understand the syntax of the singular Hebrew noun איש when it is used as a pronominal substitution in reciprocal and distributive expressions occurring in the scrolls from the eleven caves at Qumran. In the midst of this ongoing conversation I attended an SBL Syriac session in 2017 where my longtime friend and frequent collaborator, Ed Cook, read a paper on distributive expressions in the Syriac Old Testament;[1] I was looking for some help. And so my justification for presenting this Hebrew study in the midst of a sea of Aramaic offerings; Ed has so frequently enabled my own understanding (of this and of so many other things!) that I offer up this paper as a token of my thanks for his friendship with the hope that it might demonstrate my appreciation for all of his support and encouragement over the years.

In the specific cases examined below—certainly not the entirety of the reciprocal/distributive world—the qualification

[1] Edward M. Cook, 'Distributive Expressions in the Syriac Old Testament, Especially in the Book of Numbers', (paper presented at the Society of Biblical Literature conference, Boston, 2017).

for admittance to my data set is that the singular inflection of איש is a member of either the plural subject, or, in a few cases with distributives, the plural verbal complement. The distributive statement, ויעשו איש הישר בעיניו ('They did each what he pleased', CD 8.7; CD 19.19-20), is a simple example of these parameters. In this clause the predicate ויעשו is a third masculine plural verb and איש is a member of the covert subject, 'they'. Or, in other words, the verbal action is distributed over each member of the subject. In the reciprocal statement, ידבר̇ו̇ איש אל רעה̊ו ('they will speak each to his fellow [to one another]', CD 20.17–18), the predicate ידבר̇ו̇ is likewise a third masculine plural verb and איש, as well as רע, are members of the covert subject, 'they', and the verbal action is reciprocal: the speaking takes place among members of the plural subject. In a few cases we will also discover that the distributive איש does not always pertain to the subject, but rather the members of the plural object. An example of this is ויורישם איש נחלתו ('He caused them to inherit each his own inheritance', 4Q418 81 + 81a 3), where איש is a member of the object of the verb יוריש. As we will see from the evidence below, this is possible with distribution but not reciprocity.

In the next section of the study I will first note the thirty-four instances of reciprocity in the Qumran corpus and then the forty-three cases that are distributive in function.[2] I have made every effort to identify all the instances that fit my parameters among the Qumran scrolls. Following this section I will briefly consider how the components of these expressions might be understood in the syntax of the host clause. I will then report on an examination of 1QS 6.1b-2a where the difficult syntax of the passage has produced notable differences in translation and interpretation; I propose that this present study has proved helpful in identifying the solution.

---

[2] The frequency data both here and in the following section account for multiple occurrences due to coincident manuscripts but do not include reconstructions.

1. RECIPROCITY

ידבּרו איש אל רעהו

They will each speak to his fellow (CD 20.17–18)

This simple statement illustrates the elements of the structure:

1. ידבּרו – a plural verb, normally preceding the reciprocal expression,
2. איש – in the singular expressing 'each' or 'one' in the reciprocal statement,
3. אל רעהו – a phrase—adjunct or complement—in accordance with the semantics of the plural verb,
4. רע – the noun expressing the 'other' in the reciprocal statement. אח is also common and in one case עמית ('friend, neighbor') is used (4Q271 3 5),
5. הו – the third singular pronoun whose antecedent is the singular איש rather than the plural subject of the verb.

1.1. Observations

1. There are no cases in the Qumran corpus of the feminine אשה used in a reciprocal expression. This is due in part to subject matter (cf. Exod. 26.3 and Isa. 34.15) but predominantly as a result of the masculine orientation of the Qumran texts.
2. When the main verb is singular the structure is not reciprocal. In such cases איש is normally the subject and רע, or its equivalent, is the verbal adjunct or complement.[3]
3. Reciprocity is common among the Qumran Scrolls in clauses where the predicate is an infinitive absolute or construct. To satisfy the qualifications of this study the subject of the infinitive must be plural (as determined by

[3] Robert D. Holmstedt, 'Anaphora in Biblical Hebrew: A Generative Perspective', *JSem* 28 (2019), pp. 1–15 (6–7), 'a singular verb used with the collocations איש רעיהו and איש אחיו are not reciprocal anaphors but subjects and their objects (see, e.g., Exod. 21.18 וְהִכָּה־אִישׁ אֶת־רֵעֵהוּ '(when) a man strikes his neighbor')'. For examples from the Qumran corpus see CD 7.1; 1QS 6.1 (4Q258 2.5); 4Q258 2.5; 4Q377 1 i 6; and 4Q422 3.9.

the context), encompassing both איש and אח. This is quite rare in Biblical Hebrew: see Jer. 34.15, 17.

4. Although distributive expressions can relate to the object (complement) as well as the subject, the reciprocal syntagm cannot; reciprocity requires the components of the expression to be members of the subject of the verbal action.

1.2. Reciprocal Expressions (34x)

איש and רע or אח are members of the subject (34x) and:

a. the predicate is a finite verb (## 6, 7, 8, 10, 13, 16, 18, 19, 20, 21, 23),
b. the verbal inflection is first person plural (#20),[4]
c. second person plural (#21),[5]
d. third person plural (## 6, 7, 8, 10, 13, 16, 18, 19, 23),
e. the predicate is an infinitive construct (## 1, 2, 3, 9, 11, 12, 15, 17, 22),
f. the predicate is an infinitive absolute (## 4, 5),
g. the clause is nominal (#14),[6]
h. the subject is overt (## 10, 11, 16),[7]
i. the reciprocal expression precedes the verb (#7),[8]
j. the representation of 'the other/fellow' can be adjunct to a noun phrase (#2).[9]

---

[4] See Gen. 31.49 and Mal. 2.10.

[5] See Lev. 15.14; Ezek. 24.23; 47.14; Zech. 3.10; 7.9, 10; 8.16, 17.

[6] See Jer. 23.30 and Neh. 4.13.

[7] See Gen. 43.33.

[8] See Jer. 9.3–4; 19.9; Ezek. 33.26; Joel 2.8; Zech. 8.17; Job 41.9.

[9] See Holmstedt, 'Anaphora', p. 7, 'Intriguingly, BH allows reciprocals to combine with another NP to form a possessive construction similar to English "they looked at each other's clothes," as in: לֹא יִשְׁמְעוּ אִישׁ שְׂפַת רֵעֵהוּ׃ "they will not understand each other's speech" (Gen 11:7)'. See also 2 Sam. 2.16 and Hag. 2.22.

1.2.1. Examples

(1) לאהוב איש את אחיהו

They shall love, each his fellow. (CD 6.20)[10]

(2) ולדרוש איש את שלום אחיהו

They shall seek each the welfare of his fellow. (CD 6.21–7.1)[11]

(3) להוכיח איש את אחיהו

They shall reprove each his fellow. (CD 7.2)[12]

(4) וניטור איש לאחיו

They bore a grudge each against his fellow. (CD 8.5–6; 19.18)[13]

(5) ושנוא איש את רעהו

They hate each his fellow. (CD 8.6; 19.18; 4Q266 3 iv 4)[14]

(6) ויכתבו בׄשׄמׄוׄתיהם איש אחר אחיהו

They shall be recorded by their name, each after his fellow. (CD 14.4–5, 4Q267 9 v 8)

---

[10] Note the governing finite verb at CD 6.14: ישמרו.

[11] Note the governing finite verb at CD 6.14: ישמרו.

[12] Note the governing finite verb at CD 6.14: ישמרו.

[13] Note the governing finite verb at CD 8.5 (CD 19.17): ויתגוללו.

[14] Note the governing finite verb at CD 8.5 (CD 19.17): ויתגוללו.

(7) איש את רׄעיהׄו יצׄדׄו חרם

Each with his fellow, they trap with what is consecrated. (CD 16.15; 4Q271 4 ii 14–15)[15]

(8) ידבׄרׄו איש אל רעהו

They will speak each to his fellow. (CD 20.17–18)

(9) להׄצׄ֯דׄ֯יק אׄישׄ את אׄחיו

They shall vindicate each his fellow. (CD 20.18)[16]

(10) הכול יהיו ביחד אמת וענות טוב וׄאהבת חסד ומחשבת צדק א֯י֯ש לרעהו

All together they shall comprise a *Yahad*—whose essence is truth, genuine humility, love of charity and righteous intent—each with his fellow. (1QS 2.24–25)

(11) להשמע הכול איש לרעהו

They all shall obey each his fellow. (1QS 5.23; 4Q258 2.3)[17]

(12) להוכיח איש את רעהו

They shall reprove each his fellow. (1QS 5.24–25; 4Q258 2.4)[18]

---

[15] This is a quote of Mic. 7.2 where MT has אִ֖ישׁ אֶת־אָחִ֖יהוּ.
[16] Note the governing finite verb at CD 20.17: ידבׄרׄו.
[17] הכול is usually understood as plural in 1QS; see the plural verb at 1QS 2.24 and 6.15–16; see also the plural pronominal suffix at 1QS 5.23: וכתבם.
[18] הכול in the previous line (1QS 5.23) is also the subject here; see footnote 17 and also cf. CD 7.2 above.

(13) באל^ה^י יתהלכו בכול מגוריהם כול הנמצא איש את רעהו

By these (statutes) they shall conduct themselves in all their dwellings, (according to) all (the deep insight of the law) which is found, each with his fellow. (1QS 6.2)[19]

(14) על יפות <חליפות> איש לרעהו

These (the ten man quorum) are the reserves, each for his fellow. (1QS 6.7)

(15) לעשות אמת וצדקה ומשפט ואהבת חסד והצנע לכת איש אם רעהו

They shall work truth, righteousness, justice, loving-kindness, and humility, each with his fellow. (1QS 8.2)[20]

(16) ילכו בם אנשי התמים קודש איש את רעהו

The men of blameless holiness shall conduct themselves, each with his fellow. (1QS 8.20)

(17) להל{{○}}כ תמים איש את רעהו

They shall walk blamelessly each with his fellow. (1QS 9.19; 4Q256 18.2; 4Q258 8.3–4; 4Q259 3.18)[21]

(18) יכבדו איש מרעהו

Let them seek honor, each outdoing his fellow. (1QSa 1.18; 1QH[a] 18.29-30; 4Q418 55 10)

---

[19] For an analysis of this passage see section 4 below.
[20] The subject in 1QS 8.1 is plural: שנים עשר איש וכוהנים שלושה.
[21] The subject at the beginning of the line is plural: אנשי היחד.

(19) יעבורו איש מלפני רעיהו

They shall pass each before his fellow. (1QpHab 4.11–12)

(20) מדוע נבגוד אישׁ[ב]אחיהו

W[h]y are we faithless, each [with] his fellow?' (4Q265 3 2)[22]

(21) לוא תונו איש את עמיתו

You shall not defraud each his fellow. (4Q271 3 5)[23]

(22) להלחם אֿ[י]ש ברעהו

They shall fight each against his fellow. (4Q387 3 7)[24]

(23) ויעשוקו אישׁ את רעהו

They oppress each his fellow. (4Q390 2 i 9)

2. Distributive Expressions (43x)

ויעשו איש הישר בעיניו

They did each what he pleased (CD 8.7; CD 19.19-20)

This simple statement illustrates the elements of the structure:

1. ויעשו – a plural verb, normally preceding the distributive expression,
2. איש – in the singular expressing 'each' or 'one' in the distributive statement,

[22] Quoting Mal. 2.10.
[23] Quoting Lev. 25.17; see Lev. 25.14 with אחיו.
[24] Israel is the subject of the main clause.

3. הישר בעיניו – a phrase—adjunct or complement—in accordance with the verbal semantics of the plural verb that is distributed over the members of the subject,
4. הו – the third singular pronoun whose antecedent is the singular איש rather than the plural subject.

2.1. Observations

1. There are no cases in the Qumran corpus of the feminine אשה used in a distributive expression. This is due predominantly as a result of the masculine orientation of the Qumran texts.
2. איש with distributive clauses in which the predicate is an infinitive construct and the subject is plural are quite common in Qumran literature. They are rare in BH: Gen. 42.25; Num. 32.18; 1 Sam. 13.20; and Jer. 34.9 (2x).
3. The distributive expression—unlike the reciprocal—can relate to a plural verbal complement as well as a plural subject. I have thus organized the evidence for distribution into two groups: 1. those cases related to the subject and 2. those cases related to the complement.

2.1.1. Plural Subject

When איש is a member of the plural subject (35x) and:

a. the predicate is a finite verb, always third masculine or common plural (## 4, 5, 6, 7, 8, 10, 11, 13, 14, 15, 16, 17, 18, 20, 21, 22, 23, 26, 27, 29),
b. the predicate is an infinitive construct (## 1, 2, 3, 9, 12, 19, 24, 25, 28),
c. the subject is overt (## 7, 8, 9, 11, 13, 14, 15, 16, 17, 18, 19, 21, 28),
d. the distributive איש can precede the verb (## 8, 10, 17, 26).

2.1.1.1. Examples

(1) ולעשות איש הישר בעיניו

They did each what was right in his own eyes. (CD 3.6) [25]

(2) לעשות איש את רצונו

They did each his own will. (CD 3.12) [26]

(3) לעמוד איש על מצודו

They stood each on his own tower. (CD 4.11–12) [27]

(4) ויתעלמו איש בשאר בשרו

They were indifferent each with his closest relative. (CD 8.6; 19.18–19)

(5) ויעשו איש הישר בעיניו

They did each what he pleased. (CD 8.7; 19.19-20)

(6) ויבחרו איש בשרירות לבו

They chose to follow each in his own willful heart. (CD 8.8; 19.20)

---

[25] Note the governing finite verb at CD 3.5: הלכו.
[26] Note the governing finite verb at CD 3.11: ויתורו.
[27] Note the 3mp suffix at בעדם at CD 4.10.

(7) יבאו באי העדה איש בתרו

The members of the congregation shall enter each in his turn. (CD 14.10-11)

(8) כו]לם ^איש^ לפי רוחו ישפטו בעצת הֿקדש

All of them, each in accordance with his spirit, shall be judged in the holy council. (CD 20.24–25)

(9) לדעת כול איש ישראל איש בית מעמדו

All the people of Israel shall know each his proper standing. (1QS 2.22) [28]

(10) ואיש כתכונו ישבו לפניו

Each according to his proper place they shall sit each before him (the priest). (1QS 6.4)

(11) ושאר כול העם ישבו איש בתכונו

The rest of the people shall sit each in his proper place. (1QS 6.8–9)

(12) להשיב איש את מדעו

They answered each with his opinion. (1QS 6.9) [29]

---

[28] The overt subject, כול איש ישראל, occurs only here in Qumran Literature (cf. 11Q19 45.12–13). This expression is always plural in the Hebrew Bible with subject-verb word order (Judg. 20.33 et al.).

[29] Note the governing finite verb earlier in the same line: ישאלו.

(13) ובני לוי יעמודו איש במעמדו

The Sons of Levi shall stand each in his office. (1QSa 1.22)

(14) וישבו לפניו ראש̓ א[לפי ישראל אי]ש לפי כבודו

The heads of the th[ousands of Israel] shall sit before him each according to his rank. (1QSa 2.14–15)

כול ראשי א[בות הע]דה עם חכמׄ[י עדת הקודש]ישבו לפניהם איש
(15) לפי כבודו

All the heads of [the con]gregation's cl[ans,] together with [their] wis[e and knowledgeable men,] shall sit before them each according to his rank. (1QSa 2.15–17)

(16)[ואחר יבר]כו כול עדת היחד א[יש לפי] כבודו

[Finally,] the whole congregation of the *Yahad* [shall give a bl]essing, e[ach in accordance with] his rank. (1QSa 2.21)

(17) וראשי משמרותם איש במעמדו ישרתו

The chiefs of their courses, each in his office, shall serve. (1QM 2.3)

(18) והראשים יהיו נפשטים לסדריהם איש למעמדו

And the columns shall be deployed to their formations, each to its position. (1QM 8.6)

(19) עד התיצבם איש על מעמדו

Until they have taken their stand each man upon his station. (1QM 16.5; 17.11)

(20) ירימו איש ידו בכלי מלחמתו

They shall raise each his hand with his weapon of war. (1QM 16.6–7; 17.12; 4Q491 11 ii 5; see 4Q491 11 ii 21 below)

(21) וישובו העם איש לאהליו

The people returned each to his tent. (4Q158 7–8 5)

(22) נתנו איש כופר נפשו

They gave each a ransom for his life. (4Q159 1 ii 6)

(23) מ]לאו איש לפי גורלו

They [acco]mplish each according to his lot. (4Q181 1 5)

(24, 25) ולהכתב איש לפני רעה בסרך איש לפי שכלו ומעשיו

They shall be written each before his fellow by rank, each in accordance with his understanding and his works. (4Q258 2.2–3) [30]

(26) אישׁ רואש לבית אבותו יה[י]וֿ[

Each a head of his ancestral house, they shall be. (4Q365 26a–b 8)[31]

---

[30] A plural subject is indicated by מעשיהם at 4Q258 2.1. Passive verbs with an implicit or explicit agent do not allow איש and רע to be actors in a reciprocal action, thus here איש לפני רעה is distributive. Cf. the variant passage at 1QS 5.23 above. 4Q258 2.2–3 is the only case of two distributive expressions in the same clause. Note the simpler construction at 1QS 5.23: איש לפני רעהו לפי שכלו ומעשיו.

[31] Note the transcription יה[י]וֿ[instead of הוא as at Num. 1.4.

(27) ירי]מו ידם אׄישׄ בכלי מלחמתו

They shall raise their hands, each with his battle weapon. (4Q491 11 ii 21)[32]

(28) ובעומדם לדגליהמה אי[ש] עׄלׄ [מצבו

When they have taken their positions eac[h] at [his station.] (4Q491 13 4)

(29) והלכו איש לאוהלוׄ]

They returned each to his tent. (11Q19 17.9)

2.1.2. Plural Object (Complement)

When איש is a member of the plural object (complement)[33] of the verb (8x) and:

a. the predicate is a finite verb, always third masculine or common plural (## 3, 6),
b. the predicate is an infinitive construct (## 1, 2, 4, 5, 7),
c. the object is always overt (## 1, 2, 3, 4, 5, 6, 7),
d. when איש and רע are both members of the plural object (complement) the result is distributive rather than reciprocal (## 3, 7).[34]

---

[32] Cf. 1QM 16.6–7; 17.12 above.

[33] See Paul Joüon, *A Grammar of Biblical Hebrew* (trans. and rev. by T. Muraoka; Rome: Gregorian & Biblical Press, 2nd reprint, 2nd edn., 2009) §147d 3: 'The plural referent of this distributive syntagm can be also accusatival'.

[34] Note that Joüon-Muraoka, *Grammar*, §147d 3 also categorizes such occurrences as Jer. 13.14; 25.26 as distributive.

2.1.2.1. Examples

(1) ולאהוב כול בני אור איש כגורלו

(He [the Instructor] shall teach them) to love all the children of light, each according to his assignment. (1QS 1.9-10)

(2) ולשנוא כול בני חושך איש כאשמתו

(He [the Instructor] shall teach them) to hate all the children of darkness, each according to his guilt. (1QS 1.10)

(3) וכתבם בסרך איש לפני רעהו

They are to enroll them by rank, each before his fellow. (1QS 5.23)[35]

(4) להוכיח דעת אמת ומשפט צדק לבוחרי דרך איש כרוחו

They shall reprove—founded on knowledge, truth, and righteous judgment—those who chose the way, each according to his spiritual qualities. (1QS 9.17–18; 4Q258 8.2)

(5) ולהוציא אתכול העדה איש בסרכו

They shall lead the whole congregation out, each by his rank. (1QSa 1.23)[36]

---

[35] The verb should be vocalized כְּתָבֵם ('they are to enroll them'). In the variant recension of 4Q258 2.2 the verb is cast as a *Niphal* infinitive construct with a third masculine plural suffix. See above.

[36] The object of the verb—כול העדה—is understood as plural as indicated by both the Hebrew Bible (Lev. 9.5 et al.) and Qumran Literature (1QM 2.9).

(6) ויורישם איש נחלתו

He caused them to inherit each his own inheritance. (4Q418 81+81a 3)

(7) לסרך הכול איש לפני רע[הו]

They shall muster everyone, each before [his] fellow. (4Q421 1a i 3)[37]

3. SYNTAX

I began this study as a means of describing the syntax of the reciprocal and distributive examples above in order to analyze the text for a computer searchable syntax database of the scrolls from Qumran. Robert Holmstedt and I have experimented with three possible analyses and by way of this current discussion have tentatively settled on a fourth. I will describe these in the order of their examination.

At first blush it was tempting to overlook the disagreement in number evident in the clause, יְדַבְּרוּ איש אל רעהו ('They will each speak to his fellow', CD 20.17–18), and understand איש as the subject of the plural verb; in most cases it is clearly a member of the subject. However, the number of examples with both reciprocal and distributive expressions where the subject is overt and plural quickly dissuaded us of this solution. Note the same conclusion reached by Joüon-Muraoka: '[in] a phrase such as איש ... אִישׁ אֶל־רֵעֵהוּ here is no grammatical subject'.[38]

The second possibility was to understand the reciprocal/distributive expression as a 'small clause', i.e., an embedded clause having a subject and predicate, but lacking in tense. This interpretation would suggest amplifying יְדַבְּרוּ איש אל רעהו as 'They shall speak—each *will speak* to his fellow'; the elided verb in the small clause supplied by the predicate of the main clause. This solution had its attractions as the singular איש and

[37] For הכול as plural see footnote 17.
[38] Joüon-Muraoka, *Grammar*, §147d.

accompanying third masculine singular pronominal suffix are syntactically accounted for. However, the resulting clause by definition falls outside this discussion: i.e., איש as the subject of a singular verb is not reciprocal or distributive.

The third possibility is the one proposed by Joüon-Muraoka: 'a phrase such as אִישׁ אֶל־רֵעֵהוּ serves as an adverbial adjunct ...'.[39] However, this solution fails to explain the third masculine singular suffix which clearly has איש as its antecedent while the particle between the two nouns is determined in accordance with the verbal semantics. The relationship of each part of the expression might be understood as adjunct to the verb, but this does not clarify the association of איש to the third masculine singular suffix of רעהו.

A fourth possibility is the result of a recent discussion of these expressions between Robert Holmstedt and Todd Snider. Snider is currently a postdoctoral research fellow at the Language, Logic and Cognition Center, at The Hebrew University. To quote Holmstedt's synopsis of their discussion: '[the] best option is to take the איש as an adjunct to the plural subject and the rest of the phrase (e.g., object, PP, etc., with the 3ms pronoun) as the complement of the main verb. The 3ms pronoun is a result of the semantic restriction of the subject so that it applies in a universal way to 'every' man indicated (in a singular way)'.[40]

4. A TROUBLESOME CASE

Of all of the passages examined above, 1QS 6.2 (איש את רעהו) has proved to be the most problematic for exegetes and translators.[41] I will first present a transcription of the passage in question and then a selection of translations that have attempted to make sense of the syntax. Finally I will discuss the passage on the basis of the

[39] Joüon-Muraoka, *Grammar*, §147d.

[40] Personal communication on November 15, 2019.

[41] I considered two other passages before I settled on 1QS 6.2: the thorny syntax of 1QS 9.15–16, and the problematic reciprocal reconstructions at 4Q223–224 2 ii 18 and 4Q223–224 2 ii 49. The former requires an understanding of the overall structure of 1QS 9.12–19 and the latter requires a supporting study of reciprocal expressions in the Ge'ez of Jubilees.

global examination of reciprocal and distributive patterns that we have examined above.

באלה יתהלכו בכול מגוריהם כול הנמצא איש את רעהו וישמעו
הקטן לגדול למלאכה ולממון

(1QS 6.1b-2a)

Florentino García Martínez and Eibert Tigchelaar (*DSSSE*[42])

In this way shall they behave in all their places of residence. Whenever one fellow meets another the junior shall obey the senior in work and in money.

Elisha Qimron and James Charlesworth (PTSDSSP[43])

In these (precepts) they shall walk in all their dwelling places. Wherever they are found each one with his respect to his fellow: the lesser one shall obey the greater with respect to work and money.

Geza Vermes (*CDSSE*[44])

These are the ways in which all of them shall walk, each man with his companion, wherever they dwell. The man of lesser rank shall obey the greater in matters of work and money.

Michael Wise (WAC[45])

By these rules they are to govern themselves wherever they dwell, in accordance with each legal finding that bears upon communal life. Inferiors must obey their ranking superiors as regards work and wealth.

---

[42] Florentino García Martínez and Eibert Tigchelaar, *The Dead Sea Scrolls Study Edition* (2 vols., Leiden: Brill, 1997–1998) p. 1.83.

[43] James H. Charlesworth et al. (eds.), *Rule of the Community and Related Documents*, vol. 1 of *The Dead Sea Scrolls: Hebrew, Aramaic, and Greek Texts with English Translations* (PTSDSSP, Tübingen: Mohr Siebeck) p. 27.

[44] Geza Vermes, *The Complete Dead Sea Scrolls in English* (London: Penguin, 1997) p. 105.

[45] Michael O. Wise, Martin G. Abegg, and Edward M. Cook, *The Dead Sea Scrolls: A New Translation* (New York: HarperOne, rev. edn., 2005) p. 124. Also Donald W. Parry and Emanuel Tov (eds.), *Texts Concerned with Religious Law*, vol. 1 of *The Dead Sea Scrolls Reader* (Leiden: Brill, 2004) p. 25.

Before we discuss the proper placement of איש את רעהו within this passage we must first deal with a collateral issue faced by each of the translations presented here: how to understand the expression כול הנמצא, literally 'all that is found', that immediately precedes the reciprocal expression.

As for the first translation (*DSSSE*), one is hard pressed to find a similar context for the translation proposed by García Martínez and Tigchelaar where the phrase כול הנמצא is translated as the English conjunction, 'whenever', evidently referring to the potential *existence* of an *occasion* when one might encounter his fellow. Better sense can be made of the suggestion that 'all that is found' refers to subject of the verb יתהלכו, '*they* shall walk ... wherever *they* are found/dwell ...' (PTSDSSP and CDSSE). I would suggest, however, that the translation proposed by Michael Wise—where כול הנמצא becomes 'each legal finding' (WAC)—is best supported by the context of the passage. The exact phrase—כול הנמצא—also occurs at 1QS 9.20, ולהשכילם כול הנמצא לעשות בעת הזואת. This clause begins easily enough: 'He (the Instructor, see 1QS 9.12) shall instruct them (the members of the *Yahad*, see 1QS 9.19)', but then the modern reader is left to ask '*what* is the *all* that is found' that forms the content of the instruction? Wise's answer—it is a *legal* finding—is based on the lines immediately preceding 1QS 9.20. At 1QS 9.13, as a description of the first in a long list of infinitives that gives detail to the 'statutes for the Instructor' (1QS 9.12), we are told that the Instructor is to 'work out the will of God according to what has been revealed (הנגלה) for each period of history' by teaching 'all (כול) the deep insight (שכל) which is found (הנמצא) in accordance with the times'. Beginning at 1QS 5.21 and continuing to the end of the document (1QS 5.23, 24; 6.14, 18; and 9.15) שכל is the basis, along with 'deeds' (מעשים), by which the ranking of the initiate is established. As the deeds in this context are those determined by the law (1QS 5.21, בתורה), it is likely that 'deep insight' is also to be qualified by 'the law' (תורה), thus 'deep insight in the law'. Wise has followed this line of reasoning as well echoing P. Wernberg-Møller's early comment, 'The phrase alludes to the present amount of legal knowledge available to the members of the society; the conception of the gradual revelation of *halaka*, as this is expressed in [1QS] viii 4, ix 13, 14, 23 is one of the distinct characteristics of our community'.[46] This interpretation is also supported by P. Alexander and G. Vermes along with the final piece to the puzzle: 'The phrase should probably be taken as equivalent to (כ)כל הנמצא, "according to all that has been found", i.e., in accordance with the present state of legal knowledge within the Community (so Wernberg-Møller)'.[47] This solution—כל הנמצא understood as an adverbial adjunct to יתהלכו—also clears the way for איש את רעהו to be a part of the clause that precedes it (CDSSE, WAC) rather than the clause that follows (*DSSSE*, PTSDSSP). This is in keeping with all of the evidence presented in this study: there is never a case where a reciprocal or distributive expression precedes a verb with a *waw*, as *DSSSE* and PTSDSSP suggest for 1QS 6.2 and the following וישמעו ('and they shall be obedient').[48] So I propose to translate this passage: 'By these (statutes) they shall conduct themselves in all their dwellings, (according to) all (the deep insight of the law) which is found, each with his fellow'.

5. FINAL COMMENTS

Perhaps the most important finding advanced by this study of reciprocity and distribution is demonstrated by the disposition of the evidence. Fully 83% (28 of 34) of the reciprocal expressions noted in this study are found in three groups of documents: the Damascus manuscripts, the Community Rule manuscripts, and 1QSa,[49] although these documents account for only 12% of the Qumran corpus. Thus when Jacob Licht, of the first generation of

---

[46] P. Wernberg-Møller, *The Manual of Discipline: Translated and Annotated with an Introduction* (STDJ, 1, Leiden: Brill, 1957) p. 101.

[47] Philip P. Alexander and Geza Vermes (eds.), *Qumran Cave 4. XIX: Serekh Ha-Yahad and Two Related Texts* (DJD, 26, Oxford: Clarendon, 1998) p. 102.

[48] A constituent that precedes the verb and is connected to the following clause by a conjunction is quite common in the Qumran corpus but exists in three contexts: complex initial subject phrases (e.g., 1QS 7.4); prepositional phrases, especially with infinitives (e.g., 1QM 10.2); and left dislocations (e.g., 1QS 7.15–16).

[49] CD, 1QS, 1QSa, 4Q255–4Q264, 4Q266–4Q273, 5Q12, 5Q11, and 6Q15.

Qumran commentators, remarked that the reciprocal syntagms were 'Fixed expressions that express the mutuality of the relationship between the community members',[50] he had clearly put his finger on a vital characteristic that permeates these documents. In a similar way 84% (36 of 43) of the instances of the parallel distributive structure are found among the Damascus manuscripts, the Community Rule manuscripts, the War Scroll manuscripts, and in 1QSa.[51] These documents account for a slightly larger 17% of the Qumran corpus. Thus our study has had the collateral effect of highlighting another bit of evidence supporting the clear communal focus of these important sectarian compositions.

---

[50] 'לשונות קבועים המבטאים את ההדדיות שביחסי החברים', Jacob Licht, מגילת הסרכים: ממגילות מדבר יהודה (Jerusalem: The Bialik Institute, 1965) p. 135.
[51] Adding 1QM and 4Q491–4Q496 to those manuscripts listed in footnote 49.

THE PRAYER OF NABONIDUS AND LOST BOOKS: RECONSTRUCTING THE ARAMAIC LIBRARY OF THE PERSIAN PERIOD*

AARON KOLLER

The Jews of the Persian period must have produced dozens, perhaps hundreds of works of literature, in Aramaic and Hebrew, some of which no doubt were read by Jews (and perhaps others) from Egypt through Persia. Unfortunately, we have essentially two groups of this literature at our disposal: those that became part of the Bible[1] and those that were fortuitously buried in caves near Qumran.

Students of the latter group have often read them in light of the former, but recent scholarship has appropriately pointed out

* It is an honor to dedicate this paper in honor of Ed Cook, from whose writings I learned and continue to learn so much, and with whom it has been a pleasure to work. I owe a debt of gratitude to Dr. Ari Mermelstein for reading an earlier draft of this paper and not only pointing out the many flaws, but suggesting ways of improving it.

[1] For our purposes here, two otherwise weighty issues matter little: (a) the contours of the Bible at the time, whether comparable to Tanakh as known today, or more similar to other Hellenistic-era versions of the Bible, such as the one which eventually came to be the Christian Bible (minus the Christian books, of course); (b) how and when this canonization took place.

the contingency involved in this state of affairs. Already in the late 1970s, Michael Stone was sounding this warning:

> In principle, there is no reason to think that the body of literature that is transmitted as the Hebrew Bible is a representative collection of all types of Jewish literary creativity down to the fourth century. It is a selection of texts and the process of transmission and preservation that created this selection reflects the theological judgment of certain groups in Judah and Jerusalem before and after the Babylonian exile. It is specious, therefore, when faced by a third-century phenomenon, either to seek its roots in the Bible or to relegate it to foreign influence. Circles other than those transmitting the biblical books existed, or else those involved in transmitting the biblical books did not allow a considerable part of the intellectual culture of their day to be expressed in them.[2]

This was easiest to see when an entire genre was absent from the biblical corpus, such as astronomical literature as found in the Book of the Watchers and the Astronomical Book of Enoch.[3] These texts show us empirically what we should have expected anyway: that Jews in the fifth, fourth, and third centuries were producing literature that are neither later versions of Iron Age texts nor forerunners of texts known from later Judaism or Christianity.

Parallels to this state of affairs from the linguistic history of Hebrew may be instructive. As is well known, the Hebrew reflected in many books from the period of the Second Temple is somewhat different from that of earlier books.[4] It is even possible

---

[2] Michael E. Stone, 'The Book of Enoch and Judaism in the Third Century B.C.E.', *CBQ* 40 (1978), pp. 479–492 (490–491).

[3] In this regard, see also Annette Yoshiko Reed, '"Ancient Jewish Sciences" and the Historiography of Judaism', in Jonathan Ben-Dov and Seth L. Sanders (eds.), *Ancient Jewish Sciences and the History of Knowledge in Second Temple Literature* (New York: New York University Press and the Institute for the Study of the Ancient World, 2014) pp. 195–254.

[4] This statement, which is both methodologically obvious and empirically well-grounded, has oddly become controversial in recent years. For a classic and well-argued argument for it, see Avi Hurvitz, בין לשון ללשון: לתולדות לשון המקרא בימי בית שני (Jerusalem: Bialik, 1972); for a recent defense of it, see Jan Joosten and Ronald Hendel, *How Old Is the Hebrew*

to offer more nuanced histories, as the Hebrew of some of the literature produced in the sixth century BCE differs both from earlier texts and from later texts.

Of the many linguistic developments visible within Second Temple Hebrew, some continue on into later forms of classical Hebrew (in particular, Mishnaic Hebrew), while others are evolutionary dead ends. Thus, the single example of אנו instead of אנחנו (*ketiv* in Jer. 42.6) is a harbinger of things to come. On the other hand, the single example of זאתה instead of זאת (*ketiv* in Jer. 26.6) is a short-lived development.[5] In Late Biblical Hebrew, the word רָץ developed the meaning 'messenger', something not found later.[6] The books of Esther, Ezra-Nehemiah, and Daniel are full of new lexical items. Some are Persian loanwords, and while a few of those (פרדס 'garden, orchard', גזבר 'treasurer', פתגם 'decree') became normalized in later Hebrew, others (פרתם 'noble', אפדן 'palace', פרשגן 'copy') were never heard from again.[7] The same is true for other neologisms. נזק 'damage', רָאוי 'fitting', and תלמיד 'scholar' are *hapax legomena* in the Hebrew Bible (Est. 7.4; 2.9; and 1 Chron. 25.8, respectively), but appear hundreds of times in rabbinic Hebrew. On the other hand, צָפִיר 'male goat' exists in LBH and then never again in Hebrew.[8]

Bible? A Linguistic, Textual, and Historical Study (Anchor Yale Bible Reference Library, New Haven: Yale University Press, 2018).

[5] See Aaron D. Hornkohl, 'Transitional Biblical Hebrew', in W. Randall Garr and Steven E. Fassberg (eds.), *A Handbook of Biblical Hebrew, Volume 1: Periods, Corpora, and Reading Traditions* (Winona Lake: Eisenbrauns, 2016) pp. 31–42 at 37 (the analysis of זאתה relies on an unpublished dissertation by Colin Smith), and Hornkohl, *Ancient Hebrew Periodization and the Language of the Book of Jeremiah: The Case for a Sixth-Century Date of Composition* (Studies in Semitic Languages and Linguistics, 74, Boston: Brill, 2014) pp. 125–128.

[6] Hornkohl, *Ancient Hebrew Periodization*, pp. 352–355.

[7] See the convenient list in Hendel and Joosten, *How Old is the Hebrew Bible?*, p. 27.

[8] For all these words, see the relevant entries in Avi Hurvitz, in collaboration with Leeor Gottlieb, Aaron Hornkohl and Emmanuel Mastéy, *A Concise Lexicon of Late Biblical Hebrew: Linguistic Innovations in the Writings of the Second Temple Period* (VTSup, 160, Leiden: Brill, 2014).

The same is true in literary and intellectual history:[9] some developments became integrated into books that became biblical, or rabbinic, or early Christian; others flourished for a time and then died. This is only surprising if we see every development as striving towards the future as we know it to have developed. But history is not teleological.

The need to resist facile categorization is more subtle, and therefore takes more urging, when we encounter texts from Qumran which *are* comparable to texts known from the Bible. Eva Mroczek has in fact urged this, showing in detail how texts of psalms and texts about David have been misread because of well-known (but likely irrelevant) traditions about the biblical book of Psalms and David's involvement therein.[10]

In this brief paper, I would like to take these methodological points and push a bit harder on them. Not only should we read texts known from Qumran without biblical lenses, we should also be aware of possibilities for reconstructing the texts *not* known from either Qumran or the Bible. Normally, of course, lost books are just that, so they are not worth writing articles about. But in some cases, we seem to have enough data from Qumran and the Bible to offer at least a tentative reconstruction of the sorts of works of literature that were composed and circulated in ancient

---

[9] Examples could be given from biological evolution, as well. As the mammals radiated following the end of the Cretaceous period, numerous groups arose which are now extinct. The Mesonychia, for example, appear soon after the extinction of the non-avian dinosaurs, but the line was extinct by about 30 million years ago.

[10] Eva Mroczek, 'The Hegemony of the Biblical in the Study of Second Temple Literature', *Journal of Ancient Judaism* 6 (2015), pp. 2–35, and more fully in Eva Mroczek, *The Literary Imagination in Jewish Antiquity* (New York: Oxford University Press, 2016). It should be noted that Mroczek blurs her otherwise sharp point in lamenting that some scholars have retained 'the biblical' as 'a dominant category of analysis', and quotes, for the point, Cohen and Kugel stating that biblical interpretation was central to Second Temple Judaism. There is no contradiction between the point made by Cohen and Kugel – which seems clearly correct, in light of the large quantities of explicit and implicit biblical interpretation known from Second Temple texts – and that made by Mroczek in the rest of her work.

times although not presently in either corpus, and that is what this paper will offer.

Our investigation will start with 4Q242, the Prayer of Nabonidus. This is a text that does have obvious significance for the Bible, which is altogether different from saying that it should be read through biblical lenses. Since its initial publication, it has been obvious that this text has relevance to the *pre*-history of the story known to us as Daniel 4, in which Nebuchadnezzar is turned into an animal as punishment for hubris, and is healed only through recognition of the God of Israel as the one true God. The goal here is to show that the text also opens up much more than questions about biblical texts and the Qumran library: it opens the question of Aramaic literature in general in the Persian and Hellenistic periods.

The first step is to bring this text back out of Qumran, into the general Jewish library of Second Temple history. Of course, the Qumran texts always present us with the dilemma of idiosyncrasy: can we really be sure that these can inform us at all regarding the literature produced and consumed by anyone other than the fringe sect living at Qumran?

The original composition of this text almost certainly antedates the Qumran community. First, Schattner-Rieser argues that on linguistic grounds this text should be dated to the Persian period.[11] For example, the 3mp pronoun המון instead of אנון, the unapocopated relative particle די, and the lexeme כמה 'just as', all appear in this short text. Second, Ben Zion Wacholder pointed out that the correct identification of the Babylonian monarch suggests

[11] Ursula Schattner-Rieser, *L'araméen des manuscrits de la mer Morte, 1. Grammaire* (Instruments pour l'étude des langues de l'Orient ancien, 5, Lausanne: Éditions du Zèbre, 2004) p. 54; *idem*, 'L'apport de la philologie araméenne et l'interprétation des archaïsmes linguistiques pour la datation des textes araméens de Qumrân', in Katell Berthelot and Daniel Stökl Ben Ezra (eds.), *Aramaica Qumranica: Proceedings of the Conference on the Aramaic Texts from Qumran in Aix-en-Provence, 30 June – 2 July 2008* (STDJ, 94, Leiden: Brill, 2010) pp. 101–123 (109, 115).

an early date for this text.[12] As will be seen, the analysis below supports this view, despite some complexities.

Indeed, some scholars have suggested that no Aramaic text is really a 'Qumran text'. All Aramaic texts found at Qumran, on this view, must come from an earlier period, and probably circulated far more widely among Second Temple-era Jewish society. Stanislav Segert was among the early scholars to call attention to the fact that the Aramaic texts from Qumran contained none of the sectarian ideologies or literary motifs which are so common and so pervasive in the Hebrew texts then already known from the same site.[13] Building on this observation, and adding the assumption that non-Qumran texts composed while the Qumran community existed would not have been preserved by the community, Wacholder suggested that the Aramaic texts must, as a group, antedate the formation of the Qumran community. The argument (to paraphrase an old argument from the scholarship on the history of halakhah) is that anti-Qumran must be ante-Qumran.[14] This particular argument presumed that the Qumran community did not preserve any texts that were not 'theirs', except texts that were older than the community itself, because any text not explicitly sectarian[15] was anti-sectarian if it did not antedate the sect.

---

[12] Ben-Zion Wacholder, 'The Ancient Judaeo-Aramaic Literature (500–164 BCE): A Classification of Pre-Qumranic Texts', in Lawrence H. Schiffman (ed.), *Archaeology and History in the Dead Sea Scrolls: The New York University Conference in Memory of Yigael Yadin* (JSPSup, 8; JSOT/ASOR Monograph Series, 2, Sheffield: JSOT Press, 1990) pp. 257–281.

[13] Stanislav Segert, 'Die Sprachenfragen in der Qumrangemeinschaft', in H. Bardtke (ed.), *Qumran-Probleme: Vorträge des Leipziger Symposions über Qumran-Probleme vom 9. bis 14. Oktober 1961* (Berlin: Deutsche Akademie der Wissenschaften zu Berlin, 1963) pp. 315–339; *idem*, 'Sprachliche Bemerkungen zu einigen aramäischen Texten von Qumrān', *ArOr* 33 (1965), pp. 190–206.

[14] Wacholder, 'The Ancient Judaeo-Aramaic Literature', pp. 257–281.

[15] Carol A. Newsom, '"Sectually Explicit" Literature from Qumran', in William Propp, Baruch Halpern, and David Noel Freedman (eds.), *The Bible and Its Interpreters* (BJSUCSD, 1, Winona Lake, IN: Eisenbrauns, 1990) pp. 167–187.

A more nuanced argument was offered by Dimant.[16] She also begins with the observation that the Aramaic texts contain no distinctively Qumran elements. She does not date all of the texts early, but certainly does point out that some of them are early. She also emphasizes the eastern ties of many of the Aramaic texts, which are set in the eastern diaspora, draw on Mesopotamian motifs such as Gilgamesh and Humbaba, relate to the Persian court, and deal with astrological and magical themes.

Indeed, the use of Hebrew by the Qumran community is plausibly a matter of linguistic ideology.[17] On this reasoning, we could conclude that the Aramaic texts from among the Dead Sea Scrolls are not specifically sectarian, and we can utilize these texts

---

[16] Devorah Dimant, 'The Qumran Aramaic Texts and the Qumran Community', in Anthony Hilhorst, Émile Puech, and Eibert Tigchelaar (eds.), *Flores Florentino: Dead Sea Scrolls and Other Early Jewish Studies in Honour of Florentino García Martínez* (JSJSup, 122, Leiden: Brill, 2007) pp. 197–205. Florentino García Martínez, 'Aramaica Qumranica Apocalyptica', in Katell Berthelot and Daniel Stökl Ben Ezra (eds.), *Aramaica Qumranica: Proceedings of the Conference on the Aramaic Texts from Qumran in Aix-en-Provence, 30 June – 2 July 2008* (STDJ, 94, Leiden: Brill, 2010) pp. 443–483 suggests that the entire question of the origin of the Aramaic texts at Qumran is uninteresting: 'My answer to [the question of the origin of the Aramaic texts] is that it is irrelevant and not particularly useful, since the only context we have for most of the Aramaic compositions is the context provided by the collection in which they have been found'. While this is, in one sense, evidently correct, it also declares an entire area of inquiry off-limits, by fiat.

[17] Steve Weitzman, 'Why Did the Qumran Community Write in Hebrew?' *JAOS* 119 (1999), pp. 35–45. William Schniedewind argued something stronger – that the *form* of Hebrew at Qumran was ideologically motivated. See Schniedewind, 'Qumran Hebrew as an Antilanguage', *JBL* 118 (1999), pp. 235–252, and see Eibert J. C. Tigchelaar, 'Sociolinguistics and the Misleading Use of the Concept of Anti-Language for Qumran Hebrew', in Pieter B. Hartog, Alison Schofield, and Samuel I. Thomas (eds.), *The Dead Sea Scrolls and the Study of the Humanities: Method, Theory, Meaning - Proceedings of the Eighth Meeting of the International Organization for Qumran Studies (Munich, 4–7 August, 2013)* (STDJ, 125, Leiden: Brill, 2018) pp. 195–206. (The 'approval' expressed by myself and Bernstein regarding Schniedewind's article, criticized by Tigchelaar (p. 195), extended only to the use of sociolinguistics, not to the conclusions reached.)

as a window through which to glimpse a picture of Jewish Aramaic literature more generally.[18] There are, however, complications; in particular, even texts that are not originally Qumran compositions may have been sectarianized in the transmission process.[19] In the case of the Prayer of Nabonidus, however, there are no signs of sectarianization, and as far as we can tell, the text seems to have been preserved by the Qumran community more or less as it likely circulated elsewhere, as well.

Having established that the text as we have it can tell us something about the texts circulating among ancient Jews more generally, we can now see where this leads. The thrust of the following argument is that this text was part of a body of Jewish Aramaic literature of the Persian period, and that this body was in turn only a subset of a broader body of Aramaic-language literature in circulation throughout the Persian empire. This literature, on the whole, was probably cosmopolitan in its themes and genres, rooted in contemporary issues and utilizing current motifs and genres to explore themes of general interest. The Jewish texts likely had a Jewish lens, although it is conceivable that not all did. This literature was not 'proto-biblical', and was not 'exegetical' (presupposing a canonical or quasi-canonical text

[18] This is, however, not as simple as sometimes said. Jonathan Ben-Dov, 'הכתיבה בארמית ובעברית במגילות קומראן ובספרים החיצונים: הרקע בעולם העתיק והחיפוש אחר סמכות יהודית כתובה', *Tarbiz* 78 (2009), pp. 27–60, pointed out that although *some* of the Aramaic texts at Qumran are old, at least some of the copies (dating paleographically) are as late as the Herodian period. Ben-Dov therefore argues that the use of Aramaic has to be understood within the linguistic ideology of the Qumran community. Ben-Dov argues that despite the sect's general use of Hebrew, there were three reasons why this community might compose texts in Aramaic: (1) the use of Aramaic gives an aura of antiquity, and therefore of authority; (2) scientific compositions should be in Aramaic since that was the usual language of the genre in Persian and Hellenistic times; (3) 'historical mimesis', based on the claim that the Patriarchs spoke Aramaic, and that therefore texts they composed should be in Aramaic. None of these considerations apply to 4Q242, however.

[19] See Robert Kugler, 'Whose Scripture? Whose Community? Reflections on the Dead Sea Scrolls Then and Now, By Way of Aramaic Levi', *DSD* 15 (2008), pp. 5–23.

to be interpreted). It was also not sectarian, not related to intra-communal disputes, and not legalistic, apocalyptic, or prophetic.

We are often misled by the Bible into reading Second Temple texts in ways not intended by the authors and not experienced by the early audiences, sometimes in blatant ways (see the interpretive history of 4Q550, for example), but more often in subtle and more insidious ways. Most fundamentally, we expect texts to be religiously significant, even momentous. But some texts do not give us laws or theology. They give us something that is perhaps even more interesting: literature.

The text of the first three fragments of 4Q242, as read and restored by our Jubilar,[20] reads as follows:

1. מלי צ[ל]תא די צלי נ֯ב֯ני מ֯ל֯כ֯א [מלך בב]ל מלכ֯[א רבא כדי כתיש הוא]
2. בשחנא באישא בפתגמ א֯[להא עלי]א בתימן[אנה נבני בשחנא באישא]
3. כתיש הוית שנין שבע ומן [די צלית] שוי א[להא עלי אנפוהי ואתרפית]
4. וחטאי שבק לה גזר והוא֯ [הוה גבר] יהודי מ֯[ן בני גלותא ואמר לי מלכא]
5. החוי֯ וכתב למעבד יקר ור֯[בו והד]ר֯ לשם א[להא עליא אדין כתבת אנה]
6. כתיש הוית בשחנא ב[אישא כדי הוית] בתימן [בפתגם אלהא עליא אדין]
7. שנין שבע מצלא הוי[ת ובעא בעו לכל] א֯ל֯ה֯י֯ כספא ודהבא [נחשא פרזלא]
8. אעא אבנא חספא מן די [במדעי הוית סב]ר די אלהין ה[מון]
9. [ ]מיהון א֯ל֯◦[ ]ב֯ ל֯[ ]

1. The words of the p[ra]yer that King Nabonidus, king of Babylon, [great] kin[g] prayed [when he was struck]
2. with a terrible skin disease, by decree of G[od Most Hi]gh, in Teman: '[I, Nabonidus, with a terrible skin disease]
3. was struck for seven years, but because [I prayed], Go[d turned his face to me, and I was healed.]

[20] The text and translation are from our forthcoming volume: Moshe Bernstein, Edward Cook, and Aaron Koller, *Aramaic Texts from Qumran* (WAW, Atlanta: Society of Biblical Literature, forthcoming). My thanks to my collaborators for the joint work, and for permission to use that work in this article.

4. My sin – a diviner released it; he was a Jewish [man] from am[ong the exiles. He said to me, 'O King!]
5. 'Make it known and write, in order to give glory and exal[tation and ho]nor to the name of the G[od Most High!' And thus did I write: 'When]
6. I was struck by a ter[rible] skin disease [while in] Teman, [by the word of the God Most High, then]
7. for seven years I w[as] praying, [beseeching all] the gods of silver and gold, [of bronze and iron,]
8. of wood, of stone, of clay, since I t[hought] that [they we]re gods

As has been noted by virtually all commentators, this text is similar enough to Daniel 4 that some sort of genetic relationship is assured.[21] In both, the Babylonian king is stricken by God; he is stricken for 'seven periods of time'; the Jewish man advises the king to recognize God's dominion and thus be cured. There are details in which the stories differ which are easily explained as simply evolution. Most obviously, two characters in the Prayer of Nabonidus texts, the king (Nabonidus) and the Jewish seer (who is anonymous), are replaced by well-known characters who then play those roles (Nebuchadnezzar and Daniel). The movement of stories from anonymous or lesser-known characters to well-known replacements is both intuitive and well attested.

There are, however, other differences between the texts that make it clear that the texts are not just a parent and child within the development of a narrative. 4Q242 is *a* formerly missing link, but it is not *the* missing link that would allow us to draw a straight line from Neo-Babylonian history to the book of Daniel.[22] The most significant detail that irreparably separates the two is precisely what malady struck the king. In the Prayer of Nabonidus, it is שחנא באישא 'a terrible skin disease'. It seems

[21] See the discussion in Andrew Steinman, 'The Chicken and the Egg: A New Proposal for the Relationship Between the Prayer of Nabonidus and the Book of Daniel', *RevQ* 20 (2002), pp. 557–570.
[22] See Matthias Henze, *The Madness of King Nebuchadnezzar: The Ancient Near Eastern Origins and Early History of Interpretation of Daniel 4* (JSJSup, 61, Leiden: Brill, 1999) pp. 51–100.

compelling to assume that this motif originated with a writer aware of the Mesopotamian connection between the god Sin and diseases of the skin.[23] The claim that Nabonidus suffered from a terrible skin disease then drips with irony: it is a vicious mockery of the king who claimed to spend his life out in Tayma venerating the moon good Sin. Were Nabonidus' piety real, the author is implying, clearly he would not have been struck by a disease controlled by his own preferred deity. Such a cruel joke could only have originated in Mesopotamia, where the relevant theological nuances were known to writer and audience.

But the motif of skin disease is of course absent from the canonical text of Daniel, where the king – Nebuchadnezzar now – is struck by the malady of becoming like an animal. This is also likely a motif that originated in Mesopotamian circles: it seems to play on the narrative of Enkidu within the Gilgamesh epic, presumably well-known to anyone with a decent Babylonian education.[24] Alternatively, or in addition, this may allude to a complex of motifs in Mesopotamian literature regarding demons and the dead.[25]

This then necessitates the conclusion that at least two different Jewish, anti-king versions of the story circulated in Babylonia independently, and before us we have two different nodes on the family tree, not two points in an evolution. This also means that both Jewish authors were writing from, and for, an insider's perspective with regard to Babylonian culture. They

---

[23] Susan Ackerman, 'The Prayer of Nabonidus, Elijah on Mount Carmel, and the Development of Monotheism in Israel', in William G. Dever and J. Edward Wright (eds.), *The Echoes of Many Texts: Reflections on Jewish and Christian Traditions. Essays in Honor of Lou H. Silberman* (BJS, 313, Atlanta: Scholars Press, 1997) pp. 51–65.

[24] André Lemaire, 'Nabonide et Gilgamesh: l'araméen en Mésopotamie et à Qoumrân', in Katell Berthelot and Daniel Stökl Ben Ezra (eds.), *Aramaica Qumranica: Proceedings of the Conference on the Aramaic Texts from Qumran in Aix-en-Provence, 30 June – 2 July 2008* (STDJ, 94, Leiden: Brill, 2010) pp. 125–44.

[25] Christopher B. Hays, 'Chirps from the Dust: The Affliction of Nebuchadnezzar in Daniel 4:30 in its Ancient Near Eastern Context', *JBL* 126 (2007), pp. 305–325.

could draw on knowledge of that culture, and expected their audience to have the same.

Three further points ought to be emphasized, based on what we see empirically regarding the Prayer of Nabonidus. First, it traveled far. This is perhaps obvious, since our one remaining copy of the Babylonian-Jewish composition 'The Prayer of Nabonidus' was found on the Judean shores of the Dead Sea, in the collection of a group of sectarians who had moved from their regular communities to a commune in the desert. There is no reason to posit particular links between the Qumran community and the eastern diaspora; one only needs to presume – as indeed I think we must – that the text, despite its eastern origins, was copied by and circulated among Jews even in the land of Israel.[26] Similarly, the book of Esther was likely composed in the eastern diaspora, but 'Mordechai's Day' was being celebrated in second century BCE Alexandria (2 Macc. 14), and the book was being translated into Greek in first century BCE Jerusalem. Other Aramaic texts from Qumran may be similar in this regard; it has been suggested that the Targum of Job is in eastern Aramaic,[27] for example, and the Enoch literature draws on traditional Mesopotamian themes.[28] The precise routes of transmission escape us, but clearly texts traveled among Jews over the course of these centuries.

---

[26] The eastern origins are especially clear in the discussion of Paul-Alain Beaulieu, 'Nabonidus, the Mad King: A Reconsideration of His Steles from Harran and Babylon', in Marlies Heinz and Marian H. Feldman (eds.), *Representations of Political Power: Case Histories from Times of Change and Dissolving Order in the Ancient Near East* (Winona Lake, IN: Eisenbrauns, 2007) pp. 137–166, who discusses the Harran Stele, the Verse Account, the Nabonidus Chronicle, and especially the Chronicle about Shulgi, as relevant Mesopotamian texts for the background of the Prayer of Nabonidus.

[27] Takamitsu Muraoka, 'The Aramaic of the Old Targum of Job from Qumran Cave XI', *JJS* 25 (1974), pp. 425–43 (esp. 442).

[28] See discussion in Aaron Koller, 'Negotiating Empire: Living Jewishly Under the Achaemenids in Persia and Palestine', in Aaron Koller and Daniel Tsadik (eds.) *Iran, Israel, and the Jews: Symbiosis and Conflict from the Achaemenids to the Islamic Republic* (Eugene, OR: Pickwick Publications, 2019) pp. 3–23 (17–18).

The second point is the deduction that this text had a long history of transmission and transmutation. It has often been observed that the change from Nabonidus to Nebuchadnezzar is reasonable since Nabonidus was soon forgotten, whereas Nebuchadnezzar lived on in the memory of the Jews.[29] On this reasoning, the Prayer of Nabonidus could not have been a second-century, or, probably, even a third-century composition, and perhaps not even a fourth-century composition. It could have been a fifth-century composition, or even a sixth-century composition – in any event, centuries older than the copy we possess.[30]

It stands to reason that the text that happens to have been found at Qumran is not the only text that circulated in antiquity. Instead, it seems safe to assume that other texts had similar lives. It may well be that the *preservation* of the Prayer of Nabonidus is related to the fact that it belongs to a genre similar to the stories of Daniel, which extol the virtue of court Jews in the diaspora.

---

[29] See n. 12 above. For thorough discussion of the use of Nabonidus in Jewish literature, see Carol A. Newsom, 'Why Nabonidus? Excavating Traditions from Qumran, the Hebrew Bible, and Neo-Babylonian Sources', in Sarianna Metso, Hindy Najman, and Eileen Schuller (eds.), *The Dead Sea Scrolls: Transmission of Traditions and Production of Texts* (STDJ, 92, Leiden and Boston: Brill, 2010) pp. 57–79, and Newsom, 'Now You See Him, Now You Don't: Nabonidus in Jewish Memory', in Diana V. Edelman and Ehud Ben Zvi (eds.), *Remembering Biblical Figures in the Late Persian and Early Hellenistic Periods: Social Memory and Imagination* (Oxford: Oxford University Press, 2013) pp. 270–282.

[30] Contrariwise, Caroline Waerzeggers, 'The *Prayer of Nabonidus* in the Light of Hellenistic Babylonian Literature', in Mladen Popović, Myles Schoonover, and Marijn Vandenberghe (eds.), *Jewish Cultural Encounters in the Ancient Mediterranean and Near Eastern World* (JSJSup, 178, Leiden: Brill, 2017) pp. 64–75, has argued that the Jewish texts should be seen as part of an ongoing scholarly interest in Nabonidus that continued through the Hellenistic period. This scenario cannot be ruled out, but it should be stressed that the story in Daniel 4 is almost certainly older than that, and – assuming the story of Nabonidus was adapted as a Jewish story once, rather than twice – this militates for the conventional view that the Jewish story comes from the Persian period rather than later. Waerzeggers' argument would still be relevant then for the context of the *transmission* of the story, but not for its composition.

This very reasoning would therefore suggest that this text is exceptional only in its survival (which of course it is), but that in Second Temple times, there were many Jewish Aramaic tales circulating.

The Prayer of Nabonidus itself, when triangulated with the known record of Nabonidus' own inscriptions narrating his reign and the biblical story of Daniel 4, allows us to consider further just how this story developed – and thus to get an idea of what other related stories likely circulated in the intervening centuries. The complexity of the development of the narrative is shown in the following conjectural chart. In suggesting this development, I am making a number of assumptions – plausible ones, I think, but assumptions that should be noted:

1. This collection of stories began with the historical events of Nabonidus' reign. All of our sources agree that extraordinarily, he spent much of his time as king in the oasis town of Tayma, and that he focused much of his religious attention there on the god Sin.[31]
2. There was, of course, an official royal narrative that described Nabonidus' stay in the desert in positive terms, 'published' on a regular basis during Nabonidus' reign. The king himself claimed to have moved out of Babylon because of the impiety of the Babylonians, who sinned against Sin.[32]
3. At the same time, or very soon thereafter, there circulated less charitable versions of Nabonidus' actions. People decried Nabonidus' impiety and sacrilege, and criticized other aspects of his personality and reign. We have no way of knowing exactly how quickly they were put into writing, but this seems to have been done quite soon, within a few years of the end of his reign.[33]

---

[31] For a historian's account of the reign of Nabonidus, see Paul-Alain Beaulieu, *The Reign of Nabonidus, King of Babylon, 556–539 BC* (New Haven: Yale University Press, 1989). For a conjecture as to the 'real' reason for Nabonidus' move to Tayma, see p. 184 there.

[32] Beaulieu, *The Reign of Nabonidus*, pp. 62–63, 184.

[33] See Beaulieu, 'Nabonidus, the Mad King', discussing especially the Verse Account.

4. It seems unlikely that the Jews were the only, or even the first, subjects of Nabonidus' kingdom to write counter-narratives of his reign. Thus the existence of Jewish literature of this genre implies the prior and contemporary existence of non-Jewish literature of this sort.
5. This literature was likely in Aramaic.
6. There were different versions that mocked Nabonidus in different ways. Some (like the forerunner of Daniel 4) claimed that Nabonidus had retreated to the desert because he had turned into an animal. Others (like the forerunner of the Prayer of Nabonidus) mocked him as having a skin disease.

Some of the details in this chart are of heuristic value only: some of the motifs could have been introduced earlier or later than they are shown here, and there are alternative branching schema that are possible as well. The point of this is to show visually how the story could have developed into the forms actually known to us, and to emphasize just how complicated this development must have been.

As is also clear from this chart, the story did not stop developing once it adopted a particular motif, either. Rainer Albertz argued that the version reflected in the Greek is even older than that preserved in the Aramaic text,[34] and Michael Segal showed that both the MT and the Old Greek versions of Daniel 4 have elements that are secondary relative to the other.[35]

---

[34] Rainer Albertz, *Der Gott des Daniel: Untersuchungen zu Daniel 4–6 in der Septuagintafassung sowie zu Komposition und Theologie des aramäischen Danielbuches* (SBS, 131, Stuttgart: Verlag Katholisches Bibelwerk, 1988). See also Albertz, 'The Social Setting of the Aramaic and Hebrew Book of Daniel', in John J. Collins and Peter W. Flint with the assistance of Cameron VanEpps (eds.), *The Book of Daniel: Composition and Reception* (VTSup, 83, Leiden: Brill, 2001) I, pp. 171–204.

[35] Michael Segal, *Dreams, Riddles, and Visions: Textual, Contextual, and Intertextual Approaches to the Book of Daniel* (BZAW, 455, Berlin: De Gruyter, 2016) pp. 94–131. For further evidence of a pre-MT version, in part preserved in Greek, see R. Timothy McLay, 'The Old Greek

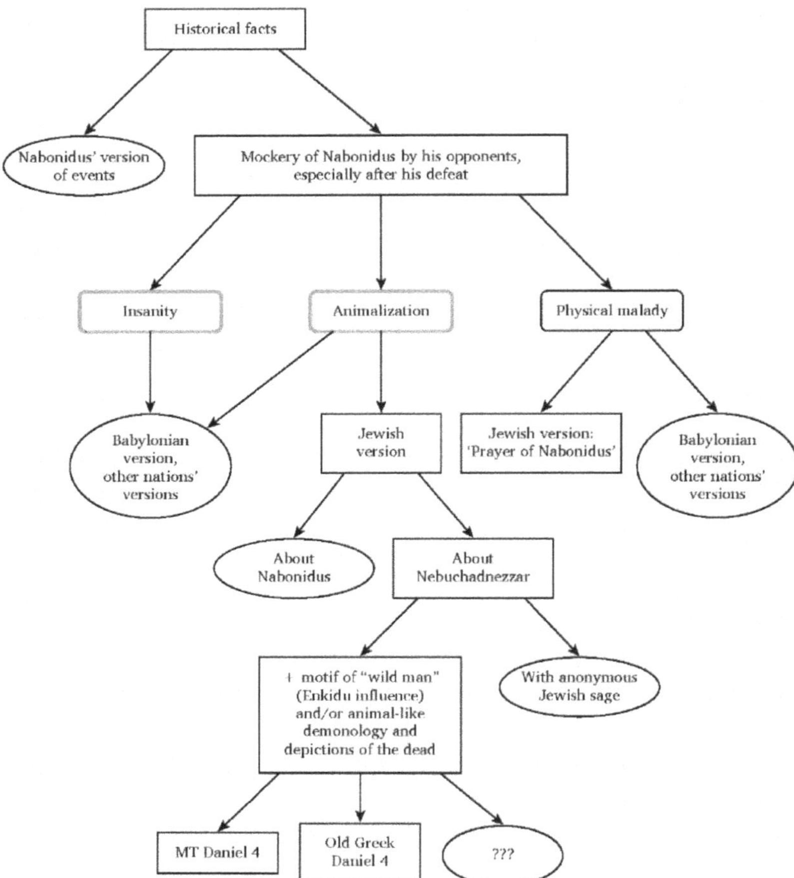

This is all to the point, however. Stories are told and re-told. All the versions of this particular story share a common basic theme: the degradation of the Babylonian king and the accompanying glory given to the God of Israel, conveyed to the king through a Jewish wise man. But so many of the surrounding details are fluid. Is the story better told with the king animalized or insane?

Translation of Daniel IV–VI and the Formation of the Book of Daniel', *VT* 55 (2005), pp. 304–323.

Should the Jewish sage be one well known or anonymous? Is the king the great Nebuchadnezzar, or the controversial Nabonidus? All these may have changed from telling to telling as the story traveled around the Near East.

Not all texts could be subjected to this type of analysis: for many texts we simply do not have the requisite data. It seems that at least three data points may be needed to start spinning out what else must have existed around those three points. There could perhaps be parallel discussions regarding the 'Persian Court Tales' of 4Q550, which may also come from between the mid-fifth century and mid-fourth centuries. There is nothing particularly Jewish about the preserved sections, raising the possibility that the Qumran community also preserves for us fragments of the broader Aramaic literature of the second half of the first millennium BCE, otherwise known to us from the tale of Inaros from Sheikh Faḍl,[36] the extraordinary P. Amherst 63, and especially the Tale of Two Brothers therein,[37] and of course the Aḥiḳar papyrus from Elephantine.

The most important point, however, is simply that there was a body of literature, primarily in Aramaic, circulating during the Persian period, and that the Jewish literature was a subset of that. The texts known to us – collected in the Bible or accidentally preserved at Qumran, for example – are the most fragmentary remains, the faintest echoes of this literature.

---

[36] Tawny Holm, 'The Sheikh Faḍl Inscription in Its Literary and Historical Context', *AS* 5 (2007), pp. 193–224.
[37] See Karel van der Toorn, *Papyrus Amherst 63* (AOAT, 448, Münster: Ugarit-Verlag, 2018), and especially Richard C. Steiner, *The Aramaic Text in Demotic Script: Text, Translation, and Notes*, online publication (2017, available at https://www.academia.edu/31662776/The_Aramaic_Text_in_Demotic_Script_Text_Translation_and_Notes).

SURVEY OF THE INTERPRETATIONS OF THE 'SON OF GOD' IN 4Q246

PETER Y. LEE

1. INTRODUCTION

In the Aramaic text 4Q246, an enigmatic figure appears who is referred to as the 'Son of God' (ברה די אל), and an enormous amount of scholarship has been devoted to identifying this figure. Because of the great interest in this question, 4Q246 has become known as the 'Son of God' text. Only two columns of the text itself are preserved with the first column torn in half.[1] It reads as follows:

Column 1[2]

1. [......ע]לוהי שרת נפל קדם כרסיא
2. רגז ושניך[4] אתה[3][.....מ]לכא [ ]עלמא
3. [.......]א חזוך וכלא אתה עד עלמא

[1] The Israel Antiquities Authority has provided online photographs of this manuscript at http://www.deadseascrolls.org.il/explore-the-archive/manuscript/4Q246–1.

[2] Translations are my own.

[3] The parchment has a lacuna preceding this word, below which the scribe has drawn something resembling a circle. Some have read this circle as a *mem*.

[4] I follow Edward M. Cook, who takes אתה in 1.2, 3 as the G-participle 'to come' and not as the 2ms independent pronoun, which would be אנתה ('4Q246', *BBR* 5 [1995], p. 49).

4. [.....ר]ברבין עקה תתא על ארעא
5. [.......]ונחשירון רב ב[מ]דינתא
6. [.......]מלך אתור [ומ]צרין
7. [.......]רב להוה על ארעא
8. וכלא יש[מ]שון[5][.....יע]בדון
9. [.....ר]בא יתקרא ובשמה יתכנה

1. [....] settled on him. He fell before the throne
2. [....kin]g? forever. Wrath is coming and your years
3. [....] your vision and everything is coming forever
4. [....] great ones. Tribulation will come upon the land
5. [....] and slaughters. A great one in the [pr]ovince
6. [....] the king of Assyria [and E]gypt
7. [....] he will be great on the land
8. [....] they [will do] and all will se[rv]e
9. [.... g]reat he will be called and by his name he will be designated

Column 2

1. ברה די אל יתאמר ובר עליון יקרונה כזיקיא
2. כן מלכותהן תהוה שני[ן] ימלכון על[6]די חזיתא
3. ארעא וכלא ידשון עם לעם ידוש ומדינה למד[ינ]ה
4. *vacat* עד יקים עם אל וכלא יניח מן חרב
5. מלכותה מלכות עלם וכל ארחתה בקשוט ידי[ן]

---

[5] On this reconstruction, see Edward M. Cook, *Dictionary of Qumran Aramaic* (Winona Lake, IN: Eisenbrauns, 2015) p. 171.

[6] Many understand this word as חזותא, reading the *yod* as a *waw*, and thus parsing this as a noun meaning 'vision' rather than as a verb. Émile Puech observes that the distinction between *yod* and *waw* orthographically is difficult ('Fragment d'une apocalypse en araméen (4Q246 = pseudo-Dan[d]) et le "royaume de Dieu"', *RB* 99 (1992), pp. 98–131 [105]). Cook comments that the determined state of 'vision' would be חזוא, not חזותא, and therefore, this cannot be the noun 'vision', but rather the verb 'you saw' ('4Q246', pp. 46, 55). This word is part of a larger phrase that begins at the end of 2.1 and continues into 2.2, כזיקיא די חזיתא 'like the comets which you saw'. Given the proper verbal identity, this line is significant since it provides the only piece of information in the manuscript that reveals the content of a previous dream.

6. ארעא בקשט וכלא יעבד שלם חרב מן ארעא יסף
7. וכל מדינתא לה יסגדון אל רבא באילה
8. הוא יעבד לה קרב עממין ינתן בידה וכלהן
9. ירמה קדמוהי שלטנה שלטן עלם וכל תהוסי

1. It will be said (that he is) the son of God and the son of the Most High they will call him. Like the comets
2. which you saw, so shall be their kingdom. (A few) year[s] they will rule over
3. the earth and they will trample everything, people will trample people and provinces (will trample[7]) provi[nc]es.
4. [*vacat*] Until he establishes the people of God and brings rest to everything from the sword.
5. His kingdom will be an eternal kingdom and all his ways will be righteous. He will jud[ge]
6. the earth justly, and he will make everyone to be at peace. The sword shall cease from the land,
7. and every province shall pay homage to him. The great god will be his strength.
8. He himself will make war for him/them. He will give the nations into his hand, and all of them
9. he will place before him. His dominion will be an eternal dominion and all of the deeps...

The fragmentary nature of the text makes it difficult to be certain of the activities, events, and even the persons who are described within it. There is, however, a clear mention of distress that will come upon the land and the disastrous reign of enemies, which will be short-lived. This will last 'Until he establishes the people of God and brings rest to everything from the sword' (2.4). The opening lines of the completely preserved second column mention a significant figure who is referred to as the 'Son of God' and 'Son of the Most High'. Scholars have long linked these epithets with the same titles used in the New Testament, particularly in Lk. 1.32–35 in reference to Jesus of Nazareth. However, the interpretations on the identity of this mysterious 'Son of God'

[7] The verb 'trample' is gapped, suggesting the possibility that this text is poetic.

figure in its pre-Christian, Jewish setting have been wide-ranging. Many have proposed different restorations of the fragmentary first column, based on their interpretations of this 'Son of God' figure. The purpose of this essay is to survey the major, proposed interpretations by scholars on the identity of the 'Son of God' figure.[8]

Tucker S. Ferda, whose interpretation will be described below, has provided a helpful taxonomy of the numerous views for the 'Son' of 4Q246 as either positive or negative.[9] Although he does not define what is meant by these terms, their basic meaning is clear. The 'positive' view sees the 'Son' as someone who is fulfilling a divine purpose or plan against the enemies of God—a protagonist. The 'negative' view is simply the opposite: someone who is generally hostile against God, opposing his divine will—an antagonist. Within this broad categorization, more specific views have been proposed. This essay will follow this general approach by grouping the various views into their interpretative genus then further elaborating on their particular species.

2. NEGATIVE INTERPRETATIONS

2.1. The Seleucid King Alexander Balas

Any discussion of the interpretation of the 'Son of God' in 4Q246 must begin with the work of J. T. Milik, who was the first to present this text in a lecture given at Harvard University in

---

[8] Martin Hengel interprets the 'Son of God' as 'the Jewish people, like the Son of Man in Daniel 7:13' (*The Son of God: The Origins of Christology and the History of Jewish-Hellenistic Religion* [Philadelphia: Fortress Press, 1976] p. 45), but his interpretation has not stirred much of a following.

[9] Tucker S. Ferda, 'Naming the Messiah: A Contribution to the 4Q246 "Son of God" Debate', *DSD* 21 (2014), pp. 153–157. He says that there have been two general arguments used to support one of the two general views. The first, in support of a negative view, presumes a chronological development in the text. The second, in support of a positive view, focuses on the literary background of the titles 'Son of God' and 'Son of the Most High'. As will be discussed later, Ferda proposes a third option based on a rhetorical-critical analysis.

1972.[10] His views were made known within the published works by Joseph A. Fitzmyer.[11] According to Milik, the text describes a seer who, moved by the spirit,[12] kneels down before the throne of God and gives a historical description of the Seleucid period, as far as the *vacat* in 2.4. From this point begins the description of a global peace which is to come. The narrative of the coming evils would thus have a historical (not eschatological) character and the 'Son of God' would be a Seleucid king. In this case, Milik proposes Alexander Balas, son of Antiochus IV Epiphanes and successor to Demetrius I Soter. According to Milik, those titles would suit him admirably since he appears as 'Deo Patre Natus' and θεοπάτωρ on coins. Thus, Milik reconstructs 1.8–9 as follows:

וכלא ישמשון [לה חלפת מלכא ר]בא יתקרא ובשמה יתכנה

> And all of them will serve [him. Successor of the G]reat [King] he will be called and with his name will he name himself

The reference to the 'Great King' would be none other than Alexander the Great, and, in fact, Alexander Balas bore his very name.

Some scholars have criticized Milik's view. First, it does not seem likely that a Jewish text would tolerate an exalted title as 'Son of God', 'Son of the Most High', or even 'Great King' (his restoration of 1.9) for a pagan king. As John J. Collins says, 'If this reference was to a Syrian king, we would expect to find some indication in this Jewish text that the title was inappropriate. If

---

[10] Although this text was entrusted to J. T. Milik for publication in 1958, he never did so. He refers to it in two other writings: *The Books of Enoch: Aramaic Fragments of Qumran Cave 4* (Oxford: Clarendon Press, 1976) p. 60, and 'Les modèles araméens du livre d'Esther dans la grotte 4 de Qumrân', *RevQ* 15 (1992), pp. 321–406 (383–384).

[11] Joseph A. Fitzmyer, 'The Contribution of Qumran Aramaic to the Study of the New Testament', *NTS* 20 (1973–74), pp. 382–407, reprinted with a supplement in *A Wandering Aramean: Collected Aramaic Essays* (Missoula, MT: Scholars Press, 1979), pp. 85–107. Fitzmyer also set out the parallels between this text and the Gospel of Luke in his commentary, *The Gospel According to Luke I-IX* (AB, 28, Garden City, NY: Doubleday, 1981) pp. 205–206, 347–348.

[12] According to Fitzmyer ('Contribution', p. 111), Milik would restore [רוחה] at the beginning of 1.1, '[and his spirit] rested up[on him]'.

the Son of God was viewed negatively, we would expect the text to tell of his downfall'.[13] Frank Moore Cross also criticizes the identity of a pagan king and says that the titles found in 2.1 ('Son of God' and 'Son of the Most High') are given in their Hebrew forms. He suggests that this makes it implausible that they be applied to anyone but an Israelite king.[14]

Of a more serious nature and with no textual basis is the introduction of the 'Great King' and of the idea of succession. Even if one admits that the mysterious personage referred to is Alexander Balas, what is the meaning of the titles applied to him in this text? We do know Balas bestowed the high priesthood on Jonathan, but are we to conclude from this that the author of the text was a member of the Maccabean party and that he was therefore satisfied with the pagan titles of the Seleucid king, or whether he was an opponent of the Maccabees and the Seleucids and his inclusion of the titles has no other purpose than that of identifying the enemy?

2.2. Antiochus IV Epiphanes

Émile Puech interprets the 'Son of God' similarly to Milik. Whereas Milik identified the 'Son of God' as the Seleucid king Alexander Balas, so Puech identifies him as Antiochus IV Epiphanes, although he does not rule out the possibility that this can be a positive messianic figure.[15] He agrees with Fitzmyer that

---

[13] John J. Collins, 'A Pre-Christian "Son of God" among the Dead Sea Scrolls', *BR* 9 (1993), pp. 34–38 (36).

[14] Frank Moore Cross, 'Notes on the Doctrine of the Two Messiahs at Qumran and the Extracanonical Daniel Apocalypse (4Q246)', in D. W. Parry and S. D. Ricks (eds.), *Current Research and Technological Developments on the Dead Sea Scrolls* (STDJ, 20, Leiden: Brill, 1996) pp. 1–13 (12). We should also note that it is not certain that the throne in this context is to be seen as the throne of God, as Milik suggested. It seems more fitting to picture the throne of a king here. A description of the sequence of the story before the king is perfectly in line with prophetic conduct and with the Book of Daniel, whose influence in column two is without dispute.

[15] Émile Puech, 'Some Remarks on 4Q246 and 4Q521 and Qumran Messianism', in D. W. Parry and S. D. Ricks (eds.), *The Provo International Conference on the Dead Sea Scrolls: Technological Innovations, New Texts,*

the absence of the word משיח confirms that this is not a messianic figure. However, where Fitzmyer continues to view the 'Son of God' as a protagonist (i.e., a Jewish king in the line of David), Puech views him as an antagonist, specifically Antiochus IV Epiphanes.[16]

One defense of Puech's view is in his analysis of the overall structure of the text, an argument commonly used by those who hold to a negative interpretation of the 'Son of God'. Puech sees the structure of this text as being in two parts. The first covers 1.1–2.3, in which negative descriptions are given (i.e., tribulations on earth, wars, slaughters between nations).[17] It is in this section that the 'Son of God' is mentioned, and Puech suggests that this mysterious figure is using this title to identify himself with the prerogatives of deity. Puech says that such a description fits well with Antiochus IV Epiphanes, who in 2 Macc. 9.8–12 is described as possessing a near superhuman boastfulness and in Dan. 11.36–38 as arrogant and blaspheming, magnifying himself above every god. Only with the *vacat* in 2.4 does the positive part of the text begin with the rise of the people of God and their subsequent reception of the kingdom of peace.

---

and Reformulated Issues (STDJ, 30, Leiden: Brill, 1996) pp. 545–565; 'Le fils de Dieu, le fils du Très-Haut, messie roi en 4Q246', in Oliver Artus et al (eds.), *Le jugement dans l'un et l'autre testament: Mélanges offert à Raymond Kuntzmann* (LD, 197; Paris: Ed du Cerf, 2004) pp. 271–286. In two earlier articles, Puech had not yet established an opinion on the identity of the 'Son of God' (*pace* e.g., Cross, 'Extracanonical Daniel Apocalypse', p. 5), only allowing for the possibility of a messianic interpretation, without explicitly holding to such a view ('Fragment', pp. 98–131, and 'Notes sur le fragment d'apocalypse 4Q246 – <le fils de Dieu>', *RB* 101 [1994], pp. 533–558). Later, he took the negative interpretation of Antiochus IV Epiphanes.

[16] Émile Puech, '4QApocryphe de Daniel ar', in George Brooke et al. in consultation with James VanderKam (eds.), *Qumran Cave 4. XVII: Parabiblical texts, Part 3* (DJD, 22, Oxford: Clarendon, 1996) pp. 165–184 (173–174).

[17] Ferda ('Naming the Messiah', pp. 156, 158–163) argues against using chronology and general structure as support for a negative interpretation of the 'Son of God'.

Edward M. Cook also has identified the 'Son of God' as Antiochus IV Epiphanes.[18] He suggests that the identity of this figure is clarified when we see that the literary tradition most influential on the text is not the biblical Book of Daniel (as many earlier interpreters had presumed), but rather the Akkadian prophecy texts.[19] In fact, Cook argues that there is a direct relationship between several Akkadian prophetic texts and the 'Son of God' text. Provided below is a chart that he produced to show this correlation:[20]

4Q246	Akkadian Prophecies
'tribulation will come upon the land' (1.4)	'there will be a hard time in the land' (Uruk, ob., line 9) 'confusion, disturbance, and disorder in the land' (Text A, first side, ii.13)
'a prince of nations [will arise]' (2.4) 'the people of God will arise' (2.4) 'he will be master over the land' (1.7)	'a prince will arise' (common to all texts) 'he will become master over the land' (Uruk, rev., 10, 16; Marduk Prophecy III.20)
Oppression and submission	'he shall oppress the land' (Dynastic Prophecy ii.14) 'the lands will be given together to the king of Babylon and Nippur' (Shulgi Prophecy III.1)
'[his son] will be called Great, and by his name he will be designated' (1.9)	'after him his son will arise as king in Uruk and become master over the world' (Uruk, rev., 16) 'after him his son shall sit on the throne' (Dynastic Prophecy ii.9)
'like the meteors that you saw, so will be their kingdom' (2.2)	Astronomical omens of Text B

[18] Cook, '4Q246', p. 63.

[19] For more detailed comments regarding these Akkadian texts, see A. K. Grayson and W. G. Lambert, 'Akkadian Prophecies', *JCS* 18 (1964), pp. 7–30; Herman Hunger and Stephen A. Kaufman, 'A New Akkadian Prophecy Text', *JAOS* 95 (1975), pp. 371–375.

[20] Cook, '4Q246', pp. 60–61.

'people will crush people, nation will crush nation' (2.4) 'the sword' as a symbol of violence (2.4, 6)	'city against city, tribe against tribe' (Text B 15) 'friends will cast one another to the ground with the sword, comrades will destroy one another with the sword' (Shulgi V)
'(a few) years they will reign over the land' (2.2) 'his/their kingdom is an eternal kingdom' (2.5) 'he/they shall judge the land in truth' (2.5–6)	'he shall reign for X years' (common to all texts) 'his dynasty shall be established forever' (Uruk, rev., 17) 'he will provide justice in the land, he will give right decisions for the land' (Uruk, rev., 17)
'The Great God is his help, he himself shall fight for him' (2.7–8)	'Enlil, Shamash, and Marduk will go at the side of his army' (Dynastic iii.15–16) 'I [Marduk], god of all, will befriend him, he will destroy Elam' (Marduk 21–22)

In addition to common literary elements and expressions, Cook also suggests that 4Q246 shares the method of Akkadian prophecies to 'foretell' history in terms of the rise of a series of unnamed rulers, their reigns characterized as either disastrous or propitious. The final ruler in the series always inaugurates an era of prosperity. He suggests that the purpose of 4Q246, like the Akkadian prophecies, was for political propaganda to support and justify the final reign.[21] According to Cook, if we assume that 4Q246 is to be characterized as political propaganda, then the Maccabean revolt immediately suggests itself as the true referent of the rise of the people of God. This is what leads Cook to identify the 'Son of God' as Antiochus IV Epiphanes. Cook also suggests that the expansion of the Seleucid realm under Antiochus III to include Judea and Samaria might be referred to in the fragmentary first column, and the continued battles with the Ptolemies is the phrase עם לעם ידוש ומדינה למדינה 'people will crush people, nation (will crush) nation' (2.3).

[21] Cook, '4Q246', pp. 64–65.

There is a significant difference between the Akkadian prophecies and its alleged Qumran counterpart. The message in 4Q246 is almost a near reversal of the Akkadian prophecy that it allegedly resembles, namely the Uruk prophecy. The end of that Akkadian text tells of the rise of a benevolent ruler, who is succeeded by a son, who then initiates an eternal dynasty. For Cook, 4Q246 reflects a similar scenario with the rise of a father and son, but their reign is brief: כזיקיא די חזיתא כן מלכותהן תהוה 'like the comets which you saw, thus shall be their kingdom' (2.1–2). The eternal kingdom belongs to the people of God, as does the eternal dynasty and peace. In response to this clear reversal, Cook suggests that this text is to be understood as an example of Judean 'counter-prophecy' to the prophecies possibly used by the Seleucids. According to Cook, it is conceivable that the advent of the Seleucids was accompanied by the dissemination of these Akkadian-type prophecies as propaganda to speak favorably of the Seleucid reign. Seen from this perspective, Cook suggests that 4Q246 is best understood as a sample of Jewish counter-propaganda to the Seleucids, 'which resulted in turning the Akkadian prophecy genre against itself'.[22]

The entire notion of Akkadian prophecy texts as the literary background to 4Q246 is a novel suggestion that has merit. However, scholars who hold to a positive interpretation of the 'Son of God' are not persuaded. In response to Cook, Collins states that he is ultimately unconvinced by Cook's suggestions, although very intrigued by them.[23] The reasons for his rejection are as follows:

1. The parallels to the Akkadian prophecy texts are still conjectures, whereas the allusions to Jewish apocalypticism, such as the Book of Daniel (specifically Daniel

[22] Cook, '4Q246', p. 66.
[23] John J. Collins, 'The "Son of God" Text from Qumran', in Martinus De Boer (ed.), *From Jesus to John: Essays on Jesus and Christology in Honour of Marinus de Jonge* (JSNTSup, 84, Sheffield: JSOT Press, 1993) pp. 51–62.

7[24]) are explicit and obvious. The apparent parallels with the Akkadian prophecy texts may be indirect since the Book of Daniel and the Akkadian prophecies share similar features.

2. Antiochus IV Epiphanes was never called 'the Great' and Antiochus III was never king of both Syria and Egypt. In fact, no Seleucid king ever reigned over those two regions.
3. If the 'Son of God' figure was indeed a reference to a Seleucid king at the time of the Maccabean revolt, it stands to reason that such a figure would be subject to judgment. No such judgment is passed when the people of God arise.[25]
4. As we have seen Collins argue before, the sequential logic of the text does not require us to regard everything prior to the rise of the people of God as negative since apocalyptic texts often repeat an event multiple times.[26]
5. The closest parallel to the titles found in 2.1 are those found in Lk. 1.32–35.[27]

---

[24] It is possible that 1.8 uses the same verb ישמשון as in Dan. 7.10. However, the verb דוש clearly appears in 2.3 (twice) and Dan. 7.23 within an apocalyptic context. Also, the phrase מלכותה מלכות עלם in 2.5 also occurs in Dan. 3.22; 7.27.

[25] It is possible that such a judgment could have been described in a non-extant col. 3 of this text.

[26] Collins, 'The "Son of God" Text', p. 70. Collins uses Daniel 7 as an example of such repetitiveness in apocalyptic literature. Cook ('4Q246', pp. 60–61) correctly notes that the example of Daniel 7 is misconceived since the giving of the kingdom is not narrated over and over again; he says it is narrated once and interpreted twice. He also says that the rise of the 'people of God' and the 'Son of Man' are discrete events separated by tribulation, not reiterations or reinterpretations of the same event.

[27] Cook ('4Q246', p. 60) says that although there is a likeness between 4Q246 and Lk. 1.32–35, the study of this text has suffered from a tendency to read it in light of that Gospel passage. He suggests that this is reading Christian interpretations back into a text that only shares *prima facie* similarities.

2.3. Proto Anti-Christ

David Flusser offers another negative proposal. He identifies the 'Son of God' as the leader of the destructive nations mentioned throughout the text and as the figure who will develop into the Anti-Christ, infamously mentioned within later Christian writings.[28] According to Flusser, the true protagonist of the text 'is not a messiah, but Israel, the people of God who will be then the guarantor of world peace'.[29] For Flusser, the *vacat* that opens 2.4 is the beginning of a new section, describing the rise and victory of the people of God. Thus, everything that precedes this line describes this destructive leader. All those who hold to a negative interpretation of the 'Son of God' make this similar argument regarding the structure of the text with the transition from a negative section to a positive one at 2.4.

Flusser compares the 'Son of God' to the 'man of lawlessness' in the New Testament, specifically in 2 Thess. 1.1–12, the 'Beast of the Sea' in Rev. 13.8–12, as well as with other extrabiblical, apocalyptic texts, such as Asc. Isa. 4.2–16 and the *Oracles of Hystaspes*. Asc. Isa. 4.2–16 speaks of the incarnation of an antagonist in whom all peoples will believe and to whom they will sacrifice; the *Oracles of Hystaspes* describes one who will destroy humanity, call himself God, and order that he himself be worshipped. Thus, the Qumran texts speak of the hubris of such a figure.

As noteworthy as these parallels are, Flusser's position rests primarily on understanding the verb יע[בדון (1.8) as a Hebraism to mean 'worship'. Also, as noted by both Florentino García Martínez and Fitzmyer, another weakness in Flusser's interpretation is that the literary evidence he uses comes from the Christian sources about the Anti-Christ mentioned in the previous paragraph.[30] Although he insists that the concept of a figure like

---

[28] David Flusser, 'The Hubris of the Antichrist in a Fragment from Qumran', *Immanuel* 10 (1980), pp. 31–37.

[29] Flusser, 'Hubris', p. 33.

[30] Florentino García Martínez, 'The Eschatological Figure of 4Q246' in *Qumran and Apocalyptic: Studies on the Aramaic Texts from Qumran* (STDJ, 9, Leiden: Brill, 1996) pp. 162–179 (171); Joseph A. Fitzmyer, 'The Aramaic "Son of God" Text from Qumran Cave 4', in Michael O. Wise,

the Anti-Christ exists in Jewish and pre-Christian literature, it seems that he is too heavily influenced by these Christian texts. It is true that there are wicked opponents found in Qumran sectarian texts (e.g., Melchi-Resha who opposes Melchizedek in 11QMelchizedek; the 'sons of darkness' in 1QS and 1QM), but such antagonists are not necessarily *anti-messiah*. Flusser correctly points to a transition in the text in 2.4. It does not follow, however, that everything that precedes it is negative. It is characteristic of apocalyptic texts to describe themes or time-periods repeatedly through various different perspectives. As an example, Collins suggests that Daniel 7 narrates the giving of the kingdom to the people of God three times, and this is not to be interpreted as three different events.[31]

2.4. The Fourth Beast of Daniel 7

Another proposed identification of the 'Son of God' comes from Michael Segal.[32] Daniel 7 has already been well documented as a literary background to 4Q246. In addition to that, Segal suggests there is an allusion to Psalm 82 that has been unnoticed by previous scholars. According to Segal, the epithet 'Son of the Most High' (בר עליון), which occurs as a second title in 2.1, is not attested in the Hebrew Bible with the singular 'Son'. The plural 'sons', however, is found in Ps. 82.6, 'sons of the Most High' (בְּנֵי עֶלְיוֹן), which he suggests marks a clear connection between this psalm and 4Q246. Segal says that Psalm 82 is a record of divine beings, who are called 'gods' (אֱלֹהִים) and 'sons of the Most High' (בְּנֵי עֶלְיוֹן). Their actions, however, were not consistent with their

---

Norman Golb, John J. Collins, and Dennis G. Pardee (eds.), *Methods of Investigation of the Dead Sea Scrolls and the Khirbet Qumran Site: Present Realities and Future Prospects* (Annals of the New York Academy of Sciences, 722, New York: New York Academy of Sciences, 1994) pp. 163–178 (169–170); Fitzmyer, *The Dead Sea Scrolls and Christian Origins* (Grand Rapids, MI: Eerdmans, 2000) p. 57. Future references will be to the version in *The Dead Sea Scrolls and Christian Origins* (hereafter, *DSSCO*).

[31] Collins, 'Son of God', p. 36.

[32] Michael Segal, 'Who is the "Son of God" in 4Q246? An Overlooked Example of Early Biblical Interpretation', *DSD* 21 (2014), pp. 289–312.

divine designations in that they were unjust judges and showed partiality to the wicked (v.2). Because of these wicked actions, they lost their divine status and became mortals, subject to death 'like men' (v.7). Segal suggests that the 'Son of God' and 'Son of the Most High' of 4Q246 are paraphrases of the 'sons of the Most High' of Ps. 82.6. In both cases, the 'name of the object does not match its reality'.[33] Meaning, like the 'sons of the Most High' in Ps. 82.6, the 'Son' of 4Q246 no longer retains his divine status, but rather is punished for an immoral or unjust act that is not mentioned in the extant manuscript.

Segal says that Psalm 82 is also the literary background of Daniel 7. Just as Psalm 82 describes the fall of divine beings, so Daniel 7 describes the fall of four bestial creatures who arose from a great sea (v.2). Since the fall of the 'Son of God' of 4Q246 parallels the fall of the divine beings of Psalm 82 and these divine beings are the referent to the fall of the four beasts of Daniel 7, Segal suggests that the 'Son' of 4Q246 is to be identified with one of the beasts of Daniel 7. He proposes the fourth beast, which he takes as representative of Greece.[34] For Segal, therefore, this individual is not connected with the 'one like the son of a man' in Dan. 7.14, nor is he a 'human sovereign over an earthly kingdom nor a divine messianic figure'.[35]

The connection between the 'Son of the Most High' in 2.1 with the 'sons of the Most High' in Ps. 82.6 is intriguing. In other proposed negative interpretations, however, the title 'Son of God'

---

[33] Segal, "Who is the 'Son of God'", p. 307. To support his argument, he cites Noam Mizrahi's unpublished M.A. thesis, *The Aramaic 'Son of God' Scroll from Qumran (4Q246): Exegetical Problems in Linguistic Perspective* [Hebrew] (M.A. Thesis, Hebrew University of Jerusalem, 2001). Segal notes, however, this his interpretation of the text differs from that of Mizrahi ('Who is the "Son of God"', p. 306, n. 39).

[34] Segal ('Who is the "Son of God"', p. 312) gives three arguments for identifying the 'Son' with the fourth beast. First, he takes the reference to the 'king(s) of Assyria and Egypt' in 1.6 as representing the Seleucid and Ptolemaic kingdoms. Second, the verb דוש, which is used twice in 2.3, also occurs in Dan. 7.23, describing the fourth kingdom. Third, he says the fighting in 1.4–2.3 is similar to the battles of the Hellenistic empire in Daniel 11.

[35] Segal, 'Who is the "Son of God"', p. 311.

and 'Son of the Most High' have within them a negative connotation. For Segal, these divine titles are not negative in themselves, but rather, those with these titles are viewed as negative because they do not behave consistently with their *positive* title. As Segal states, the 'name originally assigned to an object ceases to correspond to its essence'.[36]

3. POSITIVE INTERPRETATIONS

3.1. Messianic Interpretations

The majority of scholars who have studied this text hold to the interpretation that the 'Son of God' is a positive figure. Of this group, many identify the 'Son' as a messianic figure.[37] This survey will describe the works of three such scholars, namely Collins, Cross, and Ferda.[38] Collins considers the use of the title 'Son of God' to be an early interpretation of the 'one like the Son of Man' in Dan. 7.14.[39] He admits that the word 'messiah' is not (and most likely was not) used in 4Q246. However, in defense of his messianic identification of the Son of God figure, he says that

---

[36] Segal, 'Who is the "Son of God"', p. 310.

[37] Others not discussed in this survey who hold to a messianic interpretation include the following: Seyoon Kim, *The "Son of Man" as the Son of God* (WUNT, 30, Tübingen: J. C. B. Mohr, 1983) pp. 20–22; Robert Eisenman and Michael Wise, 'The Son of God (4Q246)', in *The Dead Sea Scrolls Uncovered* (Shaftesbury, Dorset: Element, 1992) pp. 68–71; Johannes Zimmermann, 'Observations on 4Q246—The "Son of God"', in James H. Charlesworth et al. (eds.), *Qumran Messianism: Studies on the Messianic Expectations in the Dead Sea Scrolls* (Tübingen: Mohr, 1998) pp. 175–190.

[38] Collins, 'A Pre-Christian "Son of God"' and 'The "Son of God" Text'; Cross, 'Extracanonical Daniel Apocalypse'; Ferda, 'Naming the Messiah'. In addition to his aforementioned articles, Collins also analyzes 4Q246 in 'The Messiah as the Son of God', in *The Scepter and the Star* (New York: Doubleday, 1995) pp. 154–172; 'The Background of the "Son of God" Text', *BBR* 7 (1997), pp. 51–62; 'Messiahs in Context: Method in the Study of Messianism in the Dead Sea Scrolls', in *Methods of Investigation of the Dead Sea Scrolls and the Khirbet Qumran Site* (Annals of the New York Academy of Sciences, 722, New York: New York Academy of Sciences, 1994) pp. 213–229.

[39] Collins, 'The "Son of God" Text', p. 80.

during the times when there was no longer a Davidic king in Jerusalem and when the Jewish people looked increasingly to the future, the word 'messiah' took on a meaning beyond its base etymological sense of 'the anointed one'. Collins says that reference to 'the anointed one of the Lord' in Ps. 2.2 was originally written with reference to an earthly king, not of someone who was expected in the future. But he also says that passages like Ps. 2.2 in the Psalter as well as in the Prophets were commonly interpreted during the exile and beyond as referring to that expected 'messianic' figure who would restore the kingdom of Israel and who was often conceived of in a highly idealized way. Thus, Collins states, 'At the turn of the era, an heir to the Davidic throne, in an apocalyptic context, cannot be distinguished from the Davidic messiah, and we are fully justified in speaking of a messiah here, even though the word does not appear in the text'.[40]

Cross also identifies the 'Son of God' as a messianic figure, restoring the fragmentary lines 1.7–9 as follows:[41]

7 [ויקום בר אנש מלך] רב להוה על ארעא

8 [וכל אנש לה י]עבדון וכלא ישמשון כלה

9 [לה קדיש אלהא ר]בא יתקרא ובשמה יתכנה

> 7 [And there shall arise a son of man] / He shall be a great [king] over the [whole] earth
>
> 8 [And all mankind] shall serve [him], / And all shall minister [9 to him.]
>
> [The Holy One of the g]reat [God] he shall be called, / And by his name he shall be surnamed.

Cross reconstructs the sequence of messianic epithets from 1.7 to 2.1, 'Son of Man', 'Great King', 'Holy One of the great God', all of which fit in the lacunae. Not only do these epithets fit well within

---

[40] Collins, 'Pre-Christian "Son of God"', pp. 36–37. For further reading on Collin's view on messianism in the Dead Sea Scrolls, see his article 'Messiahs in Context', and his monographs *The Scepter and the Star* and *Apocalypticism in the Dead Sea Scrolls* (London: Routledge, 1997) pp. 71–90.

[41] Cross, 'Extracanonical Daniel Apocalypse', pp. 6–7.

the allotted space in the manuscript, but they also fit the conceptual context of the preserved titles ('Son of God' and 'Son of the Most High'). They also are the same titles found in Lk. 1.32–35. Cross says that the epithets in Luke 'are so striking as to suggest, if not require, that the author of the hymn quoted in Luke is dependent on a Danielic text very much like the one in 4Q246'.[42]

Ferda's identification the 'Son of God' is similar to the messianic interpretation of others, such as Collins and Cross.[43] To support his view, he contributes a new method to the study of this text and presents three arguments. First, he begins by demonstrating the literary connection (or *Tendenz*) between 4Q246 and sections of the Book of Daniel, specifically Daniel 2, 4, and 7.[44] Specifically, he notes that the importance of the verb 'serve' in 1.8 (ישמשון) is often overlooked. It also occurs in Dan. 7.10 (יְשַׁמְּשׁוּנֵּהּ), a biblical *hapax* that refers to a positive act of 'serving' by a 'thousand thousands'. He concludes, therefore, that the 'all will serve' (ישמשון) in 1.8 is most likely a positive presentation of the 'Son of God'.

Second, he uses a rhetorical-critical approach to show from biblical and extrabiblical evidence that the usages of the naming verbs in 1.9 (יתאמר and יתכנה) and 2.1 (יתאמר and יקרונה) conform to divine naming traditions, where the naming agent is God himself (less frequently, an unspecified collective). According to Ferda, the biblical occurrences of this divine designation support a positive activity of the named individual, 'for there are no cases in the Hebrew Bible of a naming activity + mention of God's name used in a negative, polemical fashion'.[45]

---

[42] Cross, 'Extracanonical Daniel Apocalypse', p. 12.

[43] Ferda, 'Naming the Messiah', pp. 150–175.

[44] Although his understanding of the background of Daniel 7 is not unique to him, he uniquely observes a close structural similarity of 4Q246 with the dream/interpretation pattern in Daniel 2 and 4. He says this observable parallel with Daniel 2 and 4 challenges a general position held among scholars that the 'Son' must be grouped with the negative activities of the 'they' in 2.2.

[45] Ferda, 'Naming the Messiah', p. 171. Ferda cites Deut. 28.10; 2 Sam. 6.2; 12.28; 1 Chr. 13.6; 2 Chr. 7.14; Isa. 43.7 as biblical examples to support his claim.

The specific *messianic* identification of the 'Son' is further clarified in his third argument where he suggests that the previously mentioned naming tradition is used to designate and commission an individual to accomplish a divinely appointed mandate. He points out how Lk. 1.32–35 follows similar patterns of naming for the purpose of accomplishing a messianic task.

Although Ferda's observations regarding the Danielic background of 4Q246 are not unprecedented, his comments regarding the importance of the verb 'serve' (ישמשון) in 1.8 are helpful, and he provides literary evidence to support his view of the naming tradition.

As popular as this interpretation of the 'Son of God' may be, it has also faced opposition. Fitzmyer has rejected this messianic interpretation for the following reasons:[46]

1. The word משיח does not occur in the text, and to impart it is gratuitous.[47]
2. The titles 'Son of God' and 'Son of the Most High' have a background in the Old Testament, but there is no clear Old Testament passage where either of these titles is used of a figure called משיח.
3. Many Old Testament passages that speak of a person being 'anointed' must be understood generically as indicative of a divine guarantee for the future of the Davidic household, or dynasty, and that 'anointed one' may be part of the continuation or even restoration of that monarchy of old. In other words, such passages express eschatological hope, but not directly eschatological messianism.

Fitzmyer does say that a lively messianic expectation existed in the Qumran community, that such an expectation was bipolar, expecting both a Davidic and priestly messiah. But he insists that there is nothing in the Old Testament or in the pre-Christian

---

[46] Fitzmyer, *DSSCO*, pp. 59–60. He makes a similar, but fuller, list of objections to a messianic interpretation in his article, '4Q246: The "Son of God" Document from Qumran', *Bib* 74 (1993), pp. 153–174 (170–173).

[47] Puech makes the same critique in '4Q246 and 4Q521', pp. 549–550.

Palestinian Jewish tradition that shows that the title 'Son of God' has a messianic nuance. To read any messianism into this text is to force a Christian interpretation upon a pre-Christian, Jewish text.

3.2. Coming, Non-Messianic Jewish Ruler

In contrast to the various messianic interpretations above is Fitzmyer's position. He considers the 'Son of God' to be a coming Jewish ruler, perhaps a member of the Hasmonean dynasty and a successor to the Davidic throne. Rather than envisaging this figure as a messiah, Fitzmyer argues that 'the text should be understood as a sectarian affirmation of God's provision and guarantee of the Davidic dynasty'.[48] Therefore, he restores 1.9 as [והוא בר אל ר]בא יתקרא '(For) he shall be called son of the great God'. He bases this restoration on 2.7, where the phrase אל רבא appears.[49] He also says that the title may be inspired by 2 Sam. 7.14. Although this passage (along with Ps. 2.7–8) refers to a future, enthroned figure from the line of David as the 'son of God', he does not believe that this title refers to a messianic figure. In fact, Fitzmyer believes that many Old Testament passages used to support the messianic interpretation of the 'Son of God'[50] are to be understood generically as a guarantee of the future Davidic household or dynasty. He bases his conclusion on the fact that the title משיח does not occur in any Old Testament text before Dan. 9.25–26 with a future sense of an awaited anointed one.[51]

García Martínez raises several objections to Fitzmyer's interpretation.[52] He says that Fitzmyer implies a link between the

---

[48] Fitzmyer, '4Q246', p. 174; 'Aramaic "Son of God" Text', p. 175; *DSSCO*, p. 60.

[49] García Martínez ('Eschatological Figure', p. 170) criticizes Fitzmyer's restoration as repetitious of what is said in the immediate context in 2.1, where the title 'Son of God' is explicit.

[50] Fitzmyer questions such Old Testament passages like 2 Sam. 7.12–16; 23.5; Gen. 49.10–12; Pss. 2; 89; 110; Isa. 9–11; Zech. 3.8; 6.12 as references to a messiah, i.e., a future, expected anointed figure to be raised up by God for the good or salvation of his people.

[51] For further details of Fitzmyer's understanding of messianism, see 'Qumran Messianism' in *DSSCO*, pp. 73–81.

[52] García Martínez, 'Eschatological Figure', pp. 170–171.

emergence of the mysterious 'Son of God' figure and the pacification, which is not found in the preserved text. He also states that it does not seem likely that, after an apparent peace-making arrangement, according to his reconstruction, the text continues to talk of one people crushing another people and one city crushing another one.

3.3. Heavenly Super Messiah

García Martínez also offers his own interpretation of the 'Son of God'.[53] After analyzing various interpretations and finding them insufficient,[54] he proposes interpreting the 'Son of God' as an 'eschatological liberator of angelic (or nonhuman) nature'.[55] The figure that García Martínez envisions is one similar to Melchizedek in 11QMelch, the Prince of Light in 1QM, the archangel Michael, or even the 'Son of Man' figure in Daniel 7. He uses the term 'angelic' to describe this figure; however, he admits that such a term can be misleading since angels did not receive an anointing. For that reason, the better term that he prefers is 'superhuman' because there is a human component to this figure as well.[56]

Not only does he see the 'Son of God' as a 'superhuman' agent of eschatological salvation, but he also says that this is in fact a 'heavenly messiah'. Defending his notion that such a 'Super-Messiah' was anticipated in Judaism at the time of the Qumran community, he states the following, 'And yet it seems difficult to

---

[53] Although García Martínez says that the 'Son of God' is a messianic figure, he suggests a special type of messiah, 'a heavenly messiah'. Since this is not exactly the same position as other scholars who hold messianic interpretations (i.e., Collins, Cross, Ferda), he is given a separate treatment and discussion.

[54] García Martínez, 'The Eschatological Figure', pp. 162–179. García Martínez only focuses upon the views of Milik (described above), David Flusser ('Hubris'), and Fitzmyer, 'The Aramaic "Son of God" Text'; '4Q246'.

[55] García Martínez, 'Two Messianic Figures in the Qumran Texts' in Donald W. Parry and Stephen D. Ricks (eds.), *Current Research and Technological Developments on the Dead Sea Scrolls* (STDJ, 20, Leiden: Brill, 1996) pp. 14–40 (27).

[56] García Martínez, 'Two Messianic Figures', pp. 29–30.

avoid using the adjective *messianic* to characterize this figure, since the functions attributed to him are messianic in nature. This seems to require a semantic widening of the term messiah to enable us to apply it to figures which are presented not only as human but also as superhuman'.[57] Specifically in reference to the 'Son of God' in 4Q246, he says, 'He [Son of God] is thus a messiah, an almost divinized messiah, similar to Melchizedek and the heavenly Son of Man'.[58] Thus he believes it is justified to use the term 'heavenly messiah' in reference to this 'Son of God' figure in this text, in spite of the fact that the term 'messiah' does not seem to be used.

4. FUTURE PROSPECTS

As evident in this survey, scholars have taken many approaches in attempting to identify the 'Son of God'/ 'Son of the Most High', mentioned in 2.1. As the survey above seems to indicate, the favored position among scholars is to interpret the 'Son of God' as a positive, messianic protagonist. However, approaches that address literary backgrounds or use different methodologies have created new avenues of interpretation.[59] Recently, Ferda and Segal have utilized rhetorical-critical methods on the naming verbs in 1.9 and 2.1. Interestingly, this has led them to reach diametrically opposed conclusions.[60] Further study in these areas may bring forth helpful results.

The work of Cook goes beyond the identification of the 'Son of God' and comments on the language and literary nature of the text. In that regard, he is one of the few to properly identify this

---

[57] García Martínez, 'Two Messianic Figures', p. 20. He also refers to several Jewish writings not from Qumran where such 'superhuman' agents are mentioned yet referred to as 'messiah'. For example, *Parables of Enoch* 48.10; 52.4, where the term 'messiah' is occasionally used together with the more common titles of 'Chosen One' and 'Son of Man' to denote an existing, transcendental figure; and 4 Esdras 13, where a person 'like a man' (called 'messiah' in 7.28 and 12.32) is clearly presented as a person of heavenly origin.

[58] García Martínez, 'Two Messianic Figures', p. 30.

[59] For example, the Akkadian prophecies by Cook, Psalm 82 by Segal.

[60] Recall that Ferda proposed a messianic view; Segal proposed the fourth beast of Daniel 7.

as an early example of Aramaic poetry.[61] Apparently, a prosaic narrative is presumed among the scholars surveyed in this essay. Because of column 1's state of preservation, only column 2 can provide any clues to this text's poetic nature. A careful observation reveals several possible poetic features (e.g., terse lines, parallelism, verb gapping, etc.).

Cook comments on the parallelism and meter of this text, and even attempts a stichometric breakdown (as does Puech). He also says that characteristic of the parallelism of this text is the fact that the poet 'prefers to begin the second colon with the conjunction *waw*'.[62] If such prosodic constraints can be determined (or measured), what of the larger structure? The lines in column two seem to be grouped together into what can be called 'strophes'. 1.9 and 2.1 focus on the naming of this significant figure with the use of naming verbs like יתקרא, יתכנה, and יתאמר. 2.2–3 deals with the destruction of a group (perhaps kings) whose kingdom will be like 'the comets' (2.1) from the vision. 2.4 can be considered a unit in itself due to the possible twin *vacats* at the beginning and end of that line; if the proposed second *vacat* at the end of that line is merely an open space, then line four most likely is to be grouped with what follows. 2.5–7a describes the activity of either the 'Son of God' or the 'people of God', depending on how one identifies the 3ms verbs and pronominal suffixes. 2.7b–9a shows a relationship between either the 'Son of God' or the 'people of God' with אל himself; it also describes the activity of God on behalf of his son/people.

Similar strophic organizations can be discerned within the extant sections of column one as well. 1.2–3 provides an opening

---

[61] Cook, '4Q246', pp. 46–60. Puech ('4QApocryphe de Daniel ar', pp. 167–170) and Cross ('Extracanonical Daniel Apocalypse', pp. 10–11) also recognize the poetic features of the text. For a detailed poetic analysis of column 2, see Peter Y. Lee, *Aramaic Poetry in Qumran* (Saarbrücken, Germany: Scholars' Press, 2015), pp. 181–202. I am very influenced by the poetic analysis of Cook. My own analysis differs only slightly from his.

[62] Cook, '4Q246', 49. This is similar to the parallelism in the description of Sarah's beauty in the *Genesis Apocryphon,* 1QapGen 20.2–8b. For a detailed poetic analysis of this poem, see Lee, *Aramaic Poetry*, pp. 311–346.

to the interpretation where we are told that 'wrath is coming'.[63] 1.4–5a describes the destruction that may be associated with a powerful group (possibly ר]ברבין). 1.5b-6 focuses upon a particular figure, or possibly two significant figures (רב ... [...]מלך אתור [ומ]צרין). 1.7–8 seems to describe the activity of the figure(s).

Perhaps further application of the literary-critical analyses of genre, poetry, rhetoric, and literary backgrounds will continue to yield valuable clues in the quest to grasp the nature of this ancient text and its key figure. If, in fact, the messianic interpretation begins to lose its majority hold and those who hold to an antagonist interpretation champion their cause, this would have a significant impact on our understanding of messianism and messianic expectations within a pre-Christian, Jewish setting. The evidence provided thus far, though favoring a positive messianic view, is hardly conclusive. This has led some, like Fitzmyer, to say, 'the debate over this important sectarian Qumran text is far from over'.[64] I must agree.

---

[63] Most restore at least two transitive verbs at the beginning of line three since the text mentions two objects (שניך, חזוך), both with 2ms pronominal suffixes.

[64] Fitzmyer, *DSSCO*, p. 61.

THE CASE OF THE REQUISITIONED COW: A NEW STUDY OF MUR 42*

MICHAEL OWEN WISE

In this discussion I will deal with Mur 42. Editions of the letter are as follows:

Editio princeps. J.T. Milik in P. Benoit, J.T. Milik and R. de Vaux, eds., *Les Grottes de Murabbaʿat* (DJD, 2, Oxford: Clarendon Press, 1961) pp. 155–159, plates 2, 45.

Editio maior. Ada Yardeni, *Textbook of Aramaic, Hebrew and Nabataean Documentary Texts from the Judaean Desert* (2 vols, Jerusalem: The Hebrew University, 2000) pp. 1.155–156, 2.64.

1. PHYSICAL DESCRIPTION

The letter is inscribed on the upper half of a rectangular sheet of papyrus measuring 15.2 x 21 cm. The archaeologists discovered the letter rolled up like a scroll in Murabbaʿat Cave 2. This was the Roman fashion for archiving a letter. For original delivery the letter was first folded in half vertically, then three times horizontally, bottom to top. Minor damage mars the top and left sides, but otherwise the sheet is complete, and apart from a few

* I offer this study as a small token of my friendship and admiration for Ed Cook. I have learned much from his scholarship over the years and immensely enjoyed working as collaborators in the study of the Dead Sea Scrolls. I can only hope for more of each in years to come.

damaged letters the same is true concerning the text, although ink bits have abraded from the writing throughout.

2. PALEOGRAPHY

Unaccustomed to the formal script, the writer attempted it nevertheless, adorning letters such as *resh* and *lamedh* with tittles. The lines are irregularly spaced and descend toward the left. Scholars differ whether the writer was a professional scribe or merely an experienced letter writer, perhaps a soldier at hand. Given the writer's apparent role as affiant and final signatory, the flowing signature strongly argues that he was indeed a scribe. The writing is on the *recto,* that is, in the direction of the fibers.

3. DRAWING[1]

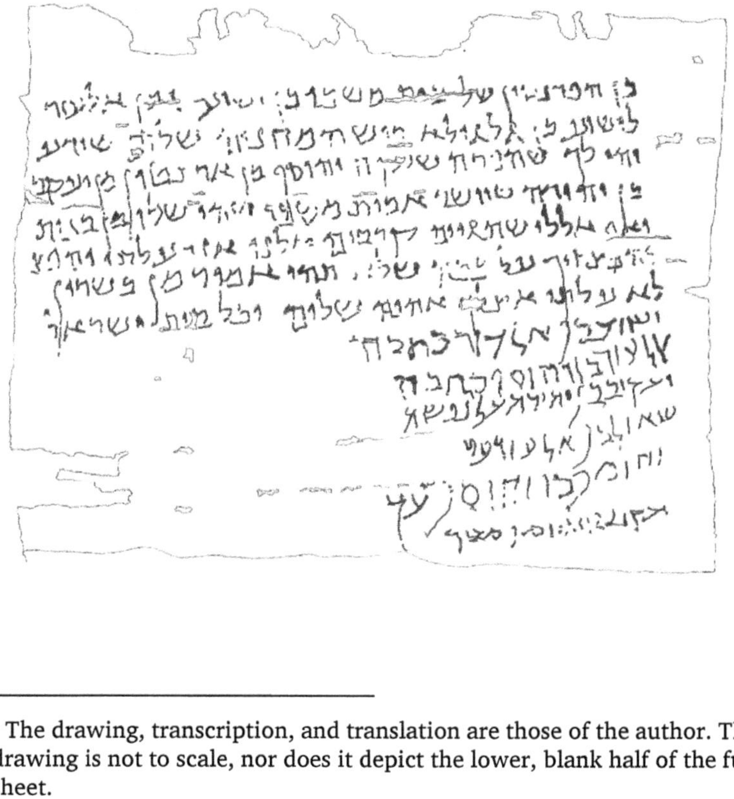

[1] The drawing, transcription, and translation are those of the author. The drawing is not to scale, nor does it depict the lower, blank half of the full sheet.

4. TEXT

1. מן הפרנסין של בית משכו מן ישוע ומן אלעזר
2. לישוע בן גלגולא רוש המחניה שלום שידע
3. יהי לך שהפרה שלקח יהוסף בן ארצטון מן יעקוב
4. בן יהודה שיושב אבית משכו שהי שלו מן בנות«ים»
5. ואף אללי שהגוים קרבים אלנו אזי עלתי {והפצ}
6. והפצתיך על ככה שלא תהי אמור מן בשרון
7. לא עלתי אצלך אהוה שלום וכל בית ישראל
8. ישוע בן אלעזר כתבה
9. אלעזר בן יהוסף כתבה
10. יעקוב בן יהודה על נפשה
11. שאול בן אלעזר עד
12. יהוסף בר יהוסף עד
13. יעקוב בן יהוסף מעיד

5. TRANSLATION

[1]From the administrators of Beth Mashiko, Jesus and Eleazar, [2]to Jesus ben Galgula, the commander of the camp: Greetings! Be it known [3]to you that the cow that Joseph ben Ariston took from Jacob [4]ben Judah, inhabitant of Beth Mashiko, is indeed his by mutual agreement. [5]Also, if the Gentiles were not near us, then I would have come up [6]and indemnified you on the matter. So, you should not be thinking that [7]I failed to come up to you out of neglect of duty. Be well—and all Beth Israel!

[8]Jesus ben Eleazar issued it. (second hand)

[9]Eleazar ben Joseph issued it. (third hand)

[10]Jacob ben Judah (gives witness) concerning himself. (fourth hand)

[11]Saul ben Eleazar, witness. (fifth hand)

[12]Joseph bar Joseph, witness. (sixth hand)

[13]Jacob ben Joseph, affiant. (seventh hand)

6. DISCUSSION

Mur 42 stands out among the Murabbaʿat letters for several reasons. First, only Mur 42 was discovered by the archaeologists. All of the other Murabbaʿat letters were obtained by purchase from the Bedouin (with the concomitant loss of much scientific information that an *in situ* discovery would have afforded). Second, this letter is unique for intertwining legal with epistolary structures. In effect, it is two documents combined, a letter and an affidavit. Lines 2–4 assert a legal claim concerning a cow whose ownership has evidently been a disputed matter. In lines 8–13 two village magistrates, two witnesses, a principal and an affiant then support this claim with their signatures. This portion of the document expresses a plural and legal perspective. In between, in lines 5–7, one of the two magistrates—presumably Jesus ben Eleazar, since he signs in first position—speaks, using singular verb forms to explain why he is not coming personally to Herodium. He defends himself prospectively against a potential accusation of neglect of duty. These lines constitute the body of a letter. Mur 42 was apparently elicited by a written or oral dispatch from Jesus ben Galgula requiring the truth regarding the cow. The message ordered Jesus ben Eleazar to report to the commander and provide answers.

Third, Mur 42 stands out from the other Murabbaʿat letters (and the bulk of the Bar Kokhba correspondence) in being fully published in a preliminary treatment shortly after discovery. Nearly a dozen substantive studies responded to Roland de Vaux's readings and analysis.[2] These contributions greatly improved the *editio princeps* when it appeared some eight years later at the hands of the official editor, J.T. Milik. His interpretation of the letter was as follows:[3]

> Joseph ben Ariston, from an undetermined village, buys a cow from a resident of Bet-Mashiko, Jacob ben Judah. To bring him home, he must have the purchase certificate which he will submit to the approval of the 'camp chief', Jesus ben Galgula. The latter, in turn, will deposit the document in his archives which he will transport later, at the same time as his

---

[2] In addition to the literature cited in note 2 above, cf. O.H. Lehmann and S.M. Stern, 'A Legal Certificate from Bar Kochba's Days', *VT* 3 (1953), pp. 391–396 and Mathias Delcor, 'Murabbaʿat' in *Dictionnaire de la Bible, Supplément 5* (1957) cols. 1390–1399.

[3] Milik, *DJD* 2, pp. 155–156 (author's translation). Names have been modified to accord with the style used in this study.

> 'camp', to the caves of Murabbaʿat. The authors of the certificate, administrators of the village, add a few lines of personal interest and report the movements of Roman troops.

Milik's interpretation leaves unexplained precisely what prompted the camp commander, Jesus ben Galgula, to take such an active interest in the bovine transaction. By Milik's lights he has no real stake in the proceedings. Why would not Joseph ben Ariston himself simply write or send, or even come to Jacob ben Judah to obtain the writ? Milik's reading of Mur 42 perceives no implicit tension that may be motivating the commander. Compare the global interpretation Dennis Pardee and his co-authors offered some twenty years later:[4]

> This is a letter serving to authenticate that a cow taken from an inhabitant of Beth-Mashko belongs rightfully to the member of the Jewish army who took it. There had apparently been a dispute of some kind over Yehosef's right to the cow in question, and Yeshua ben Galgula had probably sent a message to the village managers of Beth-Mashko asking them why they had not cleared up the matter of the cow's ownership. They reply apologetically and furnish a full attestation of ownership for Yehosef. (Is it possible that the cow has indeed been seized and that Yaaqov ben Yehuda has been constrained to furnish a deed for fear of reprisal from the soldiers?)

The deficits of Milik's interpretation have here been made good. The matter of the cow is roiling the camp and this unrest has become a problem for the commander. This is why he takes an active role in collecting testimony of the animal's true ownership. He may have a more personal issue as well. Something like what Pardee tentatively suggests may have happened. Citizen-soldiers from Beth Mashiko, mustered in the camp at Herodium, have recognized the cow and are now charging Jesus with seizing it by force. Joseph ben Ariston may have been the lieutenant who did so at his orders. Alternatively, perhaps Joseph did compensate Jacob ben Judah for the animal.

---

[4] Dennis Pardee et al., *Handbook of Ancient Hebrew Letters* (Chico, CA: Scholars Press, 1982) p. 127.

Naturally, other readings of the situation have been offered. Most of them turn on four words in the text. As to the first, scholars have differed on the question of which man the two administrators assert the legal owner to be, whether Joseph or Judah. The question is thus the referent of שלו in line 4. The word לקח in line 3 is likewise ambiguous; beyond its common meaning of 'take', it often means 'buy' in Tannaitic Hebrew. Whether Joseph bought the cow, or simply took it, matters considerably. But the difficulties of שלו and לקח probably resolve themselves if the puzzles posed by the second pair of terms are solved. The reading of מן בנות at the end of line 4 is the most difficult philological problem Mur 42 presents. Much hinges on the direction taken here. Understanding the text in its totality, however, rests even more upon the meaning of the first word in line 6, והפצתיך.

In his preliminary publication De Vaux had proposed to read מן בנות and understood it to mean 'au su de tous' ('at the knowledge of all'). He explained, 'Nous interprétons בנות par בינות écrit défectivement; ce pluriel abstrait (cf. Is. XXVII, 11) forme avec מן une locution adverbiale'.[5] This shallowly rooted solution convinced no one. It was quickly deracinated and the discussion moved on. J.J. Rabinowitz argued that בנות means 'daughters', explaining that the cow was among (מן) a number of cows (the daughters) born to an animal belonging to the man in question.[6] Unconvinced, Isaiah Sonne proposed that 'the sense of בנות here is that of villages, farms, settlements surrounding Bet-Mashko. This term is well known not only in the biblical idiom 'x-city and its villages' (Neh. 11.25ff.), but . . . is found also as a legal term in Tannaitic sources'.[7] Thus, Sonne understood that the cow would be taken from the surrounding group of villages. He conceded that connecting בנות with יקח (as he read the word in the middle of line 3) was syntactically awkward, so much distance lying between the terms. He thought that legal precision required

---

[5] 'We interpret בנות as בינות written defectively; this abstract plural (cf. Is. XXVII, 11) forms with מן an adverbial locution'.

[6] Rabinowitz, 'Legal Document', p. 200.

[7] Sonne, 'Bar Kokeba Letters', p. 89.

the writer to separate the phrase מן בנות from the names of the men, lest someone think human daughters were in question.

Neither of these rather strained suggestions for מן בנות garnered much support. Yet almost from the first another reading for the phrase in question was in play. Two scholars independently arrived at the reading בזבנות, 'by purchase'. W.F. Albright and Isaac Rabinowitz published their suggestions in the same October 1953 fascicle of the *Bulletin of the American Schools of Oriental Research.*[8] They adduced Syriac and Jewish Palestinian Aramaic cognates for their proposal, adding that זבנות itself was morphologically good Hebrew (the syntactically requisite *status absolutus* would be זבנו in Aramaic, not זבנות). When Milik published the *editio princeps* he adopted a slightly different reading, מזבנות, but the meaning was essentially the same. This reading also became that of Ada Yardeni in her *editio maior,* and it is commonly adopted in the literature today.[9] Thus, the cow was a legal possession of the man who held it. He had bought the cow.

Pardee and his co-authors, however, did not buy the suggestion. They wrote: 'The *zayin* in Milik's reading *mzbnwt* … is impossible, and the *mem* appears more like *bet.* The meaning of *bn bnwt* (or *mn bnwt*) is unsure'.[10] This judgment echoed that of the master paleographer, Solomon A. Birnbaum, writing shortly after De Vaux's original publication:[11]

> It has been suggested that the subsequent sign [after *mem*] is a Z, superimposed onto the lower half of the long-tailed final N from the line above. However, not all the downstrokes of

---

[8] See note 2 above.

[9] E.g., E.Y. Kutscher, 'לשונן של האיגרות העבריות והארמיות של בר כוסבה ובני דורו'. The study originally appeared as two parts, divided by language, in *Leshonenu* 25 (1961), pp. 7–23 and 117–33. The study was then reprinted as part of Kutscher's collected works, here cited: Kutscher, מחקרים בעברית ובארמית (ed. Z. Ben Hayyim et al., Jerusalem: Magnes Press/Hebrew University, 1977) p. 64; Klaus Beyer, *Die aramäischen Texte vom Toten Meer: Ergänzungsband* (Göttingen: Vandenhoeck & Ruprecht, 1993) p. 218; Hanan Eshel and Boaz Zissu, מרד בר כוכבא העדות הארכאולוגית (Jerusalem: Israel Exploration Society/ Yad Izhak Ben-Zvi, 2015) p. 81.

[10] Pardee et al., *Hebrew Letters,* pp. 127–128.

[11] Birnbaum, 'Beth Mashku', p. 24.

> this writer's finals are of such extraordinary length. The *nuns* in l. 1 and the *k* in l. 3 do not run beyond the ceiling of the subsequent line. Careful inspection of what is supposed to be the lower half of our final *nun* shows that it is slightly further to the left than the alleged upper half. In other words, the two do not form a continuous line. If they did, the stroke would unaccountably have changed its direction, and that just at the ceiling of the lower line. It is most unlikely that the writer wrote a Z straight onto the tail of the final *nun*. If he had done so it would have caused a thickening of the underlying stroke, but not the slightest indication of that is apparent. ... In addition, the head of the Z at the end of line 1 is horizontal, but the triangle we have here at the line ceiling, is caused by a narrow curve like that in all the specimens of final N. Our sign is therefore not a Z but a final N (also De Vaux's reading). It is, in fact, a perfect replica of the letter above it. Our word is accordingly מן, and it remains for us to deal with בנות.

Birnbaum could, however, find no satisfying suggestion for that word. As a *reading* בנות seemed secure, but he ended by asking, 'How is one to work it into the interpretation of the document as a whole?' The *meaning* was opaque.

The solution proposed here is to read and restore מן בנות«ים»: literally, 'from between the two of them'; in acceptable English, 'by mutual agreement'. The word is probably a dual; מן refers to source. The puzzling form בנות resulted from scribal error and a consequent need to abbreviate by suspension, the writer trusting that a scribal reader could supply the missing two letters and divine the sense. (Actually, he may himself have been the prospective reader, as discussed below.) Insufficient space remained to write a *yod* followed by a final *mem*. Splitting words between lines, as might happen in contemporary Greek literary texts, was not a practice usual to the Semitic languages of Palestine in the first-second centuries C.E.[12] Hence the suspension.

---

[12] Only the Copper Scroll (3Q15) is an exception here, and that metallic production is exceptional in many respects, not least in that the scribe(s) wrote in 'river of letters' fashion, as was usual with Greek literature. Spacing between words was the normal practice for the Semitic

As a legal term or otherwise, בנותים was unknown when Mur 42 was originally published. Today we know it thanks to the publication of the materials from the Cave of Letters. The word occurs in a contract written at En Gedi in late November of 134 C.E. In this document, *P.Yadin* 44, two pairs of partners divide certain parcels of land between them. The text stipulates as to this division, '[The two sets of persons] hereby divide consensually between the two of them (רצו וחלקו בנותים) of their own free will ... the plots that they leased from Jonathan ben Mahanaim, Simon ben Kosiba's administrator in En Gedi' (lines 2–7).[13] As is evident, the forensic context in which the proposed בנותים appears in Mur 42 is like that of the En Gedi contract. In both cases a legal transaction is described that involves two parties, making the dual form natural.

Close inspection of the superior photographs on the DSSDL website shows that as the writer came to the word מן preceding בנותים, he made a mistake. Likely a draft lay before him, as commonly with official letters in the Greco-Roman world. The draft would be in cursive script, providing a model, but an imprecise one for his formal script with its somewhat differing proportions of letter and line. By parablepsis, or perhaps through an error of the mind, the writer skipped over מן to בנותים. He began to write that word, penning a *beth.* Immediately realizing his omission, he modified the letter as best he could to create a *mem.* He closed in the letter's base stroke at the right lower corner so it would not extend so far beyond the descending vertical. He inked the short descender at the tip of the *beth,* thickening its aspect so it would assume a more medial position on the horizontal. The writer was able to repair the letter and produce an acceptable form of the מן he had skipped. But now he faced a further problem. He had begun to write בנותים only after a glance at the draft affirmed that he had the space. After repair he realized

---

languages, as the materials from Murabbaʿat and Nahal Ḥever amply display. They evidence no example of a word split between lines.

[13] Yigael Yadin et al., *The Documents from the Bar Kokhba Period in the Cave of Letters: Hebrew, Aramaic and Nabatean-Aramaic Papyri* (JDS, 3, Jerusalem: Israel Exploration Society/Institute of Archaeology, Hebrew University/Shrine of the Book, Israel Museum, 2002) p. 44.

he had room for only four letters, not six. The מן had eaten two letter spaces. Seeking to retain the word and line positions of the draft, the writer decided on the strategy of abbreviation by suspension. This was a commonplace on the coins of the day, common also in economic documents of various types. As so often with strange words and forms in ancient texts, here as well: scribal error at the heart of a crux. Behind the error, distraction.

The text itself provides a possible clue to the cause of the writer's lapse. As he approached the end of line 4, it seems he was beginning to think about re-inking his pen. He observably performed that action at the beginning of each line. Note how the initial words of lines 1–7 are darker, the ink visibly thicker at first, the stylus beginning to thirst for ink as he proceeded toward the left.[14] Re-inking of pens underlies numerous scribal errors in the history of manuscript copying and transmission. This is because 'the constant necessity to re-ink one's pen provided the opportunity for scribal distraction at the level of eye, memory, judgment and pen'.[15]

If the proposed solution for בנות is correct, then the ambiguity of שלו in line 4 also resolves. In context that word can now refer only to Joseph ben Ariston. Moreover, the meaning of לקח in line 3 also seems to come clear. The reasoning is as follows. If it meant 'bought'—as is possible in Tannaitic Hebrew—then the explicit statement in line 4 that the exchange of the cow was 'by mutual agreement' serves no purpose. מן בנותים becomes redundant. Such excess verbiage is unexpected, since Mur 42 is a legal text, so presumably carefully worded. The words are not needed because, as a matter of law, sale reifies mutual agreement. Of course, mutual agreement need not mean mutual happiness. We might imagine that Jacob ben Judah was resentful or unhappy about the transaction for any number of reasons. Nevertheless, *res ipsa dicit*. However conflicted, once he exchanged the animal for money, that act would constitute the resolution of his internal

---

[14] This phenomenon is most clearly observable on DSSDL photographs B-276958 (*quondam* PAM 40.187) and B-283841 (*quondam* PAM 42.553).
[15] P.M. Head and M. Warren, 'Re-Inking the Pen: Evidence from P.Oxy. 657 (P^{13}) Concerning Unintentional Scribal Errors', *NTS* 43 (1997) pp. 466–473 (473).

struggle. Thus, the wording that the exchange was by mutual agreement almost certainly means no sale occurred. What happened was that Joseph ben Ariston 'took' (לקח) the animal.

The very shape of Mur 42 reinforces this understanding of לקח if we presume that the legal shaping of Mur 42 responds to the legal need. If what was in question was a legal *sale,* then the response would need to include a bill of sale or equivalent wording legitimating that transaction. We learn something of what such an affirmation would need to include from *P.Yadin* 8, an Aramaic bill of sale found among the documents of the Babatha Archive.[16] As with Mur 42, so here too, an animal changes hands. One brother sells another brother a white donkey, together with a second, female animal (נקבה—possibly another donkey). The document is issued by a village administrator, the analog of Jesus ben Eleazar. Like the Jesus of Mur 42, he affirms his issuance by signature. And the sale is witnessed by the seller, who signs as a principal, potentially the analog to our Jacob ben Judah. Thus far, *P.Yadin* 8 and Mur 42 are arguably parallel. What is missing from the latter, however, is a critical third element found in *P.Yadin* 8: *the sale price.* In the customary law of the region, bills of sale included that fundamental information. Mur 42 does not. Hence it does not speak of a sale, and לקח does not mean 'bought'. Mur 42 is shaped to justify an exchange that was not a sale.

This understanding gains impetus as we come to terms with line 6. Seen contextually, the verb והפצתיך at the beginning of that line should elucidate what the lead official at Beth Mashiko, Jesus ben Eleazar, understood the commander to require of him. The stated action must respond to that requirement. Therefore, this verb is the fulcrum of the letter. It necessarily colors Mur 42 in its entirety. Although other readings of the word were early proposed, De Vaux's original והפצתיך quickly won the assent of scholarship and is today the consensus reading. Discussion has focused on what root the Hebrew represents, and what the meaning of that root is. De Vaux argued for the verb פצה.

[16] Yadin et al., JDS, 3.109–113.

Ginsberg proposed the root פיס. Both options have won distinguished defenders.

De Vaux wrote of והפצתיך that it is 'une forme *hiphil* de פצה, non attestée en hébreu biblique mais correspondant au *pael* de l'arm. פצא ... qui a le sense de 'libérer,' comme l'a exceptionnellement le *qal* de פצה dans la Bible'.[17] J.J. Rabinowitz applauded De Vaux's understanding, while adding, '[he] was, however, unaware of the technical sense of ridding a person of an adverse claim with respect to certain property in which the word is used in our document'. He then cited an Egyptian Aramaic parallel from 437 B.C.E. and referenced a passage from the Babylonian Talmud, demonstrating thereby a thousand years of Aramaic legal nuance for the verb.[18] Given that Mur 42 functions in part as an affidavit, any legal nuance to the verb in line 6 would clearly be fundamental to proper understanding of the text.

The Aramaic verb פצא is not merely ancient. It is also widespread in the Aramaic dialects. Beyond its use at Elephantine, it appears in texts composed in Qumran Aramaic, Jewish Palestinian Aramaic, Christian Palestinian Aramaic, Samaritan Aramaic, Parthian Middle Aramaic, Jewish Babylonian Aramaic, Syriac and Mandaic. Across these dialects the root functions in four stems: G, D, AtD, and C, broadly meaning 'to rescue, to save', or the passive of those glosses. The causative stem in Samaritan Aramaic, also meaning 'rescue', particularly stands out since the usage in Mur 42 is causative. And the forensic nuance that J.J. Rabinowitz drew to scholars' attention is common in Jewish Babylonian Aramaic, more widespread than his single citation might suggest.[19] Both Syriac

---

[17] Translated, 'a *hiphil* form of פצה, not attested in Biblical Hebrew but corresponding to the *pael* of Aramaic פצא ..., which has the sense of "set free," as does the *qal* of פצה exceptionally in the Bible'. He referred to Ps. 144.7, 10, 11 and Ecclesiasticus 51.2 (Hebrew). Quotation from 'Quelques Textes', p. 272.

[18] Quotation from 'Legal Document', p. 201. The ancient Aramaic document was Kraeling 3.19–23 (Emil G. Kraeling, ed., *The Brooklyn Museum Aramaic Papyri* [New Haven: Yale, 1953]). The Talmud passage was b. B. Bat. 45a.

[19] Cf. Michael Sokoloff, *A Dictionary of Jewish Babylonian Aramaic* (Ramat Gan, Israel: Bar Ilan University / Baltimore: Johns Hopkins University, 2002) s.v.

and Christian Palestinian Aramaic further attest this nuance. The lexical data thus appear friendly to the notion that the forensic coloring was possibly familiar to Aramaic speakers in second-century Judea.

The next requirement would be that these semantics enter the Hebrew of Judean bilinguals at some point by the process of semantic extension. As we saw above, פצה was a Hebrew word already in biblical times, and it continues in evidence in later Hebrew texts roughly coeval to Mur 42.[20] Important details of this Hebrew usage were still unknown when De Vaux and his early respondents wrote. In particular, one more recently available text, 4QTobit[e] (4Q200), may use the *hiphil*.[21] Further important, it is striking that Greco-Roman translators of Tobit 13.2 from Hebrew and Aramaic read פצא/פצה as a *qal/peal* with the meaning 'escape' (even if it were not so intended originally). Thus, the Greek 'long version' (Codex Sinaiticus): καὶ οὐκ ἔστιν οὐδέν, ὅ ἐκφεύξεται τὴν χεῖρα αὐτοῦ, 'and there is nothing that will escape his hand'; and the 'short version' (Codices Alexandrinus and Vaticanus): οὐκ ἔστιν ὅς ἐκφεύξεται, 'there is none who will escape'. The *Vetus Latina* is *et non est qui effugiat manum eius*, 'and there is none who will escape his hand'. Modern Semitic lexica do not capture the meaning 'escape' for the simple stem, but these evidences from Tobit are clearly of potential importance for understanding Mur 42. A Hebrew *hiphil* meaning 'set free, rescue'

---

[20] Rabinowitz cited Ecclesiasticus 51.2. The passage is extant in Hebrew only in MS B; see Pancratius C. Beentjes, *The Book of Ben Sira in Hebrew* (VTSup, 68, Leiden: Brill, 1997) p. 91. The particular phrase lacks a parallel in the Greek. Patrick W. Skehan and Alexander A. DiLella, *The Wisdom of Ben Sira* (Anchor Bible, 39, New York: Doubleday, 1987) p. 560 translate פציתני here as 'you delivered me', reading the verb as a *qal*. It may as easily be a *piel*, of course.

[21] Edited by Joseph Fitzmyer in M. Broshi, et al., *Qumran Cave 4. XIV Parabiblical Texts, Part 2* (DJD, 19, Oxford: Clarendon Press, 1995). The passage in question, Frag. 6 vii (Tob. 13.2) is treated on pp. 70–72. It reads ומה אשר יפצה מידו which Fitzmyer renders, 'What is there that can snatch from his hand?' He suggests that the verb is probably best read as D but notes that since it is unmarked it could be G or even N. Fitzmyer does not make the observation, but the unmarked form as written could also be *hiphil*, paralleling the stem usage of Mur 42.

would be expected for a *qal* 'escape', since the *hiphil* is most frequently causative with respect to the *qal*.[22] Hebrew speakers using the *qal* as the Greco-Roman translators understood it would naturally use a *hiphil* as the writer of Mur 42 arguably does. This understanding fits Mur 42 contextually, and the base meaning 'set free' could well carry Rabinowitz's forensic nuance.

Since De Vaux's original publication, the principal argument against deriving הפצתיך from פצה has been the claim that the Aramaic verb is not used in the causative, most commonly appearing in the *pael*.[23] Today this does not seem a strong argument. The evidences of Samaritan Aramaic, 4QTobit[e], and the Greek and Latin translations of Tobit undermine it on its face, as we have seen. But put those aside for the moment: the premise of the argument is problematic. Can one really insist for loans that Aramaic stem patterns mandate corresponding Hebrew stem patterns? That may be common, but it is surely no axiom. Too many counterexamples urge the contrary. Just within the Bar Kokhba letters, for example, one finds in *P.Hever* 30 that the Hebrew טרף has extended its semantic domain under the influence of Aramaic to mean 'strike'. Yet the stems do not correspond; this meaning, expressed by the *hiphil*, corresponds to the semantics of the simple stem in Aramaic, not the causative.[24] Furthermore, the *hiphil/haphel* not infrequently overlaps with the

---

[22] Emil Kautzsch, ed., *Gesenius' Hebrew Grammar,* trans. A.E. Cowley (2nd edn., Oxford: Clarendon, 1910) §53c; Paul Joüon, *A Grammar of Biblical Hebrew,* (trans. and rev. Takamitsu Muraoka; Rome: Pontificio Instituto Biblico, 2nd edn., 2006) §54d; Bruce K. Waltke and Michael O'Connor, *An Introduction to Biblical Hebrew Syntax* (Winona Lake, IN: Eisenbrauns, 1990) 27.1.e.

[23] E.g., Kutscher, 'לשונן של האיגרות', p. 64 and Uri Mor, עברית יהודאית (Jerusalem: Academy of the Hebrew Language, 2013) p. 106 and n. 122. Neither considers the evidence of Samaritan Aramaic.

[24] *P.Hever* 30 line 10 is a *post scriptum* not previously deciphered. It reads, [כפר] בריו העיר שהטרפ[ו], '[Kephar] Baru is the city that the[y] struck'. Among the Aramaic dialects the causative of טרף is attested only in Samaritan Aramaic, where it means 'to reject', and Syriac, where it means 'to smash the ground'. The meaning 'strike' appears in the *peal* in multiple dialects, and less commonly also in the *pael*. In Hebrew the passive is expressed by the *niphal* in the same letter, line 7.

piel/pael semantically, and this overlap occurs in the Aramaic dialectal usage of פצא, as noted. Accordingly, the interchange to which the argument objects would hardly be surprising.[25]

Beginning with the initial publications, those who have rejected derivation from פצה have largely followed Ginsberg in deriving הפצתיך from the verb פיס.[26] This term, meaning 'appease, persuade', is itself a loan into Aramaic from Greek πεῖσαι, aorist infinitive of πείθω. The Greek verb's meanings include 'appease, persuade'. From Aramaic, Ginsberg implied, the word then passed into Hebrew. He accounted for the *tsade* of הפצתיך by regressive assimilation to the first letter of the root:[27]

> By π I represent the sound of the letter *pe* in Greek loanwords. That a *pe* in Greek loanwords was pronounced differently from either the dageshed or undageshed native *pe,* is sometimes indicated diacritically in Syriac and always in Christian Palestinian Aramaic. ... Being unaspirated ... this p < π was treated like *tet* and *qoph,* which are likewise unaspirated ... and like them tended to render neighboring sounds emphatic.

Ginsberg's understanding of the Greek π as a nonaspirated stop or occlusive at the time πεῖσαι was borrowed has held up under research by phoneticians into the development of Classical occlusives in Koine Greek.[28] As a matter of phonology his suggestion was possible.

---

[25] The sole monograph-length study of the *hiphil* is W.T. Classen, *The Hiphil Verbal Theme in Biblical Hebrew,* (PhD Diss., University of Stellenbosch, 1971). From this dissertation Classen broke out two journal articles of importance to the relations in question, 'On a Recent Proposal as to a Distinction Between Piel and Hiphil', *JNES* 1 (1971), pp. 3–10, and 'The Declarative-Estimative Hiphil', *JNSL* 2 (1972), pp. 5–16.

[26] Ginsberg, 'Notes', pp. 26–27, n. 15.

[27] *Idem.*

[28] E.B. Petrounias, 'Developments in Pronunciation During the Hellenistic Period', in A.-F. Christidis (ed.), *A History of Ancient Greek from the Beginnings to Late Antiquity* (Cambridge: Cambridge University Press, 2007) pp. 606–607; Claude Brixhe, 'Linguistic Diversity in Asia Minor During the Empire: Koine and Non-Greek Languages', in Egbert J. Baker (ed.), *A Companion to the Ancient Greek Language* (West Sussex, UK: Wiley-Blackwell, 2010) pp. 234–235. For the exceptional pronunciation of π in Greek loans into Syriac, contrary to the usual rules for *qushoyo*

Nevertheless, Pardee and co-authors were not persuaded by Ginsberg's derivation. His method of accounting for the *tsade* required for them that Mur 42 borrow *immediately* from Greek. This would have to be an isolated *ad hoc* borrowing, the Greek term never having entered Aramaic or Hebrew previously, because a form with *tsade* does not otherwise exist: 'The verb as far as we can determine is always spelled with *samech* in later sources. Ginsberg ... cite[s] no exceptions'.[29] The forms of פיס attested in ancient Jewish sources always spell the word with *samekh,* the authors noted, meaning that those written forms must have descended from a separate or *second* borrowing of πεῖσαι. By 'sources', then, they implicated also Hebrew. פיס becomes relatively common from Tannaitic times onward but is unknown in Hebrew writings of any earlier period.[30]

In tandem with the positive evidence for פצה, Pardee and company's objections to פיס seem close to decisive. Not absolutely decisive, of course, since one might argue for an exchange of *tsade* and *samekh* as a matter of orthography in a situation where the two phonemes were merging.[31] The notion that פיס would be borrowed into Aramaic and Hebrew twice yet be spelled differently in the two instances—especially when one such spelling can evidence in Jewish sources only a unicum, Mur 42—does appear far-fetched. No Hebrew source other than Mur 42—if Ginsberg and fellow travelers be right—treats the word as explicitly foreign. Rather, as happens generally with most loans, so here, too. The Hebrew lexical history shows פיס as regularized according to the grammar of the receiving language. Jewish Aramaic dialects (Jewish Palestinian Aramaic and Jewish

---

and *utsotso,* cf. Theodor Nöldeke, *Compendious Syriac Grammar,* (trans. James A. Crichton, 1904; Winona Lake, IN: Eisenbrauns, 2001) §25.

[29] Pardee et al., *Hebrew Letters,* p. 125. Subsequently Mor has drawn attention to an *aphel* infinitive with a *tsade* in עברית יהודאית, p. 106. See now Michael Sokoloff, *A Dictionary of Christian Palestinian Aramaic* (Leuven: Peeters, 2014) p. 347 s.v.

[30] Eliezer ben Yehuda, מלון הלשון העברית (8 vols., New York/London: Thomas Yoseloff, 1960) vol. 5 s.v.

[31] This problem would seem to require extensive exploration here only if a verb פצה could not work.

Babylonian Aramaic) likewise treat the loan according to native grammar. In short, to construe Mur 42 line 6 הפצתיך as derived from the verb פיס seems a low-percentage play. We have no compelling reason *not* to read הפצתיך straightforwardly. It is best taken as what it would first seem, a *hiphil* from פצה.[32]

7. SUMMARY INTERPRETATION OF MUR 42

In light of the foregoing discussion, one might conceive the following scenario for our letter. Jesus ben Galgula, the commander at Herodium, sent a lieutenant of his, Joseph ben Ariston, possibly originally from En Gedi,[33] to the nearby village of Beth Mashiko. There a wealthy householder, Jacob ben Judah, was known to have a cow that Jesus judged necessary for the war effort.[34] He told Joseph to requisition the animal; this was a kind of *angareia,* or perhaps of *annona:* the two forms of (normally,

---

[32] Here it is interesting to observe how Yardeni treats the question in her *Textbook* (cited above). For both her Modern Hebrew translation in vol. 1 and the English rendering in vol. 2, she allows for the possibility that either verb may be correct in line 6. But in her Concordance, vol. 2.3, p. 122, she opts for פצה and does not even list פיס.

[33] Joseph's Greek patronym was uncommon among Palestinian Jews of this period. It is attractive therefore to associate him with En Gedi as the brother of Jesus ben (A)riston, vender there of half a vegetable garden to Eliezer ben Samuel in *P.Yadin* 47. Both Joseph and Jesus are likely sons of the Ἀριστίων who was neighbor to a courtyard willed by Judah ben Eleazar Khthusion to his daughter, Shelamzion, in 128 C.E. (*P.Yadin* 19, *P.Yadin* 20.11, 34 ἀμφόδιον Ἀριστίωνος, 'Ariston's lane'). Note that Ἀριστίων is an attested biform of Ἀρίστων according to Tal Ilan, *Lexicon of Jewish Names in Late Antiquity. Part I. Palestine 330 BCE-200 CE* (Tübingen: Mohr Siebeck, 2002) p. 268. Ilan does not include the name from *P.Yadin* 47 text b 4, רצטון. The scribal spelling is explicable as an *ad aurem* rendering of ישוע בר (א)רצטון, the quiescent *aleph* not being represented between the two *reshes.*

[34] Jacob's signature makes it likely that he was wealthy. His fluent hand testifies to a well-educated person who could read with ease, and normally in antiquity, where public education did not exist, that level of education corresponded to wealth. For the connection of handwriting to degrees of literacy, see Raffaella Cribiore, *Writing, Teachers, and Students in Greco-Roman Egypt* (Atlanta: Scholars Press, 1996) esp. pp. 3–33, and Michael Owen Wise, *Language and Literacy in Roman Judaea* (New Haven Yale, 2015) pp. 36–61.

Roman) taxation overlap at the margins. 'The *annona* was the ad hoc exaction of supplies taken by the army for its own use or that of fellow soldiers elsewhere; such exactions included animals (which were then as good as lost) … *[a]ngareia* was a temporary levy of services for a particular job'.[35] In a wartime setting the temporary levy of a farmer's animal might easily slide into permanence.

Seizure of animals was a regular practice of ancient warfare. As they began a campaign in a given locale, the Romans regularly requisitioned all the animals they could find in order to provision the army from the area of its operations, rather than having to import animals from afar.[36] We must imagine that Judaea was largely denuded of its farm animals by the point in the Revolt when Mur 42 was composed. Some of the animals were held by the Romans; others, by the forces of Beth Israel and Simon ben Kosiba. The Jews were used to—and, perhaps, somewhat inured to—this oppressive practice at the hands of Rome. It was the more painful when their own government seized their animals: 'Requisitioning animals, even more than seizing food or fodder, was sorely felt by the local population, as animals represented an important part of a farmer's capital'.[37]

Perhaps accompanied by several additional soldiers, Joseph ben Ariston made the short trip to Beth Mashiko. Once there, he sought out Jacob and informed him that his cow was needed for service at Herodium. Jacob did not resist (though initially he may have had the animal in hiding), and Joseph led the heifer back to the camp and ben Galgula. Perhaps the cow was used to help with …owing. In any event, the animal was recognized by soldiers at …odium who hailed from Beth Mashiko, and they objected to

… Goodman, *State and Society in Roman Galilee, A.D. 132–212* …J: Rowman & Allanheld, 1983) p. 147. In his discussion on … Goodman draws attention to passages in the Gospels and in …ture that instance this ancient reality of Roman oppression. …o the state was of course famously familiar to the Jews …he time of Solomon.

…h, *The Logistics of the Roman Army at War (264 B.C. –* …rill, 2012) pp. 144–147.

its presence, assuming that it had been seized by force over Jacob's protestations. We may imagine that the situation was open to question from the perspective of still-evolving customary law, since *annona/angareia* was not normal Jewish practice in Roman times. Galgula found himself in the legal crosshairs. Even though he was the commander of the camp, he could ill afford to act in ways that birthed dissension among the troops, whose morale may have been questionable given the direction the war was now taking. He needed to justify the presence of Jacob's cow at Herodium.

Calling to himself a young soldier and scribe, Jacob ben Joseph, he ordered him to carry a message to the senior magistrate at Beth Mashiko.[38] Whether the message was crafted in the form of a letter, or was to be communicated orally, we have no way of knowing. The distinction is here unimportant. The message was simple: come here. Explain that the cow was not taken by force. Indemnify me. Receiving this message, Jesus ben Eleazar decided he could not safely journey to Herodium. His reason (or perhaps, excuse) was the local presence of Roman forces.[39] He did not wish to reveal his and his townspeople's present location should his movements be observed. Possibly the townsfolk were clustered together, sequestering themselves in a hiding complex, the village drained of all visible occupation. Rather than obey Galgula's command directly, Jesus conceived an alternative. He gathered his junior magistrate, Eleazar ben Joseph; that man's brother, Joseph

---

[38] It was common for a carrier, whoever he was, to read the letter aloud to recipients after arrival. Having the scribe deliver the letter guaranteed a proper reading out, aided accurate interpretation through follow-up questions, and spared the necessity of finding someone else sufficiently literate to read and guide interpretation after delivery.

[39] הגוים קרבים אלנו in line 5 is formally ambiguous, as the Hebrew may be read either 'are approaching' (participle) or '(are) near' (adjective). Commentators are about evenly split. Birnbaum's reasoning guides the translation adopted here: 'Now, if the purpose of this sentence were to inform [Jesus ben Galgula] of the approach of the enemy, two things would not be easy to understand: why so vital a piece of intelligence should have been put in the protasis of a conditional sentence, and why, in fact, the whole sentence should have been placed at the end of the document'. Thus his 'Beth Mashku', p. 26.

ben Joseph; his own brother, Saul ben Eleazar; and the principal whose cow was in question, Jacob ben Judah. Within a letter replying to Galgula and scribed by the messenger, he sandwiched an affidavit stating that the cow had changed hands 'by mutual agreement'. No force was involved. It was as much a giving as a taking. These leading citizens of Beth Mashiko then signed in accordance with their roles.[40] Folded letter in hand, the scribal messenger Jacob ben Joseph slipped away and returned to Herodium. Upon arrival, he affixed his signature to the document as the final signatory, publicly affirming the truth of the contents.[41] Then he read the letter aloud to Galgula and as many of the men of Beth Israel as the commander chose (supplying the suspended letters for מן בנות«ים», of course). Present were soldiers from Beth Mashiko. We may assume that Mur 42 had its intended effect. Jesus ben Galgula then took the letter, rolled it, and filed it away in his epistolary archive—the whole bovine affair a matter to be forgotten for some two thousand years.

---

[40] Jacob ben Judah signed as a principal, על נפשה, translated above as, '(gives witness) concerning himself'. The typical expression Jacob used was probably elliptical, expressing what written fully would be מעיד על נפשה. The evidence of this ellipsis comes from Syriac contracts of a slightly later period, where the full expression appears; these contracts share many documentary protocols with the Judaean materials. For full discussion see Wise, *Language and Literacy,* pp. 394–395, n. 8.

[41] Jacob wrote יעקוב בן יהוסף מעיד. The addition of the word מעיד is unique for witnesses among all the Bar Kokhba documentary materials, and probably does not mean precisely what the term meant for principals. 'Affiant' is an attempt to capture its essence here. For full discussion see Wise, *Language and Literacy,* pp. 233–235 and n. 103.

ARAMAIC TRANSLATIONS OF SCRIPTURE

THE RELATIONSHIP BETWEEN LAMENTATIONS 1.15, ISAIAH 63.3, JOEL 3.13, AND THEIR TARGUMIM*

CHRISTIAN M. M. BRADY

The Book of Lamentations is full of strong and evocative language as the poets seek to convey the pathos of their situation and the complexity of their feelings. In keeping with the genre of lament, there are the usual elements of calling out to God, describing the calamity, contrition, and even the commitment to return to faithful obedience to the Lord (Lam. 3.40). Yet the language of the Book of Lamentations is often far more graphic and strident than that found in the Psalter.

Lamentations 1.15 is a good example of such dramatic language and imagery.

> Lam. 1.15 [Heb.] The Lord[1] has rejected
> all my warriors in the midst of me;

* This small study is offered in honor of my friend, mentor, and colleague Edward Cook. A study of intertextual influence and borrowing seemed fitting to me, since Ed received some amount of fame outside of the world of Aramaic studies for revealing Bob Dylan's borrowing and creative use of previous sources.

[1] MT has אדני but multiple mss., including 4QLam, have יהוה and the *New Revised Standard Version*, cited here, follows this in its representation of the word with 'LORD'. The Targum has ײ which is the usual marker for the Tetragrammaton and is indicated likewise.

> he proclaimed a time against me
> to crush my young men;
> the Lord has trodden as in a wine press
> the virgin daughter Judah.

As graphic as the last line is, the Targum takes it to a new level of drama and pathos. The poetic image of the Lord treading grapes is transformed into the explicit rape of 'the virgins of the House of Judah'.

> TgLam 1.15 The Lord has crushed all my mighty ones within me; he has established a time against me to shatter *the strength of* my young men. *The nations entered by the decree of the Memra of* the Lord *and defiled* the virgins of the House of Judah *until their blood of their virginity was caused to flow like wine from a wine* press *when a man is* treading *grapes and the wine of his grapes flows.*

The biblical image of the vengeful God treading on the enemy as one would tread grapes in the wine press is found in two other biblical passages. It is most notably found in Isaiah 63.3, 'I have trodden the wine press alone, and from the peoples no one was with me; I trod them in my anger and trampled them in my wrath; their juice spattered on my garments, and stained all my robes'. Similar language is found also in Joel 4.13 [Heb.], 'Put in the sickle, for the harvest is ripe. Go in, tread, for the wine press is full. The vats overflow, for their wickedness is great'. As we shall see, the Targumim to Lamentations, Isaiah, and Joel all share a similar interpretation of their respective texts. The question arises as to the source of this interpretive tradition. Were the Targumim of these three texts influenced by the similar biblical texts, by one another, or did they simply develop their own, surprisingly similar interpretation?

1. BIBLICAL RELATIONSHIP

Chapter 63 of Isaiah begins with a dialogue, presumably between one standing watch on the city wall and God. The Lord approaches as a warrior whose clothes are stained red with the blood of his enemies.

Isa. 63.1 [Heb.] 'Who is this that comes from Edom,
from Bozrah in garments stained crimson?
Who is this so splendidly robed,
marching in his great might?'
'It is I, announcing vindication,
mighty to save'.
2 'Why are your robes red,
and your garments like theirs who tread the wine press?'
3 'I have trodden the wine press alone,
and from the peoples no one was with me;
I trod them in my anger
and trampled them in my wrath;
their juice spattered on my garments
and stained all my robes'.

The Targum of Isaiah is typically expansive, but notice the nature of the additions made to the base text (which are indicated in the translation with italics). As in TgLam the already graphic imagery is increased in its force and violence.

> TgIsa 63.1 *He is about to bring a stroke upon* Edom, *a strong avenger upon* Bozrah, *to take the just retribution of his people, just as he swore to them by his Memra. He said, 'Behold,* I *am revealed–just as I spoke–*in *virtue, there is* great *force before me* to save. 2 Why *will mountains be* red *from the blood of those killed,* and *plains gush forth* like *wine in the* press? 3 *Behold, as grapes trodden in the* press, *so shall slaughter increase among the armies of the* peoples, *and there will be no strength for them before* me; I will *kill* them in my anger and trample them in my wrath; *I will break the strength of their strong ones before me,* and I *will annihilate* all *their wise ones*'.[2]

The passage in Joel conveys a similar message to that of Isaiah 63. The Targum is more compact in its rendering, yet, even so, the Targum manages to make the text a dark and grim pronouncement. The poetic has been replaced by the literal.

[2] Bruce D. Chilton, *The Isaiah Targum: Introduction, Translation, Apparatus and Notes* (Wilmington, DE: Michael Glazier, 1987) p. 120.

> Joel 4.13 [Heb.] Put in the sickle, for the harvest is ripe. Go in, tread, for the wine press is full. The vats overflow, for their wickedness is great.
>
> TgJoel 4.13 Stretch out the sword *against them*, for the time of *their* end has arrived. Descend; trample *the slain of their warriors like one stomping when it is stomped in a wine* press. Pour out *their blood*, for their evil has multiplied.[3]

Both of these biblical passages are pronouncements of God's Day of Judgment upon the enemies of Israel. There are some differences. Joel mentions the wine press as an image of the results of divine vengeance, but God is not the active agent. Isaiah, on the other hand, includes the description of God as the warrior, returning from battle, covered in the blood of his enemies, as the very one who trod the wine press. The latter makes the comparison with Lamentations explicit.

These prophetic texts are offering assurance to Israel of God's final victory over *their* enemies and the restoration of his people. In Lamentations, however, it is Israel who has become the enemy of God and the day of judgment that has been declared is against Jerusalem, not Bozrah. 'The Lord has rejected all my warriors in the midst of me; he proclaimed a time against me to crush my young men; the Lord has trodden as in a wine press the virgin daughter Judah'.

Interestingly, modern commentators make little of this comparison between Lamentations and Isaiah. If comment is made at all, it is found in commentaries on Lamentations and they simply note that Lam. 1.15 evokes the Divine Warrior image as found in

[3] Jerome Lund, 'Targum Joel' in *Targum Onkelos, Jonathan, and the Writings (English): Accordance Bible Software* (Oak Tree Software, Inc., 2015). The determination of which words are 'added' and thus indicated in italics are my own. This verse does not have the clear one-to-one correspondence that is usually the hallmark of Targum. For example, in the last stich the Hebrew הַיְקָבִים, 'vats', seems not to be represented at all, unless we posit that דַמְהוֹן, 'their blood', is intended. That is a reasonable suggestion since instead of the vats overflowing it is 'their blood' which is 'poured out'.

Isa. 63.3.[4] Of course any such comparison would be difficult, needing to take into account genre, date and provenance, audience, and so on. The challenges, however, should not preclude the effort, although this study will only touch briefly on the relationship between the biblical texts.

The date of composition for each of the biblical texts is a complicated question in and of itself. It seems likely, however difficult to prove, that the first chapter of Lamentations is earlier than either passage under consideration in Isaiah or Joel. Assuming Trito-Isaiah and Joel *are* later than Lamentations 1, it could be that the prophets are inverting the image of Lam. 1.15, invoking the dramatic and devastating image of God allowing Jerusalem to be trodden and destroyed as punishment for her transgressions in order to describe the comeuppance of the enemies of Israel. The punishment God has leveled on his chosen people will now be meted out in the utter annihilation of their enemies. Even if it is impossible to say which text is older and whether they were each drawing upon a shared tradition or borrowing from one to the other, that there are similarities in imagery cannot be denied and it appears the Targumim took this into consideration in their interpretations.

2. TARGUMIC RELATIONSHIP

2.1. Targum Lamentations

Targum Lamentations 1.15 employs prosaic expansion, the process by which the Targumist always renders Hebrew poetry into Aramaic prose,[5] but the Targumic interpretation goes in a very different direction than the biblical text, even while

[4] See, for example, Adele Berlin, *Lamentations: A Commentary* (Louisville, KY: Westminster John Knox Press, 2004) p. 58. 'The warriors and youths are the crushed grapes, whose blood runs out like wine. Isaiah 62.3 also contains the image of God treading his enemies like grapes in a wine press (and cf. Joel 4.13 [Heb.])'.

[5] See Moshe Bernstein, 'Translation Technique in the Targum to Psalms', *SBL 1994 Seminar Papers* (Atlanta, GA: Scholars Press, 1994), pp. 326–345, and Christian M. M. Brady, *The Rabbinic Targum of Lamentations: Vindicating God*, (SAIS, 3, Leiden: Brill, 2003) p. 25.

preserving a word-for-word equivalence. The final two stichs of this verse receive the greatest attention. '[H]e proclaimed a time against me to crush my young men; the Lord has trodden as in a wine press the virgin daughter Judah' becomes 'the nations entered by the decree of the Memra of the Lord and defiled the virgins of the House of Judah until their blood of their virginity was caused to flow like wine from a wine press when a man is treading grapes and the wine of his grapes flows'. This stich demonstrates the extreme language which the Targumist was willing to employ in order to impress upon his audience the horror of Jerusalem's fate.

The image conjured by MT is already a gruesome one, although it is clearly intended as a metaphor. As elsewhere in TgLam, the Targumist has little problem speaking of God in anthropomorphic terms, but clearly this verse, particularly the description of the Lord himself trampling 'the virgin daughter Judah', was too much for his sensibilities. In the Targum, the Lord decrees by his Memra that the *nations* should enter Jerusalem. We will find a similar use of Memra in the section of Targum Isaiah under consideration (TgIsa 63.1 and 5).

So, upon entering Jerusalem at the Lord's decree, the nations raped the virgins so viciously that 'their blood of their virginity was caused to flow like wine from a wine press'. The depiction is vivid and shocking and although it removes God from the direct role of active abuser, the biblical image has been taken to an extreme. God issues the initial decree allowing the enemy to enter the Holy City (since no harm can assail Jerusalem without God's approval), but it is the nations who actually defile the innocent.

In reinterpreting this stich the Targumist ignores the word order presented in MT. אדני is still the first word represented in the Targum, but the reference to grapes being trod in a wine press is relegated to the final clause of the verse. Thus instead of the parallelism of 'warriors/young men/virgin daughter' found at the end of each stich in the Hebrew, the Targumist balances the destruction of the youths with the repetitious references to the flowing blood/wine. Although the MT is theologically problematic, it did not necessitate the graphic interpretation which the Targumist has provided. This depiction of the desecration of virgins heightens the audience's sense of dismay and brings the true nature of the siege into relief.

2.2. Targum Isaiah

While also employing prosaic expansion, Targum Isaiah 63.1–3 does not provide a simple translation of the biblical text and, in fact, it is often difficult to discern what is intended to be the word-for-word equivalence. The Hebrew *Vorlage* has been dissolved into the Aramaic as the Targumist reframes the first verse of chapter 63 from a dialogue into a report. The watchmen asking, 'Who is this that comes from Edom, from Bozrah in garments stained crimson? Who is this so splendidly robed, marching in his great might?' becomes an introductory statement. 'He who has said these things is about to bring a blow upon Edom, a strong avenger on Bozrah, to execute just retribution on behalf of His people, just as He has sworn to them by His Memra. He has said…'. God still speaks, but it is no longer in the form of a discourse with the sentry. It is a declaration 'by His Memra'.

Notice that robes and garments have disappeared from the Targum to verse 1, but in verse 2 are rendered with geographical terms. Thus, 'Why are your robes red, and your garments like theirs who tread the wine press?' becomes 'Why are *mountains* red with the blood of the slain and *valleys* bring forth like wine in a wine press?' The latter portion of verse 3, our primary focus, has an even more expansive translation that takes us farther from the base text. 'Their juice spattered on my garments, and stained all my robes' is now 'and I will break the might of their strong ones before Me, and all their wise men I will destroy' (וְאַתבַר תְקוֹף תַקִיפֵיהוֹן קֳדָמַי וְכָל חַכִימֵיהוֹן אְסַלעֵים:).

The poetry of the Hebrew text of verse 3 has been transformed into prose and the perfect tense to the imperfect, describing God's future act of vengeance. As in verse 2, the 'garments' and 'robes' are replaced, in this case by 'their strong ones' and 'their wise men' which are placed in parallel and are described as having been broken and destroyed. In this way, the poetic, if graphic, imagery of the biblical text is rendered by the specific description of the destruction of the enemy.

It is not clear why the Targumist has replaced the garments/robes of MT with completely unrelated terms ('mountains'/'valleys' in v. 2, 'their strong ones'/'their wise men' in v. 3). These renderings are too inconsistent to be following some sort of anti-anthropomorphic agenda. In this passage, God speaks (directly, not only through his Memra) as well as tramples and slaughters his enemies while saving Israel by his 'mighty arm'. Yet *something* about the image of God wearing robes stained with the blood of his enemies was just too much for the Targumist.[6] This is a point worth following up in detail in another study, but a brief examination of other instances of TgJon rendering בֶּגֶד and לבוּשׁ in Isaiah is insightful. It reveals that the Hebrew בֶּגֶד is rendered consistently with the Aramaic לבוּשׁ. For example, in Isa. 36.22, the Hebrew בְגָדִים is rendered with the Aramaic לְבוּשֵׁיהוֹן. This equivalence, where the term is referring to clothing and not 'vengeance', seems to be consistent in TgIsa. The key to the rendering in 63.3 may be Isa. 59.17.[7]

וַיִּלְבַּשׁ צְדָקָה כַּשִּׁרְיָן וְכוֹבַע יְשׁוּעָה בְּרֹאשׁוֹ וַיִּלְבַּשׁ בִּגְדֵי נָקָם תִּלְבֹּשֶׁת
וַיַּעַט כַּמְעִיל קִנְאָה׃

וְיִתגְלֵי לְמַעְבַד זָכְוָן לְעַמֵיה תְקוֹף וּפֻרקָן יַיתֵי בְמֵימְרֵיה לְדָחְלוֹהִי
לְמַעְבַד לְאִתפְּרָעָא בִתקוֹף מִסָנְאֵי עַמֵיה וְיָתִיב נִקמָא לְבַעֲלֵי־דְבָבוֹהִי

Isa. 59.17 [Heb.] He put on righteousness like a breastplate,
and a helmet of salvation on his head;
he put on garments of vengeance for clothing,
and wrapped himself in fury as in a mantle.

TgIsa Then He will be revealed to perform merits for His people, to bring strength and deliverance by His Memra to those who fear Him, to exact retribution in strength from the

---

[6] God is the speaker in Joel 4.13 (and there is no clothing involved) and so the Targum does not need to create any sort of distance. 'Stretch out the sword against them, for the time of their end has arrived. Descend; trample the slain of their warriors like one stomping when it is stomped in a wine press. Pour out their blood, for their evil has multiplied'.

[7] Perhaps the terms being in parallel caused translational issues or בגד is read as 'treachery', but in the biblical context where 'treachery' is the meaning, the Targum renders in various ways (*בזז 'plunder' and *שקר 'lie'), e.g., Isa. 33.1 and 48.8.

> enemies of His people and to return vengeance to His enemies.[8]

It is still unclear why *בגד should be rendered with *תקף but it seems to be related to the Hebrew construct בִּגְדֵי נָקָם, 'garments of vengeance'.[9] Returning to Isa. 63.3, this seems to be the same equivalence as וְיֵז נִצְחָם עַל־בְּגָדַי, 'their juice spattered on my garments', is rendered with וְאַתבַר תְקוֹף תַקִיפֵיהוֹן קֳדָמַי, 'and I will break the might of their strong ones before Me'. On the other hand, I do not yet have an explanation for the equivalence of חַכִים for the Hebrew לבוּשׁ.

2.3. Targum Joel

In the case of Joel 4.13, the Targumist offers a fairly straightforward prosaic expansion, even if at times it is difficult to determine the underlying Hebrew text.[10] This passage remains a declaration from God to his people that the end of their enemies was about to arrive. God would gather all the nations and sit in judgment over them (Joel 4.12 [Heb.]), bringing them to ruin on the Day of the Lord. The imperative of the Hebrew שִׁלְחוּ מַגָּל, 'put in the sickle', is maintained in the Aramaic אוֹשִׁיטוּ בְהוֹן חַרבָא, 'stretch out the sword against them', even as the agrarian imagery found throughout the section has been replaced with the more mundane images of war. And that is the primary change found in this verse and throughout the Targum to this section; the poetic agricultural allusions to warfare and judgment are made explicit and graphic. The command to 'tread, for the wine press is full' is replaced with ponderous 'trample the slain of their warriors like one stomping when it is stomped in a wine press'. No longer do

---

[8] Translation by Eldon Clem, *Targum Onkelos, Jonathan, and the Writings (English): Accordance Bible Software* (Oak Tree Software, Inc., 2015). Notice Chilton's translation and italics, he sees only a handful of words as representing MT. 'He *will be revealed to do virtues for his people, strength and* salvation *he will bring by his Memra to those who fear him, to do* [*them*], *to take retribution in strength from the adversaries of his people,* and he *will return vengeance to his enemies*'. Chilton, *The Isaiah Targum*, p. 115.

[9] See also the final phrase כַּמְעִיל קִנְאָה, '...as a mantle of fury'.

[10] See the earlier footnote in reference to discerning Hebrew/Aramaic equivalents.

the vats overflow; now the imperative is directed at those who are attacking the enemy to 'pour out their blood'.

3. CONCLUSIONS

All three biblical texts under consideration in this study share a common tradition of the metaphor of treading grapes in a wine press for the destruction of God's enemies. In the case of Lamentations, the enemy is God's own people and it is the virgin daughter Judah that 'the Lord has trodden as in a wine press'. Isaiah includes the depiction of God as the Divine Warrior, perhaps implied also in Lamentations. In Joel, God commands that the 'harvest' of the enemy begin and that the vats would overflow because their wickedness was so great.

The use of agricultural imagery is found throughout the Bible, so it is not surprising that images of harvest, winnowing the wheat from chaff, and the crushing of grapes in the making of wine should be employed to evoke the image of judgment and destruction. It is impossible to determine with certainty which biblical text is older, although an argument can be made that the passage from Lamentations has primacy, with the prophets inverting the imagery of God's punishment upon his people that will now be visited upon their enemies. This distinction between Lamentations and the prophetic texts seems to be driving the Targumim in different directions in each case.

In each case, the poetic Hebrew was expanded into Aramaic prose. The rendering of TgJoel is fairly straightforward, replacing the rustic agricultural imagery with the brutal images of war. In contrast, both TgIsa and TgLam embellish the text extensively, yet in very different ways. TgIsa has a particular concern to reset the dialogue between the Divine Warrior and the guard as an exposition as well as to transform the metaphors of clothing (cloak and robe) into the actual enemies of Israel. Building upon the underlying Hebrew text's reference to the 'virgin daughter Judah', TgLam took what could have 'simply' been blood flowing like grape juice from a wine press and transformed it into a horrific account of war-rape and the flowing 'blood of their virginity'.

This sort of graphic re-presenting of the Hebrew text is likely the result of prosaic expansion, the practice of turning the poetic and metaphorical into the banal and yet gory reality of the results of war. Yet, even as they broaden the biblical text in producing their Targum, each Targumist follows the contours of their source. If the Targumists made a connection between Lamentations 1.15, Isaiah 63.3, and Joel 4.13, it is not reflected in their renderings. There seems to be no discernible influence between the Targumim. Common culture, metaphors, and translational practices seem the most likely reasons for what similarities exist between the Targumim.

GLEANINGS FROM THE COMPREHENSIVE ARAMAIC LEXICON III: TARGUMIC NOTES FROM THE UNDERGROUND -א*

STEPHEN A. KAUFMAN

In publications and in many oral presentations, I have long been urging students and scholars of Aramaic to expand the kinds of research into Aramaic texts that they are undertaking by taking advantage of the increasing availability of online and other computerized databases, which, if properly used, can enable the researcher to ask the kinds of questions never before answerable, or at least never before answerable without the thousands of hours of data collection and analysis that has gone into such projects. Nonetheless, more often than not such pleas fall on deaf ears. Even the very existence and usefulness of the Comprehensive Aramaic Lexicon (CAL) project is often ignored while the

---

* I am pleased to be able to make this contribution in honor of Ed Cook, whose long and loyal toil as a research associate in the early days of the CAL project contributed extensively to the publications and databases of the project. Earlier articles in this series were 'I. Previously Unknown Syriac Words' in M. J. Lundberg, S. Fine, and W. T. Pitard (eds.), *Puzzling Out the Past: Studies in Northwest Semitic Languages and Literatures in Honor of Bruce Zuckerman* (CHANE, 55, Leiden: Brill, 2012) pp. 93–97 and 'II: Notes on the State of Modern Syriac Lexicography' in Alejandro F. Botta (ed.), *In the Shadow of Bezalel: Aramaic, Biblical, and Ancient Near Eastern Studies in Honor of Bezalel Porten* (CHANE, 60, Leiden: Brill, 2013) pp. 137–43. Both papers are available online at Academia.edu.

typical 'scholar' demonstrates her erudition by producing extensive footnotes citing the pages in the printed dialect dictionaries where a word is dealt with, even though all of that data (and probably more) could be subsumed in a single reference to an entry in the online CAL.[1]

Now it may be that there are those who think that until a 'publication' appears in print it is irrelevant, and there may be others who simply do not know of the existence of the CAL. Others, even otherwise excellent scholars, may think that the only legitimate source for Aramaic lexicography is Syriac.[2] The goal of the current publication is to suggest to such researchers that there may be more to find in the online CAL than just a few definitions and references to other dictionaries.

There are currently (May 23, 2023) 41,694 main entries in the CAL, 68,747 glosses, and 97,769 citations, based on over 465,000 lines of parsed text. Main entries are often accompanied by notes, some quite substantial and innovative, a print publication of which would take up thousands of pages. We here begin to 'publish' some of the more extensive notes, i.e., those containing what we think to be innovative 'contributions' that might otherwise become overlooked.[3] The following selected

---

[1] A recent, disappointing example of this is the late Ada Yardeni's *The Jeselsohn Collection of Aramaic Ostraca from Idumea* (Jerusalem: Yad Ben Zvi, 2016), whose lexical footnotes read like those of a first year student of Aramaic, a fact all the more surprising given that she, along with her mentor Bezalel Porten, has been one of the most notable contributors to and benefactors of the CAL project.

[2] For a blatant example of which see how Aaron Butts points out just such an oversight in his review of Leonid Kogan's *Genealogical Classification of Semitic: The Lexical Isoglosses* (De Gruyter: Berlin, 2015) in *JNES* 77 (2018) pp. 144–49 (148). Of those who might dismiss the work of the CAL out of old-fashioned European scholarly egotism, the less said the better, other than to remind them that it is a work in progress.

[3] Most of the CAL's individual lexical notes are simply etymological references for loanwords and foreign words in the texts; these are not included here. In the overwhelming majority of cases, the extensive, unsigned notes are my own work, but there may be a few here and there that are largely due to the research of our research associates, specifically and most likely Ed Cook and Jerry Lund. Unfortunately there is now no way to verify such cases, for which *mea culpa*.

notes on words with initial *aleph* concentrate on the targumic lexicon, one of Dr. Cook's main specialties.

ʾb, ʾbʾ, ʾnbʾ (*ʾeḇ, ʾebbā, ʾinbā*) n.m. **fruit, produce**[4]

Forms with *nun* are found in Biblical Aramaic, Qumran, and Mandaic, i.e., the Official Aramaic Literary tradition; those without *nun* in JLA (> Samaritan, see *DSA*, p. 2), Syriac, and Galilean. LJLA has both forms, but the evidence suggests an original attempt in that dialect to distinguish between the two, where *nun*-minus forms mean 'fruit', those with *nun* meaning 'produce'. Also note that this word is used exclusively in the targumic tradition for the literal meaning of 'fruit'. In those cases where the biblical text uses פרי in figurative senses such as 'produce, offspring, results' and the like, the parallel targums regularly use other terms, in particular the cognate פירי.

ʾbl conj. **but**

This is a blatant Hebraism in the late targumim. Note that it appears only in the very early chapters of TgPsJ and TgSong, i.e., it is the result of scribal tampering.[5] It is, of course, a normal term in talmudic dialectic.

ʾgd, ʾgdʾ n.m. **staff**

The Palestinian targumic tradition at Num. 22.7 explaining how one can have קְסָמִים in one's hand appears differently in each text as אגדן, אגרן, גדין, and גרין. We are not certain whether the original version was meant to be arrows (*gyr*)

---

[4] The etymological relationship between this word and Syriac ܗܒܒܐ 'flower' is unclear. For the probable connection with Hebrew עֵנָב 'grape' via Akkadian *inbu* see Stephen A. Kaufman, *The Akkadian Influences on Aramaic* (AS, 19, Chicago: Oriental Institute, 1974) p. 58 [hereafter *AIOA*].

[5] I.e., it reflects the so-called 'Kaufman effect' as I outlined in 'Of Beginning, Ends, and Computers in Targumic Studies', in Maurya P. Horgan and Paul J. Kobelski (eds.), *Touch the Text: Biblical and Related Studies in Honor of Joseph A. Fitzmyer, S.J.* (New York: Crossroad, 1989) pp. 52–66, whose effects have been so ably confirmed by our honoree in 'The "Kaufman Effect" in the *Pseudo-Jonathan* Targum', *AS* 4 (2006), pp. 123–132.

for divination or this word, i.e., a staff, for which see Levy (*Ch-W,* I, p. 125 s.v. גד). The Fragment Targum reading אגרן חתימין would seem to understand it as 'sealed documents' however.

ʾgdn, ʾgdnʾ (*ʾaggəḏān*, *ʾaggəḏānā*) n.m. **silphium and/or asafoetida**[6]

A monumentally important medicinal plant and spice in Antiquity, silphium (known for its resin) became extinct, and afterward names for it were transferred to a spice derived from resin of the seeds or root of a related 'ferula' plant, the so-called 'asa foetida'. Since neither spice is normally poisonous, the cited LJLA example[7] may refer to its well-known fetid odor before processing rather than to some other drug.

ʾgwr, ʾgwrʾ n.m. **temple; pagan shrine**[8]

The example cited in *DJBA* (s.v. איגורא) is 'uncertain' and has variants.

Note that this word is regularly used in the JLA targums to render Biblical Hebrew מִזְבֵּחַ when reference is to a pagan one.

In Samaritan only איגור סהדותה for biblical יְגַר שָׂהֲדוּתָא.

ʾdr, ʾdrʾ (*ʾi/eddar*, *ʾi/eddrā*) n.m. **threshing floor, barn**

For the use as a seating arrangement, see Jastrow (*Dictionary*, s.v. גורן, p. 227). This usage, along with the similarity to the word *ʾdrwn* 'inner chamber', led to the distinctive Zohairic usages of the word as both a meeting room and a portion of the Zohar itself.

---

6 Immanuel Löw, *Die Flora der Juden* (Vienna and Leipzig: R. Löwit Verlag, 1924–34) I, p. 278. For Persian forms see Claudia A. Ciancaglini, *Iranian Loanwords in Syriac* (Wiesbaden: Reichert, 2008) p. 99 (hereafter, *ILS*). For the vocalization see Matthew Morgenstern, 'Notes in the Noun Patterns in the Yemenite Tradition of Jewish Babylonian Aramaic', *REJ* 168 (2009), pp. 51–83 (64).

7 TgPsJ Deut. 29.17: דשרוי חיטאה חלי וסופיה מ{ס}<רי>ר כאגדנא דמותא 'for its sin's beginning is sweet but its end is as bitter as deadly asafoetida'.

8 From Sumerian E.KUR > Akk. *ekurru*; *AIOA,* p. 48.

It has been suggested that the word itself is a loan from Akkadian *adru*,[9] but given the antiquity and ubiquity of the threshing floor in the Near East, as well as the generally accepted Amorite origin of the Babylonian month names (i.e., Adar refers to the time of year the *adar* was first used), almost certainly an ancient culture word. Note, too, its use in place names in the Hebrew Bible, although the common word for this in BH itself is גֹּרֶן. On the other hand, since Palestinian Arabic *bēdar* is clearly from Aramaic בי דר (see s.v. *by dry*) and the need to distinguish among various elements connected with the threshing process, that a need for a borrowed form was felt cannot be absolutely excluded.

ʾwznyqʾ n.m. **royal court (??)**
LJLA. *TgEsth³ 7.4* : לית למעיקא טומין ורוחא באזניקא דמלכא.
This interpretation assumes that this targumic variant follows the interpretation of the LXX, but it is a dubious variant at best; far preferable is the form בטוניא (< *ṭʿwn* 'burden') of the larger supplements, which accounts for the two forms טומין and באזניקא.

ʾwqyʾnws (*ʾūqīaʾnāws*) n.m. **ocean**
Greek *ὠκεανός*[10]
1 ocean JPAtg, CPA, Syr, JBA, LJLA.
2 pl. : bravo! Syr.
The use as an exclamation follows Greek *ὠκεανέ*.[11]

---

[9] Paola Pagano, *Akkadian Lexical Influences in Syriac* (PhD Diss., Università degli Studi di Napoli 'L'Orientale', 2016) pp. 149 ff., 261 ff.
[10] Samuel Krauss, *Griechische und lateinische Lehnwörter im Talmud, Midrasch und Targum* (Berlin: S. Calvary & Co., 1898–99) I, p. 25.
[11] See BDAG, p. 2416; see G. W. Bowersock, 'The Syriac Life of Rabbula and Syrian Hellenism', in Thomas Hägg and Philip Rousseau (eds.), *Greek Biography and Panegyric in Late Antiquity* (Berkeley: University of California Press, 2000) p. 260.

ʾwrdk, ʾwrdka (*ʾurdaḵ, ʾurdǝḵā*) n.m. **pestle; large needle**[12]

1 pestle LJLA. *TgProv 27.22* var.: אין מחית ליה לשטיא במכתשא בגו סיעאתא ובאורדך 'if you smash a fool in a mortar, even with a pestle [= MT בַּעֱלִי] in the midst of a crowd'.

2 large needle

The meaning 'large needle' is attested by the Syriac lexicographers, but otherwise unknown.[13] Given the text of Targum Proverbs, however, it is clear that the original Syriac version must have had this word, subsequently lost from the Syriac tradition when the Peshitta text was modified to comport with the LXX. For another example of the targum preserving a lost Syriac form see s.v. *qwṭ* 'herd'.

ʾwrh, ʾwrtʾ n.f. **nightfall**

See discussion *DJBA*, although that article fails to recognize that almost all examples refer to 'nightfall' rather than simply 'night'. See Levy, *Ch-W* for a more extensive treatment.

Probably to be connected with *ʾwry* #3 n.m.: 'west', an obvious connection that would not be noticed by rendering simply as 'night'. See also s.v. *ʾwr* div. 'divinity of darkness'.

ʾwrkh, ʾwrktʾ n.f. **power of attorney for debt collection**

See also s.v. *ʾdrktʾ* 'document authorizing collection of a debt'; the forms are regularly confused in the mss. with this form found in Geonic texts and the other in the Talmud. *DJBA* attempts to disambiguate them, claiming that this form is the 'power of attorney' while the attested form is a scribal error based on the regular JBA *aphel* of *qwm* which itself is often found in LJLA texts. The correct LJLA form should be אדרכתא, the document of property

[12] For etymology, compare Akkadian *urāku*, 'a long metal tool, perhaps a chisel' *AHw*, p. 1427b., 'copper rod or wire' *CAD* U/W, p. 206. See also Levy, *Ch-W*, s.v. אוראראנ.

[13] Johann Georg Ernst Hoffmann (ed.), *Syrisch-arabische Glossen. Erster Band: Autographie einer Gothaischen Handschrift enthaltend Bar Ali's Lexikon von Alaf bis Mim* (Kiel: Schwers'sche buchhandlung, 1874) p. 397.

seizure, but it seems to us unlikely that two different words are involved.

ʾḥl, ʾḥlʾ (*ʾă/uḥal, ʾa/oḥlā*) n.m. **alkali; saltwort**[14]
Saltworts are a class of salty plants whose burned material produces a cleansing ash, i.e., 'alkali' and whose crushed parts are used for other medicinal purposes (see *CAD* U/W s.v. *uḫūlu*). The confusion (at least among later scribes and modern lexicographers) between 'aloe' (see s.v. *ʾhl* #2) and 'saltwort' seems to be extensive in the Babylonian dialects where /ḥ/ and /h/ have generally merged.
See also s.v. *mlwḥ* 'salty; salty plant'.
The native lexicographers associate it with the Arabic word *ʾušnān*, which can be any number of different salty, alkali-producing plants as well as cleansing 'ash' in general, so it is not quite clear how broad the meaning of the Aramaic can be.

ʾḥsnw, ʾḥsnwtʾ (ʾaḥsānū, ʾaḥsānūṯā) v.n.C **inheritance (of real property)**
JPAtg, LJLA. *Cairo Geniza manuscript Z Gen. 48.4*: אחסנות עלם 'a perpetual inheritance'. *TgNeof Gen. 49.30*: די זבן אברהם ית חקלה מן לוות עפרון חתייה לאחסנו דקבורה 'that Abraham had bought from Ephron as a burial property'. *TgPsJ Num.* 34.11: אחסנות שיבט ראובן.
For the (artificial?) distinction between אחסנה and אחסנו in JPAtg, see *DJPA* note to the former. It is clear that this form can be found in the fixed expression לאחסנו, which may well be an archaic formulary (compare לאנתו, 'in marriage'), but it is not clear that this form would otherwise be attested in the absolute. Among the various dialects of Palestinian Aramaic the verbal nouns of the derived stems do vary in the construct and determined forms between forms in *-āṯ* and those in *-ūṯ*. In most cases we have chosen to combine them into a single lemma, but here separation seems justified.

---

[14] See Immanuel Löw, *Aramäische Pflanzennamen* (Leipzig: W. Engelmann, 1881) p. 42; Philippe Gignoux, *Lexique des termes de la pharmacopée syriaque* (Studia Iranica, Cahier, 47, Paris: Association pour l'avancement des études iraniennes, 2011) p. 17; =Akkadian *uḫūlu.*

ʾḥry (*[ʾa]ḥrāy*) adj. **final, last**
See also s.v. *ʾḥry* n.m.
Note the distinction between the Palestinian targumic tradition, which uses this word, and the literary tradition (JLA and LJLA) which uses *btry* adj. instead.

ʾḥry n.m. **guarantor, responsible party**
Literally the one who stands last in the line of responsibility; *DJA* 30a joins #1 (adj.) and #2 (n.m.).
This meaning, attested only in legal usage, is undoubtedly connected with similar Akkadian terminology as suggested by Greenfield (see *DJBA* s.v.), but inasmuch as the Akkadian usage only appears in Neo-Babylonian documents, it is probably an Aramaism there!

ʾṭwn, ʾṭwnʾ ([*ʾa*]*ṭwān*, [*ʾa*]*ṭwānā*) n.m. **twisted strap**
This word is probably also to be reconstructed as the original form underlying the various forms found in the Palestinian Targum tradition paralleled by the form in TgPsJ at Gen. 50.1.[15]
From Babylonian *ṭumānu*, 'braided fabric' > /ṭwān/ with prothesis, as demonstrated by the JBA variant without *aleph*.
The vocalization in *DJBA*, taken from the targumic tradition is incorrect. Interestingly enough, the sole Syriac example preserves the correct vocalization although the consonantal spelling is incorrect (though one suspects rather an error by Budge here!).
See also s.vv. *ṭwy* vb. and *ṭwnbʾ*.

ʾyhw pron. **he**
Normally only as subject, in LJLA as some kind of emphatic copula. Often it has the same extra semantic force as does *hwyw*, i.e., 'he himself', especially in the objective meanings.

[15] TgPsJ Gen. 50.1: ערס דשנדפין מחפייא דהב טב מקבעא אבנין טבן ומחזקא באטונין דבו{ין}<ץ> 'an ivory bed plated with fine gold inset with precious stones and bound with linen straps'.

The etymology has long been debated, but we are convinced that it is of the same basic type as the repeated form *hwyw* with vocalic dissimilation and loss of initial *heh.*

ʾyzgd, ʾyzgdʾ (*ʾizgad, ʾizgaddā*) n.m. **messenger**[16]
Note that in JLA and LJLA it is used for MT מלאך in reference to a human as opposed to divine messenger, while JPAtg uses שליח.

ʾyl, ʾylʾ (*ʾăyel, ʾaylā*) n.m. **stag**
In Hebrew the words *ʾayil* 'ram' and *ʾayyāl* 'stag' are distinct, but there is no clear evidence for that distinction here. The occasional bi-syllabic variant vocalizations in JLA texts are almost certainly Hebraisms, as is the meaning 'ram' at Qumran. On the other hand, the JLA vocalization of the feminine form as *ʾayyālā* seems well established.
The reading אילי at 4Q531 17.8 has been rejected in favor of איש.
The entry in *BarBahlul* demonstrates that the word was not known in Syriac outside of the biblical contexts.
For possible figurative usages see s.v. *ʾyl* #5 n.m.[17]

ʾysṭygnyn n.m.pl. **astrologers, magicians**
This is a common form from Mishnaic Hebrew (see Jastrow, *Dictionary*, pp. 89 ff.), itself apparently a corruption of an otherwise unknown Greek word combining the words for 'star', i.e., *astro-* with 'knower', i.e., *gnō*. Levy's proposed etymology ὁ στεγανος makes little sense in the contexts.
Note that all the other versions other than Pseudo-Jonathan use the standard Aramaic word for 'sorcerer', i.e., *ḥrš* in these passages. Apparently TgPsJ wanted to use a foreign-sounding word to reflect the obviously foreign word in BH, but more importantly wanted to distinguish between the dream-interpreting function of the Hebrew term in the

---

[16] From Old Persian **ažganda*, which also appears as a loan in Akkadian. For the most recent etymological discussion see *ILS*, pp. 105 ff.
[17] 1 **projecting ledge** JLAtg. 2 **ship's prow** JBA. 3 **a worm (or the like) in grapes** JBA, JBAg.

Genesis passages, for which he uses the standard חרש, and the magical actions here.[18]

ʾysr, ʾysrʾ n.m. **a type of angel, genius**
Given the dialectal distribution (JBA, LJLA) almost certainly from Akkadian, but the actual etymon is unclear. Most likely from the Assyrian *išar* adj., i.e., 'just one'. Alternatively from Babylonian *ēsiru* 'one pressing for payment', i.e., 'representative' (see *CAD* E s.v. *esēru* A).

ʾyt (*ʾīṯ, ʾīṯay/ē-*) vb./adv. **there is, exists**
See Nöldeke *CSG*, pp. 148 ff. As Wertheimer points out, the copulative usage in Syriac was undoubtedly influenced by Greek, but often appears in translated texts even where the Greek does not use the verb 'to be'![19] It must be seen as a natural development of the kind of usage found already in Standard Literary Aramaic (Biblical Aramaic [only Daniel!], JLA) with participles and other adjectives, i.e., where the existential nature of the predication is still paramount. In Syriac the participle is no longer nominal, hence *ʾīṯ* is not used with it, only enclitic pronouns. A more comprehensive study still needs to be done, though.

ʾkwl n.m. **granary (??)**
JLAtg. *TgJon Jer. 50.26* var.: פְּתַחוּ אֲבֻולַיהָא/אכולהא 'open its city-gates (var. granaries)' †.
The form is highly uncertain. Although the Hebrew source מַאֲבֻסֶיהָ surely means granary (compare אבוס), it is probable that it was interpreted as if from בוס, 'to trample' by the targum, hence the correct text simply אבוליהא, i.e., 'its gates'.

ʾlw conj./inte. **presentative particle**
In Biblical Aramaic (Daniel) both ארו and אלו occur in close proximity. This may be simple textual or even authorial variation, but if there is a semantic difference it would appear to be that most of the time אלו usually expresses a

---

[18] TgPsJ Exod. 7.22: ועבדו היכדין איצטיגנוני מצרים. TgPsJ Exod. 8.3: ועבדו היכדין אסטגניניא בלחשיהון.

[19] Ada Wertheimer, 'Syriac Nominal Sentences', *JSS* 47 (2002), pp. 1–21 (1. ff).

sudden, surprising appearance whereas ארו adds elements to an already existing scene.

ʾlmwg, ʾlmwgʾ n.m. **a type of precious wood**

An old culture word almost certainly equivalent to Akkadian *elammakku* (for whose usages see *CAD* E, pp. 75 ff.). In the targumic texts the forms are always basically a transliteration from Hebrew. It is quite unlikely that the Aramaic translators knew precisely what it was.

ʾmrkl (*ʾămarkol, ʾămarkəlā*) n.m. **administrator of finances**

Note the phonological and semantic development *hmrkr* → *hmrkl* (Qumran) → *ʾmrkl*. In Second Temple times in Hebrew clearly connected with finances (see Jastrow, *Dictionary*, s.v.), but in the targums it would appear that, with the loss of initial *heh*, the popular etymology (i.e., simply 'administrator, one giving all the orders') may have prevailed.

ʾnplyn (*ʾanpilyān*) n.m. **innermost room**

LJLA. *TgSong 4.12*: ובתול<ת>יך טמירן כגנזן {דאלפילין}<דאנפלין> וחתימן תמן 'your virgins! are hidden and sealed there like treasures of the innermost chambers' †.

Greek *ἐμπύλιος* 'gate house'; also in RH^2 (Gen. R.). This word is to be kept distinct from Jastrow's אנפלי (*Dictionary*, p. 78) 'money-box'.

ʾswr, ʾswrʾ (*ʾāsōr, ʾāsōrā*) nom.ag. **one who binds**

TgNeof Deut. 24.6: אסורי חתנין וכלין 'those who bind grooms and brides'.

Apparently the targum passage refers to a folk custom, deemed pagan, of binding the hands of (potential?) brides and grooms together. Pseudo Jonathan, however, (ולא יהוי גבר אסר חתנין וכלין בחרשין) understood this targumic interpretation to refer to bewitching: see s.v. *ʾsr* vb.

ʾrs n.m. **poison**

A connection with Latin *virus* has been posited by some,[20] but is highly dubious.

---

[20] Krauss, *Griechische und lateinische Lehnwörter*, p. 43.

1 poison, venom Gal, CPA, JBA, LJLA. *SYAP 30.42*: ואריק וארס סם בה 'I shall pour out poison and venom on it' †. *TgPs 58.5* אירסא להון כגוון אירסא דחויא 'they have venom like snake venom'.
2 a soothing ointment (?) LJLA. *TgJob 30.24* var.: אין למרעיה יסיק להון ארסא 'if for his sickness he will bring up soothing ointment for them [~? MT אִם־בְּפִידוֹ לָהֶם שׁוּעַ]'.
Levy *Ch-W* argues that the TgJob passage cited for mng. 2 should be connected rather with 'iris'; cf. s.vv. *ʾyrs, ʾwrs* in the manner of *sm*, which can clearly be both a poison and a medicine.

SOME ARCHAISMS IN TARGUM SONG OF SONGS AND LATE JEWISH LITERARY ARAMAIC*

ANDREW W. LITKE

1. INTRODUCTION

One of the notable linguistic features of Targum Song of Songs (TgSong) and the other texts written in Late Jewish Literary Aramaic (LJLA) is their use of features that are seen in older dialects of Aramaic and could be referred to as archaisms. While labeling something as archaic can suffice as a cursory explanation, the term is rarely defined, and the governing

* It is with great pleasure that I write this essay in Ed's honor, and I hope that it will be a fitting tribute to both his scholarship and friendship. I am also pleased to thank Daniel Carver, Stephen Coleman, William Fullilove, and Andrew Gross, who made valuable comments on an earlier version of this essay.

This essay was completed before I became aware of two new studies: Hsin-Chih Perng, *The Aramaic Targum to Canticles: A Critical Edition with Textual and Linguistic Studies* [Hebrew] (PhD Diss., The Hebrew University of Jerusalem, 2021); Paul R. Moore, *Studies in the Language of Targum Canticles: With Annotated Transcription of Geniza Fragments* (STAS, 18, Leiden: Brill, 2022). Though I have not been able to make an exhaustive assessment, it does not appear that Perng's study alters the conclusions made here. Moore's does not, and now see my review essay of that work, 'Targum Canticles and Linguistic Complexity', *HS* 64 (2023), pp. 201–215.

parameters of an archaism within a text are also rarely described. In this essay I will analyze three features that could be labeled as archaisms in TgSong and LJLA: (1) the -ה preformative of the Causative stem, (2) the use of historic שׂ, and (3) the third feminine singular pronoun /-ahā/ on nouns.[1] In the course of analyzing the attestations of each feature in TgSong and the other LJLA targumim, I will also address the historical development of the features in Aramaic more broadly. The point will not be to define the nebulous term archaism, but rather, I will provide a closer look at some features in LJLA that could be termed archaic on a surface analysis, the result of which will allow for a better understanding of their sources and parameters. This will in turn lead us to a more nuanced understanding of the multi-faceted nature of archaisms in LJLA.[2] The analysis will show that the –ה preformative of the Causative stem is a non-productive, occasional feature that has analogues in Biblical Aramaic. The use

---

[1] Other archaic features in LJLA have been addressed elsewhere. Edward M. Cook analyzed several in an essay on Targum Pseudo-Jonathan, 'The "Kaufman Effect" in the *Pseudo-Jonathan Targum*', *AS* 4 (2006), pp. 123–132. The features he discusses include the third masculine plural suffix הום–, the third masculine singular suffix on plural nouns והי–, and the non-assimilation of נ in certain words. He argues that some (but not all) of the older features, such as the two suffixes above, are more frequently attested earlier in the manuscript and suggest that they are the result of scribal changes. Concerning these pronouns in TgSong, see my analysis in *Targum Song of Songs and Late Jewish Literary Aramaic: Language, Lexicon, Text, and Translation* (STAS, 15, Leiden: Brill, 2019) pp. 61, 64; Hsin-Chih Perng, 'Preservation or Correction? On the Peculiarities of Ms Paris 110 and Current Trends in Targumic Studies', *AS* 18 (2020), pp. 198–212 (206–208). I also addressed the use of Biblical Aramaic terms in 'The Lexicon of Targum Song of Songs and Aramaic Dialectology', *AS* 15 (2017), pp. 78–105 (96–97).

[2] This is not to say that the LJLA targumim are a unified group of texts; in fact, each of them displays unique characteristics. They do, however, share a number of linguistic particularities and exhibit the same kind of artificial linguistic regularity. As such, they can be analyzed as a group. Generally, see Stephen A. Kaufman, 'Targum Pseudo-Jonathan and Late Jewish Literary Aramaic', in Moshe Bar-Asher et al. (eds.), *Moshe Goshen-Gottstein—In Memoriam* (Studies in Bible and Exegesis, 3, Ramat-Gan: Bar Ilan University Press, 1993) pp. 363–382 [Hebrew]; translated and reprinted in *AS* 11 (2013), pp. 1–26.

of שׁ is a Hebraism and is not an Aramaic archaism. The third feminine singular /-ahā/ suffix is a modeling of Targum Onqelos and Targum Jonathan, which fits the overall compositional approach of the TgSong targumist and is therefore not any more archaic than the rest of the Targum.

At the outset, it is important to note that TgSong is attested in two recensions, a Western recension and a Yemenite recension. While both recensions derive from the same *Urtext*, the Western recension is superior, and two of the three features discussed below show that the Western recension is more like the rest of the other LJLA targumim (several of which do not have a Yemenite recension), as opposed to the Yemenite recension, whose scribes exhibit a tendency to alter the language to be more like that of Targum Onqelos and Targum Jonathan.[3] When discussing other LJLA targumim, I have utilized the texts presented in the Comprehensive Aramaic Lexicon and the Accordance® Targum Module. I have also consulted critical editions of the targumim when possible.[4]

---

[3] Unless otherwise noted, the citations in this essay are from the Ms. Paris Héb. 110, which is from the Western recension. On the recensions, see Raphael Hai Melamed, *The Targum to Canticles According to Six Yemen MSS: Compared with the 'Textus Receptus' as Contained in de Lagarde's 'Hagiographa Chaldaice'* (Philadelphia: Dropsie College, 1921); Carlos Alonso Fontela, *El Targum al Cantar de los Cantares* (PhD Diss., Edición Critica Colleción Tesis Doctorales, 92/87, Madrid: Editorial de la Universidad Complutense de Madrid, 1987). See also Philip S. Alexander, *The Targum of Canticles: Translated, with a Critical Introduction, Apparatus, and Notes* (The Aramaic Bible 17A, Collegeville, MN: Liturgical Press, 2003) pp. 6–7; Litke, *Targum Song of Songs*, pp. 3–6.

[4] Note http://cal.huc.edu; Emanuel White, *A Critical Edition of the Targum of Psalms: A Computer Generated Text of Books I and II* (PhD Diss., McGill University, 1988); David M. Stec, *The Text of the Targum of Job: An Introduction and Critical Edition* (AGJU, 20, Leiden: Brill, 1994); Derek R. G. Beattie, 'The Targum of Ruth: A Preliminary Edition', in Paul V. M. Flesher (ed.), *Studies in Aramaic Translations and Interpretations in Memory of Ernest G. Clark* (SAIS, 2, Leiden: Brill, 2002); Peter Stephan Knobel, *Targum Qoheleth: A Linguistic and Exegetical Inquiry* (PhD Diss., Yale University, 1976).

2. CAUSATIVE STEM AND THE USE OF THE *HAPHEL*

One archaism attested in TgSong concerns the use of verbal stems. As is the case in the late dialects of Aramaic, TgSong utilizes a group of verbal stems that includes the *peal* G-stem, *pael* D-stem, and the like, but there is one exception that occurs in the Causative stem. As is standard among the late dialects, nearly every attestation of the C-stem in TgSong is an *aphel*, but on one occasion the targumist uses a *haphel* form. TgSong 2.17, in part, reads as follows:[5]

ובזעירות יומיא עבדו בני ישראל ית עגלא ... ובעא ייי להובדא יתהון מן עלמא

> And within a few days, the Israelites made the calf ... and the Lord wanted to destroy them from the world.

One wonders why the targumist used a *haphel* here instead of the expected *aphel* and what influenced this decision.

The *haphel* with its prefixed ה was the original Aramaic form of the Causative stem.[6] The transition to *aphel* likely occurred because of the loss of intervocalic ה in the prefix conjugation, where, for instance, *yəhaqṭel* > *yaqṭel*. This loss of ה then spread through the rest of the verbal paradigm by analogy, and the א stood in place of the consonant onset.[7] While it is probable that the phonological change had already occurred in at least the imperfect by the time of Imperial Aramaic, conventional spellings with ה continued for some time. Therefore, we see the presence of both the *aphel* and *haphel* in Middle Aramaic dialects, most

[5] Note that the Yemenite recension has an *aphel* instead of a *haphel*, as is attested throughout the Western recension.

[6] Rainer Degen, *Altaramäische Grammatik der Inschriften des 10.–8. Jahrhundert v. Chr.* (AKM, 38, 3, Wiesbaden: Kommissionsverlag Franz Steiner, 1969) p. 66; Holger Gzella, *A Cultural History of Aramaic: From the Beginnings to the Advent of Islam* (HdO, 1, 111, Leiden: Brill, 2015) p. 34.

[7] Klaus Beyer, *Die aramäischen Texten vom Toten Meer* (*ATTM* I) (Göttingen: Vandenhoeck & Ruprecht, 1984) p. 148.

notably in Biblical Aramaic.[8] By the late dialects, the *haphel* fully gives way to the *aphel*.[9]

Returning to the TgSong passage, since Biblical Aramaic modeling would be a likely explanation for the form, it is worth noting that the use of the *haphel* here is not context based. This is to say that the targumist is not mimicking a Biblical Aramaic form because the events being described in the Targum are related to the events described in Biblical Aramaic texts.[10] Rather, as is the

---

[8] Takamitsu Muraoka and Bezalel Porten, *A Grammar of Egyptian Aramaic* (HdO 1, 32, Leiden: Brill, 1998) pp. 113–116; Margaretha L. Folmer, *The Aramaic Language in the Achaemenid Period: A Study in Linguistic Variation* (OLA, 68, Leuven: Peeters, 1995) pp. 123–137; Franz Rosenthal, *A Grammar of Biblical Aramaic* (PLO, 5, Wiesbaden: Harrassowitz Verlag, 7th edn., 2006) p. 46; Muraoka, *A Grammar of Qumran Aramaic* (ANES, 38, Leuven: Peeters, 2011) pp. 109–111; Jean Cantineau, *Le nabatéen: 1 notions génerales — écriture grammaire* (Paris: Librairie Ernest Leroux, 1930) pp. 68–70; Cantineau, *Grammaire du palmyrénien épigraphique* (Le Caire: Imprimerie de l'institute français d'archéologie orientale, 1935) p. 87.

[9] Concerning the morphology of the C-stem in the late dialects, see Steven E. Fassberg, *A Grammar of the Palestinian Targum Fragments from the Cairo Genizah* (HSS, 38, Atlanta: Scholars Press, 1990) p. 171; Elitzur A. Bar-Asher Siegal, *Introduction to the Grammar of Jewish-Babylonian Aramaic* (Lehrbücher orientalischer Sprachen, III/3, Münster: Ugarit-Verlag, 1st edn., 2013) pp. 124–128; Theodor Nöldeke, *A Compendious Syriac Grammar. Translated from the Second and Improved German edition by James A. Crichton. And with an Appendix: The Handwritten Additions in Theodor Nöldeke's Personal Copy edited by Anton Schall and translated by Peter T. Daniels* (London: Williams & Norgate, 1904; Winona Lake: Eisenbrauns, 2001) p. 107; Christa Müller-Kessler, *Grammatik des Christlich-Palästinisch-Aramäischen: Teil 1* (TSO, 6, Hildesheim: Georg Olms Verlag, 1991) pp. 173–177; Abraham Tal, *Samaritan Aramaic* (Lehrbücher orientalischer Sprachen, III/2, Münster: Ugarit-Verlag, 2013) pp. 60–61; Theodor Nöldeke, *Mandäische Grammatik* (Halle, 1875) pp. 211–212.

[10] This contrasts with the targumist's use of Biblical Aramaic words, which appears to be more context based. Words in TgSong that are more characteristic of Biblical Aramaic often occur in contexts that would welcome the use of an older term, such as the use of כהל 'to be able' in 7.9 (as opposed to יכל) in a passage describing Daniel's colleagues or similarly, the use of אשתדור 'sedition' (6.1) when giving the reasoning for Israel's exile. See Litke, 'The Lexicon of Targum Song of Songs', pp. 96–97.

case in about half of the Targum, the targumist is describing the events surrounding the exodus from Egypt and the wilderness wanderings, and he does not use *haphel* forms elsewhere. This is, however, the only time that the verbal root אבד is attested in the Targum, and this opens up the possibility that the use of the *haphel* is lexeme specific.

In order to gain a better understanding of the use of the *haphel* in TgSong, a broader analysis of the other LJLA targumic texts is instructive.[11] The *haphel* is attested 154 times in these texts, and their distribution is as follows:

Root	Total C-Stem Attestations	*Haphel* Attestations (% of total)	LJLA Texts with *Haphel* [12]	BA Attestation in *Haphel*	BH Attestation in *Hiphil*
אבד 'to destroy'	85	36 (42.3%)	Esth I, Esth II, TgPsJ, TgQoh, TgChr, TgSong	Yes	Yes
אתי 'to bring'	133	8 (6%)	TgPsJ	Yes	Yes[13]
חוי 'to show'	4	1 (25%)	TgJob	Yes	No
חצף 'to dare, be insolent'	2	1 (50%)	TgQoh	Yes	No
חרב 'to destroy'	12	1 (9.1%)	TgEsth II	Yes	No

[11] For a discussion of the *haphel* in TgPsJ, see also Edward M. Cook, *Rewriting the Bible: The Text and Language of the Pseudo-Jonathan Targum* (PhD Diss., University of California, Los Angeles, 1986) pp. 182–184.

[12] The numbers that include TgPsJ only refer to attestations that are unique to TgPsJ and do not include those attestations that are shared by Onqelos or the Palestinian targum tradition.

[13] There are two attestations, Isa. 21.14 and Jer. 12.9.

ידי 'to give thanks'	86	11 (12.8%)	TgPs, TgPsJ	No	Yes
ידע 'to make known'	49	27 (55.1%)	TgPs, TgJob, TgPsJ, TgEsth II, TgQoh, TgChr	Yes	Yes
יפע 'to shine'	5	2 (33.3%)	TgPs	No	Yes
נזק 'to damage'	7	5 (71.4%)	TgPsJ	Yes	No
נפק 'to send forth'	119	39 (32.8%)	TgPs, TgPsJ, TgJob	Yes	No
עדי 'to remove'	30	2 (6.7%)	TgEsth II	Yes	Yes[14]
עלל 'to make enter'	48	9 (18.8%)	TgPsJ	Yes	No
צלי 'to incline'	19	1 (5.3%)	TgPs	No[15]	No
קום 'to raise'	72	4 (5.6%)	TgPs, TgEsth II	Yes	Yes
שכח 'to forget'	129	6 (4.6%)	TgPsJ	Yes	Yes[16]
שני 'to change'	4	1 (25%)	TgPs	Yes	No

[14] There is one attestation, Prov. 25.20.
[15] The root occurs in the D-stem in Dan. 6.11 and Ezra 6.10.
[16] There is one attestation, Jer. 23.27.

Several points can be drawn from this information. First, the LJLA texts with the most *haphel* forms are TgPsJ, TgPs, and TgEsth II, and they account for 78% of the *haphel* forms.

Second, as was the case with TgSong, they do not appear to be consistently used for any contextual reasons. This includes roots that are frequently attested in the *haphel*, like the root ידע 'to make known', which occurs in the *haphel* 55% of the time, as well as roots that are rarely attested in the *haphel*, such as שכח 'to find', which occurs in the *haphel* only 4.6% of the time.

Third, with only three exceptions, every *haphel* attested in LJLA occurs with a root that is likewise attested in Biblical Aramaic in the *haphel*;[17] this accounts for thirteen of the roots and leaves only three exceptions. One exception, the root יפע 'to shine', occurs six times in the C-stem in LJLA, and there is manuscript evidence for the use of the *haphel* in four of these occurrences.[18] It is important to note that this root occurs in the *haphel* on two occasions in TgJon,[19] but perhaps more significantly, the cognate root occurs in the *hiphil* in the underlying Hebrew of these verses. In the case of TgPsJ Deut. 33.2, the Palestinian targum tradition uses the exact form attested in the Hebrew (הופיע).[20] It would be best, therefore, to view these forms as Hebraisms. The *haphel* forms of the root ידי 'to give thanks', a second exception, are similarly influenced by the Hebrew. This root occurs in the *haphel* ten times in TgPs and one time in TgPsJ.[21] Each attestation of this root in TgPs is likewise attested in the underlying Hebrew in a *hiphil* form, though the ה from the *hiphil* only occurs in the Ps. 45.18 attestation because of the

[17] The converse of this statement is not true, which is to say that the use of the *haphel* with a given root in Biblical Aramaic does not necessitate its presence in the *haphel* in LJLA.

[18] The *haphel* is attested with this root in TgPsJ Deut. 33.2, TgPs. 80.2; 94.1; TgJob 37.15 (in a minority of manuscripts).

[19] See Judg. 5.4; Ezek. 7.10; neither of these attestations have the Hebrew cognate in the underlying Hebrew.

[20] While the two remaining C-stem attestations of the root likewise have the root in the Hebrew in *hiphil* forms, the targumist uses *aphel* forms; see TgJob 3.4; 10.3.

[21] TgPs. 7.18; 45.18; 99.3; 107.8, 15, 21, 31; 118.21; 140.14; 145.10; TgPsJ Gen. 49.8.

morphology of the I-*yod* verb.[22] Both of these roots just mentioned have Hebrew cognates with attestations in Biblical Hebrew in the C-stem, and the Hebrew influence is understandable given the translational character of the targumim. The only other exceptional root, צלי 'to incline', does not have a Hebrew cognate, but it is translating the *hiphil* form הַטֵּה 'to incline' in Ps. 31.3 and may likewise be influenced by it.[23] In the end, we can point primarily to Biblical Aramaic modeling or secondarily to Biblical Hebrew influence for every attestation of the *haphel* in LJLA.

Fourth, the *haphel* is the minority form for almost every verbal root, and most of these roots use the *haphel* in fewer than 10% of the C-stem attestations. This is especially noticeable when one leaves out the verbal roots that are attested five times or fewer in the entire corpus.[24] As such, the *haphel* should be seen as an *occasional* variant, which raises questions about the intentionality of their use on the targumists' part. There are, however, two roots that are notable given their high frequency of *haphel* forms and their presence in several LJLA texts. The C-stem of the root אבד 'to destroy' is attested in the *haphel* in 42% of its eighty-five attestations.[25] The vast majority of these attestations are translating the Hebrew cognate, though most of these are not in the *hiphil*. The root ידע 'to make known' occurs in the *haphel* in 55% of the forty-nine C-stem attestations, and nearly every attestation is translating a *hiphil* form of this Hebrew cognate.[26] It is also significant that Onqelos and Jonathan use the *haphel* with this root, and it is likely that the targumists were influenced by these older and more official targumim. It is notable that these

---

[22] As for the *haphel* of this root in TgPsJ Gen. 49.8 (יהודון), Cook has argued that this form is used to strengthen the play on words with יהודאין 'Jews' later in the verse; see Cook, *Rewriting the Bible*, pp. 183–184. One might add that the verse also begins with יהודה 'Judah' in both the Hebrew and the Aramaic.

[23] According to White's edition, the *haphel* is attested in a minority of manuscripts, with the majority attesting an *aphel*.

[24] Of the sixteen verbal roots with *haphel* attestations in LJLA, nine of the roots have five or fewer attestations.

[25] These *haphel* forms occur in TgPsJ, TgJob, TgChr, TgEsth I, TgEsth II, and TgSong.

[26] These occur in TgPsJ, TgPs, TgJob, TgEsth II, TgChr, and TgQoh.

two roots which are most frequently attested in the *haphel* in LJLA have Hebrew cognates, and the root ידע is regularly *haphel* in Onqelos in Jonathan, a primary influence on the LJLA targumim.

In conclusion, the *haphel* in LJLA should be seen as an occasional variant that is not contextually based. It is not a productive verbal stem, and it is root specific. Nearly every single verbal root attested in the *haphel* is likewise attested in Biblical Aramaic, and the remainder show Hebrew influence. The two roots most frequently attested in the *haphel* are אבד 'to destroy' and ידע 'to make known'. Both have Hebrew cognates, and the latter occurs in the *haphel* throughout Onqelos and Jonathan.

3. HISTORIC שׂ

A second feature is the orthographic use of historic שׂ, as opposed to ס.[27] When Aramaic inherited the twenty-two letters of the Phoenician alphabet, Aramaic scribes enlisted certain graphemes to do double-duty to account for their larger phonemic inventory. One of these was ש, which represented both /š/ and /ś/.[28] The beginning stages of a merger of /ś/ and /s/ (represented by ס) is attested in Imperial Aramaic texts. This is initially noticeable in loan words where the exact pronunciation was unclear; this is seen, for instance, in the spellings of Sennacherib in Aḥiqar as both סנאחריב (C1.1.50) and שנאחריב (TAD C1.1.3).[29] In Middle Aramaic texts, though scribes often maintained the distinction between the letters in their spellings, it is likely that the merger was complete.[30] The letter ס is primarily used in Late Aramaic texts, though one still finds spellings with שׂ in some later Jewish

[27] In what follows, I will use the diacritical dot above the שׂ for the sake of disambiguation, though that is not a standard practice in the manuscripts.

[28] Degen, *Altararamäische Grammatik*, p. 31; Beyer, *ATTM* I, pp. 102–103.

[29] Muraoka and Porten, *Egyptian Aramaic*, pp. 6–7. Though from Middle Aramaic, see also the different spellings of the loan word 'harp' in Biblical Aramaic as both סַבְּכָא (Dan. 3.5) and שַׂבְּכָא (Dan. 3.10, 15). It is also worth noting the complicated representation of sibilants in Neo-Assyrian here. See Stephen A. Kaufman, *The Akkadian Influences on Aramaic* (AS, 19, Chicago: University of Chicago Press, 1974) pp. 140–142; many thanks to Andrew Gross for pointing out this connection.

[30] Rosenthal, *Biblical Aramaic*, p. 20; Beyer, *ATTM* I, p. 421.

texts.[31] In the targumic literature, as Dalman notes regarding Onqelos and Jonathan, the use of שׂ in these targumim is almost exclusively limited to proper names.[32] The use of שׂ is attested in the Palestinian targum tradition, but it is much more frequently seen in Neofiti than in the Cairo Genizah manuscripts or the Fragment Targum manuscripts. Notably, some of the words attested with historic שׂ in Neofiti are spelled as such early in the manuscript, but they are spelled more frequently with ס later in the manuscript. This suggests that some of the spellings with שׂ may be the result of scribal changes.[33]

Looking at TgSong, there is a stark distinction between the two recensions of the Targum. The Western recension attests the use of historic שׂ, but the Yemenite recension does not.[34] In fact, this is another example of Yemenite scribes smoothing out unusual features in TgSong and replacing them with more familiar forms from Onqelos and Jonathan. Given that the use of historic שׂ is attested in other LJLA texts, including certain ones that do not have a Yemenite recension, it is safe to assume that historic שׂ was one of those original features that was removed by Yemenite scribes. In the Western recension, the use of historic שׂ is lexeme specific and inconsistent.

The natural impulse is to assume that the targumists were modeling the older Aramaic spelling practices as seen in Biblical Aramaic. This indeed accounts for a number of words spelled with שׂ, such as בשׂר 'flesh', שׂער 'hair', and עשׂר 'ten'. But this does not account for other words, such as פרשׂ 'to spread' and שׂפה 'lip', which do not occur in Biblical Aramaic. A second option would be that all of the words with an etymological שׂ are spelled as

---

[31] Beyer, *ATTM* I, p. 421; Fassberg, *Grammar*, p. 26; Bar-Asher Siegal, *Jewish-Babylonian Aramaic*, pp. 37–38.

[32] There are occasional differences between Targum Jonathan and Targum Onqelos in this regard. Note, for instance, that Jonathan has the form חשׂיך 'poor, lean', whereas Onqelos has חסיך (all in Genesis 41).

[33] For example, the verb 'to hate' is usually spelled as שׂני in Genesis, but it is usually spelled as סני later in the manuscript.

[34] The Cairo Genizah manuscripts occasionally exhibit the use of ס in relevant environments; see Litke, 'Targum Canticles and Linguistic Complexity', p. 213.

such, but this does not follow either, since, for instance, the words סנא 'enemy' and סיתוא 'winter' are spelled with ס instead of etymological שׂ.[35] A closer look at all of the words spelled with שׂ shows that every word in TgSong spelled with a שׂ has a Hebrew cognate spelled with שׂ, and in fact, we can say that every attestation of שׂ in TgSong is due to Hebrew spelling conventions. There are two important caveats. First, not every word spelled with a שׂ in Hebrew occurs as such in TgSong, but rather, if a word is attested in TgSong with שׂ, then it occurs in Hebrew with שׂ. Second, the fact that we are dealing with Hebrew spelling conventions and not a modeling of some kind of *Aramaic* archaism is most noticeable when we look at words spelled with שׂ in Biblical Aramaic that do not have Hebrew cognates. Every one of these words, such as שׂהדו 'testimony' and שׂטר 'side' is spelled with a ס in TgSong. Therefore, the use of historic שׂ in TgSong should be considered a Hebraism, not an Aramaic archaism. Note the summary of the TgSong attestations in the following chart:

Word Spelled with שׂ in TgSong	Spelled with שׂ in BA	Spelled with שׂ in BH
בשׂר 'flesh'	Yes	Yes
כשׂדאי 'Chaldean'	Yes	Yes
מעשׂר 'tithe'	No	Yes
עשׂר 'ten, -teen'	Yes	Yes
עשׂירי 'tenth'	No	Yes
פרשׂ in G-stem 'to spread'	No	Yes

[35] It is notable that the word סיתוא 'winter' is only attested one time in Biblical Hebrew. It is in the same verse as the TgSong attestation (2.11), where it is spelled with ס. Clearly the targumist was thinking about the underlying Hebrew here.

שמאלא 'left'	No	Yes
שער 'hair'	Yes	Yes
שפה 'lip'	No	Yes
בשׂם 'spice, perfume' (less common spelling; בסם is more common)[36]	No	Yes
Notable Words Spelled with ס in TgSong	Spelled with שׂ in BA	Spelled with שׂ in BH
סנא n. 'enemy', vb. 'to hate'[37]	Yes	Yes
סכל 'to look at'	Yes	Yes[38]
סגי 'many, much'	Yes	No cognate[39]
סהדו 'testimony'	Yes	No cognate
סטר 'side'	Yes	No cognate

So what of LJLA as a whole? As was the case in TgSong, every instance of שׂ should be attributed to Hebrew influence, rather than Aramaic archaizing. First, thirty-six of the words attested with שׂ in LJLA have Hebrew cognates or corresponding roots spelled as such in Biblical Hebrew (and many of them are spelled

---

[36] This is much like the other LJLA texts and the Palestinian targum tradition, where the word is primarily spelled בסם, though exceptions occur.

[37] This word is attested one time in TgSong 2.14, and this spelling with ס is the primary spelling in LJLA more broadly. Roughly 90% of the LJLA attestations of this root are spelled with a ס, though exceptions occur with שׂ.

[38] Biblical Hebrew attests this root, but it has the nuance of thought rather than sight.

[39] There are two BH attestations of this root spelled with שׂ, Job 12.23; 36.24. Both instances should be interpreted as Aramaisms.

this way in Rabbinic Hebrew as well).[40] This accounts for all but three of the words attested with שׂ in LJLA. Second, it is possible that two of the remaining three instances have been influenced by the underlying Hebrew, though the words in question are not Hebrew cognates. Note the second half of TgPs 96.8:

(BH) הָבוּ לַיהוָה כְּבוֹד שְׁמוֹ **שְׂאוּ**־מִנְחָה וּבֹאוּ לְחַצְרוֹתָיו׃

(TgPs) הבו קדם יהוה איקר ורוממו שמיה **ושוברו** תיקרובתא ועולו לקדמוי לדרתוי׃

> Ascribe glory before the Lord and exalt his name; carry a gift and enter before his courts.

The verb סובר is spelled unusually here with a שׂ instead of the customary ס. It is interesting to note when looking at the Hebrew, that the targumist is translating the verb נשׂא 'to lift, carry'. The verb סובר is not a standard translation of נשׂא in TgPs,[41] and it is possible that the שׂ in the underlying Hebrew had an influence on the peculiar spelling of this word.[42] I have found only one word spelled with a שׂ in LJLA that does not seem to have an explanation pointing to Hebrew influence, and that is the spelling of the word יסוד 'base' with a שׂ in TgPsJ Lev. 4.7. This word

---

[40] Note the following: ארשׂ in the D-stem 'to betroth'; בשׂם 'spice, perfume'; בשׂם in the G-stem 'to be sweet', in the D-stem 'to sweeten', בשׂר 'flesh'; בשׂר in the D-stem 'to announce'; חשׂיך 'poor, lean'; חשׂך in the G-stem 'to keep back'; חפשׂ in the D-stem 'to dig'; מעשׂר 'tithe'; נשׂא in the G-stem 'to lift up', in the Dt-stem 'to be lifted up'; עשׂב 'grass'; ערשׂ 'bed'; פרשׂ in the G-stem 'to spread'; קשׂו 'jug'; שׂבע 'satiety'; שׂגב in the D-stem 'to exalt, lift up'; שׂדד in the D-stem 'to plow'; שׂטן in the G-stem 'to be hostile'; שׂיבה 'old age'; שׂיבו 'old age'; שׂיח in the C-stem 'to speak of'; שׂים in the G-stem 'to set'; שׂכל 'knowledge'; שׂמ(א)ל 'left'; שׂמאלי 'left hand'; שׂמח in the D-stem 'to make joyful'; שׂמחה 'joy'; שׂממי 'lizard'; שׂנא 'enemy'; שׂנא in the G-stem 'to hate'; שׂנאה 'enmity'; שׂער 'hair'; שׂערה 'barley' שׂפם 'upper lip'; שׂרטה 'incision'; תפשׂ in the G-stem 'to grab'.

[41] This equivalence is only used 14% of the time. Some other more common translation equivalents are זקף 'to lift, raise', שבק 'to forgive', נטל 'to lift up', רום in C-stem 'to raise'.

[42] A similar situation is seen in TgJob 41.25, where the verb עסי in the D-stem ('to press; to compel') is uncharacteristically spelled with a שׂ in the majority of the manuscripts. It is likely that this is a play on העשׂו 'the one who made him' in the underlying Hebrew.

occurs with a ס in the underlying Hebrew, and the same term is spelled with the standard ס in the other four instances in which it is attested in the same chapter in TgPsJ. This may indeed be an archaic hypercorrection, and the only one in the corpus.[43]

It is also important to note that, as was the case in TgSong, Aramaic words spelled with שׂ in Biblical Aramaic that do not have Hebrew cognates are never spelled with a שׂ in LJLA, where they are all (such as שׂטר 'side' and שׂהדו 'testimony') consistently spelled with a ס.[44]

In conclusion, with the lone exception of 'base' (which occurs one time with the spelling ישׂוד), every attestation of שׂ in LJLA should be considered a Hebraism of some kind rather than an *Aramaic* archaism. Once again, there are three caveats. First, not all words attested with שׂ in Hebrew are also attested with a שׂ in LJLA. Second, the spellings with שׂ are not necessarily dependent on whether the word occurs in the underlying Hebrew. And a third point, which I have not yet noted, is that the vast majority of words attested with שׂ are occasional variants, as was the case with the use of the *haphel*. For instance, while some words, like בשׂר 'flesh', occur frequently with שׂ (roughly 50% of the time), others, like עשׂב 'grass, herbage' are much less frequent (about 15% of the time), and others are even less.

4. THIRD FEMININE SINGULAR PRONOMINAL SUFFIX ON NOUNS

One final feature that I will address is the third feminine singular pronominal suffix /-ahā/ in environments where a simple /-ah/ is expected. Though this is attested in other LJLA texts, it is fairly infrequent outside of TgSong, where it is uniquely the only 3fs

---

[43] This term is notably spelled with a שׂ on two occasions in Qumran texts: 4Q266 5 ii 9; 8 iii 6.

[44] The same cannot be said for the Palestinian targum tradition, particularly Neofiti. Cairo Genizah MS C unsurprisingly has שׂהדו (with a שׂ) in Gen. 31.47, as it occurs in the underlying text (the lone Aramaic phrase in the Pentateuch). Neofiti spells the term with a שׂ frequently in Genesis and Exodus, though the infrequency of the spelling with שׂ in the latter half of the Pentateuch suggests that the spellings with שׂ are the result of scribal activity. TgPsJ has the word סָהִיד 'witness' in Gen. 31.47.

suffix used with nouns.[45] When looking at this feature, there are two considerations to take into account: (1) historical Aramaic considerations and (2) language contact considerations.

Aramaic historically had two types of pronominal suffixes, and the type that is utilized is determined by the phonological environment. Generally speaking, Type 1 suffixes typically follow consonants and are therefore used most frequently with masculine singular and feminine nouns. Type 2 suffixes tend to follow vowels, and that means that they are most typically used with masculine plural nouns.[46]

The Type 1 3fs suffix was always /-ah/ and was represented by ה– from the earliest inscriptions.[47] The Type 2 suffix was also represented by ה– in Old Aramaic texts and, for the most part, in Imperial Aramaic texts, though in the latter, one sees rare spellings with הה– or הא–, which arguably indicated /-ahā/.[48] Cook, following and building on the earlier work of Kutscher and Beyer, argues that the Type 2 suffix was always /-ahā/ from the earliest dialects, but the final /-ā/ was not always orthographically represented because it was unstressed.[49] In

---

[45] Outside of TgSong, there are fewer than thirty attestations of this suffix in the corpus of LJLA targuim. Cook notes some of them and attributes them to scribal carelessness; see *Rewriting the Bible*, p. 133.

[46] Concerning the phonological environment of these pronouns, see Folmer, *Aramaic Language in the Achaemenid Period*, pp. 237–238; Edward M. Cook, 'The Orthography of Final Unstressed Long Vowels in Old and Imperial Aramaic', *Maarav* 5–6 (1990), pp. 53–67 (55 n. 11).

[47] Degen, *Altaramäische Grammatik*, p. 55; Volker Hug, *Altaramäische Grammatik der Texte des 7. und 6. Jh.s v. Chr.* (HSAO, 4, Heidelberg: Heidelberger Orientverlag, 1993) p. 56.

[48] For a discussion of the attestations, see Folmer, *Aramaic Language in the Achaemenid Period*, pp. 237–241; Muraoka and Porten, *Egyptian Aramaic*, p. 50; Ursula Schattner-Rieser, 'Some Observations on Qumran Aramaic: The 3rd Fem. Sing. Pronominal Suffix', in Lawrence H. Schiffman, Emanual Tov, and James C. VanderKam (eds.), *The Dead Sea Scrolls: Fifty Years after Their Discovery: Proceedings of the Jerusalem Congress, July 20–25, 1997* (Jerusalem: Israel Exploration Society, 2000) pp. 739–745 (739–740).

[49] E. Y. Kutscher, 'Aramaic' in T. A. Sebok (ed.), *Current Trends in Linguistics* 6, Linguistics in South West Asia and North Africa (The Hague:

Qumran Aramaic, the longer /-ahā/ suffix is attested much more frequently (particularly in the Genesis Apocryphon).[50] In addition to the possibility that this long form in Qumran Aramaic orthographically represents the suffix that had always been present, scholars have alternately posited that we are dealing with situations of diglossia or language contact. Concerning language contact in particular, Fitzmyer suggests that the /-ahā/ forms in Qumran Aramaic are possible Hebraisms, but as Fassberg notes in his survey of possible Hebraisms in Qumran Aramaic, this is not a convincing explanation.[51] More recently, Schattner-Rieser states, 'we should not rule out the possibility of interference with another Semitic language, most likely Arabic, alongside the theories of "archaizing" and "hebraizing"'.[52] Regardless of how we should deal with the Qumran forms, it is unquestionably the case that the forms in Targum Onqelos and Targum Jonathan are regular with their spelling of the Type 1 suffix as ה– /-ah/ and Type 2 suffix as הא– /-ahā/.[53] Late dialects once again largely spelled the suffix with a simple final ה– which is vocalized as either /-a/ or /-e/.[54]

Mouton, 1970) pp. 347–412 (349–350); Beyer, *ATTM* I, pp. 122–125; Cook, 'Orthography', pp. 59–60.

[50] E. Y. Kutscher, 'The Language of the "Genesis Apocryphon": A Preliminary Study', *Aspects of the Dead Sea Scrolls = Scripta Hierosolymitana* 4 (Jerusalem: Magnes, 1958) pp. 1–34 (11); Schattner-Rieser, '3rd Fem. Sing. Pronominal Suffix', p. 741.

[51] Joseph A. Fitzmyer, *The Genesis Apocryphon of Qumran Cave 1: A Commentary* (BibOr, 18A, Rome: Biblical Institute Press, 2nd, rev. edn., 1971) pp. 26; Steven E. Fassberg, 'Hebraisms in the Aramaic Documents from Qumran', in *Studies in Qumran Aramaic* (Abr-Nahrain Supplement, 3, Louvain: Peters, 1992), pp. 48–69 (53–54).

[52] Schattner-Rieser, '3rd Fem. Sing. Pronominal Suffix', p. 745.

[53] Thomas O. Lambdin, *An Introduction to the Aramaic of Targum Onqelos*, revised by John Huehnergard (Cambridge: Harvard University, 2002, unpublished manuscript) pp. 15, 21; Douglas M. Gropp, *The Aramaic of Targum Onkelos and Jonathan: An Introduction* (unpublished manuscript) pp. 25–26, 42, 53–54.

[54] Fassberg, *Grammar*, p. 114; Bar-Asher Siegal, *Jewish-Babylonian Aramaic*, pp. 89–90; Tal, *Samaritan Aramaic*, pp. 37–39; Müller-Kessler, *Christlich-Palästinisch-Aramäischen*, pp. 69–70; Nöldeke, *Syriac Grammar*, p. 46; Nöldeke, *Mandäische Grammatik*, p. 88.

From a historical Aramaic perspective, this 3fs /-ahā/ suffix in TgSong would be a modeling of the suffixes that would have been primarily (or exclusively) known from Onqelos and Jonathan. In Type 2 contexts there are words with the expected /-ahā/ suffix, such as בנהא 'her sons' (1.8; 8.5) and עולימהא 'her lads' (6.10). What is unique is that the paradigms have leveled in TgSong, and in Type 1 contexts we see, for example, עפייהא 'its foliage' (2.2),[55] כספהא 'her money' (8.9),[56] and שלמהא 'her welfare' (8.10).[57] As was the case with the Qumran forms, one other significant possibility is that these suffixes are the result of language contact, and given the late date of this text, the most logical Semitic language is Arabic.

There is one 3fs suffix in Arabic, and in fact, it is /-hā/, but in contrast to what is seen in TgSong, the Arabic suffix is used in all environments: on nouns, verbs, and particles.[58] In TgSong, the /-ahā/ suffix is only used with nouns; otherwise, the targumist uses the simple final ה– /-ah/. If Arabic was influencing the targumist's decisions, why would he stop with the nouns? Rather, all of the unquestioned Arabisms in the Targum are limited to a list of gemstones in the Western recension of 5.14.[59] It seems more likely that the targumist was composing TgSong in a place, such as southern Italy, where Greek or some other Indo-European language would have been a more likely native language than Arabic. With this in mind, these 3fs suffixes should be seen as a

---

[55] The form עֲפִיַּהּ is expected. Compare the comparable form of the same morphological noun class פּוּתְיַהּ 'its width' (TgOnq Exod. 37.6).

[56] The form כַּסְפַּהּ is expected. Compare the Type 1 3ms suffix with this word, e.g., כַּסְפֵּיהּ (TgOnq Gen. 17.23).

[57] Compare בִשְׁלָמַהּ in TgJon Jer. 29.7. The TgSong manuscripts are not unanimous on this last form. Paris 110 has שלמה, which is either an emphatic form with the unusual (for this text) emphatic form with ה (instead of א) or it is a 3fs suffix with ה. Some other Western manuscripts have the unambiguously emphatic שלמא.

[58] John Huehnergard, *Introduction to the Comparative Study of the Semitic Languages* (Cambridge: Harvard, 2002, unpublished manuscript) p. 58. Note that these comments refer specifically to classical Arabic.

[59] Andrew W. Litke, 'Following the Frankincense: Reassessing the *Sitz im Leben* of Targum Song of Songs', *JSP* 27 (2018), pp. 289–313 (292–293); Alexander, *Targum of Canticles*, pp. 210–213.

modeling of Onqelos and Jonathan, not an Arabic influence. Analysis shows that nearly every grammatical category in TgSong begins with Onqelos and Jonathan being the primary models, and it is from their dialect that the targumist occasionally diverges. It is entirely possible that the targumist saw the /-ahā/ suffix and perceived that it was the older/more original *targumic* form (since they are not Biblical Aramaic forms),[60] and as such, he used this form in his own targumic composition. This feature is then archaic, insofar as it exhibits an attempt to utilize an older targumic form. In actuality, however, it is a modeling of Onqelos and Jonathan, which is the primary compositional approach of our targumist and is therefore not surprising, though the leveling to the Type 1 environments is notable.

5. EXCURSUS ON SCRIBAL CULTURE

One theme that runs through all of the features addressed in this essay is the role of scribes and scribal culture in the transmission (if not also the composition) of TgSong and the other LJLA targumim.[61] This does not, however, negate their devotional and synagogal use. In fact, I am not convinced that TgSong was purely a scribal invention written exclusively for scholars and divorced from a synagogal use, in spite of the fact that it is such a long targum and would take significant time to recite. To account for the sheer length of TgSong, it is important to keep in mind that the earliest comments regarding the recitation of Song of Songs stipulate that it should be read on two succeeding nights instead of in one service.[62] It is entirely possible that there were other

---

[60] Rosenthal, *Biblical Aramaic*, p. 24.

[61] I wish to thank Stephen A. Kaufman for reiterating this point after I delivered an earlier version of this essay at the 2017 Society of Biblical Literature conference in Boston. See also Leeor Gottlieb, 'Composition of Targums after the Decline of Aramaic as a Spoken Language', *AS* 12 (2014), pp. 1–8.

[62] See *Massekhet Soferim* 14.7. Concerning the date of this late tractate, see H. L. Strack and Günter Stemberger, *Introduction to the Talmud and Midrash* (trans. M. Bockmuehl; Minneapolis: Fortress Press, 2nd edn., 1996 [1991]) pp. 227–228; Deborah Reed Blank, *Soferim: A Commentary to Chapters 10–12 and a Reconsideration of the Evidence* (PhD Diss., Jewish Theological Seminary of America, 1998) pp. 59–72; M. B. Lerner, 'The

ways of breaking up the recitation during the Passover Holiday as well. Additionally, in the preface to his edition of the North-Eastern Neo-Aramaic translation of TgSong, Yona Sabar fondly recalls reading TgSong while growing up in Kurdistan, and he shows the feasibility of the Targum's use in the synagogues by stating, 'It was read by individuals or, for those who could not read, recited in the synagogue by the Ḥakham in the original Targumic Aramaic, and translated into the spoken language ... during the Passover Holiday'.[63] It is clear that there was a devotional and synagogal use of TgSong.

At the same time, it is also clear that TgSong and the other LJLA targumim were transmitted and preserved in a scribal milieu, with certain scholarly and pedagogical interests at play. In such a setting, one would expect that the scribes were more familiar with Hebrew and the official targumim of Onqelos or Jonathan. This would help to explain two of the features discussed in this essay, namely the spelling of words with שׂ being a Hebraic feature and the third feminine suffix /-ahā/ being a modeling and expansion of the suffix known from Onqelos and Jonathan. The scribal setting could also help explain the *occasional* use of the *haphel* and שׂ, where accidents or mental lapses may have occasionally been a factor in the presence of different forms. The scribes were not entirely consistent, but as is the case with other linguistic features in LJLA, they contribute to the artificial regularity of the language that one finds in these targumim. Of course, the linguistic peculiarities cannot be fully explained away as scribal mistakes or alterations, and in fact, many of the features were likely original to the targumim. It does mean, however, that scribal culture had an important role to play in the creation and transmission of these targumim.

What is still unclear is how the scribal culture and process helps describe the collective and individual natures of the LJLA targumim; they are individual compositions, but they are also a

---

External Tractates', in S. Safrai (ed.), *The Literature of the Sages, Part 1* (CRINT, 3, 1, Philadelphia: Fortress Press, 1987) pp. 367–403 (397–400).

[63] Sabar, *Targum de-Targum: An Old Neo-Aramaic Version of the Targum on Song of Songs. Introduction, Eclectic Text, English Translation, Comparative Notes, and Glossary* (Wiesbaden: Otto Harrassowitz, 1991) p. 7.

loose group of texts. They can be subdivided in different ways, but many of their linguistic peculiarities are seen across the group, though in varying degrees.[64] As more linguistic work is being done on the individual LJLA texts, it is also important to continue addressing areas of convergence across the LJLA texts in order to better understand the nature of their interrelatedness.

6. CONCLUSION

In this essay I have analyzed three features in TgSong and LJLA more broadly that could be vaguely classified as archaic. Upon closer analysis, a more nuanced understanding of these features has emerged. The use of the *haphel* is an occasional variant that is root specific. It is not productive, and with very few exceptions, all of the roots are likewise attested in the *haphel* in Biblical Aramaic, the lone exceptions likely being influenced by the underlying Hebrew. Second, the spelling of certain words with שׂ is wholly attributable to Hebrew spelling conventions and should not be considered an Aramaic archaism. Third, the 3fs pronominal suffix /-ahā/ is more specific to TgSong, though it is attested elsewhere. It is a modeling of the language of Onqelos and Jonathan, but this fits the larger linguistic picture of the Targum and as such, is not out of the ordinary with this Targum. Though the leveling of the paradigm is unique, the suffix should still be seen through the lens of these older targumim. This more nuanced understanding of the features presented in this essay has not only allowed us to better understand these archaic features (two of which should not be considered archaic in the first place), but it has also provided insights into the targumists' literary influences and compositional intentions.

---

[64] Dalman argues that there is a linguistic difference between the Megilloth and the other late targumim; see Gustaf Dalman, *Grammatik des jüdisch-palästinischen Aramäisch* (Leipzig: J. C. Hinrichs Verlag, 1905; repr. Darmstadt: Wissenschaftliche Buchgesellschaft, 2nd edn., 1960) pp. 27–39. The texts can also be categorized in other ways as well. See Kaufman's distribution of the LJLA texts based on their Syriac correspondences in Steven A. Kaufman, 'The Dialectology of Late Jewish Literary Aramaic', *AS* 11 (2013), pp. 145–148.

SOME TRANSLATION FEATURES IN THE HARQLEAN VERSION OF FIRST PETER

JEROME A. LUND

The honoree has contributed studies to many dialects of Aramaic including Syriac, especially as they relate to the Bible. I wish to make a small contribution to the analysis of translation techniques employed by Thomas of Harqel in his rendering of First Peter.[1] Thomas made a recension of the Greek New Testament that incorporated variant Greek readings[2] and that

---

[1] For an informed introduction to the version of Thomas of Harqel, see Andreas Juckel, 'Ḥarqlean Version' in Sebastian P. Brock, Aaron M. Butts, George A. Kiraz, and Lucas Van Rompay (eds.), *Gorgias Encyclopedic Dictionary of the Syriac Heritage* (Piscataway, NJ: Gorgias Press and Beth Mardutho: The Syriac Institute, 2011) pp. 188–191. The text of the Harqlean used in this essay derives from *Das neue Testament in syrischer Überlieferung*, I. *Die grossen katholischen Briefe*, in Verbindung mit A. Juckel, herausgegeben und untersucht von Barbara Aland (Berlin and New York: Walter de Gruyter, 1986). For the Greek New Testament and Peshitta New Testament, the Accordance modules NA28–T, Version 2.1, containing *Novum Testamentum Graece* (28th revised edition; edited by Barbara and Kurt Aland, Johannes Karavidopoulos, Carlo M. Martini, and Bruce M. Metzger; Stuttgart: Deutsche Bibelgesellschaft, 2012) and PESHNT-T, Version 3.0, containing the text of the British and Foreign Bible Society (London, [1920]) as provided by George A. Kiraz were used.

[2] For example, he marks ※ܗܘ ܕܠܘܬܗܘܢ ܡܢ ܡܬܓܕܦ : ܠܘܬܟܘܢ ܕܝܢ ܡܫܬܒܚ↙ 'He that, on the one hand, is blasphemed with them, on the other hand, is

marked words needed for sense but lacking in his Greek sources,[3] completing his work in A.D. 616.[4] While he used the earlier Philoxenian version (A.D. 507/8) as a source, he did not aim at a revision of that translation, but purposed 'to make the Syriac text into as formal a representation of the Greek original as possible'[5] and so translated directly from Greek texts.[6] The exact relationship between the Harqlean and the Philoxenian versions of First Peter cannot be determined because the Philoxenian is not extant for this book, yet the verses culled from Philoxenus' *Commentary on the Prologue of John* for other books of the New Testament by Sebastian Brock demonstrate its influence on Thomas as well as his independence from it.[7] Thomas' translation complements the translation of the Old Testament of Paul of Tella (the so-called Syro-hexapla) made at the same time, under the same auspices, and using similar techniques of translation—they were part of the same translation project. John Gwynn has suggested that the occasion of the translation was the reunion of the Syrian and Coptic Miaphysites who had broken from each other some years earlier.[8] Viewed as such, it was an ecumenical translation aimed at mending the schism.[9] After the Islamic

---

glorified with you' (1 Pet. 4.14) as appearing in some Greek source(s), but not all. The reading *κατα μεν αυτους βλασφημειται κατα δε υμας δοξαζεται* 'On the one hand, he is blasphemed by them, but, on the other hand, he is glorified by you' is known from some manuscripts.

[3] For example, he translated *ἐν πάσῃ ἀναστροφῇ* 'in all conduct' as ܒܟܠܗ ܗܘܦܟܐ ⁺ܕܝܠܟܘܢ↘ 'in all conduct of yours', adding the vocable ܕܝܠܟܘܢ 'yours' for clarity.

[4] Juckel, 'Ḥarqlean Version', p. 188.

[5] Sebastian Brock, 'The Resolution of the Philoxenian/Harclean Problem', in Eldon Jay Epp and Gordon D. Fee (eds.), *New Testament Textual Criticism, Its Significance for Exegesis, Essays in Honour of Bruce M. Metzger* (Oxford: Clarendon, 1981) pp. 325–343 (341).

[6] Juckel, 'Ḥarqlean Version', p. 190.

[7] See, for example, Brock's discussion of John 16.12–13 (Brock, 'Resolution', p. 331).

[8] John Gwynn, 'Paulus (48) Tellensis', in William Smith and Henry Wace (eds.), *A Dictionary of Christian Biography* (London: John Murray, 1877) pp. 4: 266–271 (267).

[9] Juckel, 'Ḥarqlean Version', p. 189.

conquest, 'the "ecumenical" perspective ... was replaced by a scientific and philological attitude'.[10]

The translation is best described as a source-oriented translation as opposed to a reader-oriented translation. The sometime description 'mirror translation'[11] can be misleading as the translation goes only as far as the Syriac language allows it to go. Thomas does attempt to represent every Greek word, including particles, which makes retroversion of his Syriac into Greek relatively certain. Analysis of the translation will be divided into the following broad categories: the treatment of Greek vocabulary, the treatment of Greek grammatical categories, the treatment of Greek syntax, and theological translation. This study is not exhaustive, but selective. At times, the Harqlean will be compared with the Peshitta to bring out its preciseness in rendering the Greek.

1. TREATMENT OF GREEK VOCABULARY

1.1. Divergence from the Peshitta

Changes in vocabulary from the Peshitta point the reader to a clearer understanding of the Greek *Vorlage*: ܫܝܢܐ 'peace' replaces ܫܠܡܐ 'well-being, peace' of the Peshitta as the translation equivalent of Greek εἰρήνη 'peace' (1 Pet. 1.2; 3.11 H1 margin);[12] ܦܘܪܩܢܐ 'salvation' replaces ܚܝ̈ܐ 'life, salvation' of the Peshitta for Greek σωτηρία 'salvation' (1 Pet. 1.9-10; 2.2); ܦܪܩ 'save' replaces ܚܝܐ 'live, be saved' of the Peshitta for σῴζω 'save' (1 Pet. 3.21; 4.18) and διασῴζω 'rescue, deliver, bring safely through' (1 Pet. 3.20); ܒܣܪܐ 'flesh' replaces ܦܓܪܐ 'body'—an interpretive rendering—of the Peshitta (1 Pet. 4.2), more closely reflecting the Greek σάρξ; the loanword ܦܪܨܘܦܐ 'face' replaces ܐܦܐ 'face, nostrils' of the Peshitta for πρόσωπον 'face', a singular (1 Pet. 3.12); the loanword ܐܘܢܓܠܝܘܢ 'evangel' replaces ܣܒܪܬܐ 'message, gospel' of the Peshitta for εὐαγγέλιον 'good news' (1 Pet. 4.17), but

---

[10] Juckel, 'Ḥarqlean Version', p. 189.

[11] Juckel, 'Ḥarqlean Version', pp. 188 and 190.

[12] Thomas does use ܫܐܠ ܫܠܡܐ 'greet' and ܫܠܡ (D-stem) 'greet' as translations of the verb ἀσπάζομαι 'greet' in 1 Pet. 5.13–14.

the Harqlean retains the verb ܣܒܪ 'proclaim the gospel' from the Peshitta for εὐαγγελίζω 'proclaim the good news' (1 Pet. 1.12, 25; 4.6). Moreover, the Harqlean renders the noun ἐπισκοπή 'visitation' as ܣܘܥܪܢܘܬܐ 'visitation' against ܒܘܚܪܢܐ 'testing' of the Peshitta (1 Pet. 2.12). The noun ἐπίσκοπος 'overseer, guardian' is rendered as ܐܦܝܣܩܘܦܐ 'overseer' by the Harqlean but as ܣܥܘܪܐ 'overseer' by the Peshitta (1 Pet. 2.25). The present participle of the verb ἐπισκοπέω 'oversee' is translated as ܟܕ ܣܥܪܝܢ ܐܢܬܘܢ 'while you oversee' by the Harqlean and by ܣܥܘܪܘ 'oversee' (imperative) by the Peshitta (1 Pet. 5.2). Then, too, the Harqlean uses ܝܗܒ ܡܠܬܐ to render ἀποδίδωμι λόγον 'give an account' against the Peshitta translation ܝܗܒ ܦܬܓܡܐ, a Syriac idiom usually meaning 'respond, reply' (1 Pet. 4.5). In this Thomas maintained consistency in rendering λόγος, the other five cases in First Peter also being rendered as ܡܠܬܐ. These examples demonstrate the source text orientation of the Harqlean version as opposed to the Peshitta.

1.2. Treatment of Greek Compounds

Greek compounds are often, but not always, represented etymologically by two or more words in the Harqlean version.[13] Of the seventy-eight Greek verbs formed from multiple elements in First Peter, the Harqlean translates fifteen (19%) by more than one word using etymology. Of the fifty-six Greek nouns formed from multiple elements, the Harqlean uses etymology as the key in translation in thirteen cases (23%). In an additional four cases (7%), it uses the Greek loanword equivalent to the source-text

[13] Compare Andreas Juckel, 'Should the Harklean Version be Included in a Future Lexicon of the Syriac New Testament?' in A. Dean Forbes and David G. K. Taylor (eds.), *Foundations for Syriac Lexicography I* (Perspectives on Syriac Linguistics, 1, Piscataway: Gorgias, 2005) pp. 167–194 (186–189), and 'Toward an Analytical Concordance of the Harklean New Testament', in P. J. Williams (ed.), *Foundations for Syriac Lexicography II* (Perspectives on Syriac Linguistics, 3, Piscataway: Gorgias, 2009) pp. 99–154 (137–146).

word.[14] In three cases, or four if one includes the heading, the Harqlean uses multiple words to translate, but in non-etymologically generated idiomatic Syriac.[15] So, while Thomas wanted to accurately represent the Greek for his Syriac audience, he was also concerned that they understand what they read without obfuscating the text. His source-text oriented translation was also user friendly, produced in palpable Syriac of his day. The *alpha*-privatives, as a special class of compound, will be treated separately under 1.3.

- *ἀγαθοποιέω* 'do good', the compound of *ἀγαθόν* 'good' and *ποιέω* 'do', is rendered as ܥܒ݂ܕ ܛܒ̈ܬܐ 'do good': ܟܕ ܥܒ݂ܕܝܢ ܐܢܬܘܢ ܛܒ̈ܬܐ 'when you do good things' renders *ἀγαθοποιοῦντας* 'by doing good' (1 Pet. 2.15) and ܟܕ ܛܒ̈ܬܐ ܥܒ݂ܕܝܢ ܐܢܬܘܢ 'while doing good' renders *ἀγαθοποιοῦντας* 'by doing good' (1 Pet. 3.17).
- *ἀγαθοποιΐα* 'doing good', a noun formed from *ἀγαθόν* 'good' and *ποιέω* 'do', is translated by ܥܒܘܕܘܬ ܛܒ̈ܬܐ 'doing good' versus the Peshitta: ܥܒ̈ܳܕܐ ܛܳܒ̈ܐ 'good works' (1 Pet. 4.19).
- *ἀγαθοποιός* 'doer of good', related to the two foregoing words, is rendered as ܥܒ݂ܕ ܛܒ̈ܬܐ 'doer of good' (1 Pet. 2.14).
- *ἀλλοτριεπίσκοπος* 'busybody, meddler',[16] a combination of *ἀλλότριος* 'belonging to another (i.e., another person's affairs)' and *ἐπίσκοπος* 'guardian, overseer', is translated as ܐܦܝܣܩܘܦܐ ܢܘܟܪܝܐ 'foreign overseer' (1 Pet. 4.15). The

---

[14] The *alpha*-privative ܐܣܘܛܘܬܐ for *ἀσωτία* 'incorrigibleness' (1 Pet. 4.4), ܐܦܝܣܩܘܦܐ for *ἐπίσκοπος* 'overseer' (1 Pet. 2.25); ܐܘܢܓܠܝܘܢ for *εὐαγγέλιον* 'gospel' (1 Pet. 4.17); ܦܪܨܘܦܐ for *πρόσωπον* 'face' (1 Pet. 3.12).

[15] *ἀπολογία* 'defense' is rendered idiomatically as ܡܦܩ ܒܪܘܚܐ 'defense' (1 Pet. 3.15), *ἐπιστολή* 'epistle' as ܐܓܪܬܐ ܩܬܘܠܝܩܝ 'catholic letter' (heading), *οἰκονόμος* 'household manager, steward', the compound of *οἶκος* 'household' and *νέμω* 'manage', as ܪܒ ܒܝܬܐ 'steward' (lit., 'chief of the house') (1 Pet. 4.10), and *ὑπόκρισις* 'hypocrisy' as ܢܣܒܘܬ ܐܦ̈ܐ 'putting on of faces, hypocrisy' (1 Pet. 2.1).

[16] For discussions of the meaning of the Greek see BDAG and Joseph Henry Thayer, *Greek-English Lexicon of the New Testament* (sixth printing 1967; Grand Rapids: Zondervan, n.d.) p. 29.

Peshitta does not translate ἀλλοτριεπίσκοπος either because the translator condensed the text or because it was missing in his *Vorlage*.

- ἀναγεννάω 'beget again', a combination of ἀνά 'anew' and γεννάω 'beget', is rendered as ܡܚܕܬ ܝܠܕ 'beget again'. Once, the Harqlean renders ἀναγεννήσας ἡμᾶς as ܡܚܕܬ ܝܠܕ ܠܢ 'he begat us again', whereas the Peshitta renders it as ܐܘܠܕܢ ܡܢ ܕܪܝܫ 'he begat us again' (1 Pet. 1.3). The Harqlean uses the *peal* conjugation, while the Peshitta the *aphel* conjugation. Another time, the Harqlean translates ἀναγεγεννημένοι 'being born again' as ܡܚܕܬ ܐܬܝܠܕܬܘܢ 'you were born again' (1 Pet. 1.23). The Peshitta is identical to the Harqlean, except for writing ܡܢ ܕܪܝܫ as two words.
- ἀντιλοιδορέω 'revile in return', a compound made up of the preposition ἀντί 'in return' and the verb λοιδορέω 'revile', is rendered as ܗܦܟ ܨܥܐ 'revile back'. Thomas thus distinguishes it from λοιδορέω 'revile', which he renders ܨܥܐ 'revile' earlier in the same verse (1 Pet. 2.23).
- ἀντιτάσσω 'oppose', composed of the elements ἀντί 'against' and τάσσω 'arrange', is rendered as ܣܕܪ ܠܘܩܒܠ 'arrange against' in ܡܛܠ ܕܐܠܗܐ ܠܘܩܒܠ ܡܥܫܩ̈ܠܐ ܣܕܪ 'For God sets himself against the proud' (1 Pet. 5.5).
- ἀπογίνομαι 'be removed from', composed of ἀπό 'from' and γίνομαι 'become', is rendered as ܗܘܐ ܠܒܪ ܡܢ 'be apart from' (1 Pet. 2.24).
- ἀποτίθημι 'put away', made up of ἀπό 'from' and τίθημι 'put', is realized as ܣܝܡ ܡܢ 'put away from' in ܟܕ ܣܝܡܝܢ ܐܢܬܘܢ ܡܢܟܘܢ ... ܟܠܗ ܒܝܫܘܬܐ 'while you put away from yourselves ... all evil' (1 Pet. 2.1).
- ἀρχιποίμην 'chief shepherd', the constituents of which are the prefix ἀρχ- 'chief' and ποιμήν 'shepherd', is rendered as ܪܝܫ ܪ̈ܥܘܬܐ 'head of the shepherds' (1 Pet. 5.4).
- εἰδωλολατρία 'idolatry', composed of the elements εἴδωλον 'image' and λατρεία 'worship', finds its realization in ܦܘܠܚܢܐ ܕܦܬܟܪ̈ܐ 'worship of idols' (1 Pet. 4.3).

- εὐπρόσδεκτος 'acceptable', comprised of εὖ 'well' and προσδεκτός 'received',[17] is translated as ܫܦܝܪ ܡܩܒܠܝܢ 'well received (ܠܐܠܗܐ by God)' (1 Pet. 2.5).
- εὔσπλαγχνοι 'having tender feelings', a compound of εὖ 'well' and σπλάγχνον 'seat of the passions', translates as ܡܪܚܡܢܝܢ ܫܦܝܪ 'well compassionate' (1 Pet. 3.8).
- κακοποιέω 'do evil', the compound of κακόν 'evil' and ποιέω 'do', is translated as ܥܒܕ ܒܝ̈ܫܬܐ 'do evil' (1 Pet. 3.17).
- κακοποιός 'evil doer', made up of κακόν 'evil' and ποιέω 'do', is translated as ܥܒܕ ܒܝ̈ܫܬܐ 'doer of evil' (1 Pet. 2.14).
- καταλαλέω 'speak against', the compound of κατά 'against' and λαλέω 'speak', finds its counterpart in ܡܠܠ ܥܠ 'speak against' both in the active ܟܡܐ ܕܡܡܠܠܝܢ ܥܠܝܟܘܢ 'inasmuch as they speak against you' (1 Pet. 2.12) and in the passive ܟܡܐ ܕܡܬܡܠܠ ܥܠܝܟܘܢ 'inasmuch as it is spoken against you' (1 Pet. 3.16).
- καταλαλιά 'defamation', cognate to the preceding verb, is represented by ܡܡܠܠܐ ܕܥܠ ܚ̈ܕܕܐ 'speech against one another' (1 Pet. 2.1).
- μακροθυμία 'patience', a compound based on μακρός 'long' and θυμός 'spirit', finds its counterpart in ܢܓܝܪܘܬ ܪܘܚܐ 'patience' (lit., 'long of spirit') (1 Pet. 3.20).
- οἰνοφλυγία 'drunkenness' (lit., 'wine babbling'), a compound of οἶνος 'wine' and φλύω 'babble', translates as ܫܠܗܒܘܒ ܚܡܪܐ 'inflaming of wine' (1 Pet. 4.3).
- ὁμόφρονες 'being like-minded', a compound of ὁμός 'common' and φρήν 'mind', is translated as ܫܘ̈ܝ ܬܪܥܝܬܐ 'equal of mind' (1 Pet. 3.8).
- πατροπαράδοτος 'handed down from one's forefathers', a compound of πατήρ 'ancestor, father' and παραδίδωμι 'hand over, deliver', is rendered as ܡܢ ܡܫܠܡܢܘܬ ܐܒܗ̈ܝܟܘܢ 'from the transmission of your forefathers' (1 Pet. 1.18).
- πολυτελής 'of high value', consisting of πολύς 'much' and τέλος 'cost, end', is rendered as ܣܓܝ ܡܫܡܠܝܐ 'very mature, quite perfect' (1 Pet. 3.4). In rendering the same adjective

[17] The adjective προσδεκτός 'received as completely satisfactory' (BDAG) itself is a compound of πρός 'with, to' and δεκτός 'acceptable'.

when modifying 'ointment of pure nard' (Mk. 14.3) and 'attire' (1 Tim. 2.9), he uses the compound ܣܓܝ ܕܡܝܐ 'expensive' (lit., 'much of cost').

- πολύτιμος 'very valuable', consisting of πολύς 'much' and τιμή 'value', appearing as a comparative, is rendered ܣܓܝ ܝܬܝܪ ܡܝܩܪ 'much more valuable' (1 Pet. 1.7).
- πρόγνωσις 'foreknowledge', a combination of πρό 'pre-' and γνῶσις 'knowledge', is rendered as ܡܩܕܡܘܬ ܝܕܥܬܐ 'prior knowledge, foreknowledge' (1 Pet. 1.2). The Peshitta also uses two words, rendering ܒܩܕܡܘܬ ܝܕܥܬܐ 'foreknowledge'.
- προγινώσκω 'foreknow', combining πρό 'pre-' and γινώσκω 'know', is translated as ܩܕܡ ܝܕܥ 'know beforehand' in ܗܘ ܕܩܕܡ ܐܬܝܕܥ ܡܢ ܩܕܡ ܬܪܡܝܬܗ ܕܥܠܡܐ 'He that was known beforehand before the foundation of the world ...' (1 Pet. 1.20).
- προμαρτύρομαι 'testify beforehand', composed of the elements πρό 'before' and μαρτύρομαι 'testify', is realized as ܩܕܡ ܣܗܕ 'testify beforehand' (1 Pet. 1.11).
- συγκληρονόμος 'joint heir', as substantive, comprised of σύν 'together' and κληρονόμος 'heir', is rendered ܫܘ̈ܝܬ ܝܪܬܘܬܐ 'equals of inheritance, co-inheritors' (1 Pet. 3.7). Thomas correctly understood the dative plural form συγκληρονόμοις to be feminine in gender.[18]
- συμπαθεῖς, a compound of σύν 'together' and πάσχω 'suffer' is reflected in the translation ܚܫ̈ܝܢ ܐܟܚܕܐ 'suffering together' (1 Pet. 3.8).
- συμπρεσβύτερος 'fellow elder', a compound of σύν 'together' and πρεσβύτερος 'elder', is represented by ܩܫܝܫܐ ܕܥܡܟܘܢ 'an elder with you' (1 Pet. 5.1).
- συνοικέω 'live with', consisting of σύν 'with' and οἰκέω 'dwell', finds its expression in ܥܡܪ ܥܡ 'dwell with' (1 Pet. 3.7).

[18] Compare ἀθεμίτοις εἰδωλολατρίαις '(in) abominable idolatries' (1 Pet. 4.3).

- συντρέχω 'run together with', consisting of the preposition σύν 'with' and the verb τρέχω 'run', is translated as ܪܗܛ ܥܡ 'run with' (1 Pet. 4.4).
- σωφρονέω 'be of sound mind', a verb created from σῶς 'sound' and φρήν 'mind', is reflected etymologically by the translation ܐܬܬܥܝܪ ܒܪܥܝܢܐ 'be alert in mind' in ܐܬܢܟܦܘ ܗܟܝܠ ܘܐܬܬܥܝܪܘ ܒܪܥܝܢܐ ܠܨܠܘ̈ܬܐ 'be sober therefore and be alert in mind regarding prayer' (1 Pet. 4.7). The Harqlean follows the Peshitta in reversing the order of the verbs—the Peshitta reads ܐܬܢܟ̈ܦܘ ܘܐܬܬܥܝܪܘ 'be sober and be alert' against σωφρονήσατε ... καὶ νήψατε 'be of sound mind and be sober'— and then adds the prepositional phrase ܒܪܥܝܢܐ 'in mind' to bring out the nuance of the Greek.
- ταπεινόφρονες 'humble', a compound of ταπεινός 'lowly' and φρήν 'mind', is translated as ܡܟܝ̈ܟܝ ܪܥܝܢܬܐ 'humble of mind' (1 Pet. 3.8).
- ταπεινοφροσύνη 'humility', a compound of ταπεινός 'lowly' and φρήν 'mind', is rendered as ܡܟܝܟܘܬ ܪܥܝܢܬܐ 'lowliness of mind, humility' (1 Pet. 5.5).
- φιλαδελφία 'brotherly love', combining φίλος 'love' and ἀδελφός 'brother', is rendered as ܪܚܡܬ ܐܚܘܬܐ 'love of the brotherhood' (1 Pet. 1.22).
- φιλάδελφοι 'having brotherly love', a compound of φίλος 'love' and ἀδελφός 'brother', is rendered as ܪ̈ܚܡܝ ܐܚ̈ܐ 'lovers of the brothers' (1 Pet. 3.8). The form ܪ̈ܚܡܝ is the plural participle in construct to ܐܚ̈ܐ. Compare ܪ̈ܚܡܝ ܟܣܦܐ 'lovers of money' as a reflex of φιλάργυροι (2 Tim. 3.2), ܪ̈ܚܡܝ ܗܢܝܘܬܐ 'lovers of pleasure' representing φιλήδονοι, and ܪ̈ܚܡܝ ܐܠܗܐ 'lovers of God' reflecting φιλόθεοι (2 Tim. 3.4). My thanks are due Dr. Andreas Juckel for these parallels.
- φιλόξενος 'hospitable', a combination of φίλος 'love' and ξένος 'stranger', is translated ܪ̈ܚܡܐ ܐܟܣ̈ܢܝܐ 'stranger-lovers, guest friendly' (1 Pet. 4.9).

1.3. Renderings of the Greek alpha-privative

Thomas often represents the Greek *alpha*-privative by the negation ܠܐ followed by a noun, adjective, or verb. He never uses the negation ܠܘ in this way.

1.3.1. Alpha-privative Substantives Rendered with the Element ܠܐ

- ἄγνοια 'ignorance' is rendered as ܠܐ ܝܕܥܬܐ 'ignorance' (1 Pet. 1.14)
- ἀγνωσία 'ignorance' is rendered as ܠܐ ܝܕܥܬܐ 'ignorance' (1 Pet. 2.15)
- ἄφθαρτος used as a substantive 'incorruptability' is rendered as ܠܐ ܡܬܚܒܠܢܘܬܐ 'incorruptability' (1 Pet. 3.4)

1.3.2. Alpha-privative Adjectives Rendered with the Element ܠܐ

- ἄδολος 'unadulterated' is rendered as ܠܐ ܢܟܝܠ 'non deceptive' (1 Pet. 2.2)
- ἀθέμιτος 'illicit' is rendered as ܠܐ ܢܡܘܣܝ 'not lawful' (1 Pet. 4.3)
- ἀμαράντινος 'unfading' is rendered as ܕܠܐ ܚܡܐ 'which does not wither' (1 Pet. 5.4)
- ἀμάραντος 'unfading' is rendered as ܕܠܐ ܚܡܐ 'which does not wither' (1 Pet. 1.4)
- ἄφθαρτος 'imperishable' is rendered as ܠܐ ܡܬܚܒܠܢ 'not corruptible' (1 Pet. 1.4, 23)
- ἀμίαντος 'undefiled' is rendered as ܠܐ ܡܬܛܠܫܢ 'not defiled' (1 Pet. 1.4)
- ἀνεκλάλητος 'inexpressible' is rendered as ܠܐ ܡܬܡܠܠܢ 'not utterable' (1 Pet. 1.8)
- ἀνυπόκριτος 'unhypocritical' is rendered as ܠܐ ܢܣܒ ܒܐ̈ܦܐ 'not handling with faces' (1 Pet. 1.22)

1.3.3. Alpha-privative Verbs Rendered with the Element ܠܐ

- ἀπειθέω 'disobey' is translated as ܠܐ ܐܬܦܝܣܘ 'not obey' (ܦܝܣ in the Ct stem) (1 Pet. 2.8; 3.1, 20; 4.17)
- ἀπιστέω 'disbelieve' is translated as ܠܐ ܗܝܡܢ 'not believe' (1 Pet. 2.7)

1.3.4. Alpha-privative Adverb Rendered with the Element ܕܠܐ *'without'*

- ἄμωμος 'unblemished' is rendered as ܕܠܐ ܡܘܡܐ 'without defect' (1 Pet. 1.19)
- ἀπροσωπολήμπτως 'impartially' is translated as ܕܠܐ ܡܣܒ ܒܦܪ̈ܨܘܦܐ 'without handling with a face' (1 Pet. 1.17)
- ἄσπιλος 'spotless' is rendered as ܕܠܐ ܟܘܬܡܐ 'without spotting' (1 Pet. 1.19)

1.3.5. Alpha-privatives Rendered Without the Element ܠܐ

- ἄδικος 'unjust' is rendered as ܥܘܠܐ 'wicked' (1 Pet. 3.18; Peshitta ܚܛܝܐ 'sinner')
- ἀδίκως 'unjustly' is rendered as ܥܘܠܐܝܬ 'wrongfully' (1 Pet. 2.19; Peshitta ܒܥܘܠܐ 'in the wrong')
- ἀλήθεια 'truth' is rendered as ܫܪܪܐ 'truth' (1 Pet. 1.22; Peshitta ܫܪܪܐ 'truth')
- ἀληθής 'true' is rendered as ܫܪܝܪ 'true' (1 Pet. 5.12; Peshitta ܫܪܝܪ 'true')
- ἀσεβής 'impious' is rendered as ܪܫܝܥܐ 'wicked' (1 Pet. 4.18; Peshitta ܪܫܝܥܐ 'wicked')
- ἀσέλγεια 'immorality' is rendered as ܦܚܙܘܬܐ 'wantonness' (1 Pet. 4.3; Peshitta condenses the text and so does not clearly translate it)
- ἀσθενής 'helpless' is rendered as ܡܚܝܠ 'weak' (1 Pet. 3.7; Peshitta ܡܚܝܠ 'weak')
- ἀσωτία 'incorrigibleness' is rendered as ܐܣܘܛܘܬܐ 'intemperance', a Greek loanword in Syriac (1 Pet. 4.4; Peshitta ܐܣܘܛܘܬܐ 'intemperance')
- ἄφρων 'witless' is rendered as ܣܟܠ 'foolish' (1 Pet. 2.15; Peshitta ܣܟܠ 'foolish')

In these nine cases of non-negation in translation, the Harqlean follows the Peshitta five times. The etymology of the words ἀλήθεια 'truth' and ἀληθής 'true' had long been forgotten in Greek itself, so it would have been highly artificial to create a Syriac counterpart based on etymology. With respect to the one case of a Greek adverb (ἀδίκως 'unjustly'), the Harqlean carefully uses the same word class (ܥܘܠܐܝܬ 'wrongfully') rather than substituting a prepositional phrase used adverbially (ܒܥܘ̈ܠܐ 'in the wrong') as the Peshitta had done. The most remarkable case is the translation ܦܚܙܘ̈ܬܐ 'wantonness', possibly a plural of intensification, for Greek ἀσέλγεια 'immorality'.

1.4. Greek Pronouns

1.4.1. Personal Pronouns

In general, Thomas showed awareness of case and nuance in rendering the personal pronoun. He rendered the nominative ἐγώ 'I' as ܐܢܐ 'I' (1 Pet. 1.16), ὑμεῖς 'you' as ܐܢܬܘܢ 'you' (1 Pet. 2.9; 4.1), and αὐτός 'he' as ܗܘ 'he' (1 Pet. 2.24; 5.10). But where the pronoun αὐτός highlights the subject, he renders it according to its context. The two cases attested are in the plural (αὐτοὶ) referring to the second person plural and so are rendered as ܐܢܬܘܢ 'you'. He rendered ἀλλὰ κατὰ τὸν καλέσαντα ὑμᾶς ἅγιον καὶ αὐτοὶ ἅγιοι ἐν πάσῃ ἀναστροφῇ γενήθητε 'But according as he who called you is holy, you also be holy in all conduct' as ܐܠܐ ܐܝܟ ܗܘ ܕܩܪܐ ܠܟܘܢ ܩܕܝܫܐ . ܐܦ ܐܢܬܘܢ ܩܕܝ̈ܫܐ ܒܟܠܗ ܗܘܦܟܐ * ܕܝܠܟܘܢ ↘ ܗܘܘ 'But according as he who called you is holy, you also be holy in all your conduct' (1 Pet. 1.15). He rendered καὶ αὐτοὶ ὡς λίθοι ζῶντες οἰκοδομεῖσθε οἶκος πνευματικὸς 'and you as living stones are being built a spiritual house' as ܐܦ ܐܢܬܘܢ ܐܝܟ ܟܐ̈ܦܐ ܚ̈ܝܬܐ ܐܬܒܢܘ ܒܝܬܐ ܪܘܚܢܝܐ 'also you as living stones be built a spiritual house' (1 Pet. 2.5).

He represented the genitive by attaching the personal pronoun to the particle ܕܝܠ, rendering μου 'my' as ܕܝܠܝ 'my' (1 Pet. 5.13), ἡμῶν 'our' as ܕܝܠܢ 'our' (1 Pet. 1.3; 2.24), ὑμῶν 'your' as ܕܝܠܟܘܢ 'your (masculine)' (1 Pet. 1.7 etc.) and ܕܝܠܟܝܢ 'your (feminine)' (1 Pet. 3.2), αὐτοῦ 'his' and αὐτῆς 'its' as ܕܝܠܗ 'his, its' (1 Pet. 1.3 etc.), and αὐτῶν 'of them, their' as ܕܝܠܗܘܢ 'of them, their' (1 Pet. 3.14; 4.19). Rarely is the pronoun attached directly to the noun: ܒܦܘܡܗ 'in his mouth' corresponds to ἐν τῷ στόματι αὐτοῦ 'in his mouth' (1 Pet. 2.22), found in a citation from Isa. 53.9, where the Peshitta reads ܒܦܘܡܗ 'in his mouth' against the Syrohexapla ܒܦܘܡܐ ܕܝܠܗ 'in his mouth'; ܠܒܥܘܬܗܘܢ 'to their request' corresponds to εἰς δέησιν αὐτῶν 'to their request' (1 Pet. 2.22). When the genitive case is governed by a preposition, he joins the personal pronoun to the corresponding preposition. He renders ἀφ' ἡμῶν 'from us' as ܡܢܢ

'from us' (1 Pet. 4.17), *ὑπὲρ ὑμῶν* 'instead of us' as ܚܠܦܝܟܘܢ 'instead of us' (1 Pet. 2.21), *περὶ ὑμῶν* '(he cares) about you' as ܚܠܦܝܟܘܢ '(he cares) about you' (1 Pet. 5.7), and *δι' αὐτοῦ* 'by him' as ܒܐܝܕܗ 'by him' (1 Pet. 1.21; 2.14). In the case of the genitive absolute where the pronoun serves as the subject of the verb, he translates it by the corresponding pronoun. He renders *μὴ συντρεχόντων ὑμῶν* 'when you do not run with them' as ܕܠܐ ܪܗܛܝܢ ܐܢܬܘܢ ܥܡܗܘܢ 'that you do not run with them' (1 Pet. 4.4). In the case of the partitive, he renders the idiom *τις ὑμῶν* 'anyone of you' into good Syriac as ܐܢܫ ܡܢܟܘܢ 'anyone of you' (1 Pet. 4.15).

He renders the dative *ὑμῖν* 'to you' and 'for you' as ܠܟܘܢ 'to you' (1 Pet. 1.2 etc.) and 'for you' (1 Pet. 2.7); *αὐτῷ* 'to him' as ܠܗ 'to him' (1 Pet. 1.21; 3.22 etc.). He represents the dative governed by a preposition by the corresponding preposition with a suffixed personal pronoun. He translates *ἐν ὑμῖν* 'in/among you' as ܒܟܘܢ 'in/among you' (1 Pet. 3.15; 4.12; 5.1); *ἐν αὐτῷ* 'in him' as ܒܗ 'by it' (1 Pet. 2.2); *ἐπ' αὐτῷ* '(believe) on him' as ܒܗ '(believe) on him' (1 Pet. 2.6); *ἐν αὐτοῖς* 'in them' as ܒܗܘܢ 'in them' (1 Pet. 1.11).

He marks the accusative with the preposition *lamadh* and attaches the pronoun: *ἡμᾶς* 'us' is realized as ܠܢ 'us' (1 Pet. 1.3); *ὑμᾶς* 'you' as ܠܟܘܢ 'you' (1 Pet. 3.18); *αὐτὸν* 'him' and *αὐτὸ* 'it' as ܠܗ 'him/it' (1 Pet. 3.6; 4.10); *αὐτήν* 'her' (feminine referent) as ܠܗ 'her' (feminine referent ܛܒܬܐ 'good'; 1 Pet. 3.6); *αὐτὰ* 'them' as ܠܗܘܢ 'them' (1 Pet. 1.12). For the accusative with a preposition, he joins the personal pronoun to the corresponding preposition. He renders *εἰς ὑμᾶς* 'for/to you' as ܒܟܘܢ 'for/to/among you' (1 Pet. 1.4, 10, 25); *δι' ὑμᾶς* 'because of you' as ܡܛܠܬܟܘܢ 'because of you' (1 Pet. 1.20); *ἐφ' ὑμᾶς* 'upon you' as ܥܠܝܟܘܢ 'upon you' (1 Pet. 4.14); *ἐπ' αὐτόν* 'upon him' as ܥܠܘܗܝ 'upon him' (1 Pet. 5.7). Twice the pronoun in the accusative is attached to the verb in translation: ܐܝܟܢܐ ܕܢܪܘܪܒܟܘܢ 'that he might exalt you' renders *ἵνα ὑμᾶς ὑψώσῃ* 'that he might exalt you' (1 Pet. 5.6); ܗܘ ܕܐܩܝܡܗ ܡܢ ܡܝ̈ܬܐ 'who raised him from the dead' renders *τὸν ἐγείραντα αὐτὸν ἐκ νεκρῶν* 'who raised him from the dead' (1 Pet. 1.21). The phrase *ἀσπάζεται ὑμᾶς* 'she greets you' is rendered idiomatically as ܫܐܠܐ ܫܠܡܐ ܕܠܟܘܢ 'she greets you' (lit., 'she inquires after your welfare'; 1 Pet. 5.13).

What this section shows is the adaptability on the part of the translator to convey the Greek text as he knew it into readable Syriac, while staying as close as possible to the source text.

1.4.2. Demonstrative Pronouns

Thomas renders the masculine singular οὗτος 'this', referring back to masculine λίθος 'stone', as masculine ܗܢܐ 'this', referring back to masculine ܟܐܦܐ 'stone' (1 Pet. 2.7). He renders the feminine singular αὕτη 'this' in ταύτην εἶναι ἀληθῆ χάριν τοῦ θεοῦ 'that this is the true grace of God' as feminine ܗܕܐ 'this', reading ܕܗܕܐ ܐܝܬܝܗ̇ ܛܝܒܘܬܐ ܫܪܝܪܬܐ ܕܐܠܗܐ 'that this is the true grace of God' (1 Pet. 5.12). In both languages, the item pointed to is feminine (χάρις and ܛܝܒܘܬܐ). His renderings of the neuter singular τοῦτο 'this' are conditioned to a great extent by agreement in Syriac. He renders τοῦτο χάρις 'this is grace' as ܗܕܐ ܗܝ ܛܝܒܘܬܐ 'this is grace', where the referent ܛܝܒܘܬܐ is feminine (1 Pet. 2.19-20). By contrast, he renders ἐν τῷ ὀνόματι τούτῳ 'in this name' as ܒܫܡܐ ܗܢܐ 'in this name', where the nominal head ܫܡܐ is masculine (1 Pet. 4.16). When τοῦτο 'this' sums up the preceding, Thomas uses the feminine singular, translating εἰς τοῦτο γὰρ ἐκλήθητε as ܠܗܕܐ ܓܝܪ ܐܬܩܪܝܬܘܢ 'since to this you were called' (1 Pet. 2.21), ὅτι εἰς τοῦτο ἐκλήθητε as ܡܛܠ ܕܠܗܕܐ ܐܬܩܪܝܬܘܢ 'for to this you were called' (1 Pet. 3.9), and εἰς τοῦτο γὰρ καὶ νεκροῖς εὐηγγελίσθη as ܠܗܕܐ ܓܝܪ ܐܦ ܠܡܝܬܐ ܐܣܬܒܪܬ 'since for this it was announced to the dead' (1 Pet. 4.6). The idiom τοῦτ' ἔστιν meaning 'that is' is rendered as ܗܘܝܘ 'that is' (1 Pet. 3.20). For the use of the masculine ܗܢܐ in rendering τοῦτο δέ ἐστιν τὸ ῥῆμα τὸ εὐαγγελισθὲν εἰς ὑμᾶς as ܗܢܐ ܕܝܢ ܐܝܬܘܗܝ ܡܠܬܐ ܗܝ ܕܐܣܬܒܪܬ ܒܟܘܢ 'Now this is the Word that was preached among you' (1 Pet. 1.25), see below under 'Theological Translation'. The plural demonstrative ταῦτα 'these' is rendered by ܗܠܝܢ 'these' (1 Pet. 1.11).

1.4.3. Indefinite Pronouns

When the indefinite pronoun τις 'someone' functions as the subject of the clause, Thomas renders it by ܐܢܫ 'someone' (1 Pet. 2.9; 4.11). He renders the negated partitive μή τις ὑμῶν as ܠܐ ܐܢܫ ܡܢܟܘܢ 'none (no one) of you' (1 Pet. 4.15). For the plural τινες 'some', he uses the plural ܐܢܫܝ̈ܢ 'some' (1 Pet. 3.1), translating ἵνα εἴ τινες ἀπειθοῦσιν τῷ λόγῳ as ܐܝܟܢܐ ܕܐܢ ܐ̈ܢܫܝܢ ܠܐ ܡܬܛܦܝܣܝܢ ܠܡܠܬܐ 'that if some (of the husbands) do not obey the word'. When the indefinite pronoun functions as the direct object, he uses ܡܢܘ 'whom' marked by the preposition *lamadh* to indicate the accusative, rendering ζητῶν τινα καταπιεῖν as ܟܕ ܒܥܐ ܕܠܡܢܘ ܢܒܠܘܥ 'seeking to devour someone' (lit., 'that he might devour someone') (1 Pet. 5.8). In Syriac the verb ܢܒܠܘܥ governs the object ܠܡܢܘ, reflecting the understanding that καταπιεῖν governs τινα in the source-text; the verb ܒܥܐ governs the purpose clause beginning with conjunctive ܕ.

1.4.4. Interrogative Pronouns

When the interrogative pronoun τίς 'who' stands at the head of the question, Thomas translated it by ܡܢܘ /mannu/ in ܘܡܢܘ ܗܘ ܕܡܒܐܫ ܠܟܘܢ 'Who is it that will harm you?' (1 Pet. 3.13). When the interrogative pronoun τί 'what' stands at the head of the question, he rendered it as ܡܢܘ /mānāw/ in ܡܢܘ ܫܘܠܡܐ 'What is the end?' (1 Pet. 4.17).

In rendering ἐραυνῶντες εἰς τίνα ἢ ποῖον καιρὸν ἐδηλοῦτο[19] ἐν αὐτοῖς πνεῦμα Χριστοῦ, Thomas offers ܟܕ ܒܨܝܢ ܗܘܘ ܕܠܐܝܢܐ ܐܘ ܒܐܝܢܐ ܙܒܢܐ ܂ ܡܬܝܕܥ ܗܘܐ ܒܗܘܢ ܪܘܚܗ ܕܡܫܝܚܐ 'while they were investigating whom or what time the Spirit of the Messiah was revealing in them' (1 Pet 1.11). The active meaning of the Gt-stem of ܝܕܥ is remarkable[20] and owes its existence in the Harqlean to the Greek reading ἐδηλοῦτο, a middle/passive form. The fact that the Harqlean uses two prepositions (ܠ and ܒ) against one in the Greek (εἰς) seems to indicate a distinction in meaning between the

[19] Thomas read the middle/passive form ἐδηλοῦτο and not the active form ἐδήλου plus the neuter article τό. Hence, he uses the middle/passive form ܡܬܝܕܥ in his translation, although the Gt-stem of ܝܕܥ normally expresses the passive. This is an exception.

[20] Michael Sokoloff, *A Syriac Lexicon, A Translation from the Latin, Correction, Expansion, and Update of C. Brockelmann's Lexicon Syriacum* (Winona Lake: Eisenbrauns and Piscataway: Gorgias, 2009) p. 564, lists only the passive ('to be known') and middle ('to disclose oneself') meanings for the Gt-stem of ܝܕܥ. On the problem of voice extension, see Rachel Aubrey, 'Motivated Categories, Middle Voice, and Passive Morphology', in Steven E. Runge and Christopher J. Fresch (eds.), *The Greek Verb Revisited* (Bellingham, WA: Lexham, 2016) pp. 563–625.

first ܐܝܢܐ and the second ܐܝܢܐ, the first referring to a person and the second modifying the noun ܙܒܢܐ. The interrogative pronoun ποῖος is rendered by the feminine interrogative when the referent is feminine in the target language: Thomas renders ποῖον γὰρ κλέος, εἰ ... as ܐܢ… ܐܝܢܐ ܗܝ ܓܝܪ ܬܫܒܘܚܬܐ 'For what is the glory if ...' (1 Pet. 2.20).

1.4.5. Reciprocal Pronouns

Thomas renders the reciprocal pronoun 'one another' appearing in the accusative as ἀλλήλους (1 Pet. 1.22; 4.9; 5.14) and the dative as ἀλλήλοις (1 Pet. 5.5) by ܚܕ̈ܕܐ 'one another'. In addition, he translates the pronoun ἑαυτοὺς functioning as a reciprocal[21] as a reciprocal, rendering τὴν εἰς ἑαυτοὺς ἀγάπην 'love for one another' by ܚܘܒܐ ܕܠܘܬ ܚܕ̈ܕܐ 'love for one another' (1 Pet. 4.8).

1.4.6. Reflexive Pronouns

Thomas expresses reflexivity through repetition of pronouns. He renders ἑαυτοῖς '(ministering not) to themselves' as ܠܗܘܢ ܕܠܗܘܢ 'to themselves' (1 Pet. 1.12). He renders οὕτως ... αἱ ἅγιαι γυναῖκες ... ἐκόσμουν ἑαυτὰς 'thus ... the holy women ... used to adorn themselves' as ܗܟܢܐ ... ܢܫ̈ܐ ܩܕ̈ܝܫܬܐ ... ܡܨܒ̈ܬܢ ܗܘ̈ܝ ܢܦܫܗܝܢ ܠܗܝܢ 'thus ... the holy women ... used to adorn themselves' (1 Pet. 3.5).

He renders εἰς ἑαυτοὺς αὐτὸ διακονοῦντες 'ministering it (the χάρισμα) to themselves/one another' as ܟܕ ܡܫܡܫܝܢ ܐܢܬܘܢ ܠܗ ܐܢܬܘܢ ܒܟܘܢ 'while you minister it among yourselves' (1 Pet. 4.10). The repetition of ܐܢܬܘܢ seems to be due to the reflexive idea in ἑαυτοὺς, although this is not wholly clear.

1.4.7. Relative Pronouns

In general, Thomas rendered the Greek relative pronoun as the demonstrative pronoun + the particle *dalath* as in ܠܗܘ ܕܟܕ ܠܐ ܚܙܝܬܘܢ ܡܚܒܝܢ ܐܢܬܘܢ 'Him that while you have not seen you love' rendering ὃν οὐκ ἰδόντες ἀγαπᾶτε 'whom having not seen you love' (1 Pet. 1.8); ܗܘ ܕܚܛܝܬܐ ܠܐ ܥܒܕ 'that one who did not commit sin' standing for ὃς ἁμαρτίαν οὐκ ἐποίησεν 'he who did not commit sin' (1 Pet. 2.22); ܣܪܐ ... ܕܗܝ ܕܗܘܝܬܝܢ ܐܢܬܝܢ ܒܢ̈ܬܐ 'Sarah, whose daughters

---

[21] See BDAG, entry ἑαυτοῦ, meaning 2, 'marker of reciprocal relationship'.

you are', the initial ܕ of ܕܗܝ representing the genitive case,[22] mirroring Σάρρα ... ἧς ἐγενήθητε τέκνα 'Sarah, whose daughters you are' (1 Pet. 3.6).

2. TREATMENT OF GREEK GRAMMATICAL CATEGORIES

2.1. Treatment of the Greek Adjective

The Harqlean version, in contrast to the Peshitta, uses the adjective form extensively due to the Greek. For example, ܪ̈ܓܝܓܬܐ ܒܣܪܢܝܬܐ 'carnal desires' reflecting τῶν σαρκικῶν ἐπιθυμιῶν appears in the Harqlean over against the rendering ܪ̈ܓܝܓܬܗ ܕܒܣܪܐ 'the desires of the flesh' of the Peshitta (1 Pet. 2.11). Then again, Thomas expresses 'the Holy Spirit' by ܪܘܚܐ ܩܕܝܫܬܐ, reflecting the Greek syntagm noun + adjective, against ܪܘܚܐ ܕܩܘܕܫܐ of the Peshitta (1 Pet. 1.12).[23] As a further example, ܒܚܕܘܬܐ ܠܐ ܡܬܡܠܠܢܝܬܐ ܘܡܫܒܚܬܐ 'with inexpressible and glory-filled joy' represents χαρᾷ ἀνεκλαλήτῳ καὶ δεδοξασμένῃ in contrast to ܒܚܕܘܬܐ ܡܫܒܚܬܐ ܕܠܐ ܡܬܡܠܠܐ 'with glory-filled joy that is inexpressible' of the Peshitta (1 Pet. 1.8).

2.2. Treatment of the Greek Infinitive

The Greek infinitive appears seventeen times in the *Vorlage* of Harqlean First Peter,[24] for which the Harqlean uses a construction consisting of *lamadh* + infinitive eight times, *dalath* + verbal form eight times, and *dalath* + ܐܝܬ once.

---

[22] Compare ܕܗܘ ܕܒܡܚܘܬܗ ܐܬܐܣܝܬܘܢ 'by whose stripes you were healed' (1 Pet. 2.24) and ܕܗܝܢ ܕܨ̈ܒܬܐ 'whose adornments' (1 Pet. 3.3).

[23] The Peshitta consistently uses the construction ܪܘܚܐ ܕܩܘܕܫܐ throughout the New Testament with one exception where the unique syntagm ܪܘܚܐ ܩܕܝܫܬܐ ܕܐܠܗܐ 'the Holy Spirit of God' appears (Eph. 4.30).

[24] In 1 Pet. 2.11, the imperative form ܐܬܪܚܩܘ 'keep away (from)' seems to reflect the reading ἀπέχεσθε 'abstain (from)', an imperative form, rather than the infinitive form ἀπέχεσθαι 'abstain (from)'. In 1 Pet. 4.5, the participial form ܕܐܢ 'will judge' seems to go back to the Greek reading κρίνοντι, a present active participle in the dative, rather than to its variant ἔχοντι κρῖναι 'is able to judge' or 'holds himself in readiness to judge', which variant contains an infinitive.

2.2.1. Greek Infinitive Represented by lamadh + Infinitive

The reflex *lamadh* + infinitive appears as the complement of a verb in ܒܗܠܝܢ ܕܡܬܪܓܪܓܝܢ ܡܠܐܟܐ ܠܡܕܩܘ 'into which the angels desire to look' (εἰς ἃ ἐπιθυμοῦσιν ἄγγελοι παρακύψαι; 1 Pet. 1.12) and ܗܘ ܓܝܪ ܕܨܒܐ ܚܝܐ ܠܡܪܚܡܘ : ܘܝܘܡܬܐ ܛܒܐ ܠܡܚܙܐ 'For whoever wants to love life and to see good days' (ὁ γὰρ θέλων ζωὴν ἀγαπᾶν καὶ ἰδεῖν ἡμέρας ἀγαθὰς; 1 Pet. 3.10). The same construction appears as the complement of a passive participle functioning as an adjective in ܦܘܪܩܢܐ ܕܡܛܝܒ ܠܡܬܓܠܝܘ 'salvation ready to be revealed' (σωτηρίαν ἑτοίμην ἀποκαλυφθῆναι; 1 Pet. 1.5) and ܕܫܘܒܚܐ ܗܘ ܕܥܬܝܕ ܠܡܬܓܠܝܘ 'of the glory about to be revealed' (τῆς μελλούσης ἀποκαλύπτεσθαι δόξης; 1 Pet. 5.1). This syntagm expresses purpose in ܐܦ ܐܢܬܘܢ ܐܝܟ ܟܐܦܐ ܚܝܬܐ ܐܬܒܢܘ ܒܝܬܐ ܪܘܚܢܝܐ . ܠܟܗܢܘܬܐ ܩܕܝܫܬܐ . ܠܡܣܩܘ ܕܒܚܐ ܪܘܚܢܝܐ 'Also you as living stones be built a spiritual house, as a holy priesthood, to offer spiritual sacrifices' (καὶ αὐτοὶ ὡς λίθοι ζῶντες οἰκοδομεῖσθε οἶκος πνευματικὸς εἰς ἱεράτευμα ἅγιον ἀνενέγκαι πνευματικὰς θυσίας; 1 Pet. 2.5) and ܠܡܐ ܕܠܐ ܬܘܒ ... ܠܡܚܝܐ 'so as no longer ... to live' (εἰς τὸ μηκέτι ... βιῶσαι; 1 Pet. 4.2). Then, too, the construction *lamadh* + infinitive expresses the nominalized infinitive (note the Greek genitive case) in ܙܒܢܐ ܗܘ ܠܡܫܪܝܘ ܕܝܢܐ 'it is time to begin judgment' (ὁ καιρὸς τοῦ ἄρξασθαι τὸ κρίμα 'it is time for judgment to begin'; 1 Pet. 4.17).

2.2.2. Greek Infinitive Represented by dalath + Verbal Form

The rendering *dalath* + prefix conjugation appears in ܒܥܐ ܕܠܡܢܘ ܢܒܠܘܥ 'desiring that he should devour (lit., swallow) someone' (ζητῶν τινα καταπιεῖν; 1 Pet. 5.8) as the complement of a verb and in ܡܝܬܪܐ ܗܝ ܓܝܪ ܕ.... ܬܚܫܘܢ 'For it is better that ... you should suffer' (κρεῖττον γὰρ ... πάσχειν; 1 Pet. 3.17) as the complement of an adjective. It also expresses purpose in ܐܝܟܢܐ ܕܗܝܡܢܘܬܐ ܕܠܟܘܢ ܘܣܒܪܐ ܢܗܘܘܢ ܐܝܬܝܗܘܢ ܒܐܠܗܐ 'so that your faith and hope might be in God' (ὥστε τὴν πίστιν ὑμῶν καὶ ἐλπίδα εἶναι εἰς θεόν; 1 Pet. 1.21), where the periphrastic construction ܢܗܘܘܢ ܐܝܬܝܗܘܢ appears. The following cases are similar to the foregoing: ܡܛܠ ܕܗܟܢܐ ܐܝܬܘܗܝ ܨܒܝܢܗ ܕܐܠܗܐ : ܕܒܕ ܥܒܕܝܢ ܐܢܬܘܢ ܛܒ̈ܬܐ : ܬܒܠܡܘܢ ܠܠܐ ܝܕܥܬܐ ܕܒܢܝ̈ܢܫܐ ܣܟ̈ܠܐ 'For thus it is the will of God that when you do good deeds, you muzzle the ignorance of foolish people' (ὅτι οὕτως ἐστὶν τὸ θέλημα τοῦ θεοῦ ἀγαθοποιοῦντας [variant: + υμας] φιμοῦν τὴν τῶν ἀφρόνων ἀνθρώπων ἀγνωσίαν; 1 Pet. 2.15); ܢܢܝܚ ܠܫܢܐ ܕܝܠܗ ܡܢ ܒܝܫܬܐ . ܘܣܦܘܬܗ ܕܠܐ ܢܡܠܠܢ ܢܟܠܐ 'Let him rest his tongue from evil and his lips that they do not speak deceit' (παυσάτω τὴν γλῶσσαν ἀπὸ κακοῦ καὶ χείλη τοῦ μὴ λαλῆσαι δόλον; 1 Pet. 3.10).

The syntagm *dalath* + participle appears in ܟܕ ܝܕܥܝܢ ܐܢܬܘܢ . ܕܗܢܘܢ ܟܕ ܗܢܘܢ ܕܚܫܐ . ܒܐܚܘܬܐ ܕܒܥܠܡܐ ܡܫܬܡܠܝܢ 'while you know that the same kinds of sufferings are being perfected by the brotherhood that is in the world' (εἰδότες τὰ αὐτὰ τῶν παθημάτων τῇ ἐν κόσμῳ ὑμῶν ἀδελφότητι ἐπιτελεῖσθαι; 1 Pet. 5.9). The periphrastic participle appears in ܠܗܝ، ܕܠܐ ܗܘܝ، ܡܬܦܣܩܢ ܨܠܘܬܐ ܕܝܠܟܘܢ 'so that your prayers might not be cut off' (εἰς τὸ μὴ ἐγκόπτεσθαι τὰς προσευχὰς ὑμῶν; 1 Pet. 3.7).

The Greek infinitive is represented by *dalath* + suffix conjugation in ܣܦܩܐ ܗܘ ܓܝܪ ܙܒܢܐ ܗܘ ܕܥܒܪ . ܕܨܒܝܢܐ ܕܥܡܡܐ ܦܠܚܬܘܢ 'For sufficient is the time that has passed that you wrought the will of the nations' (ἀρκετὸς γὰρ ὁ παρεληλυθὼς χρόνος τὸ βούλημα τῶν ἐθνῶν κατειργάσθαι; 1 Pet. 4.3).

2.2.3. Greek Infinitive Represented by dalath + ܐܝܬ

The syntagm *dalath* + inflected ܐܝܬ is attested in ܟܬܒܬ ܠܟܘܢ . ܟܕ ܡܒܝܐ ܐܢܐ ܘܡܣܗܕ ܐܢܐ . ܕܗܕܐ ܐܝܬܝܗ̇ ܛܝܒܘܬܐ ܫܪܝܪܬܐ ܕܐܠܗܐ 'I have written to you, persuading and testifying that this is the true grace of God' (ἔγραψα παρακαλῶν καὶ ἐπιμαρτυρῶν ταύτην εἶναι ἀληθῆ χάριν τοῦ θεοῦ; 1 Pet. 5.12).

2.3. Treatment of the Greek Adverb

The Harqlean version has a proclivity to render Greek adverbs by Syriac adverbs ending in ܐܝܬ-. It renders ἀδίκως 'unjustly' as ܥܘܠܐܝܬ 'wrongfully' (1 Pet. 2.19; Peshitta ܒܥܘܠܐ), ἀεί 'always' as ܐܡܝܢܐܝܬ 'always' (1 Pet. 3.15), ἀναγκαστῶς 'under compulsion' as ܡܩܛܪܐܝܬ 'by force' (1 Pet. 5.2; Peshitta ܒܩܛܝܪܐ), δικαίως 'justly' as ܟܐܢܐܝܬ 'justly' (1 Pet. 2.23), ἑκουσίως 'willingly' as ܨܒܝܢܐܝܬ 'willingly' (1 Pet. 5.2; Peshitta ܒܨܒܝܢܐ), ἐκτενῶς 'earnestly' as ܡܬܝܚܐܝܬ 'prolongedly (for an extended time)' (1 Pet. 1.22),[25] ἑτοίμως 'readily' as ܡܛܝܒܐܝܬ 'readily' (1 Pet. 4.5), προθύμως

[25] The Greek verb τείνω can mean 'stretch out' like the Syriac verb ܡܬܚ, the etymology Thomas uses in his translation.

'eagerly, cheerfully' as ܚܕܝܐܝܬ 'gladly' (1 Pet. 5.2; Peshitta ܡܢ ܟܠܗ ܠܒܟܘܢ), πρῶτον 'first' as ܩܕܡܐܝܬ 'first' (1 Pet. 4.17), and τελείως 'completely' as ܡܫܡܠܝܐܝܬ 'completely' (1 Pet. 1.13; Peshitta ܠܚܡܝܪܐܝܬ). This stands in sharp contrast to the Peshitta that only uses this type of adverb three times in First Peter, only one of which is the reflex of a Greek adverb.[26]

Thomas used the following simple equivalents for other adverbs: ܒܠܚܘܕ 'only' for μόνον 'only' (1 Pet. 2.18), ܩܠܝܠ 'for a little while' for ὀλίγον 'for a little while' (1 Pet. 1.6), ܚܕܐ ܙܒܢ 'once' (idiomatic Syriac) for ἅπαξ 'once' (1 Pet. 3.18), ܗܫܐ 'now' for ἄρτι 'now' (1 Pet. 1.6, 8) and νῦν 'now' (1 Pet. 1.12; 2.10 twice, 25; 3.21), ܡܢ ܠܒܪ 'from outside' for ἔξωθεν 'from outside' (1 Pet. 3.3), ܠܐ ܬܘܒ 'not again' for μηκέτι 'no longer' (1 Pet. 4.2), ܠܡܚܣܢ 'scarcely' for μόλις 'scarcely' (1 Pet. 4.18), and ܗܟܢܐ 'thus' for οὕτως 'thus' (1 Pet. 2.15; 3.5). He used ܒܗ ܒܡܕܡܝܘܬܐ 'in the same vein' as the translation of ὁμοίως 'likewise' (1 Pet. 3.1, 7; 5.5), whereas the Peshitta had used ܗܟܢܐ 'thus' for both ὁμοίως 'likewise' and οὕτως 'thus'.

In some cases, Thomas used etymological exegesis in rendering a Greek compound adverb. In 1 Pet. 1.17, he rendered ἀπροσωπολήμπτως 'impartially', consisting of three elements, α 'not' (*alpha*-privative), πρόσωπον 'face' and λαμβάνω 'take', as ܕܠܐ ܡܣܒ ܒܦܪܨܘܦܐ 'without partiality' (lit., 'without putting on a face'). The use of the singular ܦܪܨܘܦܐ 'face' in the idiom ܡܣܒ ܒܦܪܨܘܦܐ 'partiality' is conditioned by the Greek singular πρόσωπον 'face' and replaces ܐܦ̈ܐ 'nostrils, face' in the more usual Syriac idiom ܡܣܒ ܒܐܦ̈ܐ 'partiality'. In 1 Pet. 5.2, he employs ܒܝܘܬܪ̈ܢܐ ܨܥܝܪ̈ܐ 'for vile gains' to render αἰσχροκερδῶς 'greedily', the compound of αἶσχος 'base' and κέρδος 'gain'. The translation ܗܘ ܕܠܘܩܒܠܐ 'that which is the opposite' reflects the adverbial accusative τοὐναντίον 'contrariwise', having come about through crasis of the article τὸ 'the' and the substantive ἐναντίον 'opposite' (1 Pet. 3.9).[27]

---

[26] 1 Pet. 1.13, where ܠܚܡܝܪܐܝܬ 'completely' represents τελείως 'completely'. The Peshitta translator adds the adverbs ܪܘܚܢܐܝܬ 'spiritually' (1 Pet. 5.2) and ܫܪܝܪܐܝܬ 'firmly' (1 Pet. 5.5) for clarity and emphasis.

[27] Henry George Liddell and Robert Scott, *An Intermediate Greek-English Lexicon* (New York: Harper and Brothers, 1889) p. 258, ἐναντίος, II.1.c.

2.4. Treatment of Negation

Thomas reserves the use of the negation ܠܘ 'not' to specific contexts.[28] Everywhere else he uses ܠܐ 'not'. As noted above, only ܠܐ appears in representations of the Greek *alpha*-privative, whether it be an adjective, noun, or verb. He uses ܠܘ in the construction ... ܐܠܐ ... ܠܘ 'not X, but Y' to represent οὐ ... ἀλλὰ ..., οὐ ... δὲ ... and μὴ ... ἀλλὰ ..., all expressing contrast and meaning 'not X, but Y' as in ܠܘ ܒܣܐܡܐ ܐܘ ܕܗܒܐ ܕܡܬܚܒܠܝܢ . ܐܬܦܪܩܬܘܢ ... ܐܠܐ ܒܕܡܐ ܝܩܝܪܐ 'not with silver or gold that are perishable were you redeemed ... but by the precious blood' that renders οὐ φθαρτοῖς, ἀργυρίῳ ἢ χρυσίῳ, ἐλυτρώθητε ... ἀλλὰ τιμίῳ αἵματι 'not by perishable things, by silver or gold, were you redeemed ... but by precious blood' (1 Pet. 1.18–19; cf. 1.23; 2.18; 3.3–4, 21), ܗܠܝܢ ܕܒܙܒܢ ܠܘ ܥܡܐ . ܗܫܐ ܕܝܢ ܥܡܐ ܕܐܠܗܐ 'those which once were not a people but now are the people of God' that translates οἵ ποτε οὐ λαός, νῦν δὲ λαὸς θεοῦ 'which once were not a people, but now are the people of God' (1 Pet. 2.10; cf. 1.12), and ܟܕ ܡܣܥܪܝܢ ܐܢܬܘܢ ܠܘ ܩܛܝܪܐܝܬ . ܐܠܐ ܨܒܝܢܐܝܬ 'while you act not forcefully, but willingly' that renders ἐπισκοποῦντες μὴ ἀναγκαστῶς ἀλλ' ἑκουσίως 'overseeing not by constraint but willingly' (1 Pet. 5.2).

But when translating a Greek compound form in a contrast, he employs ܠܐ as in ܠܐ ܥܘܕ 'no longer' for μηκέτι 'no longer' and ܘܠܐ or ܐܦ ܠܐ for μηδέ 'and not'. Compare ... ܠܐ ܥܘܕ ... ܐܠܐ in representing μηκέτι ... ἀλλὰ ... in ܠܐ ܥܘܕ ܠܪܓܝܓܬܐ ܕܒܢܝܢܫܐ . ܐܠܐ ܠܨܒܝܢܐ ܕܐܠܗܐ 'no longer for the desires of humans, but for the will of God' representing μηκέτι ἀνθρώπων ἐπιθυμίαις ἀλλὰ θελήματι θεοῦ 'no longer for humans' desires, but for the will of God' (1 Pet. 4.2). The following contrastive example is instructive, where both ... ܐܠܐ ... ܘܠܐ and ... ܐܠܐ ... ܐܦ ܠܐ appear as a rendering of μηδὲ ... ἀλλὰ ... 'and not ... but ...' and ... ܐܠܐ ... ܠܘ 'not ... but ...' appears for μὴ ... ἀλλὰ ... 'not ... but ...' (1 Pet. 5.2–3):

> ܪܥܘ ܠܡܪܥܝܬܐ ܗܝ ܕܒܟܘܢ ܕܐܠܗܐ . ܟܕ ܡܣܥܪܝܢ ܐܢܬܘܢ ܠܘ ܩܛܝܪܐܝܬ
> . ܐܠܐ ܨܒܝܢܐܝܬ ܐܝܟ ܐܠܗܐ. ܘܠܐ ܒܡܘܬܪܢܐ ܥܠܝܠܐ. ܐܠܐ ܚܦܝܛܐܝܬ.

[28] Etymologically, ܠܘ is formed by crasis of ܠܐ and ܗܘ (Sokoloff, *A Syriac Lexicon*, p. 675).

> ܐܦ ܠܐ ܕܝܢ ܐܝܟ ܗܘ ܕܐܝܬܝܟܘܢ ܡܪ̈ܘܬܐ ܕܩܠܝܪܘܣ. ܐܠܐ ܟܕ ܛܘܦ̈ܣܐ
> ܗܘܝܢ ܐܢܬܘܢ ܠܡܪܥܝܬܐ
>
> Shepherd the flock, that is among you, of God, while you act not forcefully, but willingly like God, and not for shameful benefits but joyfully, and neither like you being lords of the clergy but as you being examples for the flock.
>
> ποιμάνατε τὸ ἐν ὑμῖν ποίμνιον τοῦ θεοῦ ἐπισκοποῦντες μὴ ἀναγκαστῶς ἀλλ' ἑκουσίως κατὰ θεόν, μηδὲ αἰσχροκερδῶς ἀλλὰ προθύμως, μηδ' ὡς κατακυριεύοντες τῶν κλήρων ἀλλὰ τύποι γινόμενοι τοῦ ποιμνίου·
>
> Shepherd the flock, that is among you, of God, overseeing not by constraint but willingly according to God, and not greedily but eagerly, and not like those lording over the clergy but being examples of the flock.

While ܠܐ appears in a contrastive adverbial phrase which in Greek has *μή*, the negation ܠܐ appears as part of the reflex of the Greek compound *μηδέ* twice.

3. TREATMENT OF GREEK SYNTAX

3.1. Compact Structure and Word Order

Treatment of Greek compact structure, in which the Greek places adnominals between the definite article and its nominal head, shows that the Harqlean is not bound by the Greek word order when it violates Syriac idiom. Hence, its description as a 'mirror translation' fails here. For example, ܠܢܓܝܪܘܬ ܪܘܚܐ ܕܐܠܗܐ 'the patience of God' renders *ἡ τοῦ θεοῦ μακροθυμία* 'the of God patience' (1 Pet. 3.20). In this example, Thomas puts the genitive 'of God' ·er the noun 'patience' in accordance with standard Syriac m, whereas the Greek puts it between the definite article and ·un to which it belongs. Similarly, he renders *τὴν τῶν ἀφρόνων* ·ν *ἀγνωσίαν* 'the of foolish people ignorance' as ܠܠܐ ܝܕܥܬܐ ܕܣܟ̈ܠܐ 'the ignorance of foolish people' (1 Pet. 2.15) and · *γυναικῶν ἀναστροφῆς* 'through of the wives conduct' as · ܒܝܕ 'through the conduct of the wives' (1 Pet. 3.1). In ·ferent example, he translates *ταῖς πρότερον ἐν τῇ ἀγνοίᾳ* ·ις 'the formerly in your ignorance passions' as ܗ ܕܐܝܬ ܗܘܝܢ ܡܩܕܡܝܬܐ ܕܠܘܬܟܘܢ ܠܪ̈ܓܝܓܬܐ 'your former passions that were in ignorance' (1 Pet. 1.14). In the Syriac, the nominal head precedes the adnominals. By contrast, in the Greek, the adnominals come before the nominal head but after its definite article. In like manner, Thomas renders ὁ κρυπτὸς τῆς καρδίας ἄνθρωπος 'the hidden, of the heart, person' as ܗܘ ܒܪܢܫܐ ܡܛܫܝܐ ܕܠܒܐ 'the hidden person of the heart' (1 Pet. 3.4), περὶ τῆς ἐν ὑμῖν ἐλπίδος 'concerning the in you hope' as ܡܛܠ ܣܒܪܐ ܕܒܟܘܢ 'concerning the hope that is in you' (1 Pet 3.15), τὸν ἀμαράντινον τῆς δόξης στέφανον 'the unwithering of the glory crown' as ܟܠܝܠܐ ܕܠܐ ܣܚܐ ܕܫܘܒܚܐ 'the unwithering crown of glory' (1 Pet. 5.4), τὴν εἰς ἑαυτοὺς ἀγάπην 'the unto one another love' as ܚܘܒܐ ܕܠܘܬ ܚܕ̈ܐ 'love for one another' (1 Pet. 4.8), and εἰς τὸ θαυμαστὸν αὐτοῦ φῶς 'into the marvelous of his light' as ܠܢܘܗܪܐ ܬܡܝܗܐ ܕܝܠܗ 'into his marvelous light (lit., the light marvelous of his)' (1 Pet. 2.9).

3.2. Other Altered Word Order

In the following case, Thomas moved the position of the indirect object from interrupting an apposition near the beginning of the sentence to after the verb. He renders Διὰ Σιλουανοῦ ὑμῖν τοῦ πιστοῦ ἀδελφοῦ, ὡς λογίζομαι, δι' ὀλίγων ἔγραψα 'By Silvanus — to you —, our faithful brother, as I reckon, by a few [i.e., briefly] I have written' as ܒܝܕ ܣܝܠܘܐܢܘܣ ܐܚܐ ܡܗܝܡܢܐ . ܐܝܟ ܕܚܫܒ ܐܢܐ ܒܝܕ ܒܨܝܪܬܐ ܟܬܒܬ ܠܟܘܢ 'By Silvanus, our faithful brother, as I reckon, by a few [i.e., briefly] I have written to you' (1 Pet. 5.12). The indirect object 'to you' immediately follows the verb 'I have written'. Rather than using mirror translation that would have led to awkward Syriac, Thomas transforms the structure into smooth Syriac.

3.3. Use of the Emphatic State

The Harqlean uses the determined form for predicate adjectives without the determining function in cases where the Greek has anarthrous forms. This must be interpreted as reflecting current Syriac usage of the early seventh century. The Harqlean renders the anarthrous predicate adjective εὐλογητὸς by the determined form ܡܒܪܟܐ in ܡܒܪܟܐ ܗܘ ܐܠܗܐ ܘܐܒܐ ܕܡܪܢ ܝܫܘܥ ܡܫܝܚܐ 'Blessed be the God and Father of our Lord Jesus the Messiah' (1 Pet. 1.3). By contrast, the Peshitta uses the absolute form ܡܒܰܪܰܟ݂.

The Harqlean employs determined forms of the adjective ܩܕܝܫ 'holy' for Greek anarthrous forms of ἅγιος in ܐܠܐ ܐܝܟ ܗܘ ܕܩܪܐ ܠܟܘܢ ܩܕܝܫܐ ܆ ܐܦ ܐܢܬܘܢ ܩܕܝܫܐ ܒܟܠܗ ܗܘܦܟܐ ※ ܕܐܠܟܘܢ ↙ ܗܘܘ. ܡܛܠ ܕܟܬܝܒ ܕܩܕܝܫܐ ܬܗܘܘܢ ܆ ܡܛܠ ܕܐܢܐ ܩܕܝܫܐ ܐܢܐ 'But as he who called you is holy, also you be holy in all your behavior. For it is written, Be holy for I am holy'. By contrast the Peshitta uses absolute forms of ܩܕܝܫ all four times.

The subject of the concessive clause appears in the determined form in ܐܝܟ ܗܘ ※ܕܡܕܡ↙ ܐܟܣܢܝܐ ܓܕܫ ܠܟܘܢ 'as though something strange happened to you' (1 Pet. 4.12) against the Peshitta translation ܐܝܟ ܕܡܕܡ ܢܘܟܪܝ ܓܕܫ ܠܟܘܢ, both reflecting the Greek anarthrous construction ὡς ξένου ὑμῖν συμβαίνοντος. Again, current Syriac usage seems to be the *raison d'être*.

Thomas renders the indefinite τέκνα ὑπακοῆς 'children of obedience' as ܒܢܝܐ ܕܡܫܬܡܥܢܘܬܐ 'children of obedience' with both nouns formally in the emphatic state (1 Pet. 1.14).

3.4. Expression of Sameness

Thomas expresses sameness in idiomatic Syriac, transforming the Greek pronoun αὐτός in the meaning 'the same' by repetition of the preposition with suffixed pronoun: ܒܗ ܒܗ ܒܬܪܥܝܬܐ 'with the same mind' expresses τὴν αὐτὴν ἔννοιαν 'with the same mind' (1 Pet. 4.1), ܠܗ ܠܗ ܠܐܫܝܕܘܬܐ ܕܐܣܘܛܘܬܐ 'the same pouring out of intemperance' expresses εἰς τὴν αὐτὴν τῆς ἀσωτίας ἀνάχυσιν 'the same pouring out (excess) of debauchery' (1 Pet. 4.4), and ܗܢܘܢ ܒܗ ܗܢܘܢ ܕܚܫܐ 'the same kinds of sufferings' conveys τὰ αὐτὰ τῶν παθημάτων 'the same kinds of sufferings' (1 Pet. 5.9). He consistently translates the adverb ὁμοίως 'likewise' as ܒܗ ܒܕܡܘܬܐ 'in the same manner' (1 Pet. 3.1, 7; 5.5).

4. Theological Translation — ܡܠܬܐ Treated as Masculine When Referring to Jesus Christ

Whereas the word ܡܠܬܐ 'word' is feminine in gender in Syriac, Thomas treats it as masculine in the phrase ܒܗ ܡܠܬܐ ܚܝܐ ܘܡܩܘܝܢܐ ܕܐܠܗܐ 'by the living and abiding Word (λόγος) of God' (1 Pet. 1.23), the adjectives ܚܝܐ 'living' and ܡܩܘܝܢܐ 'abiding' being masculine. By contrast, the Peshitta used feminine agreement by rendering ܒܡܠܬܐ ܚܝܬܐ ܕܐܠܗܐ ܕܡܩܝܡܐ ܠܥܠܡ 'by the living word of

God that abides forever', apparently referring to the Scriptures. This is also the case in ܡܠܬܗ ܕܝܢ ܕܡܪܝܐ ܀ ܡܩܘܐ ܠܥܠܡ ܀ ܗܢܐ ܕܝܢ ܐܝܬܘܗܝ ܡܠܬܐ ܗܘ ܕܐܣܬܒܪ ܒܟܘܢ 'And the Word (ῥῆμα) of the Lord abides forever. And this is the Word (ῥῆμα) that was proclaimed among you' (1 Pet. 1.25). Here, again, the Peshitta uses the feminine: ܘܡܠܬܗ ܕܐܠܗܢ ܩܝܡܐ ܠܥܠܡܝܢ ܘܗܕܐ ܗܝ ܡܠܬܐ ܗܝ ܕܐܣܬܒܪܬܘܢ 'And the word of our God abides forever. And this is the word that you were proclaimed'.

A comparison with the Harqlean version of the Gospel according to John[29] reveals that Thomas treats the word ܡܠܬܐ as feminine in non-references to the person of Jesus, as in ܒܗܕܐ ܓܝܪ ܐܝܬܝܗ ܡܠܬܐ ܗܝ ܫܪܝܪܬܐ 'For in this the saying (λόγος) is true' (John 4.37) and ܐܠܐ ܐܝܟܢܐ ܕܬܬܡܠܐ ܡܠܬܐ ܗܝ ܕܟܬܝܒܐ ܒܢܡܘܣܐ ܕܝܠܗܘܢ 'But that the word (λόγος) that is written in their law might be fulfilled' (John 15.25). By contrast, he seems to handle ܡܠܬܐ as masculine in the references to Jesus as the Word, such as ܒܪܫܝܬ ܐܝܬܘܗܝ ܗܘܐ ܡܠܬܐ 'In the beginning was the Word (λόγος)' (John 1.1), where he uses the masculine construction ܐܝܬܘܗܝ ܗܘܐ. Thomas does use the feminine ܐܝܬܝܗ ܗܘܬ in the Gospel according to John: ܐܝܬܝܗ ܗܘܬ ܕܝܢ ܫܒܬܐ 'And it was the Sabbath' (John 9.14); ܐܝܬܝܗ ܗܘܬ ܕܝܢ ܒܝܬ ܥܢܝܐ ܥܠ ܓܢܒ ܐܘܪܫܠܡ 'Now Bethany was beside Jerusalem' (John 11.18); ܐܝܬܝܗ ܗܘܬ ܕܝܢ ܟܘܬܝܢܐ ܕܠܐ ܚܝܛܐ ܡܢ ܠܥܠ ܀ ܙܩܘܪܬܐ ܟܠܗ 'Now the tunic was seamless on top, all of it woven' (John 19.23). The sentence ܐܝܬܘܗܝ ܗܘܐ ܡܥܪܬܐ 'it was a cave' (John 11.38) does not contradict this analysis since the referent is the masculine ܩܒܪܐ 'tomb'.

It seems certain, then, that Thomas interpreted the λόγος in 1 Pet. 1.23 and the ῥῆμα in 1 Pet. 1.25 as referring to Jesus Christ as 'the Word' and therefore made ܡܠܬܐ masculine, as demonstrated by its agreement with other sentence constituents.

5. CONCLUSION

The study of the text of the Harqlean version of 1 Peter shows it to be a 'source-oriented translation', a better description than a

---

29 George Anton Kiraz (ed.), *Comparative Edition of the Syriac Gospels, Aligning the Sinaiticus, Curetonianus, Peshîṭtâ and Ḥarklean Versions*, Volume Four: *John* (NTTS, 24, Leiden: Brill, 1996).

‘mirror translation’. Thomas resourcefully used etymology as a translation tool to represent the Greek except in cases where it would have proved misleading. While the translation closely adheres to the Greek, it disallows certain features like the fronting of adnominals in relation to their nominal heads. Further, the version reflects the Syriac of its time by the non-use of the absolute form against the Peshitta to reflect the Greek anarthrous construction. Some expressions are odd in Syriac like the use of the Gt-stem of ܚܫܒ conveying an active meaning, but yet fully understandable. The translation of ܡܠܬܐ ‘the Word’ as masculine was motivated by its reference to Jesus Christ. The translation pushes the limits of Syriac, yet does not violate them. It is constrained by the target language in representing the source language.

THE SEMANTICS OF THE D STEM IN THE SYRIAC OF THE PESHITTA*

ALEXANDRA LUPU

1. INTRODUCTION

In Semitic linguistics research, the semantic function of the D stem has been notoriously difficult to pin down. Early modern grammars of Semitic languages argued that the D stem produces factitive forms out of stative G stems, and 'intensifies' fientive G stems.[1] The conception of a two-fold function for the D stem that

* This paper was adapted from my Ph.D. dissertation, which was carried out under Edward Cook's supervision at the Catholic University of America. I am deeply grateful for his invaluable academic insights and his kind mentorship over the years.

[1] For Arabic, cf. William Wright, *A Grammar of the Arabic Language* (Vol 1, Cambridge: Cambridge University Press, 1896) pp. 31–32; Henri Fleisch, *Traité de Philologie Arabe. Vol. II: Pronoms, Morphologie Verbale, Particules* (Beirut: Dar el-Machreq, 1979) p. 288. For Ge'ez, cf. August Dillmann, *Ethiopic Grammar* (London: Williams & Norgate, 1907) pp. 143–146. For Hebrew, cf. Paul Joüon, *A Grammar of Biblical Hebrew* (trans. Takamitsu Muraoka; Rome: Pontifical Biblical Institute, 1993) p. 155.
The notion of the D stem as an intensifier was particularly prevalent in the early modern grammars of Semitic: thus, Carl Brockelmann, *Grundriss der vergleichenden Grammatik der semitischen Sprache* (Vol. 1, Berlin: Reuther & Reichard, 1908) p. 508; Emil F. Kautzsch, *Grammatik des Biblisch-Aramäischen* (Leipzig: Vogel, 1884) p. 55; Gotthelf Bergsträsser, who calls the D stem 'intensive', and links it symbolically to the lengthened ('strengthened') middle radical (*Introduction to the Semitic*

is conditioned on the semantic profile of the corresponding G stem is not original to modern grammarians; as far back as the eighth century CE, the Arabic grammarian Sibawaih grouped the Arabic stem II into two classes: those that behaved like C stems, with a causative force (analogous to the Hebrew *hiphil*, the Aramaic *aphel*, and stem IV in Arabic); and those that behaved basically like G stems. The C-like verbs functioned as transitive counterparts to stative and intransitive G stems, while the G-like verbs conveyed a notion of plurality.[2]

More recent scholarship has re-evaluated the textual evidence and identified two broad functions for the stem: the factitive (or factitive-resultative) and the pluractional. A pluractional verb explicitly encodes multiple actions, which may be distributed in time, in space, or among multiple participants. Much debate has focused on the question of whether and how these two seemingly distinct functions of the D stem ought to be reconciled. Different scholars have ascribed primacy to one function over the other, marshaling linguistic and philological evidence to support their preferred meaning.

One of the primary exponents of the theory that the factitive meaning is foundational to the D stem is Ernst Jenni, in his seminal work on the *piel* in Biblical Hebrew. He described a resultative *piel* which functioned alongside non-stative *qal* verbs in a way analogous to that of the factitive *piel* with stative *qal* verbs: while factitive verbs put the direct object into the state described by the *qal* verb, resultative verbs put the object into the state that results from the action described by the *qal* verb (thus, since the *qal* of the Hebrew root שׁבר means 'to break', the *piel* would mean 'to make broken'). In order to cover all the usages attested for the *piel* in the Bible, Jenni's arguments necessarily rest on a perhaps overly-broad understanding of grammatical cate-

---

Languages: Text Specimens and Grammatical Sketches [Winona Lake, IN: Eisenbrauns, 1983] p. 14).

[2] Frederik Leemhuis, 'Sibawaih's Treatment of the D stem', *JSS* 18 (1973), pp. 238–256 (242–243).

gories like factitivity and resultativity.[3] Nevertheless, his detailed analysis is linguistically valuable and has proven hugely influential in research on the Semitic verbal system; other scholars have expanded on this conception of the D stem, while maintaining that its primary meaning is as a factitive-resultative.[4]

The other side of this debate, which would ascribe primacy to the pluractional meaning of the D stem, is smaller but also comprises important linguistic studies. Some of these studies are language-specific while others pertain to the Semitic D stem more generally; broadly speaking, however, they all postulate an originally intensive or repetitive meaning for the D stem based on the assumption that the characteristic doubled form of the stem signals its fundamental function.[5]

The current paper, which is based on a more comprehensive survey of the D stem across nearly one hundred verbal roots in the Peshitta, attempts to add to this ongoing conversation in two main ways. First, it casts the factitive and pluractional meanings

---

[3] Ernst Jenni, *Das hebräische Piʿel: Syntaktisch-semasiologische Untersuchung einer Verbalform im Alten Testament* (Zürich: EVZ-Verlag, 1968) pp. 123–173.

[4] Stuart A. Ryder, *The D-Stem in Western Semitic* (Paris: Mouton, 1974); Stuart A. Creason, *Semantic Classes of Hebrew Verbs: A Study of Aktionsart in the Hebrew Verbal System* (PhD Diss., University of Chicago, 1995); Bruce K. Waltke and Michael P. O'Connor, *An Introduction to Biblical Hebrew Syntax* (Winona Lake, IN: Eisenbrauns, 1990). Mention should also be made here of the work done by Albrecht Goetze on the D stem in Akkadian (Albrecht Goetze, 'The So-Called Intensive of the Semitic Languages', *JAOS* 62 (1942), pp. 1–8) which predated Jenni's monograph. Goetze hypothesized that the D stem was directly linked to the Akkadian stative (or 'permansive'), an inflected adjectival form, rather than to a finite verb form.

[5] In general Semitics: Joseph H. Greenberg, 'The Semitic 'Intensive' as Verbal Plurality', in Alan S. Kaye (ed.), *Semitic Studies: In Honor of Wolf Leslau on the Occasion of His Eighty-fifth Birthday, November 14th, 1991* (Wiesbaden: Harrassowitz, 1991) pp. 577–594. In Akkadian: Norbertus J. C. Kouwenberg, *The Akkadian Verb and Its Semitic Background* (Winona Lake, IN: Eisenbrauns, 2010). In Biblical Hebrew: Jan Joosten, 'The Functions of the Semitic D stem: Biblical Hebrew Materials for a Comparative-Historical Approach', *Or* 67 (1998), pp. 202–230. In Syriac: Steven E. Fassberg, 'Is Pael An Intensive/Plural Form of Peal in Syriac?', *JA* 287 (1999), pp. 424–428.

of the Syriac D stem as semantically-conditioned manifestations of a single, overarching function, which is to raise the transitivity of the basic verb. This overall function was determined from the survey data by observing the D stem's tendency to occur with multiple cross-linguistically attested parameters of high transitivity. Second, it applies this understanding of the D stem to evaluate the semantic profiles of the G and D forms of the root **knš*, as attested in the Peshitta, a root which is ideally suited to illustrate the hypothesis under discussion.

2. Factitivity and Pluractionality as Two Manifestations of Heightened Transitivity

2.1 Factitivity in the Peshitta

A verb is called 'factitive' if it encodes an action that brings about a particular state for the verbal object. Such a state could be permanent or temporary, physical or emotional. This paper also subsumes the so-called 'declarative' and 'estimative' meanings under the factitive label.[6] A declarative verb describes a speech act that confers a resulting state onto the verbal object, while an estimative verb describes an act of judgment or conception that has a similar effect.

2.2 Pluractionality in the Peshitta

There are many different categories of pluractionality attested across the world's languages. The three which are most relevant to the Syriac D stem are participant plurality, time-distributed plurality, and space-distributed plurality. Participant plurality is the pluralization of verbal arguments—either agentive or patientive—indicated through verbal morphology, noun phrase (NP) morphology, or a combination of the two. Time-distributed plurality indicates the repetition of an action either on a single occasion or on a series of separate occasions. Finally, space-distributed plurality involves an action repeated simultaneously at different locations in space. Of course, many pluractionals

[6] Cf. Waltke and O'Connor, *An Introduction to Biblical Hebrew Syntax*, p. 402.

combine two or more of these categories of plurality into their interpretations.[7]

Most pluractional D stems in the Peshitta pluralize arguments, which is reflected in the plural morphology of the relevant noun phrases. The D stem tends to pluralize the patient of the verb, but occasionally plural agents are also attested with pluractionals, especially when the action is directed against a single affected object. A secondary use of the D stem pluractional is to indicate time-distributed plurality. Indeed, this type of plurality may be regarded as the more fundamental interpretation of the pluractional D stem since there are D stems which clearly encode repeated actions on a single patient, and which therefore preclude a participant distributive interpretation. On the other hand, D stems with plural patients can almost always be understood to also involve repetition in time; in fact, if the actions are carried out by a single agent, then the situation requires it. Thus, repetition in time in some ways underlies most if not all usages of the pluractional D stem. It is more difficult to identify this time-distributive plurality in the surface text, however, since it usually relies on semantic and pragmatic clues endemic to each individual situation; identifying participant distributivity, in contrast, often involves simply looking for morphologically plural nominal forms. The temporal repetition marked by the pluractional usually takes place on a single occasion, though there are a few cases in which multiple-occasion repetition, such as that found in habitual constructions, is also indicated with the D stem. Time-distributed plurality and participant-distributed plurality can occur together, encoded in the same D stem verb; such considerations have to be contextually determined in each case. The third type of pluractionality mentioned, spatially-distributed plurality, is much less frequently attested for D stems. It too must be identified from accompanying adverbial modifiers and other contextual information.

[7] Esther J. Wood, *The Semantic Typology of Pluractionality* (PhD Diss., University of California at Berkeley, 2007) pp. 63–64.

2.3 The Continuum of Semantic Transitivity

The factitive and pluractional functions of the D stem can be understood as separate but related manifestations of a general transitivity-raising function of the D stem. This definition requires broadening the traditional conception of verbal transitivity. While transitivity is most often viewed as a binary, syntactic feature, hinging on the presence or absence of a direct object, linguists Paul Hopper and Sandra Thompson define transitivity along a semantic continuum, as the degree to which an action is transferred from an agent (with whom it originates) to a patient (whom it affects).[8] According to their definition, which is based on cross-linguistic evidence, transitivity is a property that belongs to the entire clause rather than the verb alone, and is determined by a number of parameters apart from the presence of a direct object, as laid out in Table 1:[9]

Table 1. Parameters affecting transitivity

Feature	Higher transitivity	Lower transitivity
Number of arguments/valence	2+	1
Dynamicity	action	non-action
Telicity	telic	atelic
Durativity	punctual	non-punctual
Mode	*realis* (indicative)	*irrealis*
Affirmation	affirmative	negative

[8] Paul J. Hopper and Sandra A. Thompson, 'Transitivity in Grammar and Discourse', *Language* 56 (1980), pp. 251–299.
[9] Chart adapted from Hopper and Thompson, 'Transitivity in Grammar and Discourse', p. 252; they refer to arguments as 'participants'; dynamicity as 'kinesis'; telicity as 'aspect'; and durativity as 'punctuality'.

Feature	Higher transitivity	Lower transitivity
Agency of subject	high	low
Volitionality of subject	volitional	non-volitional
Affectedness of object	totally affected	not affected
Individuation of object	highly individuated	not individuated

These parameters include the number of noun phrases or 'arguments' that may be constructed with the verb (also known as the valence of the verb); the temporal contours of the verbal event (i.e., its *Aktionsart*); and the characterization of the agent and patient of the action in terms of agency, volitionality, degree of affectedness by the action, and individuation. The final parameter, individuation, is itself a scalar quantity which encompasses features like determination, agency, and countability (that is, whether a noun is mass or count): a highly individuated object is determined, animate, and a count noun. The degree of transitivity of a clause depends on the number of features that appear in that clause with high transitivity values. Thus, a highly transitive clause is characterized by two or more of the following: an instantiated process involving two or more participants; a subject NP exhibiting a high degree of agency and volitionality; and an object NP that is highly individuated and highly affected by the action.[10]

In their study, Hopper and Thompson do not rank these parameters according to their relative importance in determining

[10] Hopper and Thompson note that while no unifying semantic principle has yet been formulated to relate all the features of transitivity to one another ('Transitivity in Grammar and Discourse', pp. 279–280), there is a unifying pragmatic principle: the cluster of morphosyntactic properties which tend to signal foregrounding of an action are also those properties that characterize high transitivity (pp. 283–284).

transitivity; however, when characterizing the transitivity differences commonly observed between the G and D stems in the Peshitta, certain features emerged that correlated more strongly with the D stem. These features were the dynamicity of the verbal event, the verbal valence, the subject's volitionality, and the object's affectedness; and to a lesser extent, the verb's mode, the agency of the subject, and the object's individuation also played a role. The D stem consistently correlated with the higher transitivity values of each of these parameters in Peshitta Syriac.

Using the Hopper and Thompson model of transitivity, the two commonly identified functions of the D stem—factitivity and pluractionality—can both be understood as transitivity-raising operations. The factitive D stem primarily increases transitivity by increasing the valence of a verb: in the root **sbʿ*, the G stem encodes the single-argument meaning 'to be sated, full', while the D stem encodes the two-argument 'to satisfy'. The factitive D stem can also increase transitivity by encoding a dynamic event, in contrast to the state encoded by the G stem, and by requiring the new subject to have higher agency and/or volitionality than the subject of the corresponding G stem. For instance, the G of **rḥm* is a stative verb meaning 'to love', while the D stem of the same root has the more dynamic sense of 'to have (or show) mercy'. When the D stem corresponds to a non-stative, intransitive G stem, its dynamicity parameter may remain unchanged, but the D verb still exhibits increased valence and a tendency to take a highly agentive, volitional subject: thus, while the G of **bṭl* means 'to come to a stop/end', the D stem has the two-argument meaning of 'to put an end to'.

The pluractional meaning of the D stem correlates with an increase in the object affectedness of a situation; in participant-distributed pluractional events, the action affects plural objects, or multiple parts of a collective, thus raising the overall object affectedness. Alternately, in time-distributed pluractional events, an object is more highly affected by a repeated action committed against it. Object individuation is also often higher in clauses containing pluractional D stems, since these tend to occur with countable plural noun patients. Finally, the pluractional D stem tends to pluralize concrete, instantiated actions that have occurred in the narrative past or are occurring in the narrative present, rather than hypothetical, conditional, generic, or simple future actions that have not yet occurred at the time of the narrative. This suggests that, in Syriac at least, concrete actions are easier to pluralize than generic or hypothetical actions. According to Hopper and Thompson's model, specific, instantiated actions exhibit the higher-transitivity values of the mode and affirmation parameters; this is therefore another example of how the D stem aligns with grammatical categories denoting higher transitivity.

It is important to note that according to this model, nothing prevents the G stem from expressing a plural action; rather, the G and D stems form a marked~unmarked contrasting pair. The first criterion of markedness is that the two values must represent 'paradigmatic alternatives of a linguistic category'.[11] The G stem in this pair functions as the unmarked form, and encodes a simple action—that is, an action that is not explicitly marked as plural, repeated, or in any way composed of multiple sub-phases or sub-events—while the marked D stem is restricted to expressing such complex, repeated, or plural actions. Additionally, markedness requires that one value of a conceptual category—the typologically unmarked of the pair—be capable of greater grammatical versatility in the language than its complement.[12] The distribution of a typologically marked value can be curtailed by semantic restrictions in addition to syntactic considerations.[13] This is borne out in Syriac, where the D stem often has a much narrower semantic range than the G stem: while the G stem may take a variety of concrete and abstract meanings and be used in idioms and other figurative language, the D stem usually pluralizes only the most literal, concrete meaning of these G stem meanings.

Finally, it must be emphasized that the semantics of the G stem verb determine the nature of the D stem's increased transitivity: thus, stative and other low-transitivity G stems tend

[11] William Croft, *Typology and Universals* (Cambridge: Cambridge University Press, 2nd edn., 2003) p. 90.
[12] Croft, *Typology and Universals*, p. 95.
[13] Croft, *Typology and Universals*, p. 99.

to correlate with factitive/causative D stems with increased valence, while G stems that already exhibit high transitivity may produce intensive, completive, and/or pluractional D stems. According to this model, then, the D stem does not encode a single meaning; rather the meaning of the D stem is determined by the semantic characteristics of the corresponding G stem. The following section illustrates the ways in which the D stem co-occurs with high transitivity grammatical categories in the Peshitta by examining the semantic fields of the G and D stems of **knš*.

3. THE D STEM OF **KNŠ* EXHIBITS BOTH FACTITIVE AND PLURACTIONAL MEANINGS

The root **knš*, which basically means 'to gather', is extremely common in the Peshitta, occurring 78 times in the G stem and nearly 200 times in the D stem across the Peshitta Old and New Testaments. Its G stem also demonstrates some of the largest variances in usage of any Syriac verb, since it is attested with both syntactically intransitive and transitive meanings. Correspondingly, the D stem of this root exhibits both a factitive-causative meaning and a pluractional meaning. This is therefore an ideal root to illustrate the multiple ways in which the D stem encodes a more transitive verb than the G stem.

The following section presents an evaluation of the semantics of both stems in the Peshitta, in terms of the parameters of transitivity discussed previously. I show how the D stem, unlike the G stem, consistently occurs in higher-valence clauses (involving at least two argument NPs); how it tends to act on more highly individuated objects; and how, more frequently than the G stem, it conveys a greater sense of object affectedness, as gauged by its co-occurrence with adverbial modifiers such as ܟܠ ('all' or 'every'). It is important to acknowledge at the outset that the Peshitta is not a linguistically synchronic text.[14] The Old and New

[14] The source text used for the Old Testament was the Peshitta manuscript 7a1 (Milan: Ambrosian Library). A morphologically tagged transcription of this text was accessed through the Old Testament Peshitta module in Accordance Bible Software. Forms with identical consonantal patterns

Testaments belong to different strata in the development of the Syriac language, with their compositions separated by about 200 years.[15] For the sake of diachronic comparison, I have also made reference where applicable to the Old Syriac gospels which are judged to be contemporaneous with the OT Peshitta.[16] The consonantal text of the Old Syriac matches that of the NT Peshitta, except where noted.

---

were checked against their vocalized analogs in the Mosul Edition (1887–91). On the accuracy of the printed editions, cf. Joshua Bloch, 'The Printed Texts of the Peshitta Old Testament', *The American Journal of Semitic Languages and Literatures* 37 (1921), pp. 136–144 (137, 142); Bas ter Haar Romeny, 'Editing the Peshitta Old Testament: From the Nineteenth Century until Today', *Bibbia e Corano: edizioni e ricezioni. Orientalia Ambrosiana* 5 (Milan: Biblioteca Ambrosiana–Rome: Bulzoni Editore, 2016), pp. 253–258. For the New Testament text, the New Testament Peshitta module in Accordance Bible software provides a morphologically tagged text of the Peshitta based on G. A. Kiraz, Syriac Electronic Data Research Archive (SEDRA) III (1991), as well as the Old Syriac Codex Sinaiticus and Codex Curetonianus Gospel manuscripts.

[15] Different parts of the Old Testament can be dated variously to the late first-second century CE, while the New Testament was finished around the early fifth century CE (S. P. Brock, *The Bible in the Syriac Tradition* (Kottayam: St. Ephrem Ecumenical Research Institute, 1988) pp. 17–22, 28–30). On the origin and dating of the Old Testament Peshitta, cf. M. P. Weitzman, *The Syriac Version of the Old Testament: An Introduction* (University of Cambridge Oriental Publications, 56, 1999) pp. 1–7. On the different linguistic strata of the Old and New Testament Peshitta, cf. Aaron Michael Butts, 'The Classical Syriac Language', in Daniel King (ed.), *The Syriac World* (New York: Routledge, 2019) pp. 222–242. The development of the Syriac language at this time, with particular reference to the Gospel of Matthew, is also examined in Jan Joosten, *The Syriac Language of the Peshitta and Old Syriac Versions of Matthew: Syntactic Structure, Inner-Syriac Developments and Translation Technique* (Studies in Semitic Languages and Linguistics, 22, Leiden: Brill, 1996).

[16] The Peshitta NT was not a new translation, but rather a revision of the Old Syriac, the latter of which is thought to date to the late second-early fourth centuries CE; cf. Brock 28–30; Andreas Juckel, 'Research on the Old Syriac Heritage of the Peshitta Gospels', *Hugoye* 12 (2009), pp. 41–115.

3.1 The G Stem

The G stem can be separated into two primary categories, which correspond to its syntactically intransitive and transitive uses. In the first category, it refers to acts in which a single argument—the subject of the verb—gathers itself under its own power. About one-fourth of all G stems fall into this category. The argument is almost always a plural or collective NP, which is highly animate (usually human) and displays high volitionality. The following examples illustrate this usage in the OT and NT:

> ܘܬܩܪܒܘܢ ܩܘܪܒܢܐ ܠܡܪܝܐ. ܘܬܬܟܢܫܘܢ ܟܢܫܝܢ. ܘܟܠ ܥܒܕ ܕܦܘܠܚܢܐ ܠܐ ܬܥܒܕܘܢ.
>
> You will bring an offering to the Lord as you *assemble*, and you must not do any act of labor (Lev. 23.36)[17]

> ܘܐܬܐ ܪܚܒܥܡ ܠܐܘܪܫܠܡ · ܘܟܢܫܘ ܟܠܗܘܢ ܕܒܝܬ ܝܗܘܕܐ ܘܫܒܛܐ ܕܒܝܬ ܒܢܝܡܝܢ · ܡܐܐ ܘܬܡܢܝܢ ܐ̈ܠܦܝܢ ܓܒܪܐ ܥܒ̈ܕܝ ܩܪܒܐ · ܠܡܬܟܬܫܘ ܥܡ ܕܒܝܬ ܐܝܣܪܝܠ
>
> Rehoboam came to Jerusalem, and all those of the house of Judah and the tribe of Benjamin *assembled*, 180,000 warriors, to fight with those of the house of Israel (1 Kgs. 12.21)[18]

> ܡܰܢ ܕܠܳܐ ܟܳܢܶܫ ܥܰܡܝ ܡܒܰܕܳܪܽܘ ܡܒܰܕܰܪ
>
> He who does not *assemble* with me actually scatters (Mt. 12.30)[19]

---

[17] Also Num. 29.35.

[18] Also 2 Sam. 2.30; Isa. 24.22; Ezra 10.9; Sus. 4, 26; Acts 2.6; 9.39; 13.44; 14.20; 28.23.

[19] Also Lk. 11.23.

ܘܟܢܫܘ ܠܘܬܗ ܦܪ̈ܝܫܐ ܘܣܦܪ̈ܐ ܕܐܬܘ ܡܢ ܐܘܪܫܠܡ

> The Pharisees and scribes, who had come from Jerusalem, *gathered* before him (Mk. 7.1)[20]

In addition to the single-argument clauses, the G stem participates in two-argument constructions, with both an agent and a patient, in a little less than half of all cases. The patient argument can include single objects, collectives, or unbounded mass nouns. Single-object patients are quite rare and can best be interpreted as metaphorical rather than literal acts of gathering: in 1 Sam. 14.19, Saul's command to the priest to 'gather in' his hand may mean something like 'draw back' the hand. Similarly, the idiom 'gather one to one's ancestors', as in 2 Kgs. 22.20, is a reference to dying:

ܘܐܡܪ ܫܐܘܠ ܠܟܗܢܐ ܟܢܘܫ ܐܝܕܟ

> Saul said to the priest, '*Draw back* [lit., 'gather in'] your hand' (1 Sam. 14.19)

ܡܛܠ ܗܢܐ ܗܐ ܐܢܐ ܟܢܫ ܐܢܐ ܠܟ ܠܘܬ ܐܒܗܝܟ ܘܬܬܟܢܫ ܠܩܒܪܟ ܒܫܠܡܐ

> Thus I *will gather* you to your ancestors [i.e., *allow to die peacefully*], and you shall be gathered into your tomb peacefully (2 Kgs. 22.20)[21]

Literal acts of gathering, in contrast, require mass noun or collective noun patients, or patients that are morphologically marked as plurals—that is, entities that are easily understood as extended in some way or made up of constituent sub-parts that can be gathered together. There are many examples of the G stem

---

[20] The Old Syriac gospel has a Gt stem here, emphasizing the intransitive sense of the action.

[21] The only other attestation in the OT is 1 Sam. 14.52, which refers to gathering up an individual to join an existing group of other gathered individuals, which is semantically closer to gathering a collective. There is also an instance in the NT, in Acts 5.6, of a group 'gathering' (up) a dead body for burial (perhaps with reference to gathering up the limbs of the corpse).

that construct with mass or collective noun patients in the OT, only a few of which are cited below:

ܟܢܘܫܘ ܥܡܐ ܩܕܫܘ ܟܢܘܫܬܐ

Gather the people, consecrate the congregation! (Joel 2.16)

ܘܢܟܢܘܫ ܓܒܪܐ ܕܕܟܐ ܩܛܡܗ ܕܬܘܪܬܐ

A man who is pure should *gather* the heifer's ashes (Num. 19.9)

ܘܢܗܘܐ ܐܝܟ ܗܘ ܕܟܢܫ ܚܨܕܐ ܕܩܝܡܬܐ

He shall be as one who *gathers* the standing harvest (Isa. 17.5)[22]

There are fewer cases in which the G stem takes a morphologically marked plural noun patient (7 cases in the OT, or 17% of all attestations; and 4 in the NT, or 10%):

ܗܐ ܥܕܟܝܠ ܝܘܡܐ ܣܓܝ. ܠܐ ܗܘܐ ܙܒܢܐ ܠܡܟܢܫ ܒܥܝܪܐ.

It is still day(time)—it's not the time to *gather* in the cattle (Gen. 29.7)

ܘܥܐܕܐ ܕܡܛܠܐ ܒܡܦܩܗ ܕܫܢܬܐ. ܡܐ ܕܟܢܫ ܐܢܬ ܥܠܠܬܟ ܡܢ ܚܩܠܐ

... (and) the Feast of Ingathering, at the end (lit., 'exit') of the year, when you *gather* your produce from the field (Exod. 23.16)

[22] There are about five cases (two in the OT, three in the NT) in which the mass or collective noun patient is modified using the adverb *kull*. As can be seen below, this adverb much more commonly modifies the patients of the D stem.

ܗܘ ܕܪܦܫܐ ܒܐܝܕܗ ܘܡܕܟܐ ܐܕܪ̈ܘܗܝ ܘܡܟܢܫ ܚܛܐ ܠܐܘܨܪ̈ܘܗܝ ܘܬܒܢܐ
ܡܘܩܕ ܒܢܘܪܐ ܕܠܐ ܕܥܟܐ

That one, with a winnowing fan in his hand, will be purifying his threshing floors and *gathering* the wheat into his store-houses; and the chaff he will burn with fire that never goes out (Mt. 3.12)[23]

ܘܐܝܠܢܐ ܕܚܨܕ ܐܓܪܐ ܢܣܒ ܘܡܟܢܫ ܦܐܖ̈ܐ ܠܚܝ̈ܐ ܕܠܥܠܡ

He who reaps takes pay and *gathers* fruit for eternal life (Jn. 4.36)

The patients in these cases are frequently non-human or inanimate, which are features of a less highly individuated object.

The categories mentioned above do not include any of the G passive participles found in the Peshitta, which constitute nearly one-third of all occurrences of the G stem. These are also found in single-argument constructions; however, since these participles describe the resulting state after the act of gathering and say nothing about the gathering event itself, it is often impossible to tell whether the event was a single-argument or a two-argument act of gathering. In his Syriac grammar, Rubens Duval describes the passive participle as denoting a state that was entered into the past, in some way, while the active participle expresses a process that is happening in the present.[24] Compare, for instance:

ܘܒܝܘܡܐ ܕܬܡܝܢܝܐ ܗܘܝܬܘܢ ܟܢܝܫܝܢ ܘܟܠ ܥܒܕ ܕܦܘܠܚܢܐ ܠܐ ܬܥܒܕܘܢ

On the eighth day, you *shall gather* and must not do any act of labor (Num. 29.35)

[23] Cf. also Lk. 3.17, which is not morphologically marked as plural in the Old Syriac. Mt. 3.12 is morphologically marked for plurality, but uses the verbal root **ḥml*.

[24] Rubens Duval, *Traité de Grammaire Syriaque* (Paris: F. Vieweg, 1881) pp. 312–315.

ܚܙܝܬ ܕܐܬܒܕܪ ܠܗ ܥܡܐ ܡܢܝ ܘܐܢܬ ܠܐ ܐܬܝܬ ܠܙܒܢܐ ܕܘܥܕܬܐ
ܘܦܠܫ̈ܬܝܐ ܟܢܝܫܝܢ ܒܡܟܡܣ

I saw people were scattering away from me, and you had not come at the appointed time, and the Philistines *had gathered/were gathered* at Michmas (1 Sam. 13.11)

The passive participle thus does not necessarily express the result of an action with an external agent; it can also describe the state produced by a single-participant change-of-state verb. Such forms therefore cannot be accurately classified according to number of arguments.

3.2 The D Stem

Unlike the G stem, the D stem is exclusively found in two-argument clauses with an agent and a patient. In such clauses, the agent is highly animate and volitional, and the patient is frequently a morphologically marked, countable plural noun, rather than a collective or mass noun. This semantic profile fits about 60% of D stem clauses in the Peshitta. The following constitutes a sample of these in the OT:

ܘܟܢܫ ܠܒܢ ܠܟܠܗܘܢ ܐܢ̈ܫܝ ܐܬܪܐ

Laban *gathered* all the men of the place (Gen. 29.22)

ܘܟܢܫܘ ܦܠܫ̈ܬܝܐ ܡܫܪ̈ܝܬܗܘܢ ܠܩܪܒܐ ܠܢܚܠܐ

The Philistines *assembled* their troops for war at the wadi (1 Sam. 28.1)

ܘܟܢܫ ܡܠܟܐ ܕܐܝܣܪܝܠ ܢܒ̈ܝܐ ܐܝܟ ܐܪܒܥܡܐܐ ܓܒܪ̈ܝܢ

The king of Israel *gathered* prophets, around four hundred men (1 Kgs. 22.6)

The NT attests the following examples, among many others:

ܘܟܢܫ ܟܠܗܘܢ ܪܒܝ ܟܗܢܐ ܘܣܦܪܐ ܕܥܡܐ

He *assembled* all the chiefs of the priests and the scribes of the people (Mt. 2.4)[25]

ܘܢܫܕܪ ܡܠܐܟܘܗܝ ܥܡ ܫܝܦܘܪܐ ܪܒܐ ܘܢܟܢܫܘܢ ܠܓܒܝܢܘܗܝ ܕܝܠܗ ܡܢ ܐܪܒܥܬ
ܪܘܚܐ ܡܢ ܪܫܝܗܘܢ ܕܫܡܝܐ ܘܥܕܡܐ ܠܪܫܝܗܘܢ

He sent his angels with a great trumpet, so that they *would assemble* his chosen ones from the four winds, from one end of the sky to the other (Mt. 24.31)[26]

ܘܠܐ ܒܠܚܘܕ ܚܠܦ ܥܡܐ ܐܠܐ ܐܦ ܕܒܢܝܐ ܕܐܠܗܐ ܕܡܒܕܪܝܢ ܢܟܢܫ ܠܚܕܐ

Not just on behalf of the people, but also so that he could *assemble* together the sons of God that were scattered (Jn. 11.52)[27]

The D stem is found around 30% of the time with a collective or mass noun direct object, or with two or more collective or mass noun objects that are each morphologically singular:

ܘܟܢܫ ܟܠܗ ܟܢܘܫܬܐ ܠܬܪܥܐ ܕܡܫܟܢ ܙܒܢܐ

Assemble the whole congregation at the entrance to the Tent of Meeting (Lev. 8.3)[28]

---

25 Old Syriac (Curetonian) has ܠܟܠܗܘܢ, with the accusative *lamadh* emphasizing the transitivity of the verb; Sinaiticus omits the *lamadh*.
26 Old Syriac (Sinaiticus) has ܢܟܢܫ ܠܓܒܝܘܗܝ, an unambiguous D stem consonantal form which refers back to God as the agent.
27 Old Syriac has a t-stem, 3 m. pl. verb, denoting either an intransitive act of gathering by the people, or a passive act of gathering of the people.
28 Also Num. 1.18; 8.9; 16.19; 20.10; Ezek. 38.13.

ܟܢܘܫ ܠܝ ܥܡܐ ܘܐܬܠ ܠܗܘܢ ܡ̈ܝܐ

Gather the people for me, so that I may give them water (Num. 21.16)[29]

ܟܢܘܫ ܩܕܡܝ ܠܟܠܗ ܥܡܐ ܘܐܫܡܥܢ ܐܢܘܢ ܦܬܓ̈ܡܝ

Gather all the people before me, that I may tell them my words (Deut. 4.10)[30]

ܘܟܢܫ ܣܝܚܘܢ ܠܟܠܗ ܚܝܠܗ

Sihon *mustered* all of his army (Num. 21.23)

ܘܟܢܫ ܚܝܠܐ ܘܚܪܒ ܠܥܡܠܝܩ

(Saul) *mustered* his army and destroyed Amalek (1 Sam. 14.48)

ܘܠܟܠܗ ܒܙܬܗ ܟܢܘܫ ܠܓܘ ܫܘܩܗ

Gather all (of the town's) spoils in the middle of its open square (Deut. 13.17)

The collectives in these cases tend to be groups of people—'congregation', 'people', 'army'— which are highly animate and volitional entities, and therefore make more highly individuated patients. Judg. 4.10 is an example with two collective objects, each of which is marked as singular:

---

[29] Also 1 Sam. 10.17; 2 Sam. 12.28 ('the remainder of the people'); patient is 'Israel': Isa. 49.5; Jer. 31.10; 2 Chron. 24.6.

[30] Also Judg. 11.20; 2 Sam. 12.29; 2 Kgs. 10.18; 1 Chron. 11.5; patient is 'all of Israel': 1 Sam. 7.5; 28.4; 2 Sam. 3.21; 10.17; 1 Chron. 13.5; 15.3; 19.17; patient is 'all of Jacob': Mic. 2.12.

ܘܟܢܫ ܒܪܩ ܠܙܒܘܠܘܢ ܘܠܢܦܬܠܝ ܠܪܩܡ. ܘܣܠܩܘ ܥܡܗ ܥܣܪܐ ܐ̈ܠܦܝܢ ܓܒܪ̈ܝܢ

Barak *assembled* Zebulun and Naphtali to Rekem, and ten thousand men went up with him (Judg. 4.10)[31]

In Eccl. 2.8, the D stem takes multiple mass noun objects, each of which is marked as singular:

ܟܢܫܬ ܠܝ ܐܦ ܟܣܦܐ ܘܕܗܒܐ. ܘܩܢܝܢܐ ܕܡ̈ܠܟܐ ܘܕܡ̈ܕܝܢܬܐ

I *assembled* for me silver and gold, the assets of kings and countries (Eccl. 2.8)[32]

The use of the modifier ܟܠ, 'all of, the entirety of', is very common with the D stem, appearing in almost half of all cases where the patient is a mass noun or a collective noun. This modifier conceptualizes the patient as an extended entity, or, if it is countable, as an entity with distinct plural subparts. It implies that multiple acts of gathering, distributed across these subparts, are required; therefore, its occurrence alongside the D stem in such cases further suggests a pluractional interpretation for this verb form. In addition, by explicitly stating that the action affects the totality of an object, it marks high object affectedness for the modified patient.[33] It seems reasonable to conclude, then, that the use of this modifier indicates a higher transitivity situation.

In addition to ܟܠ and plural noun morphology, there are other prepositional and adverbial modifiers that indicate the plurality of the action or of the patient. Plurality of action may be

---

[31] Other cases where the patient is made up of several groups of people: 1 Kgs. 18.19; Dan. 3.2; 1 Chron. 28.1; 2 Chron. 15.9.

[32] Also taking as patient multiple mass nouns (gold and silver, property): Zech. 14.14; 2 Chron. 5.1; 24.5.

[33] Indeed, cross-linguistic studies have shown that in languages which morphologically mark high object affectedness on the verbal form by means of completive grams, such grams co-occur with adverbs of universal plurality like ܟܠ. Completive grams 'indicate that an action has been performed thoroughly or to completion', and are thus indicative of high object affectedness; cf. Joan Bybee, Revere Perkins and William Pagliuca, *The Evolution of Grammar: Tense, Aspect, and Modality in the Languages of the World* (Chicago: University of Chicago Press, 1994) pp. 18, 57–60.

distributed over a designated period of time, which draws attention to the acts of gathering occurring on multiple occasions:

ܘܢܟܢܫܘܢ ܟܠܗ ܥܒܘܪܐ ܕܫܢܝܐ ܗܠܝܢ ܛܒܬܐ ܕܐܬܝܢ

> They must *gather* all the grain of these (seven) good years that are coming (Gen. 41.35)

ܘܩܡ ܥܡܐ ܟܠܗ ܐܝܡܡܐ ܗܘ ܘܟܠܗ ܠܠܝܐ ܘܟܠܗ ܐܝܡܡܐ ܕܒܬܪܗ
ܘܟܢܫܘܗܝ ܠܣܠܘܝ

> The people stood all that day and all night and all the following day, and *gathered* the quail (Num. 11.32)

In each of these cases, temporal modifiers are employed to signal a duration of time. The multiple parts of the action can also be distributed in space, with emphasis placed on the spatial separation between the different gathering acts:

ܘܐܢ ܢܗܘܘܢ ܡܒܕܪܝܟ ܐܝܣܪܝܠ ܕܢܫܬܩܠ ܒܣܘܦ ܫܡܝܐ ܡܢ ܬܡܢ
ܢܟܢܫܟ ܡܪܝܐ ܐܠܗܟ

> Though your scattered ones, O Israel, may be far off at the ends of the sky, the Lord your God *will gather* you from there (Deut. 30.4)

ܘܐܢܐ ܐܟܢܫ ܫܪܟܐ ܕܥܢܝ ܡܢ ܟܠܗܘܢ ܐܬܪܘܬܐ ܕܒܕܪܬ ܐܢܘܢ ܠܬܡܢ

> But I, I *will gather up* the remnant of my flock from all the places where I have scattered them (Jer. 23.3)[34]

ܘܟܢܫ ܕܘܝܕ ܠܟܠܗ ܐܝܣܪܝܠ. ܡܢ ܢܗܪܐ ܕܡܨܪܝܢ ܘܥܕܡܐ ܠܡܥܠܢܐ
ܕܐܢܛܝܘܟܝ

> Then David *gathered* all of Israel, from the river of Egypt to the outskirts of Antioch (1 Chron. 13.5)[35]

---

[34] Also Ezek. 28.25; 34.6.
[35] Also 2 Chron. 34.9.

In each of these three cases, prepositional phrases indicating spatial or geographic spread necessitate an interpretation involving plural acts of gathering. Plurality of participants may also be highlighted through literary devices like simile:

ܘܬܟܢܫ ܟܣܦܐ ܐܝܟ ܥܦܪܐ ܘܐܝܟ ܚܠܐ ܕܢܚܠܐ ܕܗܒܐ ܕܐܘܦܝܪ

> You *gather up* silver like dust, gold of Ophir like the sand of a wadi (Job 22.24)[36]

The great quantity of the collective patients 'silver' and 'gold' is conveyed via the references to dust and sand, two substances that are only notable for their abundance. Even in cases in which the patient is not explicitly mentioned, the context often implies a plural or extended entity:

ܠܚ̈ܛܝܐ ܝܗܒ ܥܢܝܢܐ ܠܡܟܢܫܘ ܘܠܡܟܢܫܘ

> To sinners he gives the response to *keep gathering* [or *gather more and more*] (possessions) (Eccl. 2.26)

ܟܰܢܶܫܬܽܘܢ ܠܟܽܘܢ ܠܝܰܘܡܳܬܳܐ ܐ̱ܚܪ̈ܳܝܳܐ

> You *gathered* [gold and silver] for yourselves for the last days (Jas. 5.3)

In these cases, the repeated gathering acts occur on multiple occasions, producing frequentative or even habitual actions.

In contrast to the more common use of the D stem with plural patients, there is a small number of cases in which the D stem is used with singular and/or abstract patients:

ܟܢܫܝ ܡܢ ܐܪܥܐ ܨܥܪܟܝ ܝܬܒܬ̇ ܒܐܘܠܨܢܐ

> *Gather up* your shame, you who dwell under oppression (Jer. 10.17)

---

[36] Also Job 27.16.

ܘܝ ܠܕܥܠܒ ܘܡܟܢܫ ܒܝܫܬܐ ܠܢܦܫܗ

> Woe to he who takes advantage and *gathers* wickedness to himself (Hab. 2.9)

ܐܦܪܘܩ ܠܡܟܝܫܬܐ ܘܠܪܚܝܩܬܐ ܐܟܢܫ

> I will redeem the one beaten down, and the distant one I *will gather* in (Zeph. 3.19)

Most of these cases involve habitual or general present situations, and they could be construed as instances of repetition on multiple occasions. The first two examples are figurative, with the authors perhaps portraying wickedness and shame as concrete extended entities that can be gathered up. Nonetheless, they seem to be exceptions to typical D stem usage. Such cases more commonly employ the G stem. There are also three instances in Matthew 25 in which the D stem patient is a single individual, and the action corresponds to a single occasion:

ܟܦܢܬ ܓܝܪ ܘܝܗܒܬܘܢ ܠܝ ܠܡܐܟܠ ܘܨܗܝܬ ܘܐܫܩܝܬܘܢܢܝ ܐܟܣܢܝܐ ܗܘܝܬ ܘܟܢܫܬܘܢܢܝ

> For I was hungry, and you gave me to eat; I was thirsty, and you gave me to drink; I was a stranger, and you *took* me *in* (Mt. 25.35)[37]

The D stem takes on an unusually figurative meaning here, roughly translated as 'to take in, to show hospitality'. It is possible that this is an automatic translation of the underlying Greek συνηγάγετέ. This verb normally means 'to bring together', and hence is translated into Syriac with the D stem of **knš*; however, in these three cases it appears to function as an idiom meaning 'to take someone in, to show hospitality'.[38] This idiom is found nowhere else in the Greek NT, nor is this meaning attested elsewhere for the Syriac D stem of **knš*.

---

[37] Also Mt. 25.38, 43.

[38] The Old Syriac gospel (Sinaiticus manuscript) uses the same root in the D stem.

Finally, there are a few cases in the NT in which the G and D stems can be compared directly, either because they appear in the same verse or with the same or similar patients. These comparisons highlight that the D stem preferentially expresses specific, instantiated action, thus exhibiting the higher transitivity value of the mode parameter. The G stem, in contrast, does not face this restriction and readily encodes uninstantiated actions. The following example illustrates this difference in usage:

ܟܡܐ ܙܒܢܝܢ ܨܒܝܬ ܕܐܟܢܫ ܒܢܝܟܝ ܐܝܟ ܕܟܢܫܐ ܬܪܢܓܠܬܐ ܦܪܘܓܝܗ
ܬܚܝܬ ܓܦܝܗ

How many times have I wanted to *gather* (D) your sons, as the hen *gathers* (G) her chicks beneath her wings? (Mt. 23.37)[39]

In this case, the use of the D stem for the first occurrence of **knš* reflects the explicit repetition of the gathering (thus the rhetorical 'how many times…?'). The G participle, on the other hand, is used to indicate a general present condition which is not explicitly instantiated in any single action or series of actions.[40] The following series also illustrates the contrast between the G participle and D finite form for the same patient:

ܗܘ ܕܪܦܫܐ ܒܐܝܕܗ ܘܡܕܟܐ ܐܕܪܘܗܝ ܘܚܛܐ ܟܢܫ ܠܐܘܨܪܘܗܝ

That one, with a winnowing fan in his hand, will be purifying his threshing floors, and *gathering* (G) the wheat into his storehouses (Mt. 3.12)[41]

---

39 This verse is found again in Lk. 13.34, with a D infinitive replacing the D imperfect.

40 It is also possible that the difference comes down to object individuation, yet another parameter of transitivity—the D stem takes a human patient, which is higher on the object individuation scale than the non-human animate patient of the G stem, and thus correlates with a higher transitivity feature than the G stem in this case (cf. Hopper and Thompson, 'Transitivity in Grammar and Discourse', p. 253). However, since both objects are concrete, countable, animate plural nouns, this does not seem to amount to a huge difference in transitivity.

41 Also Lk. 3.17. Both Old Syriac gospel manuscripts to Mt. 3.12 employ the root **ḥml* here, a near-synonym also meaning 'collect, put away'.

ܓܒܘ ܠܘܩܕܡ ܙܝܙܢܐ ܘܐܣܘܪܘ ܐܢܘܢ ܡܐܣܘܪ̈ܝܬܐ ܕܢܐܩܕܘܢ ܚܛܬܐ ܕܝܢ
ܟܢܫܘ ܐܢܘܢ ܠܐܘܨܪ̈ܝ

> Pick out the weeds and bind them into bundles so they will burn; but the wheat you must *gather* (D) into my store-houses (Mt. 13.30)

The G participle in the first example is used with a general future sense, while the D stem imperative in the second instance encodes a specific set of instructions given by a man to his servants on a single occasion. The multiple acts of gathering in Mt. 13.30 must take place on a single occasion (the occasion defined here as the entire wheat harvest), but are distributed across plural agent participants; meanwhile, the temporal distribution of the acts in Mt. 3.12 is not specified, and the framing allows that they may take place on one harvest or be spread out across multiple harvests. Thus, the D stem expresses both pluractionality and a more highly instantiated, *realis* situation, both of which raise the transitivity of the clause.

The preceding data suggests that the difference in usage between the D stem and the single-argument G stem for the root **knš* lies in the verbal valence parameter, while the difference between the D stem and the two-argument G stem lies in the parameters of object affectedness and individuation, all of which affect transitivity. The higher values of the affectedness and individuation parameters associated with D stems also promote a pluractional understanding. Data on the animacy and plurality of verbal arguments—two of the key features that determine individuation—bears out this relationship: the two-argument G stem is more commonly used with non-human and inanimate verbal patients (30% of all cases) than the D stem (which attests non-human patients in 20% of cases); furthermore, the G stem generally occurs with undifferentiated mass noun patients (65% of all cases), while the D stem preferentially takes plural, countable patients (60% of all cases). In addition to indicating pluractionality, the higher percentages of plural countable, animate patients contribute to overall higher object individuation for the D stem. Moreover, the high percentage of D stem clauses containing the ܟܠ modifier attests to both pluractionality and higher object affectedness for D stem patients, since an object modified by ܟܠ is more entirely (and therefore more highly) affected than an object not modified in this way. There is also some indication that the D stem prefers more highly instantiated situations represented by the higher transitivity value of the mode parameter. Finally, low-transitivity single-argument event structures are available only to the G stem, suggesting an overall lower transitivity. Perhaps the D stem originally encoded a true transitive alternant for the G stem, before the G stem began to encroach on its semantic range.

4. CONCLUSIONS

The root **knš* provides an ideal example of the syntactic-semantic profiles of D stems found in the Peshitta, and of their corresponding G stems. In this corpus, the D stem correlates with the parameters of high clause transitivity defined by Hopper and Thompson, suggesting that the D stem produces more highly transitive verbs. Thus, in situations in which the G stem of a root encodes a state or a low transitivity event, the D stem will raise the transitivity by increasing the valence of the verb. If the G stem already takes multiple arguments, the D stem raises the transitivity by increasing the value of parameters like object affectedness and object individuation. A pattern therefore emerges that links low-transitivity G stems to high-transitivity D stems with a factitive-causative sense on the one hand, and high-transitivity G stems to D stems with pluractional and intensive/completive meanings on the other hand. In this way, the traditionally-defined factitive and pluractional subsets of the D stem may be considered exponents of the same underlying tendency of the D stem to raise the transitivity of a verbal clause.

This work has implications for the way in which the D stem is conceptualized in Aramaic, and perhaps in the Semitic languages more broadly. By subsuming the various meanings attributed to the D stem under one overall function, it proposes a simpler framework to understand the D stem in relation to the G stem—one which is perhaps straightforward enough to serve as a tool in Syriac pedagogy. The methodology employed in this paper, moreover, can be applied in a similar manner to other semantic studies of the verbal system in Syriac and other Semitic languages. For instance, one line of inquiry that proved beyond the scope of this paper was an investigation into the ways in which the semantics of the D stem and those of the inflected verb forms intersect and affect one another. It is clear that the system of inflections—including the participle—carry at least some aspectual information, and it stands to reason that aspectual considerations may affect the nature of transitivity involved in a given D stem, though the exact aspectual dimensions of the Syriac verbal system have yet to be rigorously defined.

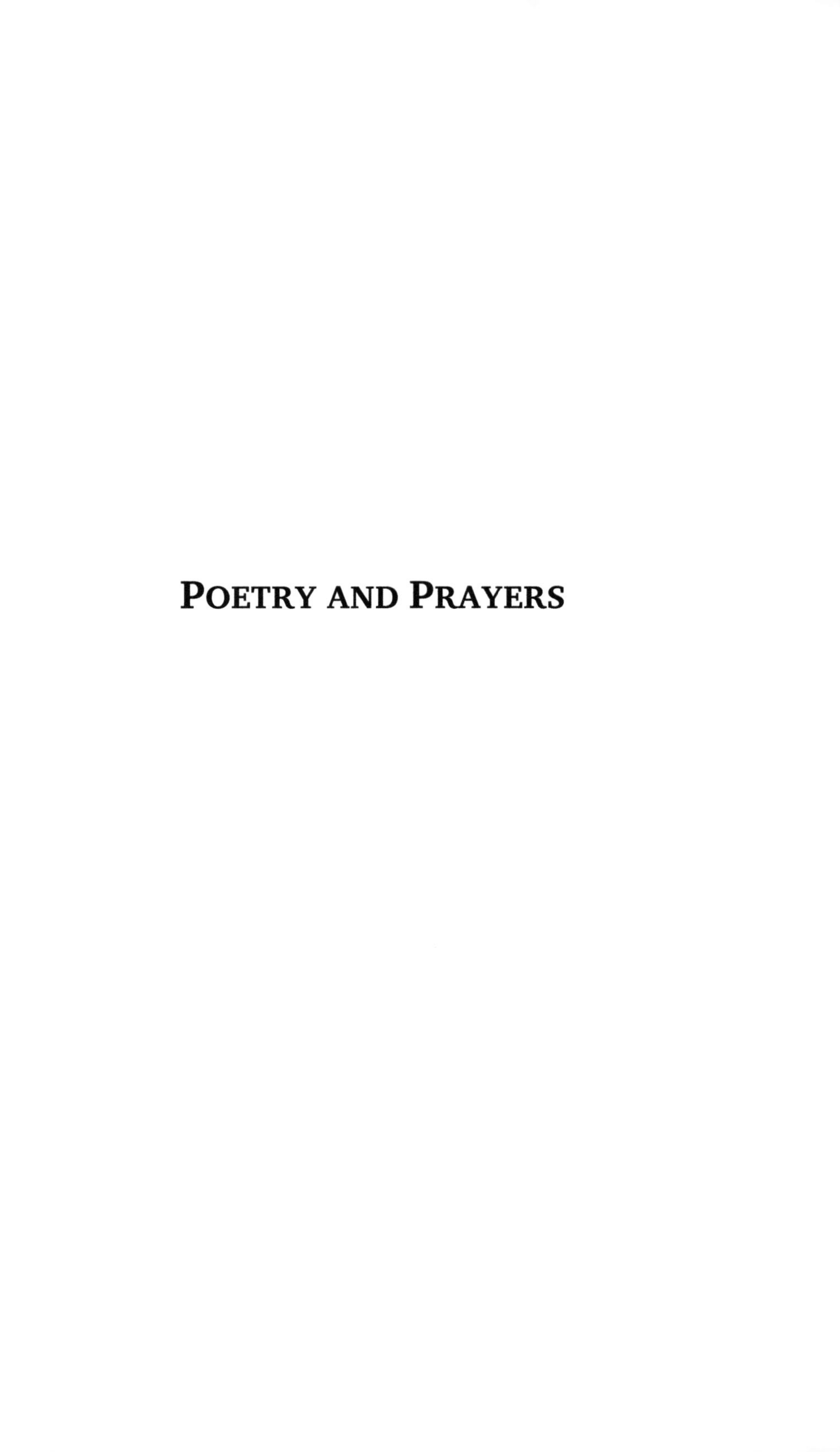

Poetry and Prayers

AN ARAMAIC POEM *FOR* PURIM, BUT IT'S NOT *ABOUT* PURIM!*

MOSHE J. BERNSTEIN

1. INTRODUCTION

Ophir Münz-Manor opens his discussion of 'Hanukkah and Piyyut (Part 1)' with 'Late antique piyyutim for Passover elaborate on the Exodus, those for Shavuoth on the giving of the Torah at Sinai, those for Purim on the story of Esther and Mordecai...'.[1] Regarding most of the Jewish Palestinian Aramaic poetry for Purim published by Yahalom and Sokoloff, this is an accurate

* Dedicated to Professor Edward M. Cook, in appreciation for more than four decades of friendship, collegiality, and scholarly cooperation in the study of Aramaic, the targumim, and the Dead Sea Scrolls.

Versions of this essay were presented at the 9th International Meeting of the International Organization for Targumic Studies (IOTS) at University College London in July 2018, and at a Jewish Studies Colloquium at Yeshiva University in March 2019. My gratitude is extended to colleagues who commented on those occasions, and especially to those others who reacted to earlier drafts of this essay, sometimes to more than one: Professor Emeritus Stephen A. Kaufman of HUC, Professor Aaron Koller of Yeshiva University, Professor Tzvi Novick of the University of Notre Dame, Dr. Avi Shmidman of Bar Ilan University, and Dr. Shani Tzoref.

[1] https://thetalmudblog.wordpress.com/page/16/ (posted December 20, 2011; accessed June 8, 2018).

statement.[2] The first Purim poem in their collection, אתנה בכנישתי (#26), however, belies the sweeping nature of that assertion. Its heading, קילוס לפורים ללמגלה, makes it quite clear that it is intended 'for Purim, for the *megilla*',[3] but the presence in the poem itself of material from the Purim narrative in the book of Esther is minimal. Poem #26 is not unique in this feature, as we can see by examining the three Aramaic poems for Purim that Eliav Grossman edited in his Cambridge MPhil dissertation.[4]

---

[2] Joseph Yahalom and Michael Sokoloff, *Jewish Palestinian Aramaic Poetry from Late Antiquity* (Jerusalem: Israel Academy of the Sciences, 1999) [hereafter, *SYAP*] pp. 170–219. Laura S. Lieber has recently published an English translation of these poems in *Jewish Aramaic Poetry from Late Antiquity: Translation and Commentaries* (Études sur le Judaïsme Médiéval, LXXV, Cambridge Genizah Studies, 8, Leiden: Brill, 2018). The poem under discussion in this essay is located on pp. 92–95. Menahem Kister's important review of *SYAP*, 'Jewish Aramaic Poems from Byzantine Palestine and Their Setting', [Hebrew] in *Tarbiz* 76.1–2 (2007), pp. 105–184, does not deal with this poem to any great extent.

[3] The term קילוס in the heading, which also occurs in a short Hebrew passage prefaced to *SYAP* #10 (a poem based on the book of Ruth that I hope to deal with elsewhere) and directly before #44 (a poem related to the book of Chronicles), is discussed briefly by Yahalom and Sokoloff in their introduction, pp. 33–35, where they write (p. 34), 'poems that discuss the subject of different books of the Hagiographa merited the heading *qillus*'. The three Aramaic poems with which it is associated are dissimilar in so many ways that it is unlikely that the term refers to a specific type of poem, and the term therefore demands further investigation, especially for any discussion of the *Sitz im Leben* of these poems. [As I prepared to send this essay to the editors in December 2020, I came across another (unpublished) fragmentary Purim poem in T-S NS 315.115 that has the heading קילוס לפורא]. That poem, which deals with the Purim story directly, is of a very different nature from the one I am discussing in this paper.]

[4] Pesach Eliav Braverman Grossman, 'A Critical Edition of Three Expansion Piyyutim for Purim from the Cairo Genizah with Introduction and Commentary' (Jesus College, University of Cambridge, 2017). He writes there, pp. 18–19, about one of the poems (איש חמודות חז):

> This piyyut – like all those published in the current work – was written for recitation on Purim, the holiday that celebrates the events narrated in the book of Esther. Yet, even a quick scan reveals that the piyyut does not contain even a single mention of any familiar character, event, or ritual associated with the

There can be no doubt that the poem is intended for Purim, aside from the heading in the manuscript, since the final historical reference in it is to that story and it is from there that the author proceeds to his prayer for divine salvation and redemption. If the poet had wished to extend the historical timeline further by including, let us say, the Maccabees (a perhaps unlikely possibility), he could have abridged the Jacob/Esau/Laban section, which is longer than any other episode in the poem, and still remained within the constraints of the alphabetical acrostic. The second of the two prooftexts following the poem, furthermore, comes from Est. 8.16. It is clear that the poet wants to end on the note of Purim.

MS Budapest 154 – *SYAP* #26[5]

Qillus for Purim for the megillah I shall recite in my congregation praise to the God of my ancestors I shall inform my nation what happened to me.	1 קילוס לפורים ללמגלה 2 אתנה בכנישתי שבח לאילה אבהתי 3 אהודע לאומתי מא דמטא יתי
In the days of the chosen elder, mighty Nimrod attacked him 5 Threw him into the fire, and the Awesome one saved him	4 ביומהי דסבא בחירא אתגרי ליה נמרוד גוברא (צ"ל גיברא) 5 וטלקיה ל{א}<נ>ורא ושיזב יתיה נורא

> holiday. Haman, Mordechai, Esther and Ahasuerus are entirely absent from the text, and there are no references to the reading of the megillah, nor to the Purim feasts and revelry that characterize the day's observance.

See further his article, 'Three Aramaic *Piyyutim* for Purim: Text, Context, and Interpretation', *AS* 14 (2019), pp. 198–255.

[5] Poem #26 in *SYAP* (pp. 170–175) is found in Budapest Kaufmann 154, a manuscript whose whereabouts are currently unknown. Photographs of this manuscript are not available at the website of the Friedberg Genizah Project (https://fjms.genizah.org), and I therefore had to rely on the transcription in *SYAP* in the early stages of the preparation of this paper. To my great surprise and delight, on the very night before I delivered the paper in London, I received the following email from Dr. Avi Shmidman: 'I finally located a copy of the Budapest 154 manuscript, originating from the photo in the Schocken Institute', and he enclosed a readable scan of that copy which I have employed in further study of the poem.

When Jacob brought goat-kids to his mother and fed them to his father, he loved him; Esau came immediately, and begrudged him and hated him When his mother saw his hostility, she sent him to Laban by himself His Beloved one appeared over him and spoke with him 10 For twenty years he shepherded the sheep with Laban And acquired daughters and sons, goats and sheep And when he came to return to his place, Laban pursued him He wanted to destroy him utterly, but his Guardian watched over him Esau roused himself (hurried?) from his sleep and went forth to greet him 15 He wanted to destroy him, were it not for the God of his ancestors The King of kings sent him troops of angels, Who should march with him, and proceed before him.	6 גדיין כד איתי יעקב לאימיה ואוכיל לאבוהי רחמיה 7 אתא עשו מן יומיה ונטריה ושטמיה 8 דבבותיה כד חמת אימיה שלחת יתיה לגב לבן לגרמיה 9 ואתגלי עלוהי רחימיה ומליל עימיה 10 הא עשרין שנין הוה רעי עם לבן עאנין 11 וקנה בנן ובנין ועיזין ואמרין 12 וכד אתא למחזור לאתריה רדף לבן בתריה 13 ובעא למובדא עיקריה ונטורא נטריה 14 זרז עשו מן שנתיה ונפק לקדמותיה 15 ובעא למובדא יתיה לולי אילה אבהתיה 16 חילוון דמלאכין שלח ליה מלך מלכין 17 דיהוון עימיה דרכין וקדמוהי מהלכין
His sons carried him straightaway (or upright) down to Egypt, with a cohort of seventy And they dwelt there for two hundred and ten years 20 That bastard Pharaoh threw their children into the river And the mighty God drowned him in the sea like lead.	18 טענו יתיה בנוי כיון ונחתו למצרים בשבעין חילון 19 ואיתותבו תמן שנין עשר ותרתין מאוון 20 ילדיהון לנהרא זרק פרעה ממזירא 21 וטבע (אפשר צ"ל וטמע) יתיה אלהא גיברא בימא כאיברא
When they came out of the sea at the command of the Most High The cursed Amaleq came to defeat them Exalted Moses lifted his hands to the Most High 25 And Amaleq was handed over for destruction to young Joshua.	22 כד נפקו מן ימא במימריה דרמא 23 אתא עמלק מחרמא מנהון למתגרמא 24 לאילה עיליא תלא ידוהי משה מעליא 25 ואתיהב עמלק לכליא ביד יהושע טליא

Wicked Sisera hoped to exact punishment from them And wished to destroy them from the midst of the earth He hurled down fire upon him from the heavens, from the stars And they arrayed battled against him on behalf of the beloved people.	26 מנהון סכי למתפרעא סיסרא רשיעא 27 ולשיציא יתהון בעא מן גו ארעא 28 נורא מן שמיא זרק עלוהי [מ]כוכביא 29 וסדרו עימיה קרביא בגין עמא [ר]חימיא
30 Sennacherib drove his hosts and gloried in his realm But he blasphemed in his foolishness against the One who created his spirit The Warrior sent angels on behalf of the beloved ones And killed of the troops young and old, 185,000, according to Scripture	30 סנחריב גרש חילותיה ואתגאי במלכות[יה] 31 [ו]חרף בנבלותיה למן די ברא נשמתיה 32 עביד קרבין של[ח מלא]כיה בגין חביבין 33 וקטל מן אוכלסוי טליין וסבין מאה ותמנן וחמשה אלפי כת[יבין]
The king of the Babylonians rushed and brought with him the Chaldeans 35 He destroyed the House of the Hebrews and exiled the Judean people When the four righteous ones arose, prayed and fasted They took over (?) his kingdom from him and saw his downfall	34 פרא מלכהון דבבלאיי ואיתי עמהון כשדאיי 35 חרב ביתהון דעבראיי ואגלי עמא יהודאיי 36 צדיקין ארבעה כד קמון וצלון וצמון 37 מלכותא מיניה אשלמון ובמפלתיה חמון
Shimshai the scribe arose and multiplied his wealth And he weighed out ten thousand to destroy the nation that tithes 40 The Most High One debased his currency and sank his ship, Confounded his end and his corpse was hanged/crucified on his own beam.	38 קם שמשאי ספרא ואסגי בעותרא 39 ותקל אלפין עשרה לאובדא אומא מעשרא 40 רמא פסל כספיה וטמע אלפיה 41 ובלבל סופיה ועל שריתיה אצטלב גופיה
May the Almighty, Lord of Heaven, stir up miracles And cause to sprout in these days salvation for the beloved children May the hour/time approach and may the nation be redeemed And may joy increase for us and you as it was in Shushan the capital	42 שדי מרי שמיה יעורר ניסייא 43 ויצמח באלין יומיא ישועה לבניא רחימיא 44 תקרב שעתא ותתפרק אומתא 45 ותיסגי לן ולכון חדותא היך דהוה בשושן בירתא

May the Ruler look down with mercy from the exalted heavens To redeem a people more beloved than (or 'from') seventy nations He Who exacted punishment from the first, may He destroy the last And take vengeance from Romans and Saracens by the hand of the Jewish people	46 שליטא ידיק ברחמין משמי מרומין 47 למפרוק עם רחימין משבעין אומין 48 מן דאתפרע מן קדמיא הוא ישיצי אחריא 49 ויתנקם מן רומיא וסרקיא ביד עמא יהודאי
As it is written, 'I shall place my vengeance on Edom by the hand of my people Israel', (Ezek. 25.14) And it is said, 'The Jews had etc. [light, joy, rejoicing and honor]' (Est. 8.16)	50 ככ׳ ונתתי נקמתי באדום ביד עמי ישראל (יחזקאל כ"ה 14) 51 ונ׳ ליהודים היתה וג׳ (אסתר ח׳ 16)

2. BRIEF OUTLINE OF CONTENTS

The poem delineates a list of opponents who sought to damage or destroy the Jewish nation, dating back to the days of the first patriarch, Abraham, and his midrashic opponent Nimrod. It includes Esau, Laban, Pharaoh, Amaleq, Sisera, Sennacherib, 'the Babylonian king' (Nebuchadnezzar), and Shimshai the scribe, whose appearance in the next-to-last stanza (38–41) is the one connection, albeit somewhat obscure, to the Purim story, in the poem.[6] A figure known from chapter 4 of the biblical book of Ezra, Shimshai is a stand-in for Haman in some other Purim poems, and there is a midrashic tradition that makes him a son of Haman, but neither Mordechai, nor Esther, nor Haman nor Ahasuerus is mentioned in our poem.[7] The penultimate stanza

---

[6] *SYAP* #33, a very lengthy but incomplete poem for Purim, also contains a list of figures who have attempted to destroy the Jewish people, with many of them, of course, being the same as those found in Poem #26. The Purim connection in that text, however, stands out much more blatantly because they are all presented as in dialogue with Haman.

[7] For a discussion of Shimshai's role as 'Haman substitute' in this and similar Aramaic poems, as well as in targumic tradition, see the collection of sources and discussion in Grossman, 'Critical Edition', pp. 21–22 and 32; for his relationship to Haman, see also *SYAP*, p. 173. Grossman goes as far as to suggest that in our poem Shimshai is *identified* with Haman, and on p. 22 n. 48 points to other poetic sources that adopt

(42–45), which, like the final one (46–49), contains a prayer for divine salvation, creates a further connection to Purim by requesting that the miraculous redemption be followed by 'rejoicing such as took place in fortified Susa' specifically. Despite the fact that the text of the poem, as a whole, is reasonably well-preserved, without many difficult readings, it leaves its reader with one significant question which is fraught with difficulty: what might have been its liturgical function and location? I am, however, going to postpone consideration of that issue until after the literary analysis of the poem.

3. READING THE POEM

Turning our attention to the consideration of the poem itself, I begin with a remark made by Ephraim Hazan in his review of Yahalom and Sokoloff, שירת בני מערבא,

> after reading the erudite and instructive introduction, I felt the lack of a chapter that summarizes and illustrates the poetic aspects of the wonderful poetry that is presented to us. Although the introduction sets out different poetic techniques in various places, this is done in an unsystematic manner.[8]

In response to this critical observation, with which I am in wholehearted agreement, the editors could certainly claim that they never intended their edition to encompass every facet of the poetry that it includes, and that the analysis of the poetic aspects

---

the same stance. I think that his position is quite plausible, and I add in support of it the poet's assertions that Shimshai became fabulously wealthy (38 ואסגי בעותרא), and that he was hanged/crucified on his [own] beam (41 ועל שריתיה אצטלב גופיה). Rabbinic tradition emphasizes that Haman was the wealthiest non-Jew ever: שני עשירים עמדו בעולם קרח מישראל והמן מאומות העולם (Tanḥuma B *Maṭṭot* 8), and the biblical text (Est. 7.9–10) emphasizes his having furnished the means for his own execution. The identification of Shimshai with Haman makes the poet's claim more understandable. Perhaps the editors of *SYAP* are making the same assumption since they refer the crucifixion/impalement of line 41 to Haman and not to 'Shimshai'.

[8] Ephraim Hazan, review of *Jewish Palestinian Aramaic Poetry from Late Antiquity* (Jerusalem: Israel Academy of the Sciences, 1999), by Joseph Yahalom and Michael Sokoloff, in *JQR* 93 (2002), pp. 293–298 (297).

of the texts has been left to subsequent scholars. But Hazan's comment nevertheless points to an understandable lacuna in our study of Jewish Palestinian Aramaic poetry, understandable because literary analysis of newly published texts (or long-published texts that have only recently been republished in accessible form) takes some time to develop. But such lacunae do have to be filled eventually, and I shall take the opportunity offered by this paper to do some gap-filling.

I am going to read the poem closely, paying attention to a variety of the literary features that makes this, in my view, a fine example of the art of the Jewish Palestinian Aramaic poet, and I admit to employing the term 'literary' somewhat loosely. We shall observe very carefully worked out use of language by the author, which differs appreciably, it appears to me, from that found in many other Jewish Palestinian Aramaic poems. He uses language carefully, often doubling and more than doubling his employment of certain terms, often using the same words to express both positive and negative sentiments. These repetitions aid in creating a sense of unity for the poem, as well as contributing to it a certain aesthetic dimension. We shall also examine the use of epithets, some of them unusual, to refer to some of the characters in the poem.

3.1. Structure and Genre

The poem is structured as a rhymed acrostic. Each pair of the first forty-four lines is headed by a letter of the Hebrew alphabet, and each line is divided into two bicola. All four bicola in each letter of the acrostic maintain the same rhyme. The final quatrain (46–49), after the alphabet has been exhausted, did not appear to adhere to a pattern until Dr. Michael Rand ז״ל of Cambridge University pointed one out following my oral presentation of this paper at the IOTS meeting. The author of the poem has embedded an encoded message in the final quatrain. Taking the initial words of the last four lines of the poem, after the alphabetical acrostic has been completed, we read שליטא, למפרוק, מן, ויתנקם, and then continuing on the final line מן בומיא וסרקיא ביד עמא יהודאיי. Their first letters spell out שלמו מרובעי, 'my quatrains have been completed'. Were it not for Rand's remarkable insight, I wonder whether this unusual poetic device would ever have been observed. I know of no other examples of this technique in JPA poetry. Regardless of whether such examples exist or not, what impelled the poet to do it here?

The generic structure of the poem is one that Tzvi Novick has recently characterized as 'serial narrative', 'a form that strings together, in chronological order, discrete episodes from the biblical past that are in one way or another similar'.[9] It belongs to the subcategory he calls *Heilsgeschichte,* in which 'an individual or group praises (or thanks) God for his salvific interventions on behalf of Israel throughout history'.[10] In this poem, the fundamental story-line, repeated over and over, is: antagonist assails the Jews, and God protects or saves them.[11] The Jews (and their ancestors) rarely act in their own defense. God alone is responsible for the foiling of the attempts of all the enemies in the list, with the exception of Nebuchadnezzar, whose deposition and downfall (lines 36–37 מלכותא מיניה אשלמון ובמפלתיה חמון) is attributed to the fasting and prayer of 'four righteous individuals'

---

[9] Tzvi Novick, *Piyyut and Midrash: Form, Genre, and History* (JAJSup, 30, Göttingen: Vandenhoeck & Ruprecht, 2019) p. 97. Lieber, *Jewish Aramaic Poetry*, p. 92, calls it 'A Poetic History', writing 'This poem, a simple alphabetical acrostic of the type called a *qillus* (literally, "praise"), retells the history of Israel from Abraham to the present'. I am not convinced that we can be sure what a *qillus* is (or whether it actually is a 'type') since, as noted above n. 3, the term is associated with only three generically disparate poetic pieces in the JPA corpus, and I also do not see the poem as a retelling of history in any usual sense of the term. I prefer Novick's term because it emphasizes the punctuated nature of the 'narrative', moving from instance to instance across the Bible with no concern for the intervening years or centuries. The text which this poem brought to my mind, for both themes and structure, when I first read it, is the well-known medieval (13th century) poem מעוז צור recited on Ḥanukkah, which surveys, in a similar fashion, the confrontations of the Jews with Egypt, Babylonia, Persia, and Greece (and Rome, as well, if we accept the plausible view of Avraham Fraenkel, "הזמר על הצלת ורמייזא וזמן חיבורו של 'מעוז צור'" *Hamaayan*, 54.2 [2013–14], pp. 9–21 [16–18], that the final stanza is original).

[10] Novick, *Piyyut and Midrash*, p. 98.

[11] Nowhere in the poem is there any confession of sin or suggestion that the abuses of the enemy might have been deserved.

(Daniel and his friends).[12] It is not immediately clear what caused the poet to deviate from his fairly rigorous pattern here.

The order of the poem is strictly chronological, with no deviation such as the one found in Poem #33 where Jesus somewhat oddly precedes Nebuchadnezzar. The poet moves from Genesis to Exodus to Judges to Kings to Ezra/Esther. The story is generally told simply without much in the way of midrashic additions.[13]

The first ten quatrains of the poem move from enemy to enemy systematically and gradually through the biblical period, but with the eleventh there is a leap across the centuries, and with the move from past to present, there is a concomitant move from 'history' to prayer. The shift to a jussive mood or future tense in יעורר...ויצמח (42–43) is the first hint,[14] and then the context is made clear with the words באלין יומיא, 'in these days'. The shift is strongly confirmed by לן ולכון, 'for us and for you', as the prayer reaches out to draw in the audience. It is as if the reference to Shimshai in the context of the Purim story has reminded the poet to call on God to have celebration increase as it did in the fortified Susa. The language of the final quatrain seems to be related to a passage in Pesiqta deRav Kahana ויהי בחצי הלילה 11: ר' לוי בשם ר' חמא בר' חנינא מי שפרע מן הראשונים הוא יפרע מן האחרנים, 'He who exacted punishment from the first will exact punishment from the last', with the first being Egypt and the last being Edom.[15] Our

---

[12] But see n. 17 below. It is striking to note that the language describing the 'four righteous ones' is remarkably similar to that used to describe Esther in #33.105 צניעתא צמת ובצלו קמת ובמפלתך חמת ('the modest one fasted, arose in prayer, and saw your downfall'; all five of the underlined words occur in 26.36–37).

[13] See the commentary in *SYAP* for a range of the biblical and midrashic references.

[14] The language in line 43, ויצמח...ישועה is a bit unusual, since ישועה is not an Aramaic word, and the idiom ויצמח פורקן would seem to be readily available. It appears to have been borrowed from rabbinic liturgical language מצמיח ישועה, as is found in the second blessing of the *Amidah* and elsewhere.

[15] Bernard Mandelbaum, ed., *Pesikta de Rav Kahana* (New York: JTSA, 1962) 1.133. The language of the Pesiqta is very similar to passages in Yannai, Qedushta 53 (ed. Tzvi Meir Rabinovitz, *The Liturgical Poems of*

poem turns the rabbinic assertion into a prayer (although an argument could be made for rendering it as an optimistic assertion as well).

3.2. Dramatis Personae and Epithets

The introductory lines to the poem (1–2) may be said to set its theme, introducing the reader to two of its three central 'characters', God and the Jewish people: 'I shall recite in my congregation praise to the God of my ancestors; I shall inform my nation what befell me'.[16] The third set of 'characters' is the enemies of the Jews. The Jews, however, are passive and largely acted upon in the 'narrative'; their enemies and God perform most of the major actions.[17]

The poem's focus on the enemies of the Jews is perhaps indicated by the fact that their prominence is emphasized through their being identified by name. Eight of the nine opposing figures are specified by name, with Laban mentioned three times, and Esau and Amaleq twice each. The only exception is Nebuchadnezzar who is simply called מלכהון דבבלאי, 'king of the Babylonians'.[18] Equal space, furthermore, is not allotted to each

Rabbi Yannai [Jerusalem: Bialik Institute, 1985], 1.298–1299), ישמע לאדום כשמע מצרים משא ד(ו)מה כמשא מצרים נפרעת מפתרוס בתכלית מכת עשירית ומאדום תפרע בתכלית קרן עשירית, and Qillir's אורה וישועה, a poem in the Purim *qerova* אמתך וחסדך, where the refrain is כאשר פרעת מן הצרים הראשונים כן תפ' מן האחרונים (CUL T-S H12.15 3v). Other similar formulations more closely connected with Purim will be discussed toward the end of this paper where possible liturgical contexts for the poem will be raised.

[16] I presume that 'me', needed for the rhyme, stands for 'the nation' here. The language is quite similar to that of 20.27 נתני כלמה דעבר עליי, 'we (=I) shall relate everything that has passed over me'. In the course of this essay, I shall employ 'Jew', regardless of whether the reference is to 'Hebrew', 'Israelite', or 'Jew/Judean'.

[17] Jacob is actually the subject of the verbs in lines 6 and 10–12, but he is primarily the object of the activity in that section. Moses raises his hands heavenward in line 24, but there is no active human combat described against Amaleq; Joshua simply has Amaleq given over into his hands.

[18] It is interesting that, in addition to choosing not to name Nebuchadnezzar explicitly, the poet also does not avail himself of the oft-

of the nine enemies alluded to in the poem: Nimrod gets two lines; Esau receives six, divided into two parts by Laban who also gets six;[19] Pharaoh, Amaleq, Sisera, Sennacherib, the Babylonian king (Nebuchadnezzar), and Shimshai receive four each. Each portion of the bipartite prayer for the future is also assigned four lines.[20]

In contrast to the constant explicit naming of the enemies, only three historical Jewish figures are named, and each one only once (Jacob [6], Moses [24], Joshua [25]). Once the post-patriarchal Israelites have become a nation (line 18), they are minimized, or rendered less significant, in the narrative, through the constant reference to them by nothing more than adjectives and third person plural verbs and pronouns. They are specified by name (יהודאי, עבראי) only in the reference to the destruction of the Temple (35), and in the final line of the poem. The effect is to focus the attention of the reader/listener on the opponents of the Jews.

The use of epithets is a common paytanic technique, in both Hebrew and Aramaic *piyyut*. Perhaps in order to prevent the poem from becoming monotonous and repetitive, the poet resorts to variation as a literary device which he employs with a certain amount of skill. In the seventeen places where he identifies by a title God acting in defense of the Jews, he rarely repeats himself. They range from the fairly 'ordinary' (e.g., אילה, 'God', always

---

employed epithet for him, ננסא, 'the dwarf'. Cf. *SYAP* #13 *passim*; #18.24, 34; #33.102.

[19] The Esau-Laban material (6–17), which could also be described as the Jacob material, forms a neat chiastic unit: Esau appears in lines 7 and 14, while Laban shows up in 8, 10 and 12.

[20] Simply for the purposes of comparison, we note that the enemies in the surviving portion of Poem #33 are Nimrod, Pharaoh, Amaleq, Sisera, Goliath, the Ethiopian (זרח הכושי; cf. 2 Chron. 14.8ff.), Sennacherib, Jesus (פלני), and Nebuchadnezzar (ננסא). The pattern is for each of them to have a twelve-line exchange with Haman, whose response to Nebuchadnezzar breaks off at line 106 with two lines missing. What would have occupied the last twenty-four lines cannot be ascertained. Would the poet have maintained a chronological sequence (which he has already broken by inserting Jesus before Nebuchadnezzar), finding two other post-Nebuchadnezzar figures to complete the dialogue with Haman, or were the last sections focused completely on Haman?

with a modifier [1, 15, 21, 24]; רמא, 'Exalted One' [22, 40]; מלך מלכין, 'King of kings' [16]; מרי שמיה, 'Lord of Heaven' [42]), to the rather outré. נורא ('Awesome One'; 5, 28?) is a Hebraism;[21] its possible presence in 28 depends on whether it is vocalized there as *nura* ('fire') or *nora.*[22] Among the other titles for God are: נטורא (13; 'Guardian, Watchman'; also in *SYAP* 29.18, 33.84, both Purim poems), מן די ברא נשמתיה (31; 'He who created his soul'),[23] עביד קרבין (32; 'Maker of Wars'),[24] מן דאתפרע מן קדמיא (48; 'He who exacted payment from earlier ones'). I should note the absence of any of the several divine epithets or titles which are borrowed from Greek and which appear frequently in many of the other poems in the Yahalom/Sokoloff collection.

Only twice are epithets employed to identify Jewish figures in the poem: Abraham (סבא בחירא, 'the chosen elder') and Daniel, Hananiah, Mishael and Azariah (צדיקין ארבעה, 'four righteous ones') are characterized by descriptive epithets. Neither of those epithets is perhaps uniquely recognizable as identifying those figures, but their position in the historical survey certainly serves to prevent any error in identification. On the other hand, Joshua, whose name is mentioned, receives the epithet טליא, the

[21] Noted as such in *SYAP*, p. 34, n. 33, and in their helpful index of epithets, pp. 356–357, which indicates that it also appears in 18.27, 43 and 25.6.

[22] *SYAP*, p. 173, contradicts itself here, translating the word in question in the Hebrew translation facing the Aramaic as אש, 'fire', implying the vocalization *nûrā* but listing it as an epithet of God, which therefore has to be vocalized as *nôrā*, in the index of epithets, p. 356 (which probably confirms that אש is not to be taken as referring to God). Lieber, *Jewish Aramaic Poetry*, p. 94, accepts the former reading. See further the discussion below, pp. 343–344.

[23] An unexpected descriptor of God in the context of Sennacherib, who is thus depicted as completely ungrateful, with the poet accusing him in biblical language (cf. 2 Kgs. 19.16, 22) [ו]חרף בנבלותיה blaspheming 'the One who created his soul'.

[24] This is the translation of איש מלחמה (Exod. 15.3) in the Aramaic versions of Neofiti and pseudo-Jonathan; the Fragment Targum and Geniza fragments are similar.

equivalent of biblical Hebrew נער, which is how he is identified in Exod. 33.11.[25]

As we have noted earlier, the poem is largely not concerned with individual Jews, but a small group of modifiers is employed as epithets for the Jewish people. Four of them carry the same meaning, 'beloved': עמא [ר]חימיא (29), חביבין (32), בניא רחימיא (43), עם רחימין (47).[26] Probably the most striking and meaningful epithet for the Jews as a group is found in line 39 where Shimshai is said to have weighed out his funds to destroy אומא מעשרא, 'the tithing nation',[27] creating a novel midrashic twist.

The use of epithets is considerably less common when dealing with the enemies of the Jews. Nimrod, if we accept the reading suggested by the editors of *SYAP*, is גיברא, 'mighty one', a term certainly based on his biblical description as גבר בארץ and גבר ציד (Gen. 10.8–9).[28] Pharaoh is ממזירא (20), 'bastard', an appellation that I have not found applied to his name elsewhere, while Sisera is רשיעא, 'wicked one', a term found uniquely

---

[25] I am not sure whether מעליא ('exalted') as applied to Moses (24), should be considered an 'epithet'.

[26] All but חביבין are noted in the index of epithets in *SYAP*, pp. 356–357.

[27] The translation in *SYAP*, p. 173, somewhat surprisingly is העם המעושר, 'the tenthed (or tithed) people', but the *pael* participle must be taken as active with Lieber, *Jewish Aramaic Poetry*, p. 94, who renders correctly 'the nation that tithes'. It is clearly connected to the biblical injunction Deut. 14.22 עשר תעשר את כל תבואת זרעך. The implication of the poetic text, I believe, is that the Jews' tithing protected them against the ten thousand of Shimshai, a point that surprisingly seems to have eluded the editors of *SYAP*. The 'standard' midrashic interpretation is that the Jews were saved from Haman's bribe by their giving of the half-shekel in the wilderness (y. Meg. 1.5; 70d). According to Lev. R. 28.6 || Pesiqta deRav Kahana 8.4, it was the fulfillment of the commandment of the sheaf (עומר) that preserved the Jews in the time of Haman. (My thanks to Tzvi Novick for the latter reference; see Novick, *Piyyut and Midrash*, pp. 174–176).

[28] The manuscript reads גוברא, 'man', which is certainly a plausible reading, but one that contributes virtually nothing to the art of the poem and which could easily have arisen from a misreading of *yod* for *vav*. גיברא, on the one hand, echoes the biblical epithet, and, on the other, furnishes a possible instance of contrastive doubling as well, as we shall see below.

associated with his name in a variant reading of the targum to Judg. 5.25, and (in its Hebrew form הרשע) in the standard printed texts of Leviticus Rabbah 7.6, although not in the manuscript witnesses in Margalioth's edition.[29]

3.3. Doubling and Other Word-Plays

One of the striking features of this poem is the author's repeated employment of words from the same root in different places. When used more than once in the same fashion, which I refer to as complementary doubling, the effect of the repetition is to reinforce or complement, while when used of opposing figures, for example, it highlights the divergence, and I call that contrastive doubling. Taking all the examples together, we may observe that the effect of this technique is to unify the several mini-stories out of which the poem is constructed.

3.3.1. Complementary Doubling

Let us begin with examples of complementary doubling. In the very first line of the poem, the poet refers to אילה אבהתי, 'God of my ancestors'; he uses the same term in line 15 אילה אבהתיה, 'God of his ancestors' for Jacob's protector. The tight and intimate connection between God and Israel is emphasized by the reference to God as רחימיה (line 9), who looks down ברחמין (line 46) on Israel, whom we have seen to be described with the root רחם in lines 29, 34 and 47.

---

[29] *Midrash Wayyikra Rabbah*, ed. M. Margalioth (Jerusalem: Wahrman, 1972), 1.161–163. My thanks to Professor Stephen Kaufman for confirming the rarity of the targumic usage. Our poem seems to contain several superficial links to that passage in Leviticus Rabbah, although I am not certain how significant they are, even taken together. In Leviticus Rabbah, the series of offenders who were punished with fire because of their arrogance (על ידי שנתגאה) consists of Pharaoh, Sisera, Sennacherib and Nebuchadnezzar (and, in the future, מלכות הרשעה ['the wicked kingdom' = Rome]). Those historical figures just happen to appear in that order in our poem (with the addition of Amaleq). Sisera's being punished by fire, along with the reference to Judg. 5.20 הכוכבים ממסלותם נלחמו, in נורא מן שמיא זרק עלוהי [מ]כוכביא וסדרו עמיה קרביא in lines 27–28 seems to reflect this midrash, as does the language describing Sennacherib ואתגאי במלכותיה (30).

God's punishment of Pharaoh is described as 'drowning' him (21).[30] The action (and probably the word, too) is repeated in the double metaphorical punishment of Shimshai, 'debasing his currency and sinking his boat' (40), for putting up the money to get Ahasuerus to agree to destroy the Jews. Divine protective behavior is thus seen to be consistent and repetitive, while the enemies of the Jews never seem to learn.

The same consistency is seen in God's sending angels to protect Jacob from Esau in line 16, מלאכיא שלח ליה, and the Jews from Sennacherib many years later in line 32, שלח מלאכיה. In both cases the action, based on the biblical texts, is described with virtually identical language. And the proximity, in consecutive 'stanzas' of וסדרו עמיה קרביא, '[the stars] arrayed battle with him [Sisera]', (29) and the divine epithet עביד קרבין, 'battle-maker' (32) creates another complementary doubling that emphasizes the divine and supernatural protection over Israel.

On the other hand, the consistency of Israel's enemies is underlined by the same language being used for several different foes' attempts to destroy them: of Laban ובעא למובדא עיקריה (13),[31] and of Esau ובעא למובדא יתיה just two lines later. And with very slight variation, changing only the choice of the verb meaning 'destroy', Sisera ולשיציא יתהון בעא (27). They all want, בעא, to destroy, מובדא or שיציא, but are unsuccessful. And we might add line 39 where Shimshai weighs out his silver לאובדא the Jews (although the form there is not the expected JPA form, which would have demanded another מובדא).[32] There is a common set of goals for the enemies of the Jews.

---

[30] The reading in line 21 should perhaps be וטמע since טבע is not a good JPA lexeme, and although CAL reads טבע in its text of the poem, it implicitly emends it, since clicking on the word brings up the root טמע (accessed 12/14/18).

[31] The obvious parallel to the language of the Passover Haggadah ולבן בקש לעקור את הכל is noted by the editors, p. 171.

[32] The inconsistent form is noted by *SYAP*, p. 16 n. 4, as is the 'non-Palestinian' form לשיציא, *SYAP*, p. 172.

3.3.2. Contrastive Doubling

Contrastive or antithetical doubling has perhaps a stronger literary effect, because it helps to depict the struggle and tension between the enemies of Israel who seek to destroy them and God who protects them. It should be obvious that contrastive doubling, when God is one referent and the other is an enemy of the Jews, is a natural way of expressing the notion of measure-for-measure punishment by God. To begin at the beginning, if we accept the reading גיברא (4) for גוברא of the manuscript, then we see both the enemy and God described with the same epithet, when God is called אלהא גיברא (21).

The very word אתפרע, 'to exact punishment or take vengeance', is itself employed in contrastive doubling. Sisera's desire was מנהון...למתפרעא, while the prayer to God in the penultimate line of the poem is that מן דאתפרע מן קדמיא הוא ישיצי אחריא.[33] Lest one argue that the word is too commonplace to be significant, it should be noted that according to CAL (accessed 12/14/18) these are two of the only three examples of this verb form in Jewish Palestinian (Galilean) Aramaic, so that the possible significance of their appearance in the contrastive senses for which we are arguing should not be ignored. And although the verbs employed differ, it should be clear that the juxtaposition of Pharaoh's throwing children into the Nile (20) and God's drowning him in the sea (21) also emphasizes the measure-for-measure nature of divine retribution. The measure-for-measure aspect of Shimshai's punishment is highlighted by his boat (אלפיה) being sunk in requital for his paying thousands (אלפין).[34]

The angels whom we saw before were sent by Jacob to Esau (line 16) are described as 'armies' or 'troops', חילוון. A complementary doubling of the word is found, perhaps surprisingly, a couple of lines later in the characterization of Jacob's family going down to Egypt as seventy חילון, which the editors render into Hebrew as צבאות, 'hosts'. It is not clear what impels the poet

33 ישיצי in that line should probably also be considered contrastive doubling to ולשיציא יתהון of line 27.

34 I owe this observation to Tzvi Novick.

to employ the term here.[35] But we then see a contrastive doubling, when Sennacherib's armies are חילותיה in line 30. We know before we read it that the human חיל of Sennacherib will not withstand the angelic one who will attack them in line 32. Note that in line 16, the angels God sends to defend Jacob are חילוון דמלאכין; this pair of words is split up and set as opposing forces in lines 30-32.[36]

A contrastive doubling that uses the same root in slightly different ways appears in the Jacob segment, bridging the Esau and Laban sections. When Esau returns from the field and discovers that his brother has supplanted him in his father's affections, נטריה ושטמיה (7), 'he "watched him [vengefully]" and hated him'.[37] When Jacob is fleeing Laban, we read ונטורא נטריה, 'his Watcher guarded him' (13). Although the first occurrence is idiomatic and the second two are literal, their proximity in the text and their subjects, Esau and God, who are clearly in tension with one another, allow us to see this as yet another sort of contrastive doubling.

3.3.3. Other Word-Plays

In addition to the meaning-laden use of repetitive language that we see in the employment of doubling, our poem also exhibits wordplays of a more 'ordinary' nature. Taking as our first example the passage discussed in the last paragraph, note the judiciously placed dichotomous reactions to Jacob's feeding his father at the

---

[35] The Israelites, according to Exod. 6.26; 7.4; 12.17, 41, and 51, are indeed described as צבאות on the occasion of the Exodus, but not at an earlier point in the biblical narrative. The use in the poem anticipates the later nomenclature.

[36] Might the use of טליין וסבין in reference to the dead of Sennacherib's army (33) be a contrastive doubling of the terms סבא and טליא employed to describe Abram and Joshua respectively? In the biblical text, there is no reference to 'young and old', and there is no obvious reason for the poetic line to be extended with those terms.

[37] Perhaps a hendiadys, as Tzvi Novick suggested, based on the targumic evidence discussed below. CAL notes on this use of נטר in Aramaic '(c.1) w. enemy, enmity: to maintain a state of vengeance in abeyance [Heb.]', presumably based on the pentateuchal לא תקם ולא תטר את בני עמך (Lev. 19.18).

ends of lines 6 and 7, רחמיה and ושטמיה, 'he [Isaac] loved him'[38] and 'he [Esau] hated him'. There is no better way to emphasize the point of this little piece of the story than that of juxtaposition of contrasting terms. A similar juxtaposition of contrasting terms is found in the Sisera passage. His goal is to eradicate the Jews from the earth (מן גו ארעא), so the reaction comes to him from the heavens (מן שמיא). The punishment mirrors the crime, as it were.[39]

The employment of the same root in different forms or of different roots that sound alike is a well-established type of word play and we find two or three of them in consecutive lines 24–25. 'Exalted' (מעליא) Moses lifted (תלא) his hands (ידוהי) to 'the highest' (עליא) God. This 'lifting' results in Amaleq's being given over into the hand (ביד) of young (טליא) Joshua. The repetitive roots and sounds bind the lines tightly together.

Our final example of word-play is a bit complicated, since it involves both doubling and some textual issues as well. In a non-scripturally based incident, Nimrod is said to have thrown 'the chosen elder' into the fire (5), both according to the manuscript reading לאורא and the emendation to לנורא accepted by both the editors of *SYAP* and CAL.[40] If we accept the emendation, a wonderful word-play is created in which נורא (*nôrā*), the Awesome One, saves Abram from נורא (*nûrā*), the fire. And if we are willing to think of טלק as a synonym of זרק, then, regardless of the reading in line 5, Nimrod joins Pharaoh (20) as a 'thrower' whose throwing actions are then contrastively doubled in נורא מן שמיא זרק עלוהי [מ]כוכביא (28), describing the defeat of Sisera. We

[38] This is not the way the line has usually been taken; e.g., Lieber, *Jewish Aramaic Poetry*, p. 93, 'fed his father who loved him', and Sokoloff-Yahalom, *SYAP*, p. 171, והאכיל את אביו אוהבו, both taking רחמיה as a participle in apposition with אבוהי. But the biblical text makes it clear that it was Esau whom Isaac loved (Gen. 25.28 ויאהב יצחק את עשו), leading me to read רחמיה as a 3ms perf. with obj. suffix, 'when Jacob brought the kids to his mother and fed his father, he loved him'.

[39] This latter observation is owed to Tzvi Novick.

[40] Although CAL does not acknowledge the Aramaic lexeme אור = 'fire', it is possible that the poet is playing on the exegesis of מאור כשדים (Gen. 15.7), 'from the fire of the Chaldeans', and borrowing the Hebrew root for that purpose.

see measure-for-measure punishment once again, but it is spread through history and not always immediate.

When we look more closely at that line (28), however, we are confronted with another textual issue (as noted above n. 22): we have to decide whether to read the first word as *nûrā*, 'fire', with God, the unexpressed subject, hurling fire onto Sisera from the stars, or *nôrā*, the 'Awesome One', hurling something unexpressed onto him. So we have either a doubling of the *nûrā* of Nimrod (5), with an echo of the *nôrā* of that line, or a doubling of *nôrā* with an echo of *nûrā*. Regardless, this is quite a nice piece of writing.

4. THE POEM AND THE *TARGUMIM*[41]

Although the poem does follow the order of the biblical narrative, it does not usually adhere to the biblical material very closely. On the surface, it does not appear to be very concerned with exegesis of the biblical text, nor does it seem to employ the targumim much in its composition. Closer examination, however, shows that the poet seems to be aware of subtle points in biblical interpretation and of idioms in the targumim, although he does not always employ them in the same passages where the targum does.

To begin with straightforward equivalences between the poem and the Palestinian targumim, we see that Joshua in line 25 is called טליא; that is the root used by the whole Palestinian tradition to translate the word נער that describes him at Exod. 33.11.[42] The divine epithet עביד קרבין for God (line 33) is clearly borrowed from the Palestinian targum at Exod. 15.3 ה' איש מלחמה where Neofiti reads עביד קרביא (PsJ is similar) and the other PTs (but not Onqelos) employ the same roots.

When Esau bestirs himself to confront Jacob (line 14), we read ונפק לקדמותיה, 'he went forth to meet him', which echoes the language of Jacob's messengers reporting back to him that Esau

[41] This section would probably have been included even if this paper had not been presented at a meeting of the International Organization for *Targumic* Studies.

[42] Onqelos has עולימא.

was הלך לקראתך, 'going to meet you'. Esau's foiled attempt on Jacob would have succeeded לולי אילה אבהתיה, 'were it not for the God of his ancestors', and the poet borrows here the language of Jacob to Laban in Gen. 31.42 that he would have succeeded in sending him away empty-handed לולי א-להי אבי, 'were it not for the God of my father'. The angels whom God sent to accompany Jacob, that they should be קדמוהי מהלכין, 'proceeding before him', is an echo of God's sending angels to 'proceed before' in such passages as Exod. 23.23 כי ילך מלאכי לפניך and Exod. 32.34 הנה מלאכי ילך לפניך. Jacob's sons carrying him to Egypt in line 18 טענו יתיה בנוי, is the language of Neofiti (alone among the targumim) for וישאו אתו בניו in Gen. 46.5.

Esau's reaction to Isaac's new-found love for Jacob is ונטריה ושטמיה (line 7); this is likely to be a double translation of the Hebrew <u>וישטם</u> עשו את יעקב, Gen. 27.41. Neofiti is the only targum to render ושטם for this verb both here and in Gen. 50.15, the other place where it occurs in the Pentateuch.[43] The other Palestinian targumim (PsJon; Nvar; FTP) and Onqelos employ a form of נטר, with the object in the Palestinian versions, omitted here by the poet, סנאה, 'hatred' (נטר שנא\סנה\סינאה). But note that the next line begins with דבבותיה, 'his hostility', the only time this word appears in JPA, according to CAL. So the poet virtually (but not grammatically) furnishes the object for that נטר in the previous line. And it just so happens that the Onqelos translation of וישטם, and of similar idioms, is נטר דבבו, both here and elsewhere. I wonder whether the poet was aware of that rendering, and created a juxtaposition in his poem which reflects three different targumic traditions simultaneously, or whether I am overreading a fortuitous group of juxtapositions. I hope that he did it intentionally!

---

[43] These occurrences of the root שטם, according to CAL (accessed 12/14/18), are the only ones in Jewish Palestinian (Galilean) Aramaic and in Palestinian Targumic Aramaic.

5. The Unity of the Poem and Its Possible Liturgical Function

Having now studied a variety of aspects of this poem in some detail, I believe that we are safe in confirming the conclusions that we outlined originally. The poet takes us through a series of challenges to the Jews and their ancestors throughout the biblical period. They are indeed sequential, but is there any 'glue' that holds the sequence together, that keeps the series from becoming what Novick calls, 'the paradigmatic *Beispielreihe* [that] reduces the biblical past to a chronologically ordered store of examples'?[44] I believe that there are two elements in the poem that contribute, in different ways, to elevating it to something beyond a series. The first is the poet's careful use of language in complementary and contrasting doublets that I have described earlier in this paper. In addition to contributing to the meaning or message of the poem, they function as a unifying feature of the work. The poet's employment of epithets and wordplays works in a similar manner as they cut across the lines between individual stanzas and indicate their interdependence. The more examples that we acknowledge, the tighter the structure.

The other feature is the one that Novick suggests is the way in which 'serial narrative' can cease to be mere *Beispielreihe* 'as it binds the content of the narrative organically to its audience, or put differently, integrates the biblical past into the present'.[45] In our poem there is an intimation of this already in the first stanza as the poet locates his staccato historical survey (מה דמטא יתי) 'in my congregation' (בכנישתי), drawing his audience in immediately from the beginning. But from there until the final two stanzas, with their turn from history to prayer, this poem could have remained a *Beispielreihe*, with its focus almost completely on the past. The poem leaps to the present in the next to last stanza with

---

[44] Novick, *Piyyut and Midrash*, p. 100. I am not suggesting that the techniques of the Aramaic poet are quite the same as that of the Hebrew *paytanim*, because it should be clear that those of the latter are more complex and subtle than those of the former. I employ Novick's contrast between *Beispielreihe* and 'serial narrative' heuristically in a manner consciously quite different from the way that he utilizes it.

[45] Novick, *Piyyut and Midrash*, p. 100.

באלין יומיא and the future/jussive verbs, and links the reference to the historical joy in Susa with a prayer for the contemporary לן ולכון, 'for us and for you', the members of the aforementioned congregation. The references to קדמיא and אחריא further link the narrative of the past with the prayers for the present. With the move from history to prayer, the summary is no longer a mere listing of events in the past, but a foundation for the hope that those events will serve as a model to be replicated in the present. That is the impact of 'joy as it once was in Shushan' (line 45) and 'May He who exacted punishment from the first destroy the last' (line 48).

I turn finally to the question that was one of the first that occurred to me when I began studying this poem. What might have been the liturgical location or employment of this sort of poem? What purpose did its composer have in mind? I think that we must presume that its author intended it for some sort of role in the liturgy or he would not have written it. What are the possibilities? Yahalom and Sokoloff (in the discussion cited above n. 3) imply a close connection to the book of Esther, although they do not go quite so far as to suggest explicitly that it is somehow related to a reading of the scroll of Esther or its translation into Aramaic.[46] It would appear that their thinking relies heavily on the phrase in the manuscript before the text of the poem קילוס לפורים ללמגלה. Were it not for those words, we might have understood the poem as linked to the festival of Purim, but not necessarily liturgically to the scroll of Esther. But the poem, as a whole, never gets close enough, in my view, to the book of Esther, to think that the liturgical connection lies there.

Are there any other options for locating a poem like this one in a Purim liturgical context? The three suggestions that I shall provide for this question should be viewed as theoretical thought experiments, since they lack real data-driven proof, although they are based on possible textual links. My first response comes closest to being on a solid footing, since it is modeled on the

[46] *SYAP*, p. 34. Lieber, *Jewish Aramaic Poetry*, p. 92, suggests explicitly that the poem 'could easily have functioned as a preface to the public reading of Esther'. We still know too little about reading and translation customs in antiquity for the *megillot*, despite *Soferim* chapter 14.

example of the three Aramaic Purim poems that Eliav Grossman published in his MPhil dissertation (above n. 5). Those three are expansion poems (פיוטי הרחבה) that are inserted into the repetition of the *Amidah* before a doxology. He was fortunate enough to have manuscripts that indicated that positioning. In many of them, the three poems are inserted into a *qerovat*-18 for Purim that may be Qillirian. They are positioned either before the doxology ב' המכניע or, in some cases, ב' מבטח.

Looking at the prooftexts that conclude this poem, the last two lines, I wonder whether it, too, might not have been intended (or employed) as a suitable expansion poem to be inserted before ב' המכניע. The entire poem catalogues the history of God's defeating the enemies of Israel and concludes with a prayer for God to act against the latter enemies, the Romans and Saracens, as He did against earlier ones. In a sense, then, it furnishes a set of historical precedents for the doxology. The call for vengeance (49; ויתנקם) against the recent enemies is echoed in the first prooftext ונתתי נקמתי באדום. The second prooftext from Est. 8.16 locates the poem in a Purim context, and echoes, perhaps, line 45 calling for 'joy as there was in Susa the capital'. I must stress that I have no evidence for this usage, although the coherence of the poem with the doxology ב' המכניע and the analogy to Grossman's poems make it at least plausible to me. Since, however, the employment of units of JPA poetry as elements of prayer in Hebrew is rather rare, this proposal can only be made with a great deal of diffidence.

My second and third suggestions are focused on the similarity between the penultimate line in the poem מן דאתפרע מן קדמיא הוא ישיצי אחריא, as we saw earlier, to a passage in Pesiqta deRav Kahana, as well as to a variety of other texts that are liturgically connected with Purim. Parallel formulations to our poem are found in two versions of a supplement to the blessing הרב את ריבנו (so characterized by Ma'agarim):[47] כאשר פרעתה מן הראשונים כן תפרע ותכחיד את האחרונים (Oxford f 57/69) and מי שפרע מן הצרים הראשו' הו' יפרע מן האחרונים (Oxford g 2/31); and in

[47] See https://maagarim.hebrew-academy.org.il/Pages/PMain.aspx?mishibbur=600015&page=8; viewed 4/12/19).

an expansion of על הנסים בימי מרדכי ואסתר for Grace after Meals: וכשם שניפרעתה מן הראשנים כן תפרע ותכחיד את האחרונים (CUL NS 101.12).[48] We thus have four liturgical texts for Purim, including our poem, beyond the midrash, that appear to employ very similar phraseology.[49] Is all this merely coincidental, or is there a deeper connection between the formula and Purim?

I suggest that it is not outside the realm of possibility that either the blessing הרב את ריבנו or the paragraph על הנסים בימי מרדכי ואסתר (whether in the *Amidah* or in the Grace after Meals) could have furnished a suitable locus for the placement of our poem. The added presence of יעורר ניסייא...באלין יומיא in lines 42–43 suggests על הנסים as a possible location for the poem, while the language of the last two lines, employing the verbs אתפרע and ויתנקם, could be said to echo the language of the blessing והנוקם את נקמתינו והנפרע לנו מכל צרותינו. But the liturgy for Purim contains a good deal of 'standard' language that is repeated in different forms from text to text, so that both of these suggestions are made, as I indicated above, with the greatest hesitation.

---

[48] Similar language for the על הנסים in the *Amidah* for both Hanukkah and Purim, without the key word פרע, survives in the geonic-era prayerbooks of R. Saadia Gaon כשם שעשיתה נסים לראשונים בימים ההם כן עשה לאחרונים בימים האילו כימים ההם (I. Davidson, S. Assaf and B. I. Joel [eds.], *Siddur Rav Sa'adya Ga'on* [Jerusalem: Mekitze Nirdamim, 1963], p. 257 in the critical apparatus, based on CUL T-S H18.33) and R. Shlomo b. Natan of Sijilmasa כשם שעשית נסים לראשונים כן תעשה לאחרונים ותושיעינו בימים האילו כימים ההם (S. Hagi [ed. and trans. into Hebrew], *Siddur Rabbenu Šelomo b. R. Natan zṣ"l Av bet din min ha-'ir Sijilmasa* [Jerusalem, 1995], p. 77). If, as might appear from the texts to which we have pointed, the idiom was initiated in a Purim context, it would not be surprising for it to migrate quite smoothly from there to the Ḥanukkah על הנסים. For the medieval debate on the inclusion of this phrase in על הנסים (for Ḥanukkah), see Stefan C. Reif, '*'Al Ha-Nissim*: Its Emergence and Textual Evolution', in *Problems with Prayers: Studies in the Textual History of Early Rabbinic Liturgy* (Studia Judaica, 37, Berlin: De Gruyter, 2006) pp. 297–298.

[49] There are also several occurrences of an idiom like this one in a variety of midrashim on Esther, where ראשונים is applied to Bigthan and Teresh and אחרונים to Haman (Esther Rabba 7; Midrash Abba Gorion 3; Yalqut Shimoni Esther 3).

6. MOVING ON

Having presented our close reading of the poem, emphasizing some of its literary features, and having proposed, very tentatively, some hypothetical liturgical contexts in which it might have been used, I step back and offer some brief thoughts on how the treatment of this poem might serve as a model for that of others in the JPA corpus. First, and more important, the approach to analyzing the 'poetic aspects' of this poem as a literary text that I adopted can readily be applied to the study of any other JPA poem, filling the lacuna in earlier treatments that Hazan has pointed out.[50] Not every poem, of course, will exhibit the same literary features and techniques, but a systematic analysis of the poetic elements in each poem will, on the one hand, contribute to our appreciation and understanding of it individually, and, on the other, will enable us gradually to fill out a literary portrait of JPA poetry as a whole.

Second, my attempt at suggesting a possible *Sitz im Leben* for *SYAP* #26, as fraught with uncertainty as it was, underlines the importance of attempting to locate JPA poetry in specific contexts. Eulogies and wedding poems carry internal indicators of their likely original locations, but many other poems do not. Even poems that appear to be associated with a calendrical event, such as the one we discussed, do not always 'fit' into an obvious liturgical location.[51] Because headings such as קילוס, found at the beginning of our Purim poem and in a couple of other places, do not have a clear liturgical definition, as I have argued in n. 3 above, they cannot, in my view, be employed as guides to the liturgical function or location of the poems with which they are associated. But these poems must have been composed to be recited in some context, and we need to do our best to locate

---

[50] See n. 8 above.

[51] The Aramaic poems for the 9th of Av, for example, found in *SYAP*, pp. 142–169, do not tell us when on that fast day they might have been recited. In 'Two Parallel Consolatory Poems for Tisha be'Av in Aramaic and Hebrew' in Shana Schick (ed.), *Land and Spirituality in Rabbinic Literature: A Memorial Volume for Yaakov Elman ז"ל* (BRLJ, 71, Leiden: Brill, 2022) pp. 159–171 (167). I have suggested a specific liturgical location for the final poem of the six contained in T-S H14.64.

possible contexts for them, using whatever textual information or intuition that we can. The puzzle that is the liturgical map of Byzantine Palestine still has many gaps, and there are many literary compositions, such as our JPA poetry, which are pieces that need to be located on it, even if only one piece at a time.

SPIRITUAL BUT NOT RELIGIOUS: FORM AND FUNCTION IN A SAMARITAN ARAMAIC POEM

LAURA S. LIEBER

Late Antiquity was an era of poetry. Each religious community—Jewish, Christian, and Samaritan—produced remarkable and remarkably innovative bodies of liturgical poetry, in a robust array of languages, including Hebrew, Aramaic, Syriac, and Greek. Recent decades have witnessed a terrific renewal of scholarly interest in hymnody from antiquity, from an array of perspectives, with various authors and genres studied deeply as literary corpora and contextually through the lenses of performance and material culture, as well as the subjects of more broadly ambitious comparative studies that cross confessional and linguistic boundaries.

The present essay focuses on what is typically the least familiar body of Late Antique literature, Samaritan writings. The Samaritans, who accept the Torah alone as scripture (and thus exclude the Prophets and Writings of the Jewish Tanakh from their canon), exist as a third Abrahamic tradition alongside Jews and Christians—groups with whom they coexisted and at times came into conflict in antiquity; after the seventh century, they lived in a cultural milieu dominated by the fourth Abrahamic tradition, Islam.[1] Samaritans, whose worship focuses on Mount Gerizim rather than Mount Zion, share many rituals and practices in common with rabbinic Jews (although not holidays such as Purim and Hanukkah, which reflect non- and post-Pentateuchal events), but their specific observance is often distinctive, as will be the case with the holiday of Sukkot that is of particular interest here. And just as Jews and Samaritans both share some religious traditions and differ over others, they also had separate but often aligned political experiences as minority religions under Roman and Christian rule.[2] Religion and politics will both be of concern in this essay, along with exegesis and aesthetics.

Samaritan works from Late Antiquity were written in a variety of Aramaic that is essentially Jewish Palestinian Aramaic (as distinct from the medieval Hebrew-Aramaic hybrid commonly known as 'Samaritan').[3] The surviving classical Samaritan writings are comprised of two corpora: liturgical poems (called *piyyutim*; s. *piyyut*), which were composed for use in the prayer service in the late third and early fourth centuries CE; and the exegetical work known as *Tibat Marqe* (the ark—that is, anthology—of Marqe), attributed to the great Samaritan sage Marqe ben Amram, who lived in the fourth century CE, and the earliest strata of which can be dated to that time period. This same Marqe was also one of the most important liturgical poets

---

[1] The most comprehensive and current overview of Samaritan history and traditions is Reinhard Pummer, *The Samaritans: A Profile* (Grand Rapids: Eerdmans, 2016).

[2] The most comprehensive summary, in addition to Pummer, is Hagith Sivan, *Palestine in Late Antiquity* (Oxford: Oxford University Press, 2008); see especially chapter 3, 'Recalcitrance, Riots, and Rebellion: The Samaritans and the Emergence of Intolerance' (pp. 107–142). Also note P. T. R. Gray, 'Palestine and Justinian's Legislation on Non-Christian Religions', in Baruch Halpern and Deborah H. Hobson (eds.), *Law, Politics and Society in the Ancient Mediterranean World* (Sheffield: Continuum, 1993) pp. 241–270.

[3] For an introduction to the language of Samaritan writings from Late Antiquity, see Abraham Tal, *Samaritan Aramaic* (Lehrbücher orientalischer Sprachen, III/2, Münster: Ugarit-Verlag, 2013); and also Moshe Florentin, *Late Samaritan Hebrew: A Linguistic Analysis of its Different Types* (Studies in Semitic Languages and Linguistics, 43, Leiden: Brill, 2005).

(*payyetanim*), along with his father, Amram Dare, and his son, Ninna, as well as the anonymous poet known anachronistically as al-Dustan (the Dosithean).

In this essay, I analyze an Aramaic text traditionally attributed to Marqe, but not one of his canonical piyyutim; never used in the liturgy, it is instead one of numerous short "songs" embedded in his prose work, *Tibat Marqe*. Normally *Tibat Marqe* is regarded as a prose work, but upon closer examination, it is clear that it contains significant passages that are, if not unambiguously poetry, at least strongly poetic: marked by repetition, parallelism, and even refrains. But at the same time, the poetry in *Tibat Marqe* differs in very obvious ways, both formal and rhetorical, from the liturgical poems from the same period, which raises a variety of questions concerning function, audience, and performance. Examples from the Samaritan liturgical poetry tradition that are, in some fashion, thematically related to the main poem, will help illustrate precisely what is distinctive about what we might term Samaritan exegetical poetry. I should note that this is a most preliminary kind of study, one which gestures toward a problem that merits systematic inquiry. But for the present, I hope to bring attention to two largely under-studied bodies of Aramaic literature, and to underscore just how expansive and vibrant the field of Aramaic Studies remains.

1. THE POETRY OF *TIBAT MARQE*

It is perhaps rather surprising that the festival of Sukkot, mentioned multiple times in the Torah, is not treated in the earliest stratum—the Late Antique material—of classical (non-biblical) Samaritan writings. We have no piyyutim specifically composed for recitation on the festival, nor is the observance of Sukkot a topic within *Tibat Marqe*.[4] But we do have Late Antique poems that come to be associated with Sukkot, and an evocative tradition about the place named 'Sukkot' does appear within the

[4] Presumably, the Sukkot-specific liturgy in early Samaritan practice was the recitation of collections of biblical verses (*qatafim*) that describe the observance of the festival.

earliest Aramaic portion of *Tibat Marqe*. This passage, which based on its language dates from the third or fourth century CE, begins as an exegetical comment on Exod. 12.37, which it quotes in Aramaic. After a brief prose introduction, the work offers a poetic paean to the Israelites which, by comparing them to both produce and farmers, seems to reflect an association between the place 'Sukkot' and the harvest festival celebrated by dwelling in temporary shelters (*sukkot*):

> *'And the people of Israel journeyed from Rameses to Sukkot'* (Exod. 12.37[5]); the cloud[6] was above them, and the fire was

---

[5] The biblical text here is in Aramaic translation; the language is close to but not identical with the Samaritan Targum, which dates to roughly the same period as this stratum of *Tibat Marqe*.

[6] The connection of Sukkot to 'the cloud' recalls a tradition preserved in an early rabbinic midrash on Leviticus, Sifra (*Emor* 17.11), which also draws the passage from Nehemiah 8 into its exegesis (a similar tradition, lacking the Nehemiah 8 reference but explicating Exod. 12.37 specifically, occurs in Mekhilta *Bo* 14 [Horowitz-Rabin 48]):

> And thus does Ezra say (in Neh. 8.15): 'And that they must announce and proclaim throughout all their cities and Jerusalem, saying: Go out to the mountains and bring olive leaves, and olive-tree leaves and *hadas* leaves, and date-palm leaves, and plaited-tree leaves to make booths (*sukkot*), as it is written: "So that your generations know that I caused the children of Israel to dwell in booths when I took them out of the land of Egypt" (Lev. 23.43)' (Neh. 8.15). Rabbi Eliezer says that **they were booths, literally** (סוכות ממש היו). Rabbi Akiva says that they were **clouds of glory**. 'When I took them out of the land of Egypt' (Lev. 23.43): We are hereby taught that even the sukkah is a reminder of the Exodus from Egypt.

The cloud-sukkah is the minority opinion here—rabbinic tradition accepts both the literal booth and the idea that it commemorates the Exodus—but the alternative is nonetheless known, and may indeed be the stronger case (see Jeffrey L. Rubenstein's essay 'The Sukkah and its Symbolism' *TheTorah.com* (2014, available at http://thetorah.com/sukkah-and-its-symbolism/). The prose opening of the passage, in which the divine cloud shelters all travelers, can be read as a metaphorical description for God extending protection to all who journey through life. The passage states:

> 'To Sukkot': 'Sukkot', ('booths') literally: 'And Jacob traveled to Sukkot, and for his cattle he made sukkot (booths), for which

before them—six hundred thousand appareled in humility, goodness and grace supporting them there. Sukkot was situated on a great pathway, a place to which all travelers went.

Abraham's stars were graceful
  And Sarah's chicks[7] were shining bright
Crowned were Isaac's multitudes,
  Garlanded were Rachel's young
Beautiful were Jacob's cypresses,
  Arrayed were Leah's ranks
Sukkot resembled the Garden of Eden,
  And the Israelites were the trees in it.
The House of the Oath[8] resembled the Ark,
  and Sarah's chicks were in its baskets.
The ram of Isaac[9] paced with it,
  Goring with his horns any who would smite him.
A crop in the House of the Oath,
  Sprouting up and gathered in,
And heaped up by the arm of the Good One
  And gathered by three glorious ministers,[10]
Hedged in by three great fences—
  By cloud, fire, and holy spirit
  One leading, one illuminating, one protecting
A good crop, with no end to its greatness,
  Sown among the Philistines

> reason the place was named Sukkot' (Gen. 33.17). These are the words of Rabbi Eliezer. Rabbi Akiva says: 'Sukkot' refers to the clouds of glory: 'And the Lord will create on the entire base of Mount Zion and on all of its branchings a cloud by day and smoke with a glow of flaming fire by night, on all the glory, a canopy' (Isa. 4.5). [Horowitz-Rabin 48]

(The Mekhilta of Rabbi Shimon bar Yochai reverses the positions of Akiva and Eliezer but is largely the same.)

[7] That is, her descendants.

[8] 'The House of the Oath' refers to Bethel ('the House of God') where God promised Jacob the land and Jacob made a vow to God (see Gen. 28.11–22). In Samaritan tradition, Gerizim and Beth El (as the House of God) are often conflated.

[9] Isaac here seems to be identified with the sheep of the burned offering from Genesis 22.

[10] That is, Eleazar, Pinchas, and Itamar.

And sprouting in the Land of Egypt
And it was tended after being sown,
(For) four hundred and thirty years earlier[11]
The years are weighed in truthful scales:
Half of them in the Land of Egypt
And half of them in the Land of Canaan.
At the end of these years they were gathered together[12]
And became a repository in the plain of Sukkot.
Excellent were these favored farmers,
Whose beauty was outstanding among His creatures![13]

This passage expands on a verse from Exodus 12 that mentions not the festival of Sukkot but rather the geographic region known as 'Sukkot', presumably a place of booths.[14] But despite the fact that the focus is not on the holiday, this passage displays numerous affinities for the holiday. It seems plausible that the place-name Sukkot at least hinted at the ritual practice that bears the same name; dwelling in a booth is significant.

The poetic qualities of this piece, conveyed here through the typesetting, would be evident even if it were printed as prose. The passage is composed of relatively short phrases marked by strong parallelism, both formal and thematic. Its structure lends the composition a forceful cadence and rhythm—it feels, when read aloud, like poetry. And it is also rich with figurative language, both simile and metaphor. Almost all of the imagery in this poem derives from the world of agriculture: the place, Sukkot, is compared to the Garden of Eden, and the children of Israel are the trees within it. They are the 'crop' of God's House (Beth El), planted, tended, and harvested by God and God's designated

---

[11] See Exod. 12.40.

[12] See Exod. 12.41.

[13] *Tibat Marqe* Book 1 (§71); text from Z. Ben-Hayyim (ed.), *Tibat Marqe: A Collection of Samaritan Midrashim* (Jerusalem: Israel Academy of Sciences and Humanities, 1988) p. 97. The translation is the present author's.

[14] The verse most likely refers to an area within the eastern Nile delta region, in the territory of Goshen. A tradition in Exod. R. 18.6 notes that God honored Egypt by calling it 'the Garden of Eden'. Gen. R. 78.16 connects the place-name *Sukkot* to the place where Jacob offered the water libation associated with the festival of Sukkot.

priestly leaders, fenced in protectively by the divine elemental manifestations of cloud (water), fire, and spirit (wind). The Israelites are a uniquely migratory crop (protected by their mobile hedge), thriving in exile as well as in the land. Like produce at the market, their years are weighed in accurate scales, and their assembly on the plains of Sukkot is likened to a storehouse or granary. As the poem concludes, the Israelites are praised as 'favored farmers' (אריסי רחותה). Figurative language rooted in agriculture is hardly innovative; children are often called 'seed', 'fruit', or, as here, 'chicks', to the point where such terms may not even be translated in strictly literal terms. What stands out here is the density of the imagery and the consistency with which the theme is developed. It seems at least plausible that the mention of a place named 'Sukkot' called to mind the abundance of the harvest season—particularly as it would have been experienced by a Samaritan in the expansive agrarian world of Late Antiquity—whether it was the agricultural plenty of the Nile Delta or the richness of the Land of Israel that was envisioned—or the lushness of the Garden of Eden, to which this poem explicitly compares the place called 'Sukkot'.[15]

The agrarian imagery of this passage is striking, and so, too, is the presence of poetry in what is so commonly understood to be a 'prose' text.[16] In truth, much of the text of *Tibat Marqe* should be reevaluated and understood as, if not poetry, as strongly poetic. We can understand this if we consider the passages that bracket the poem treated above, as they themselves employ a kind of intense litany-like structure. *Tibat Marqe* §70, the passage immediately prior to the poem translated above, begins with a

---

[15] On the role of agriculture in Samaritan life, see Laura S. Lieber, 'Shabbat in the Garden of Eden: Two Samaritan Hymns for Sukkot', in Shana Schick (ed.), *Land and Spirituality in Rabbinic Literature: Studies in Memory of Yaakov Elman ז"ל* (BRLJ, 71, Leiden: Brill, 2022) pp. 137–158.
[16] One of the few recent treatments of poetry, or near-poetry, embedded in *Tibat Marqe* can be found in Tzvi Novick, *Piyyut and Midrash: Form, Genre, and History* (JAJSup, 30, Göttingen: Vandenhoeck & Ruprecht, 2019), pp. 68–75. He treats the specific rhetorical structure of the 'iterative verse header', but gestures toward the larger body of embedded poetry more generally.

narrative expansion of the final plague and Pharaoh's decision to let the Israelites depart.[17] This midrash-like prose is followed by a litany that underscores the robustness with which the Israelites despoiled the Egyptians; each item begins with '*An exceedingly bitter borrowing...*' (שעילה מרירה עד מותר...). This phrase opens five lines in a row, which is then rounded off by a brief narration that describes the loot as the source of an enduring curse.

The passage that follows the Sukkot poem in *Tibat Marqe* §71 contains yet another kind of composition: a kind of catalogue marked by a clear pattern but less repetition than in *Tibat Marqe* §70.[18] In this passage, a chorus of voices from nature summons the Israelites out of Egypt and promises their assistance along the way. The Reed Sea, the waters of Marah, the Jordan River, and other features of the Exodus landscape and setting—ten in all—are personified and given voice. This evocative roster is followed by a long narrative in which the divine pillar of cloud and fire bars the pathway forward of the Israelites until they are reminded by the aged Serah bat Asher to retrieve the bones of Joseph.[19]

Each of the 'poetic' passages above reflects a different aesthetic, and a different rhetorical function: the litany of 'bitter borrowing' amplifies what the author reveals to be an enduring crime; the catalogue of natural voices augments the urgency of the Israelite flight from Egypt; and the poem about the Israelites at Sukkot embellishes the sense of fecundity, favor, and virtue of the people. Nor do these poems exhaust the poetic forms that can be found in *Tibat Marqe*; this is an important work whose formal composition awaits further study. What is clear, however, even from this brief example is that the prose of the major work of classical Samaritan exegesis is woven throughout with passages of non-narrative rhythmic prose and poetry. The line between poetry and prose can often be blurry, but as in the passage in *Tibat Marqe* §71, when a certain density of poetic features—short lines,

---

[17] *Tibat Marqe*, Book 1 (§70); Ben-Hayyim, *Tibat Marqe*, pp. 95, 97.

[18] *Tibat Marqe*, Book 1 (§72); Ben-Hayyim, *Tibat Marqe*, pp. 97, 99.

[19] On this passage, including attention to the *Tibat Marqe* tradition, see James Kugel, *In Potiphar's House: The Interpretive Life of Biblical Texts* (Cambridge: Harvard University Press, 1994) pp. 125–155 (especially pp. 138–140).

parallelism, repetition, and figurative language—cluster together, ascribing to a section the term 'poetry' seems appropriate.

While *Tibat Marqe* is rich with poetic material and even passages of true poetry, its embedded poems differ from piyyutim from the same period. Function—in terms of audience, performance, use, and reception—distinguishes the two kinds of writing. In this regard, the poem from *Tibat Marqe* §71 is useful, as it is rooted in Scripture and evokes a common ritual, but when juxtaposed with related piyyutim, its distinctive composition is self-evident. Where this passage elaborates on the Israelites at the place named Sukkot, in the following sections we will consider two poems that form part of the Samaritan liturgy relating to the festival of Sukkot.

2. CLASSICAL SAMARITAN PIYYUT

The poem above describes the place named 'Sukkot', but perhaps colored by the association of that location with the festival of the same name, it evokes the fertile abundance of the harvest. It may be surprising, then, to learn that we do not possess any Late Antique hymns specifically on the subject of Sukkot. Indeed, while we have many piyyutim from this time period, the subjects of the piyyutim and the poetic passages in *Tibat Marqe* rarely overlap.

The published versions of the Samaritan liturgy are largely modern; the two-volume edition by Cowley draws on mss. from the 18th and 19th centuries, and while this work is, at the very least, a product of its time and place (over a century old), it has not yet been replaced by a more modern scholarly edition.[20] The earliest stratum of the prayer service most likely consisted of the recitation of verses from scripture (*qatafim*); these readings were later embellished by hymns. The liturgy as published by Cowley opens with a poem by the 19th century High Priest Amram ben Solomon, modeled on the poetry of the Late Antique *payyetan* and exegete Marqe. Other hymns are scattered through the service, most from the 18th century but a few earlier, from the 14th

[20] A. E. Cowley, *The Samaritan Liturgy in Two Volumes* (Oxford: Clarendon, 1909). The liturgy for Sukkot can be found in II, pp. 716–817.

century.[21] None of the hymns in the service belong to the 'classical' period of Samaritan poetry—the period of Amram Dare, his son Marqe, and Marqe's son, Ninna, in the third or fourth century CE—and where the classical poems are written in Samaritan Aramaic, the medieval and modern poems were composed in the hybrid Aramaic-Hebrew commonly called 'Samaritan'.

In terms of the liturgy in Late Antiquity, we have little idea of what it might specifically have included. We do, however, have two hymns from that period which came to be associated with Sukkot, although we cannot know if their present usage was their original setting. The first of these poems is by Amram Dare ('Amram the Elder', who was also known by the Roman name Titus), who was a member of the circle of Samaritan reformers associated with Baba Rabbah; and the second is by his son, the great Samaritan sage, Marqe, to whom *Tibat Marqe* is also attributed.

Amram Dare's piyyut is (according to modern practice) said daily for most of the seventh month, from its first day until the conclusion of the festival of Sukkot on Shemini Atzeret. In this brief and gemlike hymn, Amram plays with numbers: seven, four, eight, and three. The seventh month is understood as analogous to the seventh day: a Sabbath among months. Akin to the way in which each week contains a day of sanctity (the Sabbath), the seventh month contains an abundance of holy days. These holy days themselves bear multiple names and serve multiple purposes, but all serve to nourish Israel in both body (through

---

[21] The hymns in the service are as follows, with page numbers indicating location in Cowley, *The Samaritan Liturgy*: one (p. 731) by Murjan b. Abraham [18th c.], another (p. 738) by Seth Aaron b. Isaac [15th c.], another (p. 742) by Solomon b. Tabiah [18th c.], another (p. 746) by Abdallah b. Solomon [14th c.], another two (p. 770 and p. 815) by Tabiah b. Isaac [18th c.], another (p. 779) by Pinchas b. Eleazar [date uncertain], another (p. 796) by Abraham b. Jacob Danfi [18th c.], another (p. 801 – very long!) by Eleazar b. Pinchas [date uncertain]. A fine resource for dating these works is Alan D. Crown's *Samaritan Scribes and Manuscripts* (TSAJ, 80, Tübingen: Mohr Siebeck, 2001).

rest and the harvest) and soul (through prayer and the purging of sin).

Just as the Sabbath is the crown of the week, the seventh month is the crown of the year, embellished with three holy gems: the Feast of the Seventh Month (celebrated on the first day of the month), Yom Kippur, and Sukkot. The holidays, likewise, are the Sabbaths of Sabbaths in their ritual observance, and Sukkot in turn contains the additional holiday of the Shemini Atzeret, the Eighth Day of Assembly. Holy days and festivals are layered within and among each other. Through the numbers and the emergent patterns, the month becomes a kind of ornate structure holding Israel and its piety within its bejeweled frame.

The full text of this hymn states:[22]

> Great is God, who thus commanded
> Concerning the beginning of the seventh month,
> Premier among all the new moons,[23]
> That it should be called, by the authority of God,
> By four exalted titles:
> *Shabbaton,*[24] Remembrance, Trumpet Blast, and Sacred Convocation[25]
> In order that it should be a Sabbath-among-Months,
> And a Sabbath[26]-of-Sabbaths among the Festivals,
> And the crown of the Festival of the Time of Favor
> Within it[27] are the Day of Repentance—
> Holy, expelling sin—
> And the pilgrimage of booths and the pilgrimage of the harvest,

---

[22] Amram Dare #21, Z. Ben-Hayyim, *The Literary and Oral Tradition of Hebrew and Aramaic Amongst the Samaritans*, III.2 (Jerusalem: The Academy of the Hebrew Language, 1967, in Hebrew) pp. 84–86 (hereafter, *LOT*).

[23] The word ארשי means, literally, 'foundation, origin'; see Avraham Tal, *Dictionary of Samaritan Aramaic* (HdO: The Near and Middle East, 50, 2 vols.; Leiden: Brill, 2000) p. 67.

[24] The seventh month is the 'Sabbath' of months.

[25] These four names appear in Lev. 23.24.

[26] For שב as 'Sabbath', see Tal, *Dictionary of Samaritan Aramaic*, p. 870.

[27] That is, within the seventh month.

And the Eighth Day of Assembly,[28]
Seventh of the Festivals and the holy of holies.
And all Israel is nourished (מהר) by them[29]
And they are all destined, one with another,
Threefold[30] within it.

May God be praised!
There is no God but the one!

This poem tells us little about the observance of Sukkot beyond its place in the calendar. It is simply one of many holidays that falls during the seventh month. The repetition of the poem throughout the seventh month ensures that the poem adorns the celebration of the many holidays it mentions: the first day of the month, the Day of Repentance, the seven days of Sukkot, and the Eighth Day of Assembly (Shemini Atzeret) that concludes the season of joy. But elements of the poem, particularly the linking of the Day of Atonement ('holy, expelling sin') to the festival of both booths and harvest suggests the practice of beginning construction of the sukkah while in a state of purity, and its association with agrarian riches. Furthermore, later in the hymn, Amram describes Israel as being 'nourished' (מהר) by these festivals, underscoring the connection between the autumnal agricultural festivals and the idea of physical as well as spiritual sustenance.

The connection of Sukkot to spiritual as well as physical nourishment is made even more explicit in the second classical Samaritan hymn associated with Sukkot, by Marqe, the son of

[28] That is, Shemini Atzeret.

[29] Israel is nourished—fed learning, as it were—by the holiday and its many names. The root of מהר is מור, lit., 'to procure food'—as befits the harvest festival.

[30] This may refer to the three holidays—Rosh Hashanah, Yom Kippur, and Sukkot—that fall within the seventh month, but the Samaritan calendar considers Shemini Atzeret a separate holiday, meaning that there are four festivals in the seventh month. Alternatively, it may be a reference to the three pilgrimage festivals. The language is clear, but the significance—and its implications for Amram Dare's calendrical conception—is not.

Amram Dare. Marqe ('Marcus') lived in the late third or fourth century CE; he is not included among the ranks of Baba Rabbah's reformers, as his father is, which suggests that he was young or at least not yet prominent at the time of the great reformer's influence. Marqe's influence on Samaritanism, however, is evidenced by his enduring literary significance. In addition to *Tibat Marqe*, he composed twenty-five liturgical poems, and among Samaritans he is considered the greatest of their hymnographers. While some of his poems are abbreviated in contemporary Samaritan liturgical usage (Ben-Hayyim published only the portions in active usage), the complete texts were preserved in earlier manuscript traditions (and thus are available in Cowley).

Compared to the piyyut by Amram Dare, this poem by Marqe is longer and, with its alphabetical acrostic, more formally structured. It is recited on the preparatory feast (*ṣimmūt*) of Sukkot, which is observed on the fifteenth day of the fifth month and serves as advance notice of the coming festival,[31] as well as from the first day of the seventh month ('the festival of the seventh month') until the Day of Atonement (the tenth day of the seventh month).[32] Its text is as follows:[33]

> א Come in peace, O day of fasting
> On which two goats for sin-offerings
> Are offered on the heights:
> One for Azazel and one for YHWH

[31] Both Passover and Sukkot are preceded by feast-days (which always fall on Shabbat), known as צמות (lit., 'meeting, conjunction'). The special Sabbath falls seven weeks prior to the Festival. See Reinhard Pummer, 'Samaritan Rituals and Customs', in Alan D. Crown (ed.), *The Samaritans* (Tübingen: Mohr Siebeck, 1989) pp. 650–690 (689). It is intriguing that the fifteenth day of the fifth month is, in the Jewish calendar Tu b'Av, which is closely linked to Yom Kippur in m. Taanit 4.8, much as this poem is linked in practice and themes to both occasions.

[32] See József Zsengellér, 'The Day of Atonement Among the Samaritans', in Thomas Heike and Tobias Nicklas (eds.), *The Day of Atonement: Its Interpretations in Early Jewish and Christian Traditions* (TBN, 15, Leiden: Brill, 2012) pp. 139–161.

[33] Marqe #17; *LOT*, pp. 238–241.

ב On the tenth of the month—it is said—
'You shall afflict your souls' (Lev. 16.31)
A Hebrew, abstaining from food,
Denies himself on account of his sin

ג Praises (accrue) to the one who fasts on it,
And great disgrace upon the one who violates it
They will depart, empty, from all goodness,
These (Hebrews) who abstain from fasting

ד A remembrance that shall never be nullified,
A remembrance of a day of fasting, for (all) generations
O choicest[34] of the nations, O Israel:
(You) fast upon it, and He grants forgiveness

ה Indeed, any soul that does not fast
Shall be cut off from the midst of its people
A word that God uttered—
Who is able to deny it?

ו Woe to them!—To these who are not fasting;
Or fasting, but not praying—
For they are like a blind man in the dark
Hurting themselves, day and night

ז The moon and the sun bear witness
To the nature of this day of forgiveness
A holy convocation in the name of the Holy One
For the holy congregation—there is none like it!

ח Lo, a jubilee comes at this very moment:
Once a year for (all) Israel
If one fasts upon it and repents
Then he merits redemption

ט Who has seen a day better than the day of fasting?
Happy is the congregation that is worthy of it
The dew of forgiveness
Glistens over all who fast upon it.[35]

י The day upon which praise is rendered
The day of forgiveness for Israel

---

[34] The term דמע can mean both 'offering' (תרומה) and 'choicest, best', which creates a resonant double-meaning here: Israel is the best of the nations but, through fasting, it also makes an offering of itself.
[35] This line evokes a metaphor rooted in the world of agriculture.

Let them fast upon it in repentance
These who are petitioning their Master

כ All nations observe fast-days[36]
But none resemble this one
All those of the nations are like nighttime
But this one, of Israel, is sunshine![37]
...[38]

ת Be repeating the day, O fasters,[39]
Lift your faces to the Abode
And say: Forgive Your people Israel
Whom You redeemed, O YHWH!

Nothing in this hymn explicitly evokes the festival of Sukkot at all; it speaks clearly, rather, to the Day of Atonement, particularly through its emphasis on the importance of fasting. It is not, in fact, said on Sukkot, but rather in anticipation of the holiday: on the preparatory feast day (*ṣimmūt*), on the fifteenth day of the fifth month (and thus eight weeks prior to the festival itself); on the first day of the seventh month, inaugurating the period of holy days that lead up to the festival; and on the tenth day of the seventh month, when the community is cleansed of its sins and, in that state of purity, begins to build the sukkahs. Even so, it makes use of imagery which is clearly agrarian: the dew which enables seeds to sprout, the sun which coaxes them to grow.

These two hymns are, in terms of form and tone, fair representatives of classical Samaritan poetry: the use of acrostics is common, as is the direct address to the community and to God, and the specifically topical and explicitly theological orientation. Indeed, while these poems are not 'liturgical' in the way that Jewish piyyutim embed elements of fixed statutory prayers—for the simple reason that Samaritan liturgy consisted primarily of Scriptural recitation and not post-biblical prayer rubrics—they are explicitly prayers. They speak to people and to God and reflect

[36] This line offers an unusual acknowledgement of non-Samaritan Israelite religious practice.
[37] Lit., 'daylight'.
[38] Presumably there is a gap of ten stanzas, based on the acrostic.
[39] Language of a liturgical formula; see Cowley, *The Samaritan Liturgy*, p. 435.

on ritual praxis even as they shape theological orientations. In this way, these two poems help us articulate what makes the religious poetry of *Tibat Marqe* distinctive: it is a poem, and it is about sacred scripture, but it is exegetical rather than practical.

While these three poems—the piyyutim by Amram Dare and Marqe, and the poem in *Tibat Marqe*—reflect different purposes and thus employ distinctive forms, rhetoric, and orientation, there is still much to be gained from reading these works, and others, together. In particular, as we have no classical period poems specifically for Sukkot, the passage in *Tibat Marqe* about the place named Sukkot may help us understand how that festival was understood liturgically in antiquity.

3. SAMARITAN COMPARANDS

While we lack any other mention of Sukkot in *Tibat Marqe*, just as we lack Sukkot piyyutim from its time period, these texts model rhetorical and exegetical strategies that suggest a latent richness in the texts we do have. In the *Tibat Marqe* poem on the place named 'Booths', the author blurs the boundary between the location 'Sukkot' and the agricultural richness celebrated by the festival of the same name. Elsewhere, we find in *Tibat Marqe* the reverse move, in which sacred time (the Sabbath) is transformed into sacred space: in Book 2 of *Tibat Marqe* (§16)—a passage also dating to the classical period—the Sabbath is described as 'a city entirely of blessing (מדינה כהלה ברכה)' and 'a place entirely holy (אתר כהלה קדיש)'.[40] If sacred time can be a city, perhaps it is not such a stretch to imagine a city as representing sacred time.

We find a similar translation of time into space in the liturgical poetry of Amram Dare, who writes: 'Woe to the one who departs from it (the Sabbath) / —The garden that tends its owner: / Every tree within it is Life!'[41] Marqe makes a similar move in his piyyutim, translating a concept into a spatial image, transforming the Torah into the Garden of Eden. In one poem, he writes: '(Torah is) an Eden, extending life / To those who drink

---

[40] *Tibat Marqe*, pp. 123–125.
[41] Amram Dare #18, lines 14–16; *LOT*, p. 80.

from it; / An Eden—that it is rooted / In eternal life'.[42] And in another poem, a somewhat softer formulation, according to which the Torah is a tendril that grows forth from the primordial garden: 'A sliver of life, unlike any other / (Torah) transmits wisdom into the world / A sliver of life eternal / and this is from Eden, / when it is opened by God / it sustains all its generations / and all are prolonged by its light'.[43] And likewise in the three poems attributed to 'al-Dustan', in which we find stated: 'The Sabbath resembles a city / built at the end of creation'; 'a beautiful garden is the Sabbath day'; 'a garden which will never close is the Sabbath'; 'the seventh day is a beautiful city'; and 'the seventh day is likened to the city of a king'.[44] The blurring of sacred time and sacred space is seamless. Indeed, the poets seem to delight in this image, one which anticipates Heschel's 'tabernacle in time' image by over half a millennium.

The references to Eden here are especially compelling in light of the poem in *Tibat Marqe* §71. That poem is rich with Edenic references, and agricultural imagery, evocative of the harvest abundance associated with Sukkot; the city Sukkot stands in for the fecundity of the festival. Similarly, in these piyyutim, Eden represents both the Sabbath and Torah, and it is both a city and a garden. It bears mentioning that among contemporary Samaritans, the Shabbat that falls during Sukkot is known as 'Shabbat Gan Eden'. While this appellation may be relatively late, it is woven out of threads that emerge from classical sources. For Sukkot to be a place in space as well as a place in time, and for it to be both a city and a garden, reflects an extension of extant

---

[42] Marqe #9, lines 61–64 (*LOT*, pp. 191–192).

[43] Marqe #21, strophe/line 17 (not in *LOT*, but in Cowley, *The Samaritan Liturgy*, I, p. 57).

[44] See *LOT*, pp. 280–287; and the discussion in Yonatan Miller, 'Sabbath-Temple-Eden', *JAJ* 9 (2018), pp. 46–74. The identity of the poet known as 'al-Dustan' ('the Dosithean') is unknown, but the language of the poems suggests they are from Late Antiquity, as indicated by their inclusion among the JPA poems in the Comprehensive Aramaic Lexicon (www.cal.huc.edu). See the discussion in *LOT*, pp. 17–18.

exegetical motifs as well as the experience (or memory) of the agricultural abundance of Samaria in Late Antiquity.

4. NON-SAMARITAN COMPARANDS

Neither Tibat Marqe nor Samaritan classical poetry has received the sustained attention given to Christian and Jewish writings from Late Antiquity; we can hypothesize various reasons for this comparative neglect but the best remedy is to illustrate the intrinsic significance of these works and their usefulness as comparands for other bodies of writing: poetry and prose, prayer and exegesis. An examination of how the poetry in classical Samaritan sources reveals not only how the ritual and exegetical poems differ from each other but also, by extension, help us to understand the choices made by non-Samaritan authors in their writings.

As noted above, comparing the poetry embedded in *Tibat Marqe* with liturgical poems from the same period highlights the different forms and functions of those two bodies of work. The separation of exegesis and prayer in these classical Samaritan writings makes readers of the wider hymnographic corpus aware of precisely how exegetical, or at least how narrative, so much of Jewish and Christian liturgical poetry is. Certain elements of the Samaritan hymns—the general stichometry, the use of acrostics and refrains, and the orientation toward a present audience (both human and divine)—are shared in common with Jewish and Christian liturgical poems. These elements, we can presume, reflect a performative, participatory dynamic. But where the poetry of Ephrem, Yose ben Yose, Romanos, and Yannai—among numerous others—often hews to a story line or narrative in some sense, the Samaritan poetry is more imagistic, impressionistic, and episodic. In this, it resembles the less-narrative elements of certain kinds of hymnody, such as the *rahitim* of classical *Qedushta'ot*,[45] but without the highly patterned formalism of those units.

---

[45] See Laura S. Lieber, 'Telling a Liturgical Tale: Storytelling in Early Jewish Liturgical Poetry', *ZRGG* 66 (2015), pp. 211–232.

At the same time, the quantity of poetic language in *Tibat Marqe* makes the prose nature of much of rabbinic and patristic literature stand out with greater clarity. This is not to underestimate the cadenced, rhythmic, and patterned structure of passages within such writings, particularly the Mishnah, which suggest their oral-rhetorical origins and lend themselves to a distinctive kind of oral performance.[46] The boundary between prose and poetry is largely one of degree. And yet, the density of figurative language, parallelism, repetition, and other formal structures in the oldest strata of *Tibat Marqe* are nonetheless distinctive. It is harder to evaluate the reasons for the prominence of poetic language in *Tibat Marqe*, as the genre of writing does not suggest performance, even if the formal features would lend themselves to such a use. Instead, it seems to reflect some approach to exegesis: one which lingers over specific phrases and images and thus amplifies and develops them—in a fashion that would be akin to what we see in Jewish and Christian hymnography in its more exegetical moments.

As these very tentative comparisons suggest, the very differences of Samaritan writings that emerge when we consider them alongside Jewish and Christian works, along with the affinities these bodies of exegetical and liturgical writings share with each other, raise a host of important questions, particularly given their geographic and cultural proximity. Are the differences purely aesthetic, or do they reflect a particular engagement with Scripture, or ritual use? Or is the preference for poetry functional, in that poetry shapes theology in a way that is distinctive from prose, even as liturgical poetry creates an experience distinctive from other forms of prayer?

5. CONCLUSIONS

As this brief study has shown, or at least gestured toward, Samaritan works from Late Antiquity can shed light on the development of later Samaritan rituals and concepts, such as the

---

[46] See Martin S. Jaffee, *Torah in the Mouth: Writing and Oral Tradition in Palestinian Judaism, 200 BCE-400 CE* (Oxford: Oxford University Press, 2001).

understanding of Sukkot; on the nature of Samaritan literary creativity in its classical period, in both liturgical and exegetical settings; and, perhaps most broadly, on the emergence of robust literary traditions throughout the Levant, among Jews and Christians as well as Samaritans, in a range of genres and for a variety of settings. Much remains unknown, but sources of writing such as those examined here—the written traditions of a small but important community living in Palestine in this pivotal period of history—offer important data that can enrich our understanding of the life of the mind and the spirit in Late Antiquity.

LITURGICAL TEXT OR MAGICAL TEXT? A MANDAEAN APOTROPAIC PRAYER*

MATTHEW MORGENSTERN

1. INTRODUCTION

Amongst the most serious impediments to the historical study of the Mandaean religion is the lack of early sources that might be used to reconstruct its development. The earliest known surviving Mandaic manuscript is the Bodleian Library's codex Marsh 691, which contains a small selection of the *rahmī*-prayers and was copied in Ḥuweiza in 936 AH (1529-1530 CE), while the earliest copy of the *Ginza,* CS 1 in the Bibliothèque nationale de France in Paris, dates from 968 AH (1560 CE) and the earliest copy of the *Sidra ḏ-Nišmata* (Book of Souls, also known as the *Qulasta),* now CS 12, was copied in 978 AH (1570 CE).[1] Most scholars are

---

* It is a pleasure to offer this article in honour of Professor Edward Cook, whose interest in all things Aramaic is apparent throughout his career. I wish to thank Professors Shaul Shaked, James Nathan Ford and Siam Bhayro for permission to cite from their unpublished materials, and Professor Gideon Bohak and Dr. Ohad Abudraham for their helpful comments on this paper. This research was supported by the Israel Science Foundation grant no. 419/13.

[1] For a seminal account of Mandaean manuscripts in general, see Jorunn Jacobsen Buckley, *The Great Stem of Souls* (Piscataway, NJ: Gorgias Press, 2010). Matthew Morgenstern, 'New Manuscript Sources for the Study of Mandaic', in V. Golinets et. al (eds.), *Neue Beiträge zur Semitistik. Sechstes Treffen der Arbeitsgemeinschaft Semitistik in der Deutschen Morgenländ-*

in agreement that the *Ginza* and the *Sidra ḏ-Nišmata* represent the earliest parts of the Mandaic corpus, both on linguistic grounds and on the basis of their similarity to the Coptic-Manichaean psalms. From the historical references it contains, the *Ginza* appears to have been redacted in the early Islamic period, while the *Sidra ḏ-Nišmata* was furbished with rubrics that judging by their language were composed in a later period.[2] Other texts, such as the *Draša ḏ-Iahia* (the so-called *Mandaean Book of John*), seem to incorporate both earlier (pre-Islamic) and later (post-Islamic) materials.[3]

However, from a period of some nine hundred years prior to the earliest surviving textual witnesses of the classical Mandaic corpus we now have in our possession a large and ever-growing corpus of materials written in the Mandaic script, i.e., the lamellae and incantation bowls.[4] While such texts have been

---

ischen Gesellschaft vom 09.–11. Februar 2013 in Heidelberg (Münster: Ugarit Verlag, forthcoming) contains further information on the history of the Mandaean collections in Western Europe, and additional manuscript sources that have now come to light.

[2] See already Theodor Nöldeke, *Mandäische Grammatik* (Halle an der Salle: Waisenhaus, 1875) pp. XXIII–XXIV, and Torgny Säve-Söderbergh, *Studies in the Coptic Manichaean Psalm-Book: Prosody and Mandaean Parallels* (Uppsala: Almqvist and Wiksells, 1949) pp. 156–159. On the historical materials in the *Ginza*, see Dan D. Y. Shapira, 'Manichaeans (*Marmanaiia*), Zoroastrians (*Iazuqaiia*), Jews, Christians and Other Heretics: A Study in the Redaction of Mandaic Texts', *Le Muséon* 117 (2004), pp. 243–280; Shapira, 'On Kings and on the Last Days in Seventh Century Iraq: A Mandaean Text and its Parallels', *ARAM* 22 (2010), pp. 133–170.

[3] Charles Häberl, 'Tense, Aspect, and Mood in the Doctrine of John', in Geoffrey Khan & Lidia Napiorkowska (eds.), *Neo-Aramaic and its Linguistic Context* (Gorgias Neo-Aramaic Studies, 14, Piscataway, NJ: Gorgias Press, 2015) pp. 397–406.

[4] On the dating of the magic bowls and lamellae to the fifth to seventh centuries, see the evidence garnered in Charles Häberl, 'The Aramaic Incantation Texts as Witnesses to the Mandaic Scriptures', in M. Wissa (ed.), *Scribal Practices and the Social Construction of Knowledge in Antiquity, Late Antiquity and Medieval Islam* (OLA, 266, Leuven: Peeters, 2017) pp. 143–159 (n. 11). The present author finds himself in agreement with Christa Müller-Kessler, that contra Mark Lidzbarksi, the lamellae are not to be regarded as earlier than the bowls, and that any

known to scholarship for over a hundred years, and their importance to the Mandaean religion had not been entirely overlooked,[5] Christa Müller-Kessler rightly protested against the lack of attention that has been paid to the evidence that these sources provide regarding the Mandaic language and Mandaean religion.[6] As more of these texts have become available, it has become increasingly apparent that they draw upon a body of religious terms shared with the later canonical works.[7]

This short paper seeks to address two issues relating to the classical Mandaean corpus: the pre-Islamic dating of many of the central tenets of Mandaean lore, and the origins of the Mandaean

---

differences between their scripts arises from the different mediums upon which they are inscribed. See Christa Müller-Kessler, 'Aramäische Beschwörungen und astronomische Omina in nachbabylonischer Zeit. Das Fortleben mesopotamischer Kultur im Vorderen Orient', in Johannes Renger (ed.), *Babylon: Focus Mesopotamischer Geschichte, Wiege früher Gelehrsamkeit, Mythos in der Moderne. 2. Internationales Colloquium der Deutschen Orient-Gesellschaft 24.-26. März 1998 in Berlin* (Berlin: Saarbrücker Druckerei und Verlag, 1999) pp. 427–443 (430); Lidzbarski, 'Ein mandäisches Amulett', in G. C. C. Maspero [ed.], *Florilegium ou recueil de travaux d'érudition dédiés à M. le Marquis Melchior de Vogüé à l'occasion du quatrevingtième anniversaire de sa naissance* (Paris: Geuthner, 1909) pp. 349–373 (350).

[5] For example, Säve-Söderbergh noted that 'Lidzbarski has published a Mandaean amulet containing the chief traits of the Mandaean myth' (*Studies in the Coptic Manichaean Psalm-Book*, p. 157), while Edwin M. Yamauchi discussed several propitious agents mentioned in the bowl texts which are characteristic of the canonical Mandaean texts (*Mandaic Incantation Texts* [New Haven: American Oriental Society, 1967] pp. 35–40).

[6] Christa Müller-Kessler, 'The Mandaeans and the Question of their Origin', *ARAM* 16 (2004), pp. 47–60.

[7] See for example the references to Classical Mandaic literature in Judah Benzion Segal, *Catalogue of the Aramaic and Mandaic Incantation Bowls in the British Museum* (London: British Museum, 2000); James Nathan Ford, review of *Catalogue of the Aramaic and Mandaic Incantation Bowls in the British Museum* by J. B. Segal in *Jerusalem Studies in Arabic and Islam* 26 (2002), pp. 237–272; Matthew Morgenstern, 'A Mandaic Lamella for the Protection of a Pregnant Woman: MS 2087/91'. *Aula Orientalis* 33 (2015), pp. 271–286; and Matthew Morgenstern and Maleen Schlüter, 'A Mandaic Amulet on Lead – MS 2087/1'. *Eretz Israel* 32 (Joseph Naveh Memorial Volume, 2016, in Hebrew), pp. 115–127; and see now Häberl, 'The Aramaic Incantation Texts as Witnesses to the Mandaic Scriptures'.

prayers. It will be shown that numerous Mandaean concepts found in the classical literature are already attested in the epigraphic sources, and that the scope of these references is wider than has previously been acknowledged or recognized. Moreover, it will be shown that at least parts of the liturgy are directly paralleled by the magical texts from the epigraphic corpus. This suggests that the relationship between the different genres was not static, but rather that the redactors of the religious texts were familiar with several genres and adopted and adapted texts to suit different contexts. In the case of the prayers that will be discussed below, it would appear that the same formula could be employed in a liturgical setting or as an amulet.

2. MANDAEAN RELIGION IN THE MAGIC BOWLS

In contrast to the Jewish and Christian magic bowl texts which frequently employ biblical verses, the Mandaean texts contain no apparent citations from the earliest classical scriptures such as the *Ginza Rabba* or the earliest parts of the prayer-book. Perhaps the closest we come to a direct citation is the description of the three uthras, Hiḇil, Šiṯil, and Anoš[8] as being **bna ḏ-šurbta hita ʿiarta uruazta unahurta utaqunta** 'the sons of the living, radiant, splendid, shining, and brilliant family'. This series of epithets appears with minor spelling variations in both the early magical corpus (MS 2087/1.b 45–7, MS 2087/9.a3–5 [fragmentary]) and in the *Ginza* and liturgy.[9]

In his article from 2017, Charles Häberl has drawn attention to several Mandaean religious terms shared by the epigraphic magic corpus and the canonical Mandaean scriptures preserved in the later manuscripts. Häberl has focused particularly on the cosmological terms relating to the worlds of light and darkness and demonic forces, and convincingly demonstrated how the

---

[8] In the lamella MS 2087/1.b45–8 these names are written **hʿbil, šʿtil** and **ʿunuš**. On the first of these names, see in detail Morgenstern, 'A Mandaic Lamella for the Protection of a Pregnant Woman', p. 275.

[9] Gy 285.8, ML 13.34, 144.9–11. It is also employed in an amulet formula preserved only in later manuscripts, *Qmaha ḏ-Bit Mišqal Ainia*. See Ethel S. Drower, 'A Mandaean Phylactery', *Iraq* 5 (1938), pp. 31–54 (48 ll. 16–17).

epigraphic texts and canonical works draw upon a common source of terms and expressions. To the examples that he has adduced we may add many more from both published and unpublished sources which reflect central tenets of the Mandaean faith. In what follows, I present examples drawn primarily from published materials, while providing some additional support for those examples from unpublished texts.

In the *Ginza Rabba* we read:

> **kḏ hašib hiia qadmaiia uqiriuia lmanda ḏ-hiia umanda ḏ-hiia qiriẖ lhibil ziua**...
>
> 'When the Primordial Life (**hiia qadmaiia**) meditated and created the Knowledge-of-Life (**manda ḏ-hiia**) and the Knowledge-Of-Life created Hibil-Ziwa' (Gy 126.4–5).

These fundamental figures of the Mandaean cosmology are all mentioned in the magic bowl corpus, as the following illustrative and non-exhaustive examples show: The Primordial Life: **hiia qdmaiia** (Lidzbarski lamella: 89, 164–5), or in plene spelling **hiia qadmaiiẖ** (Christie's lamella: 8, 15; Moussaieff 139.23 [unpublished]); the Knowledge-of-Life: **mndʿa ḏ-hiia** (Lidzbarski lamella: 16, 18, IM 114986 = Hunter 1994:8 etc.) or **mnda ḏ-hiia** (Moussaieff 139.9).[10] The Knowledge-of-Life appears together with Hibil in several texts: **mn hiia umn mndʿa ḏ-hiia umn hʿbil ʿutra** (SD 63.6 and similarly MS 2054/97.9-10, MS 1928/45).

In numerous places in the *Ginza Rabba* reference is made to the **bnia šurba rba ḏ-hiia** 'The sons of the great family of Life' (Gy 49.11, 299.20, 230.1, 21, 230.7, 232.17, 300.13, 342.13–14). The same expression is found in the corpus of magic texts: **umrdpihun lbnia šurba rba ḏ-hiia** 'and persecute the sons of the great family of Life' (Gorea I 10-11, collated reading).[11] **kulẖ**

---

[10] Published in Matthew Morgenstern, 'Five Mandaic Magic Bowls from the Moussaieff Collection', *Eretz Israel* 32 (Ada Yardeni Memorial Volume, 2021, in Hebrew), pp. 106–122 (114–118). There are many additional examples in the unpublished texts.

[11] Published in Maria Gorea, 'Trois nouvelles coupes magiques araméenes', *Semitica* 51 (2001), pp. 73–93 (73–75). Compare further **niradpinun lbnia šurba rba ḏ-hiia** 'let us persecute the sons of the great family of Life' (Gy 362.4).

kana ḏ-nišmata 'the entire stem of souls' of Gy 29.23, 185.8, 188.5, 229.16,[12] 231.10 appears in this form in Macuch Ia.7–8.[13] **iauar ʿtita**, who in Gy 291.35 is described as an uthra (**ʿutra**), is mentioned as **iauar ʿutra** in several of the magical sources (ROM 949.94 = McCullough E.7, BM 91722 = Segal 078.9). **iušamin dakia** (e.g., Gy 285.2, 286.6, 288.19 and 322.11) is also found in Lidzbarski lamella: 244.[14]

piriauis iardna rba 'Piriauis, the Great Jordan', which is mentioned in several places in the liturgy (e.g., ML 16.6 = CP 14.12–13) appears in several spellings in the epigraphic corpus, e.g., **tlata ʿutria ḏ-šria ʿl iardna rba** 'the three uthras who dwell in the Great Jordan' (Pognon 22.20-21) and **ppriuis irdna rba** 'into Piriauis, the Great Jordan' (Pognon 31.10), compare also **piriauis iardna rba** (MS 2054/61.16, unpublished), which provides a more complete parallel to the damaged **piri**[**au**]**is iardna rba** (BM 91708 = Segal 083.15).[15] On the Jordan (**iardna**), see further below.[16]

The maleficent agents of Mandaic literature are also represented in the epigraphic corpus. Thus we find **ḏ-lhuit mn**

---

[12] Following the reading of CS 2.

[13] Published in Rudolf Macuch, 'Altmandäische Bleirollen I', in Franz Altheim and Ruth Stiehl (eds.), *Die Araber in der alten Welt* 4 (Berlin: De Gruyter, 1967) pp. 91–203. Macuch noted its occurrence in the canonical texts.

[14] Additionally in forthcoming texts, JNF 40.11 and MS 2054/52.7.

[15] For this correct reading see Ford, 'review', p. 245.

[16] The statement in Christa Müller-Kessler, 'The Mandaeans and the Question of their Origin', *ARAM* 16 (2004), pp. 47–60 (57) regarding the evidence for the Jordan (**iardna**) in the epigraphic corpus is ambiguous: 'To pick out just one example, one can take the Mandaean baptism ritual, the *maṣbūtā* which is always considered to be the basis of Mandaean doctrine, but cannot be traced in the early corpus at all. The verbal root *ṣby* 'to baptize' does not occur like the river Jordan. The latter appears only in texts that are considered late according to criteria of contents, grammar and lexicography'. The formulation leaves it unclear whether Müller-Kessler regards the Jordan (**iardna**) to be mentioned in the epigraphic corpus or not. As we have seen, it is attested in magic bowl texts first published by Pognon. In any case, since there are no firm grounds for dating any part of the epigraphic corpus as later than others, a claim that the Jordan ('the latter' in Müller-Kessler's statement) is attested only in late texts would be patently unfounded.

tutia ʿdẖ ḏ-abatur uptahil 'that I came not from under the hand of Abatur and Ptahil' (Gorea I 5). It is notable that as in Gy 378.37, **abatur uptahil** is treated grammatically as singular.[17] **ptahil** is also mentioned in BM 91733 = Segal 080.4, 6, and as **pthil** in MS 2054/75.6.[18] The supernatural being **iurba** is also attested in numerous places in the epigraphic corpus: **iurba** (Pognon 1.9 and parallels, Pognon 25.8, Lidzbarski lamella: 201, Segal 081.8); it also appears as **iarba** (Gorea I.7, Moussaieff 23.4; MS 2087/9.a9).[19]

We find many of these elements appearing together in certain passages, e.g., **uamrilẖ hiia liauar bar qum qrilẖ lašgnda mn kimṣa liauar rba mn mia ulbirkta npšta mn irdna** 'And Life said to Yawar-Bar, "Arise, call the messenger from the end (of the world), the Great Yawar from the water and the extensive blessing from the Jordan"' (Lidzbarski lamella: 49–53). The following passage, drawn from the Mandaic magic bowl text BM 91709 = Segal 082M, is particularly rich in Mandaean religious lore:[20]

(5) **mn hda škinta ḏ-nhura nipqit**	I came forth from one abode of light,
qumat ḏ-zuṭa (6) **ʿtrurbat**	My stature that was small grew large,
mn t[r]tia škinata ḏ-nhura nipqit	I came forth from two abodes of light,

[17] Contrast what follows in the bowl text, **ula mn tutia ʿdaiun ḏ-mlakia ḏ-husrana** 'nor under the hand of the angels of imperfection', with the plural proleptic **–aiun** pronoun. The anomaly in the *Ginza* was already noted in August Johann Heinrich Wilhelm Brandt, *Die mandäische Religion* (Leipzig: J.P. Hinrichs, 1889) p. 55.
[18] Judging by his description as **ḏ-bnṉ lbita** 'the one who built the House (i.e., material world)', **ptaʿil** in Lidzbarski lamella: 245–246 is either a misreading or variant spelling of **ptahil**.
[19] For additional commentary see Morgenstern, 'A Mandaic Lamella for the Protection of a Pregnant Woman', p. 276.
[20] The text was originally published in Segal, *Catalogue of the Aramaic and Mandaic Incantation Bowls*, pp. 108–110, with important corrections appearing in Christa Müller-Kessler 'Die Zauberschalensammlung des British Museum', *AfO* 48/49 (2001–2), pp. 115–145 (132) and Ford, 'review', pp. 243–244.

qalai ḏ-zuṭ (7) **ʿtrurab**	My voice that was small grew large,
mn tlat škinata ḏ-nhura nipqit	I came forth from three abodes of light,
ʿutria rurbia liamina[i] qrit	I created the great uthras to [my] right,
(8) **mn arbia škinata ḏ-nhura nipqit**	I came forth from four abodes of light,
ʿutria drdqia lsmalai qrit	I created the small uthras to my left,
mn hmiš (9) **škinata ḏ-nhura nipqit**	I came forth from five abodes of light,
iardna ḏ-hiia qadmaiiẖ qrit	I created the Jordan of the Primordial Life,
mn šit škinata ḏ-nhura nipqit	I came forth from six abodes of light,
(10) **hbšaba ukna ḏ-zidqa qrit**	I created Sunday and sacred foods,[21]
mn šaba škinata ḏ-nhura nipqit	I came forth from seven abodes of light,
kʿna mana rba ḏ-hiia qrit	I created the chamber of the great spirit of Life
mn gupna (11) **ḏ-mlia btriṣuta umn ʿlana ḏ-kulẖ tušbihta**	From the vine that is full of rectitude, and from the tree that is all praise.
kḏ skina ḏ-razia bʿidai lgiṭna	As I hold the knife of mysteries in my hand
ṣairna baˆiˆta barbia zauiatẖ	I seal this house in its four (inner) corners,

[21] For the expression **habšaba ukana ḏ-zidqa,** see ML 34.1 = CP 28.17–18; the correct interpretation is presented in Ethel S. Drower, *The Canonical Prayerbook of the Mandaeans* (Leiden: E.J. Brill, 1959) p. 18 (English translation).

ṣairna (12) **hikla barbia qrnatẖ**	I seal this abode in its four (outer) corners,
ṣairna šaba dmuata ḏ-hišuka bšaba ṣurata	I seal the seven images of darkness with seven seals.
bšumaiun ḏ-hiia ṣairnalẖ lhazin baita	In the name of Life I seal this house,
(13) **bšumaiun ḏ-ʿutria ṣairnalẖ lhazin baita**	and in the name of the uthras I seal this house,
bšumaiun ḏ-pahtia pʿhta ḏ-hiia[22]	In the name of those who break the sacramental bread of Life,
ubhbšaba ukna ḏ-zidqa ṣairnalẖ lhazin baita	and by Sunday and the sacramental foods I seal this house,
(14) **uhtimnalẖ bšumẖ ḏ-iušamin dakia**	and I seal it in the name of the Pure Yušamin.
bhazin pugdama ḏ-qra hibil maria	By this spell that Lord Hiḇil invoked
ʿl šaba dmuata (15) **ḏ-hi**[**šuka ḏ-**]**hubẖ**	against the seven apparitions of da[arkness that] are within it
kḏ apka unpqa mn qudamẖ	as they turn and leave from before him,
ṭabuta uruaha ḏ-šauia hibil tihuibẖ	may the bounty and relief that Hiḇil established
bhazin baita dura hikla (16) **ubiniana**	in this house, dwelling, residence and building ...

A remarkable cluster of Mandaean religious terms appears within these few lines: the uthras, the Jordan, the Sunday and the sacred foods, great chamber of Life, the vine, the sacramental bread, the Pure Yušamin and Hiḇil. Many of the same terms are found in the prayer recited upon the conclusion of the baptism which emphasizes the particular elements of the Mandaean ritual which

[22] As Segal noted, the expression **ḏ-pahtia pʿhta ḏ-hiia** is found in the *Ginza* and the liturgy; see *Catalogue of the Aramaic and Mandaic Incantation Bowls*, p. 109.

will protect the baptized person when they return to the House of Life (**bit hiia**):[23]

iardna utrin kipẖ	**The Jordan** and its two banks
ˁlauaian nihuia bsahdia	Will bear witness for us
pihta ukušṭa umambuga	**The sacramental bread**, *kušṭā* and sacramental drink
ˁlauaian nihuia bsahdia	Will bear witness for us
habšaba ukana ḏ-zidqa	**Sunday and the sacramental foods**
ˁlauaian nihuia bsahdia	Will bear witness for us

In summary, we see that although direct citations from Mandaean scriptures are very rare, the earliest attestations of the Mandaean religion – the magical texts written upon clay bowls and lead lamellae – contain numerous allusions to the central figures and ritual concepts of classical Mandaean religion. These include elements drawn from early Jewish lore (the three sons of Adam), Christian sources (the Jordan), and Mandaean religious practice, which appear alongside Babylonian and Iranian influences. It is apparent that by the sixth century, i.e., the pre-Islamic period, Mandaean religion had already incorporated materials drawn from many religious traditions, and none may be regarded as the single origin of the Mandaean faith.

3. CP 15: A MANDAEAN APOTROPAIC PRAYER

In the first part of this paper, I have sought to demonstrate that the early corpus contains a significant body of references to classical Mandaean terms and concepts that are also found in the corpus of canonical works. In the second part, we shall discuss this relationship from the other side, and attempt to show that texts from the magical corpus have been integrated into the canonical liturgy.

At the heart of the Mandaean ritual stands the baptism, for which the *Sidra ḏ-Nišmata* provides the liturgical recitations. The

---

[23] ML 33.12–34.1 = CP 20.1–21.6.

actual baptism is preceded by several prayers of which the first is **ʿsir iama** 'Bound is the sea', as its preceding rubric indicates.[24] As we shall demonstrate in what follows, this prayer has the structure and formulation of a standard magical text as attested in the corpus of bowls and lamellae. In fact, almost every line of the prayer is directly paralleled by a similar formula from within the Mandaic magic corpus. The scope of these parallels is only apparent thanks to the large number of previously unpublished sources which now stand at our disposal. We shall begin by presenting the prayer in its entirety with its rubric, and in what follows present the parallels from the epigraphic corpus. For the sake of convenience, the elements of the prayer have been numbered.

Rubric	**hazin pugdama ḏ-gauaza qria lgauaza ḏ-zaita uduṣa biardna uhaizak qria maṣbuta**	This is the recitation for the staff – recite over an olive staff and insert it into the Jordan and then read the baptism
1	**ʿsir iama uʿsiria trin kipẖ ḏ-iama**	Bound is the sea, and bound are the two ends of the sea
2	**ʿsiria daiuia ušidia upiqdia ulihania**	Bound are the *devs*, and *šeds* and *piqdas* and servitors.
3	**uhumria zadaniata**	And seething pebble-spirits
4	**ʿsiria tlatma ušitin razia ḏ-bgu baita**	Bound are the three hundred and sixty mysteries in the House
5	**ʿsirna uhtimna ana plania br planita**	Bound am I, PN son of PN
6	**ulhalin nišmata ḏ-nahta liardna umiṣṭiba**	And these souls that are descending to the Jordan and being baptized
7	**bhatma ḏ-hiia rurbia nukraiia**	By the seal of the great transcendent Life
8	**bma rba ubaz rba baziz rba**	And by the great Ma and the great Az and the great Aziz

[24] See below.

9	**ubas rba ubasin rba ubas iama**	And by the great As and the great Asin and by the sea As
10	**ʿsiria kumria zabia uadidia ušatamia umrašmania**	Bound are the priests and sacrificers and oracle-mongers and temple-functionaries and scribes
11	**šuba razia ḏ-bgu iama**	The seven mysteries that are in the sea
12	**kul daiua bšumẖ ukul sahra bkinianẖ**	Every *dev* by his name, and every *sahir* by his family name
13	**ukul humarta upatikra**	And every pebble-spirit and idol
14	**ḏ-rišiẖ nišqul ugilia parṣupẖ nidalia**	That shall lift up its head and raise up his countenance,
15	**napšiẖ rbuta alanpia gabra nukraia tisbẖ**	And who acts presumptuously against the sublime man,
16	**hin alanpaiin ḏ-nišmata ḏ-masgia ʿl liardna lbiš niskia**	or will look towards the souls that are going to the Jordan in evil (intent) –
17	**unitimhia unišqap biaha iaha ubzha zha**	May he be struck and afflicted by Iaha Iaha and by Zha Zha
18	**ubmalakia ḏ-ʿštadar uatun ʿlauaihun**	And by the angels who were sent and came upon them.
19	**zha mn qudamaihun umn ziuẖ**	They fled before them and from his light.
20	**kbar ʿlauaihun zha uʿtazha**	'Flee' and 'Be expelled' overpowered them
21	**šuba šuria ḏ-parzla ahdrulia ldilia**	They have enveloped me with seven walls of iron, I,
	plania br planita	PN son of PN,
22	**ḏ-hadar haiašum kušṭa qadmaia lnapšiẖ**	(with) which the primordial Haia-Šum Kušṭa envelops himself
23	**uhiia zakiʿin**	And Life is victorious!

1. **ʿsir iama uʿsiria trin kipẖ ḏ-iama**. A direct parallel appears in JNF 40.7: **ʿsir ima ʿsiria trin kʿpẖ ḏ-ima** 'Bound is the sea, bound are the two ends of the sea'.

2. **ʿsiria daiuia ušidia upiqdia ulihania**. Compare: **uʿsiria diuia ʿsiria šidia ʿsiria piqdia ʿsiria lihania** 'and bound are the *devs*, bound are the *šeds*, bound are the *piqdas* and bound are the servitors' (ROM 949.94 = McCullough E.15).

3. **uhumria zadaniata**. Compare **uhumria zidaniata** 'and seething pebble-spirits' (BM 117880 = Segal 081M.7). **zadaniata** is the standard attribute of **humria** in Mandaic (and Jewish) incantation bowls.

4. **ʿsiria tlatma ušitin razia ḏ-bgu baita**. Compare **ʿsiria tlatma ušitin razia ḏ-šria bgu baita** 'Bound are the three hundred and sixty mysteries that dwell in the House' (JNF 40.16–17).

5. **ʿsirna uhtimna ana plania br planita**. Compare **ʿsirna uhtimna ana** 'Bound and sealed am I' (MS 2054/96.5).

6. **ulhalin nišmata ḏ-nahta liardna umiṣṭiba**. Since this line refers specifically to the participants in the baptism, it is not surprising that it is not paralleled in the magical corpus. Furthermore, in the surviving textual witnesses, the line appears with a grammatical anomaly. Whereas the recipients of the main argument of the verb in the previous lines are all the subjects of passive verbs, here the recipients are marked with the *l*-preposition as though the objects of an active verb, perhaps suggesting that this line has been subsequently integrated into the pre-existing text.

7. **bhatma ḏ-hiia rurbia nukraiia**. Compare **ubhatma ḏ-hiia rurbia nukraiia** 'and by the seal of the great transcendent Life' (JNF 40.14–15).

10. **ʿsiria kumria zabia uadidia ušatamia umrašmania.** Compare **ʿsiria kulhun mlakia phlẖ kumrẖ zabẖ [u]adidẖ šaṭamẖ umršmanẖ** 'Bound are all the angels, his worshippers – his priests, his sacrificers, his oracle-mongers his temple-

functionaries and his scribes' (Davidovitz lamella 1.66–68).[25] A similar list of cultic figures appears in Gs 17.10.[26]

11. **šuba razia ḏ-bgu iama**. Although the entire phrase is not yet attested in the early corpus, the expression **šuba razia** 'seven mysteries' is found in the lamellae Kelsey Museum b11(= Müller-Kessler, 'Mandaic Lead Roll': 484); MS 2087/18.19 (unpublished); and the magic bowl IM 11572(= Nuʿmān 6.9).

12. **kul daiua bšumẖ ukul sahra bkinianẖ**. Compare **kul daiua bšumẖ ukul shra bkinianh** 'Every *dev* by his name, and every *sahir* by his family name' (MS 2054/101.5–6).

13. **ukul humarta upatikra**. The word-pair is attested in plural form in the early corpus as **uhumria uptikria** 'and pebble-spirits and idols' (MS 2054/10.13), while an exact parallel is attested in a magical formula preserved only in later manuscripts: **kul sahra bšumẖ ukul daiua bkinianẖ ukul humarta upatikra** 'Every *sahir* by his name, and every *dev* by his family name and every pebble-spirit and idol' (*Šafta ḏ-Qaština*, Bod. MS Syr. g2 [R], 276–8). Note that the first part of this later parallel reflects section 12 of our prayer, but with the reversal of **daiua** '*dev*' and **sahra** '*sahir*'.

14, 16. **ḏ-rišiẖ nišqul ugilia parṣupẖ nidalia ... hin alanpaiin ḏ-nišmata ḏ-masgia ʿl liardna lbiš niskia**. Examples of this expression that occur in Mandaic magic texts have been discussed in detail by Müller-Kessler.[27] We may add that a very close parallel to our prayer appears in an unpublished text from the Martin Schøyen collection: **kul diua shra ušida uhumrta uruha ulilita ḏ-rišẖ nišqul ugilia prṣupẖ ndalia ulanpẖ ḏ-hazin bita**

---

[25] The first three figures – **kumria uzabia udidia** 'priests, sacrificers and oracle-mongers' also appear in Fitzwilliam Museum E.2–1907.23–4, according to the reading of Christa Müller-Kessler, 'Interrelations between Mandaic Lead Scrolls and Incantation Bowls', in Tzvi Abusch and Karel van der Toorn (eds.), *Mesopotamian Magic: Textual, Historical, and Interpretative Perspectives* (Ancient Magic and Divination, 1, Groningen: STYX Publications, 1999) pp. 197–212 (203).

[26] Note that in the *Ginza*, the form **šaṭamia** with ṭ accords with the form in the lamella.

[27] Müller-Kessler, 'Die Zauberschalensammlung des British Museum', p. 302.

ḏ-aziazdan lbiš niskia 'Any *dev*, *sahir*, *šed* and pebble-spirit that shall lift up its head and raise up its countenance and will look towards this house of PN with evil (intent)' (MS 1928/44.11–13). Although the list of evil agencies is somewhat more extended than in our prayer, the wording of the text is otherwise parallel.

15. **napšiḫ rbuta alanpia gabra nukraia tisbḫ**. Although this line is not directly paralleled in the early magic corpus, the expression **nasbia rbuta** 'acting presumptuously' is found in MS 2087/16.a8, while the epithet **gbra nukraia** 'sublime man' is attested in several spellings in the epigraphic texts (e.g., Pognon 22.19, Christie's lamella: 82, MS 2087/17 b 11 [unpublished]).

17. **unitimhia unišqap biaha iaha ubzha zha**. Compare **untmhia unštqip** 'and may he be struck and afflicted' (MS 1928/44.13) and **bšumḫ ḏ-iaha uiaha ubšum zha zha** 'in the name of Iaha Iaha and in the name of Zha Zha' (MS 2054/93.13).

18. **ubmalakia ḏ-ʿštadar uatun ʿlauaihun**. A parallel to this passage has not been found in the early Mandaic corpus, but compare from the magical corpus preserved in later manuscripts: **malakia ḏ-ʿštadar uatun** 'the angels who were sent and came' (*Šapta ḏ-Masihpan* BL Add 23,602b, DC 37 [unpublished]). Similar parallels are to be found in the Jewish Babylonian Aramaic magic bowls, which are contemporaneous with the Mandaean bowl texts, e.g., משבענא עליכון מלאכי בישי ותקיפי דאישתדרו [על] שידי ועל [דיוי] לנכסא [י]תהון 'I adjure you, evil and mighty angels that have been sent [against] *šeds* and *devs* to slaughter them' (MS 2053/200 = JBA 48.9-10).

20. **kbar ʿlauaihun zha uʿtazha. zha uʿtazha** 'be expelled and remove yourself' is a magical formula that appears in several published and unpublished Mandaic texts (e.g., Pognon 26.8, BM 135791 = Müller-Kessler, 'Aramäische Beschwörungen und astronomische Omina in nachbabylonischer Zeit': 46, Moussaieff 24.12, 45.11). It is also employed as the opening of Prayer 17 (ML 24.6 = CP 22.2).

21. **šuba šuria ḏ-parzla ahdrulia ldilia**. Compare **šuba šuria ḏ-przla hdirilḫ lbaitḫ ḏ-PN br PN** 'Seven walls of iron surround the house of PN son of PN' (IM 78159 = Nuʿmān 5.61–2; similarly MS 2054/121.12).

From the parallels listed here it is apparent that almost every line of our prayer is matched by a similar expression from the epigraphic magic corpus.[28] The texts are sometimes identical word-for-word. Even where a direct parallel is lacking, the phraseology may be similar, e.g., section 15. The frequency of such formulae in amulets and their relative scarcity in liturgical contexts suggests that Prayer 15 represents an apotropaic amulet formula that has been incorporated into the liturgy. The positioning of such an apotropaic prayer prior to the baptism suggests that its function is to protect the participants in the baptismal ceremony from unwanted demonic influences during this critical moment of bonding with the Light World.

It has long been recognized that the Mandaean liturgy is a composite work, drawing upon different sources,[29] while the incorporation of prayers against demonic influence into liturgical contexts is already attested in Jewish literature of the Second Temple period (c. 200 BCE ff.) as Flusser observed.[30] Herr suggested that the *Kol Nidre* prayer, now associated with the Day of Atonement, originated in similar magical formulae employed on the incantation bowls.[31] More recently, Levene, Marx and Bhayro have shown that pre-existing magical formulae that presumably originated in non-liturgical contexts were introduced into Jewish prayer rituals and ultimately achieved authoritative

[28] Many of the individual terms are shared also with magic bowl texts written in the Jewish, Syriac and Manichaean scripts. The relationship between these corpora is complex and lies beyond the scope of the present paper.

[29] See in particular Jonas Carl Greenfield, 'A Mandaic "Targum" of Psalm 114', in Ezra Fleischer and Jakob J. Petuchowski (eds.), *Studies in Aggadah, Targum and Jewish Liturgy in Memory of Joseph Heinemann* (Jerusalem: Magnes Press; Cincinnati: Hebrew Union College Press, 1981) pp. 23–31, who demonstrated that the juxtaposition of the Mandaean reworkings of Psalm 114 with a reworking of the part of the Jewish liturgical poem *Nishmat kol ḥay* implied that the *Sidra ḏ-Nišmata* drew upon elements of the Jewish prayer book.

[30] David Flusser, 'Qumrân and Jewish "Apotropaic" Prayers', *IEJ* 16 (1966), pp. 194–205.

[31] Moshe-David Herr, 'Matters of Palestinian Halakha During the Sixth and Seventh Centuries C.E.', *Tarbiz* 49 (1979), pp. 62–80 (68–70) (in Hebrew).

(if not legally binding) status.[32] It is therefore not surprising to find that the Mandaean liturgy also draws upon formulae from protective amulets.

4. CONCLUSION

In this brief article, we have attempted to demonstrate that the magical spells written upon metal lamellae and clay bowls, which are preserved in epigraphic witnesses copied in the fifth to late seventh centuries, and the early canonical texts of Mandaean literature, the *Sidra ḏ-Nišmata* and *Ginza Rabba*, preserved in manuscripts copied in the sixteenth to seventeen centuries, both reflect aspects of the Mandaean religion as it was canonized in the late Sassanid and early Islamic periods. The epigraphic corpus contains numerous references to the central religious figures and items of the Mandaean faith, while the liturgy incorporates an apotropaic text that is paralleled almost in its entirety in the early corpus of magical spells. The two genres of literature, separated by hundreds of years of copying, are closely interconnected, and as more of the epigraphic texts come to light and are deciphered, it is likely that the number of recorded parallels will be further increased.

LIST OF SOURCES

BL	British Library.
BM	British Museum, published in J. B. Segal, *Catalogue of the Aramaic and Mandaic Incantation Bowls*, London, 2000, unless otherwise stated.
Bod.	Bodleian Library, Oxford.
Christie's	Lamella published in Christa Müller-Kessler, 'Aramäische Beschwörungen und astronomische Omina in nachbabylonischer Zeit: Das Fortleben mesopotamischer Kultur im Vorderen Orient', in J.

[32] Dan Levene, Dalia Marx and Siam Bhayro, '"Gabriel is on their Right" – Angelic Protection in Jewish Magic and Babylonian Lore', in Manfried Dietrich, Kai A. Metzler and Hans Neumann (eds.), *Studia Mesopotamica, Jahrbuch für altorientalische Geschichte und Kultur*, Band 1 (Münster: Ugarit-Verlag, 2014) pp. 185–198.

	Renger (ed.), *Babylon: Focus Mesopotamischer Geschichte, Wiege früher Gelehrsamkeit, Mythos in der Moderne* (CDOG, 2, Berlin, 1999) pp. 427–443.
CP	Ethel S. Drower, *The Canonical Prayerbook of the Mandaeans*, Leiden, 1959.
CS	Codex Sabéen, Bibliothèque nationale de France, Paris.
Davidovitz	Lamella in the collection of Mr. Gil Davidovitz, to be published in Matthew Morgenstern and James Nathan Ford (forthcoming).
DC	Drower Collection, Bodleian Library, Oxford.
Gy	*Ginza Yamina.*
Gs	*Ginza Smala.*
IM	Iraq Museum, Baghdad.
JNF	James Nathan Ford magic bowl editions.
ML	Mark Lidzbarski, *Mandäische Liturgien,* Berlin, 1920.
Moussaieff	Collection of the late Shlomo Moussaieff, Herzliya, to be published in James Nathan Ford and Matthew Morgenstern (forthcoming).
MS	Martin Schøyen Collection.
Pognon	Text from Khouabir published in Henri Pognon, *Inscriptions mandaïtes des coupes de Khouabir*, Paris, 1898.
ROM	Royal Ontario Museum, published in W. S. McCullough, *Jewish and Mandaean Incantation Bowls*, Toronto, 1967.
SD	Samir Dehays bowl, published in Matthew Morgenstern, 'The Mandaic Magic Bowl Dehays 63', *JANES* 32 (2011), pp. 73–89.

EPILOGUE

ZUMMARTA D-PIṢXŪṮĀ, A SONG OF JOY

SHAWQI N. TALIA

1. FOREWORD

In the tradition of the Neo-Aramaic speaking Christians of northern Iraq (ancient Mesopotamia [ʿAbr Nahrain]), who live on the plain of Nineveh (Syriac, 'Dašte d-Ninwe'), at the arrival at a Christian village of a religious person, especially a bishop or a patriarch, the entire community joyfully meanders through the village paths to greet and welcome the honored dignitary at the special place of welcome. The long-held custom is to receive him with much jubilation, which includes the chanting of religious hymns and reading from the Gospel. But as it has been done for millennia, the most joyous testimony to this time of jubilance is the recitation of a poem(s) composed by villagers, which is usually a Soġīta. The guest is then escorted to the church or to a parish hall, where he is feted by the village. The ritual of such a reception is a long-held tradition that represents a cultural connection to the ancient Semitic world, with a very biblical orientation. The reciting and chanting of laudatory words, especially poems composed by community members is an honored convention, and those chosen to do so take the writing and reciting of their words as being representative of the whole village.

The literary aspect of the special reception could be purely religious, or a mixture of secular and religious. The aim of the various literary and religious cantillating is to express the joy of the writer and the community in this special person, who has come to the village. It is a time to honor the guest by invoking a very ancient practice of bestowing homage on the guest. It should be stated that the high dignitary is being received not only for his religious dignity but for another, deeply rooted one, namely that he has the ear of the central government in Baghdad, capital of Iraq. Hence, indirectly, they are greeting one who can speak on their behalf with the authorities of the central government. But this literary ritual of acclaiming an august person has, sadly, disappeared, as most of these villages and towns are now deserted, due to persecution, immigration, forced migration, wars, and lately the curse of ISIS. However, it is ironic but heartening that now, those who hail from the land of Nineveh, who are members of the glorious Syriac Church, have the opportunity to continue this long-held tradition, which is now vanishing in their native land of exile. This ritual of greeting is now called a Festschrift (Kṯāwā d-Piṣxūṯā).

It is indeed humbling to be asked by the editorial committee of the Festschrift for Professor Edward Cook, an 'ʾAxōnā' and 'Rabbi' to many of us, to contribute to this Festschrift on the occasion of his seventieth birthday. As one whose heritage, native tongue, and roots are from 'Dašte d-Ninwe', I find myself joining many other contributors in expressing my exultant spirit, in Neo-Aramaic, with a 'Soġītā d-Piṣxūṯā'. Like the villagers who came to greet their visitor, I come with a ritual of verisimilitude to express my esteem and extolment to an 'ʾaxōnā milyā myaqrūṯā', whose colleagues, students, and friends have come to deeply respect and appreciate his scholarship, collegiality, his love of Aramaic, his humbleness and, above all, his humanity.

In this old tradition, this Soġītā is composed and humbly presented to my ʾaxōnā Edward Cook. I and others of the Syriac Church from the land of Mesopotamia, and all the other lands, including immigrants of the diaspora, exiles and refugees, have been given hope and solace, due to what Professor Cook and others have accomplished in keeping alive the Aramaic tongue, which is the foundation of the liturgical language of the Syriac Church and its socio-cultural heritage. This hope says 'this Nation shall not die'. Today, our villages are no more, yet we, sons and daughters of these lands, while mourning for our ancestral homes, do also rejoice in the lives of those who have walked with us and proclaimed the Aramaic word.

When hearing Lušānā ʾArāmāyā chanted in a Soġītā or read in the liturgy, we hark back to the native lands of our forefathers, no matter how long the separation. And we, like our Jewish brothers and sisters, do mourn for our native motherland and sing:

> 'By the waters of the lands of our exile
> We sat and remembered the waters of Babylon'.

One of the most moving proverbs in Neo-Aramaic is always repeated by these Christians in their diaspora.

> 'Kim dabrunux w-ʾāyit zōra,
> Qay kim nāšitti?'
> 'I reared you from childhood,
> Why have you forsaken me?'[1]

How wonderful it is to know that we are surrounded by people who keep alive this language of Christ. We have been scattered like the grains of sand to the four corners of the world, but our Aramaists speak to us daily, reminding us to continue with the journey of hope.

> Poš Bišlāmā ʾaxōnan ʿazīzā

In the spirit of celebrating the presentation of this Festschrift to Professor Cook, this writer has discerned that it would be most appropriate to include a salutary epistle written in Neo-Aramaic, with an English translation. This is a historic and religious appreciation of the collective state of the Christians of Iraq.[2] That such a missive can still be written in Neo-Aramaic (i.e., Aramaic) is a testament to the enduring faith of the remnants of the Christian communities in the Levant and the diaspora. This writer has opted to compose this missive in the literary style so often used on such an occasion. It is meant to move the reader emotionally and spiritually. In sum, such a style of expression becomes a literary way of mourning for a community that is culturally and religiously at the twilight of existence.

---

[1] The intended meaning and sense is: 'Oh my people, I am your native land, why have you, my people, forgotten me and left to the land of exile?'

[2] It should be made clear that this appreciation applies to all the Christians who live in their ancient lands of the Middle East.

SAHDŪṮĀ D-MSAYABRĀNŪṮĀ

Xakma tanayāṯā ta qarāye ʾaḏ Soġītā–zummarta ta ʾaxōna ʿazīza, Rābbi Edward Cook. ʾAn tanayāṯā pišlā milṯa d-zummarta d-tašbōḥta b-lušānā ʾĀrāmāyā, d-muḥkayle b-gāway Mšīḥā Māran. Hul daha k-maḥkā b-ʾaḏ lušāna b-ʾaṯrawāṯa dīlā b-Dašta d-Ninwe b-ʾAṯra d-ʿAbr Nahrain. ʾAḏ lušāna d-bābī w d-yimmī w-lušānī ʾānā ʾīle lušāna ʿatīqa w-šappīra, lušāna d-Suraytūṯā. ʾAn yumāṯā ʾīlā milye ʿisqūṯa w-ʾōqānā. Nāše d-lušānā ʾArāmāyā ʾīlā piše zōre b-ʾaṯrawāṯa d-qamayṯa, badam kullay Surāye pliṭlā min ʾarāṯa w-maṯwāṯā m-sabab ʿillitta d-ʾōqānā rābā dimpille b-ʿalmā Suryāyā.

ʾĀni yumāṯā īlā pīše xiškāne w-ḥaššāne. Bāte w-maṯwāṯā diyyan w-ham ʾaitāṯa ʾīlā pīše xarabwāṯā, w-spīqe m-naše diyyay. ʿAlmā d-Suraytūṯā mšunayle l-ʿalmā d-nixrayūṯā, ʾāxa w-tāmā. Kud k-taxrux šimma d-mḍīta b-ʾaṯran kāwir ḥašša d-libban w-min aynan knaxṯi dime šaxīne. ʾAḏ tuxrāna w-txaryāṯā k-yāwilan šayna d-saybrānūṯā. Maṯla kāmir, 'ʾAṯran pišle bayṯa d-sahdūṯā', kud k-šamux ʿōnyāṯa b-ʾĀrāmāyā kāwir ʾil libbawaṯan šlāma d-Maryā kull ʿiddāna, in hāwux b-ʾaṯrā diyyan lo b-ʾaṯrā d-nixrāyūṯā. Min hādax kṯūli ʾaḏ Sōġītā–Zummarta ta d-paiša dukrāna to ʾAxōnan Edward, malpānā rābā d-lušānā ʾĀrāmāyā, w-ṭālan b-paiša dimyūṯa d-xāye xāṯe. Yā Ālāhā šmayyāna hallan šaina w-šlāmā, mxāliṣlan m-ʾaḏ ʾōqāna d-mōṯā, b-šimm d-Mšīḥa Māran.

Bassīmā rābā Rābbi diyyan. Alāhā yāwillux ḥubba w-raḥmānūṯa. Hāwā yumāṯux milye burukṯa, w-šimšā d-Marya maxūyālux ʾurxā mlīṯā piṣxūṯā w-mšamalyūṯa. Mšīḥa mxalṣāna hāwe immux yōmā w-layle. ʾĀnā, w-ʾaxawāṯī w-xaṯwātī b-ʾaṯra w-nixrāyūṯa, kulan kimṣālux ṭālux, w-kṭalbux min Māran ta d-šāpix illux raḥmūṯay w-ṭaybūṯay. Hāwā malāxe immux kull ʿiddāna.

Tašbōḥta ta ʾĀlāhā d-Šmayyā, w-ʾĀlāhā d-ʿAlmā

TESTIMONIAL TO PATIENT ENDURANCE

These are few remarks to the reader of this Poem-Song composed and presented to our dear friend, Professor Edward Cook. These words are an encomium in Neo-Aramaic, the language spoken by our Lord Jesus Christ. Even in these days, this tongue is spoken in villages that are on the Plain of Nineveh (Dašta d-Ninwe), in Mesopotamia, the land between the two rivers. This language of my father and mother, which is my native tongue, too, is an ancient and beautiful one, language of the Christians in the land called 'Beṯ Nahrain'.

Sadly, these days are days of suffering and grief. Native Aramaic speakers have dwindled in their ancient land, for they have left their abodes as refugees, due to persecution. These times are days of darkness and anguish. Our homes and villages and churches have become ruins and empty of their people. Natives of terra firma of Syriac Christianity have dispersed to the lands of Exile, wherever they found refuge.

When we remember the names of our villages and domiciles, our hearts are full of lamentation, and our eyes shed tears for a requiem. These remembrances and recalling bring unto us peace and solace for forbearance. The proverb speaks of 'lands and homes of the martyrs'. Every time we hear our antiphon in Aramaic, the peace of Christ enters our hearts, whether we are in our native land or that of our exile.

Hence, for this reason I have composed this Poem-Hymn as a testimonial to our brother Edward Cook, a magister of Aramaic language; yet, for us the spirit of this Soġītā is a symbol of a new life. Heavenly Father, bestow on us peace and tranquility, save us from this anguish of suffering; we ask this in the name of our Lord Jesus.

Greeting and salutation, dear illustrious teacher. We ask the Lord to grant you amity and peace. May your days be full of blessings and may the light of Jesus guide you to the path of beatitude and perfection. May the Savior be with you day and night. I and my brothers and sisters, who are in our native lands and in our places of exiles, all of us lift you in our prayers. We ask our Lord Jesus to pour on you His mercy and blessings. And may the angels be with you forevermore.

Praise God of Heaven and God of Earth

A POETICAL ENCOMIUM

Ta
Malpānā Rābā w-Rābā d-Malpānūṯā
Bār
Yulphānā d-Lušānā Ārāmāyā

We the contributors to this Festschrift do hereby take this opportunity to acknowledge Professor Cook's life and scholarly work. In unison we humbly say, 'We have come to extol, acclaim, and convey our encomium' to our esteemed colleague. Joyfully, we proclaim our laudation to our ʾAxōna, on two fortuitous and happy milestones: one, the celebration of Professor Cook's seventieth birthday; two, the presenting of a Festschrift to him for his peerless and illustrious life as a scholar of the language of Aramaic, the spoken tongue of Mšīḥa Māran. While the contribution of this writer to this Festschrift would be classically titled, 'Sōġītā d-Malphānūṯā', in Neo-Aramaic it is more appropriately called 'Zummarta d-Piṣxūṯā', a Song of Joy. But before this Sōġītā (Zummarta) is presented, it is apropos to say a few words about the geographical and linguistic presence of Neo-Aramaic in its ancient, native lands and the diaspora.

Neo-Aramaic (i.e., vernacular Syriac) is characterized by the multiplicity of its 'distinct' dialects. These various dialects have their own appellations. They are grouped together linguistically and geographically and classified as follows:

1. North East Neo-Aramaic (NENA):[3] This group has the two largest number of speakers, ʾĀṯurāyā, often referred to as Assyrian[4] in English, spoken by the members of the Church of the East, who reside in Iraqi Kurdistan, Lake Urmi district, North East Iran, and the diaspora. And Sūraṯ, generally called Chaldean, spoken by members of the Chaldean Catholic Church, throughout Iraq, especially in the Plain of Nineveh[5] and the diaspora.

---

[3] The term NENA was coined in 1988 by Robert Hoberman, Professor of Linguistics, Department of Linguistics, Stony Brook University, New York.
[4] 'Assyrian' is the Anglicized word for ʾĀturāyā, the ancient, historic name for the Assyrian civilization (Syriac ܐܬܘܪܝܐ).
[5] Since the American invasion of Iraq in 2003, most of the Chaldeans have moved to Iraqi Kurdistan and joined others in the diaspora.

An interesting linguistic phenomenon of this group is that often a certain village uses a word that is exclusive to that specific village, to the exclusion of the other surrounding villages. An example of this is that in the town of Tel Kape, a Chaldean Catholic town, the verb used to indicate the act of 'going, leaving' is 'ʾezal' (Syr. ܐܙܠ) while in Alquš, also a Chaldean town, the word used is 'nafaq' (Syr. ܢܦܩ). Often a speaker of either of these two towns might ponder why he is hearing 'nafaq' or 'ʾezal'.

2. West Neo-Aramaic: the dialect of three towns in Syria, whose population is mostly Christian. They are Maʿlūlā and the two smaller ones Jubbaʾdīn and Bakhʿah.[6] This dialect is closer to Classical Syriac. The Christian communities of these towns are of the Melkite Catholic Church and Greek Orthodox Church.
3. Turōyō: This dialect is spoken by a small community of Christians in the historic Christian land of Ṭūr ʿĀbidīn (Mountain of the Faithfuls), situated near the ancient town of Mardin, in southeast Turkey.
4. In the world of the diaspora the number of speakers in the various dialects of Neo-Aramaic is almost equal in size to the speakers of the communities that make up the Syriac churches in their native lands.
5. A very important component of Neo-Aramaic is that of Jewish Neo-Aramaic, spoken by the Jewish community in Iraq for more than two and a half millennia, until their emigration to Israel after the establishment of the State of Israel in 1948.

Though Neo-Aramaic literature is minimal compared to Syriac, it has nevertheless produced a substantial literature, in prose, poetry, and translation. This literary output includes religious and secular texts. The study of Neo-Aramaic language and literature is still in its infancy, for it only began in the nineteenth century. Initially this interest by scholars, especially Europeans, was

[6] The small Muslim communities of these three towns also speak Neo-Aramaic.

influenced by the presence of missionaries from Europe and the United States in Iraq and Urmia (Northwest Iran).

Giving a historical chronology of Neo-Aramaic literature is still problematic due to the paucity of written sources and inadequacy of scholarly research. Based on present scholarship and textual references, it appears that Neo-Aramaic literature appeared in the late 1200's or early 1300's.

Linguistically, the dialects of the Western group are connected to Middle Aramaic, while the Eastern dialects have their nexus in Babylonian Aramaic. The literature of the various dialects has been mostly oral, and historically it was not taught in schools. There have been two important centers for the literature of Neo-Aramaic: one, the town of Alquš, 35 miles north of Mosul, on the Plain of Nineveh, a Chaldean Catholic town; and two, the town of Urmia, in Northwest Iran, where the community is that of the Church of the East.

Since Neo-Aramaic has its own orthography and phonetics it was necessary to follow a phonetic Syriac script as well as transcription. This phonetic transliteration is necessary to ensure an accurate reading of the poem as a Neo-Aramaic text, with its own orthography, consonantal shift, and vocalization system.

The poem composed as my contribution to this Festschrift is written in Neo-Aramaic, following a phonetic transcription. The dialect of this poem belongs to East Neo-Aramaic, but more specifically, the dialect of Tel Kape,[7] located on the Plain of Nineveh,[8] and situated ten miles from the city of Mosul. The Christian community of Tel Kape[9] belongs to the Chaldean Catholic Church.

---

[7] Tel Kape, which was an ancient Assyrian fortification, was the largest Christian town in Iraq. According to the census of the early twentieth century, it had a population of around eleven thousand people. In 1961 its population was around eight thousand. Since 1961 its population has decreased due to wars, struggled between the Iraqi central government and Iraqi Kurdistan region. The final blow occurred in 2014, when ISIS captured the town. It was liberated in 2017. But sadly, today Tel Kape has only around 120 people.

[8] The dialect of the Plain of Nineveh is called Suraṯ. Suraṯ is the native dialect spoken by this writer.

[9] Tel Kape is the ancestral home of the Talia (Syr. ܛܠܝܐ) family, this writer's family, since the early 1700's CE.

ZUMMARTA D-PIṢXŪṮĀ

1. ܒܒܢܝܢܐ ܘܒܢܝܢܐ ܘܦܠܓܘܬܐ ܘܥܡܡܘܢ ܣܡܟܐ ܒܟܠ ܡܬܐ
ܗܐ ܐܢܫܝܢ ܐܬܘܪ̈ܝܐ ܠܚܘܕܐ ܒܗܢܐ ܝܘܡܢ ܒܫܡܫܘܢ ܒܡܒܪܟܝܢܘܬܐ
2. ܒܙܡܪܘܢ ܘܡܗܠܠܘܢ ܒܐܣܝܘܬܐ ܘܫܠܡܐ ܪܒܐ
ܦܪܚܠܗ ܒܟܘܠ ܚܝܠܐ ܘܡܪܐ ܚܝܠܬܐ ܒܪ ܚܝܠܘܬܐ
3. ܐܝܟ ܢܘܗܪܐ ܕܫܠܝܘܬܐ ܘܠܡܢܕܝ ܗܫܐ ܠܒܒܝ ܡܚܐ ܘܗܡܐ
ܡܥܝܢܐ ܗܒܢܝܗܝ ܗܐ ܚܠܡ ܐܝܟܐ ܒܗܡܐ ܘܕܪܡܢܐ ܕܫܠܝܡܘܬܐ
4. ܒܡܦܩܡ ܒܗܒܐ ܡܕܝܢܐ ܒܠܒܢܐ ܗܘܪܫܐ ܠܚܝܡܐ
ܡܕܪܫܝ ܒܗܡܐ ܘܡܪܝܝ ܐܝܟ ܗܐ ܢܠܘܦܐ ܦܝܫܘܬܐ
5. ܡܠܦܗܝ ܐܝܟܐ ܥܡܥܐ ܒܡܫܘܢ ܐܘܪܫܐ ܗܐ ܠܠܡܐ
ܒܗܘܐܝ ܦܥܠܐ ܡܕܒܐ ܘܒܝܗ ܡܥܡܠܝܘܬܐ
6. ܡܢ ܙܘܥܐ ܠܚܝܡܐ ܒܗܘܠܝ ܦܥܝܡܘܬܐ ܘܡܒܗܒܝܘܬܐ ܕܥܠܡܘܬܐ
ܗܘܠܐ ܐܡܝ ܙܠܘܪܐ ܘܪܒܐ ܗܐ ܕܥܡܠܝ ܡܥܝ ܡܕܒܪܢܘܬܐ
7. ܒܡܘܠܘܦ ܒܗܘܝ ܕܐܒܗܐܬܐ ܠܥܝܢܘܬܐ ܐܪܡܝܐ
ܐܝܟ ܡܕܒܐ ܡܠܝܠܐ ܡܠܝܐ ܡܠܬܐ ܕܡܠܝܠܘܬܐ
8. ܪܒܘܝ ܗܠܡܝܕܘܢ ܦܥܠܐ ܡܠܦܢܐ ܘܡܠܦܢܘܬܐ ܒܐܗܒܘܠ
ܒܕܡ ܡܝܘܢ ܥܡܠ ܡܕܪܒܢܐ ܘܗܒܝ ܡܗܪܝܘܬܐ
9. ܐܝܟ ܪܥܝ ܗܒܐ ܡܕܪܥܢܐ ܡܕܒܝ ܒܐܡܪ ܚܝܘܬܐ
ܒܠܘܒܥ ܠܒܥܐ ܕܡܡܪܘܢ ܗܡܘܡܐ ܕܡܠܦܢܘܬܐ
10. ܠܐ ܐܝܗ ܒܥܐ ܒܘܐܗܝ ܐܕ ܠܒܒܪܐ ܕܝܕܥܘܬܐ ܘܡܡܕܡܘܬܐ
ܒܕܡ ܐܠܗܐ ܒܡܒܪܒܠܝ ܒܝܕܥܬܐ ܕܡܦܥܡܘܬܐ
11. ܥܒܐ ܢܪܝܒ ܐܝܟ ܡܠܦܢܐ ܕܠܥܢܐ ܡܥܝܢܐ
ܡܣܒܠܐ ܒܟܘܠ ܡܥܝܢܐ ܡܪܝ ܡܪ ܡܣܠܝܘܬܐ
12. ܗܠܝܟܝ ܡܥܝܢܘܬܐ ܒܡܪܘܝ ܡܘܗܒܬܐ ܕܡܠܟܡ
ܐܝܟܐ ܡܘܗܒܬܐ ܡܠܠܬܐ ܡܢ ܡܕܝܢܘܬܐ
13. ܒܡܠܐ ܠܠܝܐ ܒܡܪܘܢ ܙܘܠܝܬܐ ܡܠܝܬܐ ܒܗܡܘܬܐ
ܡܪܝ ܡܥܘܣܬܐ ܗܐ ܡܒܪܘܙܐ ܡܪ ܦܪܘܥܐ ܘܡܗܢܪܘܬܐ
14. ܒܗܘܝ ܣܐ ܒܣܐ ܡܐܡܕ ܪܒܝ ܕܝܢ ܡܪ ܢܕܥܝܘܬܐ
ܡܗܪܦܘ ܘܡܗܠܗܠܘ ܒܦܝܣܘܬܐ ܗܐ ܡܪ ܡܥܝܢܘܬܐ
15. ܡܥܒܝܘ ܐܠܗܐ ܒܕܡ ܥܒܒܝ ܥܒܐ ܣܐ ܡܠܝ ܥܝܢܘܬܐ
ܡܪܐ ܥܡܥܐ ܢܗܒ ܒܣܝ ܢܪܝܢ ܘܣܝܘܬܐ ܕܒܪܝܘܬܐ
16. ܐܣܐ ܡܥܝܥܐ ܐܝܘܗ ܡܒܘܐܕܗ ܙܡܪܐ ܒܗܘܪܐ
ܠܐ ܥܝܡ ܐܕ ܠܥܝܐ ܕܡܣܒܠܐ ܒܟܘܠ ܒܪ ܣܝܢܘܬܐ
17. ܐܕܝܘ ܝܘܡܢ ܦܥܠܝ ܒܗܢܐ ܒܗܠܦܢܘܢ ܘܒܪܘܙܘܬܘܢ ܡܠܝܬܐ ܣܠܝܘܬܐ
ܥܦܪܐ ܒܡܦܥܡܗ ܒܗܒܐ ܡܕܝܢܐ ܐܝܗ ܒܪ ܡܗܪܝܘܬܐ

18. ܫܡܝܐ ܐܣܘܪܬܐ ܘܣܗܘܪܬܐ ܡܠܟ ܘܡܠܟܘܬܐ
ܡܢܘܪܐ ܕܝܢ ܛܠܠ ܟܘܠ ܒܠܫܢܐ ܘܡܟܬܒܢܘܬܐ
19. ܡܕܝܢܬܐ ܘܡܠܟܘܬܐ ܗܐ ܫܢܐ ܕܐܬܛܠܩܘܢ ܘܦܫܝܛܘܬܐ
ܒܪ ܕܘܝܕ ܦܠܓܐ ܫܢ ܗܐ ܕܦܘܫ ܫܘܐܐ ܘܛܘܒܢܘܬܐ
20. ܢܩܒܐ ܡܕܝܢܬܐ ܒܪܫܬܐ ܗܐ ܠܟܡ ܡܫܝܚܐ ܡܪ ܡܕܝܢܬܐ
ܡܪ ܠܫܢܬܐ ܐܠܗܐ ܒܡܫܘܠܡܘܢ ܐܘܪܚܐ ܡܠܟܬܐ ܦܘܩܕܐ ܕܡܫܡܫܢܘܬܐ
21. ܡܢ ܐܢܫܐ ܘܫܠܡܐ ܘܒܢܝܐ ܕܐܚܘܬܐ
ܡܪܝܐ ܒܡܒܟܠܢ ܡܫܡܠܐ ܛܠܠ ܒܪ ܡܫܡܪܢܘܬܐ
22. ܣܘܡܘ ܠܐ ܚܠܡܐ ܡܢܗܘ ܗܐ ܡܫܡܫܢܐ ܕܟܪܝܣܬܐ ܕܡܫܡܫܢܘܬܐ
ܒܡܫܪܐ ܐܪܡܢܐ ܫܠܘܡ ܫܒܘܩܐ ܒܡܫܘܠܡ ܟܪܝܣܬܐ
23. ܡܕܪܫܐ ܦܫܠܐ ܡܢܗܝܬܐ ܕܗܫܪܘܬܐ ܘܡܢܒܪܢܘܬܐ
ܡܢ ܒܫܡܘܗ̄ ܫܡܐ ܕܐܬܪܐ ܒܦܠܚܘܗ̄ ܒܫܘܬܐ
24. ܫܘܪ ܐܠܝ ܒܪ ܦܘܩܕܐ ܘܒܪ ܐܡܘܠܐ ܘܒܪ ܡܘܫܐ
ܡܦܪܫܐ ܕܝܢ ܠܟܡܝܐ ܒܡܛܝܐ ܡܠܟܬܐ ܡܫܘܢܘܬܐ
25. ܐܝܢ ܡܪ ܢܘܗܪܐ ܡܢܝܢܐ ܛܠܠ ܫܒܘܬܐ ܕܗܘܪܝܘܬܐ
ܠܐ ܡܫܝܚܐ ܡܪܝ ܦܠܚ ܫܠܡܐ ܒܢܝܐ ܫܡ ܕܘܡܐܢܘܬܐ
26. ܐܢܫ ܒܘܠܢ ܒܒܪܝܢܘܬܐ ܕܡܢܝܬܐ ܘܐܬܪܘܬܐ
ܛܠܘܗ̄ ܒܛܝܒܘܬܐ ܡܢ ܠܟܡ ܡܫܬܐ ܘܛܝܒܘܬܐ
27. ܡܗܘܬܝ ܒܦܠܛܐ ܒܢ ܢܘܡܐ ܗܢܫܡܐ ܡܢ ܒܐܡܪܐ
ܫܐ ܒܫܐ ܐܢܫ ܒܗܒܪܐ ܗܐ ܐܫܘܢ ܡܪ ܡܒܝܢܝܢܘܬܐ
28. ܦܘܫ ܚܡܢ ܐܢܝܘ ܘܢܦܪܐ ܢܘܡܘܗ̄ ܡܠܟ ܛܝܒܘܬܐ
ܦܠ ܫܢܐ ܗܠܟܬܐ ܗܘܪܝܐ ܒܡܫܝܚ ܒܛܘܝ ܒܪ ܢܫܐ ܘܡܪ ܕܡܠܟܘܬܐ
29. ܐܠܝ ܡܢܝܐ ܡܠܟܐ ܡܠܟܐ ܡܠܟܬܐ ܕܡܠܟܘܬܐ
ܒܡܘܠܦ ܡܘܕܥܬܐ ܘܡܘܕܥܢܐ ܕܡܘܕܥܢܘܬܐ ܕܦܫܝܛܘܬܐ
30. ܡܪܝܐ ܫܦܝ ܠܪܫܡܘܗ̄ ܒܪܚܬܐ ܢܘܡܐ ܒܗܪ ܢܘܡܐ
ܒܡܫܒܪܚܠܘܗ̄ ܗܫܡܫܬܐ ܘܐܢܫܪܐ ܘܡܫܡܪܢܘܬܐ
31. ܪܫܘܡܐ ܐܝ ܡܪܢܘܬܐ ܦܪܘܫܐ ܚܝܢܘܗ̄ ܐܡܢ ܒܢ ܦܘܫ
ܐܢܫ ܦܝܫ ܒܛܘܗ̄ ܒܢܡ ܐܢܫܐ ܛܠܠ ܡܪܫܝܢܘܬܐ
32. ܠܐ ܡܪ ܗܦܝܘܬܐ ܘܡܫܒܚܬܐ ܗܫܡܘܗ̄ ܡܫܝܚܐ ܘܡܠܫܢܘܬܐ
ܡܢ ܕܒܫܡܫܠܘܗ̄ ܒܦܫܐ ܦܘܫܐ ܘܒܪ ܡܦܘܫܘܬܐ
33. ܚܘܝܘܐ ܡܫܒܚܐ ܡܠܟܐ ܡܫܝܚܘܬܐ ܘܐܡܪܐ ܡܫܒܝܚܘܬܐ
ܗܐ ܗܘܪܝܐ ܕܚܠܡܐ ܐܠܝ ܒܡܬܐ ܦܘܫܡܐ ܘܡܢܪܒܝܢܘܬܐ
34. ܡܠܒܢ ܕܡܪܝܐ ܫܘܕܝܢܘܗ̄ ܗܢ ܡܫܘܬ ܐܘܪܚܐ ܘܐܘܪܚܬܐ
ܒܘܢ ܘܘܐ ܒܗܠܠܒܘܗ̄ ܡܢ ܦܪܘܡܐ ܗܐ ܕܢܘܠܘܗ̄ ܦܪܡܝܢܘܬܐ
35. ܡܛܦܝܐ ܘܡܫܡܫܢܐ ܒܗܫܡܝܬܐ ܡܠܟܬܐ ܒܦܪܝܐ
ܗܐ ܫܘܪܝ ܐܘܝ ܡܫܘܝܐ ܕܐܘܪܚܐ ܘܡܪ ܡܦܫܡܫܢܘܬܐ

36. ܩܘܡܘ ܡܢ ܫܢܬܐ ܗܘܘ ܫܡܘ ܡܢ ܐܕܝ ܡܪܐ ܡܕܪܒܘܬܐ
ܡܪܘ ܠܫܡܫܐ ܗܐ ܕܫܠܡܘܬܟ ܡܦܪܩܢܘܬܐ ܘܡܦܪܩܢܘܬܐ
37. ܡܫܡܠܝܐ ܒܒܘܪܝ ܣܠܠܠܐ ܕܕܗܒܐ ܘܐܠܡܣܐ
ܡܫܢܐܝ ܟܠܘܬܐ ܕܢܘܗܪܘܬܐ ܣܒܪܐ ܡܠܝܐ ܫܒܝܪܘܬܐ
38. ܐܢܝ ܒܪ ܫܒܐ ܒܦܝܚ ܒܠܘܝ ܡܫܝܚܐ ܒܪ ܟܘܒܢܝܬܐ
ܡܫܡܫܢܐ ܒܪܝܟܐ ܐܫܘܢܐ ܗܐ ܒܘܠܟ ܘ ܡܫܡܫܢܐ ܡܢ ܕܡܟܘܬܐ
39. ܝ ܡܠܟܐ ܕܡܠܟܝ ܢܘܗܪܐ ܕܢܘܠܟܝܘܬܟ ܡܫܡܫܘܬܐ
ܡܘܡܘܪܐ ܘܡܝܪܝ ܝ ܒܒܐ ܕܡܪܝܢܝܬܐ ܡܠܝܬܐ ܟܝܣܘܬܐ
40. ܦܘܫ ܒܫܠܡܐ ܡܪ ܕܡܠܟܘܬܐ ܗܘܝ ܐܡܘܟ
ܒܟܠܟܘܟ ܡܢ ܐܠܗܐ ܗܠ ܗܐ ܐܫܘܢ ܢܫܒܐ ܕܒܫܡܘܬܐ

ZUMMARTA D-PIṢXŪṮĀ

1. B-šaynā w-šaynā w-ṭawātā w-qāmux qaymā kullā māṯā
Yā ʾaxōnan Edward ʿazīzā, bhayre yoman, k-qaymux b-mšabḥūṯā
2. K-zamrux w-mḥaluxlux b-ʾaxōnūṯa ta-malpānā rābā
Pṣixlan b-gāwaye, ḥakīma w-mar ḥikimṯa bar ḥikmūṯā
3. ʾĪle nuhrā d-yulpānūṯa, talmīḏe ṯaylā gaybe, māxā w-tāmā
Qaššīšā, tašʿīṯay tā kullan ʾīllā basmā w-darmānā d-ḥalīmūṯā
4. Ki-mpāšiq kṯāwā qaddišā b-lušānā Suryāyā ʿatīqā
Madrāše bassīme w-qiryāne ʾīlā tā yalōpe naṣīhūṯā
5. Malaptay ʾīlā šimšā, k-maxūya ʾurxā tā ʿalmā
Kṯawāne pišlā madʿā w-bayt mšamlāyūṯā
6. Min zōnā ʿatīqā kṯūle pašīqūṯā w-makitbānūṯā d-šalmūṯā
Tūlā ʾimme zōre w-rābe tā d-šaqli minne mdabrānuṯā
7. K-mōlip kṯawāne d-ʾabahāṯa, lašnānūṯā ʾĀrāmāyā
ʾīle madʿā malīlā, milyā milṯā d-malīlūṯā
8. Rābōni, talmīdux, pšilā malpāne w-malpanyāṯā bʾeskōlā
Badam minux šqillā madirkānā w saggī mnahrānūṯā
9. ʾil rayše tāgā d-madaršānā, madʿay kāmir ḥaqqūṯā
K-lāwiš labāša d-maqrōyā smōqā d-malpānūṯā
10. Lā ʾīṯ xinna xwāṯay, ʾaḏ gaḇrā d-yaḏʿūṯa w-mqaḏmūṯā
Badam ʾĀlāhā ki-mbārikle b-yaḏʿīṯa d-mafišqānūṯā
11. Šinne yarīxe ʾīle malpānā d-lušānā Mšīḥāyā
Muḥkayle b-gāwe Mšīḥā Māran, mar mxalṣānūṯā
12. Ṯilayle mašīḥūṯā b-mayrūn mawhabtā d-malkan
ʾīle mawhabtā malalṯā min qadimūṯā
13. B-qālā ʿilyā k-qārux Soġītā mlīṯā bassīmūṯā
Qārin mašuḥtā ta makirzānā parōšā mar mahīrūṯā

14. Kaṯwy xā bixā, qāmiḍ rabbi diyyan mar yaḍʿānūṯā
Mṭarpu w-mhalihlu piṣxūta ta mar mašyānūṯā
15. Mšabḥu ʾĀlāhā badam šōʾiy šinne xāye milye šaynūṯā
Maryā šmayyānā yahib b-xāye yarīxe w-ḥayūṯā d-baryūṯā
16. ʾĀxā qašīšā ʾīwiṯ miḫwāḍit ṣayra bahurā
Lā našit ʾaḍ lušānā d-muḥkayle b-gāwe Bar Hannānūṯā
17. ʾīdyu yoman pišle bhīrā b-yulpānux w-kārōzuṯux xlīṯā
Šappirā ki-mpašqit kṯāwā qaddišā, ʾāyit bar mnahrānūṯā
18. Šmūʾu, ʾaxāwāṯi w-xaṯwāṯi, malpāne w-malpanyāṯā
Myuqrā diyyan, ṭālan kāwe balsāma w mnahrānūṯā
19. Marigšānā w-malīlāyā ta ḥubbā d-haymānūṯā
Bar Dāwīd halle xāye ta d-hāwā ʿōna w-ṭubānūṯā
20. Nafše marganīṯā brixtā, ta lušānā ʾAṯrāyā, mar qaddīšūṯā
Mar yalīpūṯa, ʾĀlāhā ki-myāwille ʾurxā mlīṯā puqdānā d-maskanūṯā
21. Minnan ʾīqārā w-šlāma, w-kabīra d-ʾʾaxawūṯā
Marya ki-mbaʾaylan muṯayle baynāṯan bar myāqrānūṯā
22. Qūmu yā ʿalmā maṣīṯu ta mašimʿānā d-mhadyānūṯā
K-maqre ʾĀrāmāyā, ḥalūya xdūša, k-maxwaylan šarīrūṯā
23. Madrāše pišlā qiṣṣityāṯā d-tixrōnā w-mṣaybrānūṯā
Kuḍ k-šamux šimmi d-ʾaṯran, k-naplux bixyūṯā
24. Xōr, ʾīle bar pōšāqā w-bar nafšā w-bar quštā
Mafraštā diyye li-šmayya k-maṭyā, mlīṯā mahūnūṯā
25. ʾAḍi bar nahrā mudayre ṭālan šabḥūṯā d-suraytūṯā
Yā Mšīḥā Māran hallan šlāma b-ʾāni šinne dōqānūṯā
26. Kullay yumāṯā ʾīwux b-nixrāyūṯa d-mḍīta w-ʾaṯrawātā
Ṭālux k-taʾnux min libban mintā w-ṭaybūṯā
27. Maṯwāṯan k-palṭi kuḍ yomā ta d-šami mā kāmrit
Xā bi-xā ʾīwux bi-spāra ta ʾaxonan mar mbaynānūṯā

28. Poš ʿimman ʾidyu w-ṣaprā, yumāṯux milye ṭaybānūṯā
Hal xāye ta lušānā Suryāyā, k-maḥke b-gāwe bar nāšā w-Mar d-malkūṯā
29. ʾīle maḏʿā malīlā, milyā milṯā d-malīlūṯā
K-mōlip mōdiʿṯa w-mōdʿāna d-haymānūṯā
30. Maryā šāpix l-rayšux burkāṯā ʾidyu w-kullay yumāṯā
Ki-mšadruxlux tašmaštā w-ʾīqāra w-myaqrānūṯā
31. Raḥūqā in qarīwā hāwit, gyānux ʿimman biḏ hōyā
ʾīwux pṣīxe b-gāwux, badam ʾīwut ṭālan marīmānūṯā
32. Yā mar sahdūṯā w maḥšabtā, tanayāṭux mišḥā w-malḥamūṯā
Man d-k-šāmaylux k-payeš hōnānā w-bar mahūnūṯā
33. ʿazīzā maḥkamānā milyā makkīxūṯā w-ʾimmā mšabḥānūṯā
Ta surāye d-ʿalmā ʾīle k-maṯe pušāqā w-madraknānūṯā
34. Malāxe d-maryā xawiḏrānux, ta d-maxwit ʾurxā w-ʾurxātā
Kuḏ zōnā kṭalbux min pārōqā ta d-yāwillux purqānūṯā
35. Qaṭfānā w-maqīmānā b-tanayāṯā milye bahrānā
Ta xūray ʾāwu maxzyānā durxā w-mar farīšūṯā
36. Qūmu mšinṯā, hayyō w-šmūʾu ʾil ʾādī mar farmīṯā
Qrūwu ʾil daṯ ḥakīma ta d-šaqlūtun mafargānūṯa w-mafargūṯā
37. Mšamilyānā k-bahre xiklīlā d-dehwā w-ʾalmāsā
Tanayāṯe ṣlōṯā d-yahībūṯā, gaḇrā milyā naḥšīrūṯā
38. ʾādī bar nāšā d-k-pāṣix b-gāwe Maran Mšiḥā Bar ṭubanīṯā
Mšamšānā brīḫa, ʾaxōnā ta kulan w-maqīmā min di-mxūṯā
39. Yā malkā d-malpāne, nuhrā d-yulpānux ḫaqqūṯa
Mazmōrā zmayran yā bābā d-marʿīṯā naṣīḥūṯā
40. Pōš bišlāma, Mšīḥā hāwe ʿimmux mār d-malkūṯā
Kṭalbux min ʾĀlāhā, hal ta ʾaxōnan nafšā d-bassīmūṯā

1. Peace and tranquility unto you, the village rises for you in greeting
Our beloved brother, Edward, this day is brightened as we assemble in humble praising
2. We come serenading you in brotherhood, oh cherished magister, caroling and chanting
We rejoice in him, a wise soul and lover of wisdom, who is of wisdom possessing
3. He is an ocean of omniscience, witness his pupils coming from near and afar, at his feet sitting
Hark, this our colleague, his expositions for us all blessing, and spiritually healing
4. The Holy Book he enunciates in Aramaic, the language beknown from long time passing
His discourses are mellifluous, his readings for the studious a splendid preaching
5. Having explications illuminating like the sun, for they bring to the world much evincing
His tomes are an inspiration and a fount given to perfecting
6. From days of langsyne he took to exegesis of the Holy Writ effectuated with teaching
There sat with him young and old, that from him they inherit his tutoring
7. Omnibus of the Church Fathers he analyzes, when engaged in Aramaic annotating
He is endowed with acumen, yes, and perspicacity, ordained with dialectics of reasoning
8. Oh Malphana, your pupils are now professoriate in collegiate centers of learning
For indeed, from you they received erudition and much enlightening
9. On his temple he wears a crown illuminating and exuding truthful discerning
He dons the red frock of lecturing, a symbol of his sagacious nurturing
10. None unto us is like him, he is the spirit of lucidity and apperceiving
Surely the Lord has blessed him with perspicuity penetrating
11. Many a year in Aramaic he has been initiating
This, the language of our Lord Jesus, bestower of life everlasting
12. From the Savior he has received his forte of intuition inspiring
When young, the gift of the language he took to mastering

13. Loudly we chant this Ṣoġītā imbued with sweet phrasing
These words we enunciate to our schoolman, doyen of articulating
14. One by one they assemble before our Talmudist, exemplar of schooling
Come sing and acclaim with joy, he who is always exhorting
15. Give praise to the Lord, for he is seventy in generation, all full of peacemaking
Heavenly Father, bestow on him long survivance and a pilgrimage given to creating
16. You, our brother, are the moon, always giving an illuminating
Do not forget the language of the Messiah, whose grace is ready for the giving
17. Our day is illumined by your all-knowing and your noble mentoring
God's words you interpret harmoniously, you are master of expounding
18. My brethren preceptors give heed to my saying,
Our esteemed one is for us a salutary balm, a savant for inculcating
19. A luminary endowed with insight, and fidelity in faith keeping
Oh, Son of David, on him confer a life of succor and love exceeding
20. A bread of life he is to our tongue of Mesopotamia, full of blessing
Oh, great Master, the Lord gave you a path of grace and humble living
21. In the spirit of companionship we offer you our salutation in our proclaiming
The All Merciful surely ministers to us, for he brought us one venerable, worthy of honoring
22. Come, oh you bibliophile, listen to him who comes gracefully guiding
In Aramaic, sweet as honey and for us truthtelling
23. His theological oeuvres speak to our memories and forbearing
When hearing the name of our native land, we fall into tears shedding
24. See this doyen of Aramaic exegesis, a rational soul, with truth bearing
His eloquence ascends unto heaven, full of percepting

25. This heir of light has restored us to the path of Christian anointing
Lord Jesus, bestow on us peace in these days of persecuting
26. Daily from our villages and motherland are exiles sojourning
We are grateful to you, from heart to heart we say, a heartfelt gratitude and God's blessing
27. Our community of faithfuls daily come to you listening
One by one we await you, oh confrere, and a scholar for the spirit nurturing
28. Remain with us today and the morrow, you are for us a fount of blessing exceeding
You nourish Aramaic, language of the Surāye and that of the Lord Jesus who bestows the Kingdom everlasting
29. A savant he is, endowed with rationale and lucent understanding
The wit of rumination he teaches those who approach him for schooling
30. May the All Holy shower you with his benediction, and life lasting
To you we proffer our homage and deference, these words of honoring
31. Whether far or near to us, your spirit is with us abiding
We rejoice in you, you are a spring that keeps exalting
32. Oh, master of truth and understanding, your words are fittingly to us an anointing
He who harkens to you is a literatus in the making
33. A beloved colleague, full of humility, given to Christian celebrating
The followers of the Nazarene he fosters with interpolation penetrating
34. May the angels of the Lord surround you as the pathway of life you take to showing
Every sunrise we call on Jesus the Christ to accord you his salvation everlasting
35. By his word he is the truth of the ancients restoring
To his friends he shows the way and makes their path radiating
36. Ye, awake from your dormancy, come to listen to him, he who is percepting
Approach this Solomon, that you receive from him splendorous initiating

37. A veritable paragon of knowledge, like golden diadem and diamonds his diction is edifying
His words are a gift of prayers, he is a companion given to exulting
38. In him the Son of the Virgin Mary is indeed rejoicing
This holy deacon, a companion to us all, he awakens us from our slumbering
39. Oh primus inter pares, illumination of your schooling is truth confirming
We cantillate a psalm for you, oh host of splendiferous declaiming
40. Peace be unto you, may God of the heavenly kingdom be to you safeguarding
We ask our Lord, to our master of teaching, shower on him all the blessing

BIBLIOGRAPHICAL REFERENCES

This bibliography is hereby included as reference material for readers who are interested in the comparative philology of Neo-Aramaic dialects, as well as Semitic philology.

Blanc, Haim, *Communal Dialects in Baghdad* (Harvard Middle Eastern Dialects Monographs, 10, Cambridge: Harvard University, 1964).

Fiey, Jean M., *Assyrie chrétienne: Contribution à étude de l'histoire et de la géographie ecclésiastiques et monastiques du Nord d l'Iraq* (Beirut: Institute de Lettres Orientales de Beyrouth, 1965–1969).

Hetzron, Robert D., 'The Morphology of the Verb in Modern Syriac (Christian colloquial of Urmi)', *JAOS* 89 (1969), pp. 112–127.

Heberman, Robert, *The Syntax and Semantics of Verb Morphology in Modern Aramaic. A Jewish Dialect of Iraqi Kurdistan* (AOS, 69, New Haven: American Oriental Society, 1988).

———. 'The History of Modern Aramaic Pronouns and Pronominal Suffixes', *JAOS* 108 (1988), pp. 557–575.

———. 'Reconstructing Pre-modern Aramaic Morphology: The Independent Pronouns', in W. Heinrichs (ed.), *Studies in Neo-Aramaic* (HSS, 36, Atlanta: Scholars Press, 1989) pp. 79-88.

———. 'The Chaldean Aramaic of Zakho', in R. Contini, F.A. Pennacchietti, and M. Tosros (eds.), *Semitica: Serta Philologica Constantino Tsereteli Dictata* (Turin: Silvio Zamorani, 1993) pp. 115–126.

Jastrow, Otto, *Die Mesopotamisch-Arabischen Qəltu-Dialect* (Band I, Phonologie and Morphologie, Abhandlungen für die Kunde des Morgenlandes 43/4, Wiesbaden: Franz Steiner, 1978).

———. 'Tikrit Arabic Verb Morphology in a Comparative Perspective', *Al-Abhath* 31 (1983), pp. 99-110.

Khan, Geoffrey, *A Grammar of Neo-Aramaic: The Dialect of the Jews of Arbel* (HdO, 1, The Near and Middle East, 47, Leiden: Brill, 1999).

———. 'Quelques aspects de l'expression d' 'être' en neoaraméen', in Anaïd Donabédian (ed.), *Langues des Diaspora. Langues et*

Contact (Faits de Langues de Linguistique, 18, Paris: Ophrys, 2001) pp. 139-148.

———. *The Neo-Aramaic Dialect of Qaraqosh* (Studies in Semitic Languages and Linguistics, 36, Leiden: Brill, 2002).

Krotkoff, Georg, *Neo-Aramaic Dialect of Kurdistan: Texts, Grammar and Vocabulary* (AOS, 64, New Haven: American Oriental Society, 1985).

Maclean, Arthur John, *Grammar of the Dialects of Vernacular Syriac* (Cambridge: Cambridge University, 1895).

———. *A Dictionary of the Dialects of Vernacular Syriac as Spoken by the Eastern Syrians of Kurdistan North-West Persia, and the Plain of Mosul* (Oxford: Clarendon, 1901).

Mingana, Alphonse, *Clef de langue araméenne: ou, grammaire complète et pratique des deux dialectes syriaques, occidental et oriental* (Mosul: Imprimerie des Péres Dominicains, 1905).

Mutzafi, Hezy, 'The Neo-Aramaic Dialect of Maha Khtaya d-Baz = Phonology, Morphology and Texts', *JSS* 45/2 (2000), pp. 293–322.

Nöldeke, Theodor, *Grammatik der neusyrischen Sprache am Urmi-See und in Kurdistan* (Leipzig: T.O. Weigel, 1868).

Polotsky, Hans, 'Studies in Modern Syriac', *JSS* 6 (1961), pp. 1–32.

———. 'Eastern Neo-Aramaic: Urmi and Zakho', in Franz Rosenthal (ed.), *Aramaic Handbook* (Porta linguarum Orientalium, 4 parts, Wiesbaden: Harrassowitz, 1967), ii.1, pp. 73–77; ii.12, pp. 104–111.

Rhétore, Jean, *Grammaire de langue Soureth: Mosul* (Mosul: Imprimerie des Péres Dominicains, 1912).

Rubba, J., 'Forms Derived from Verbal Roots in Tisqoopa Modern Aramaic', in R. Contini, F.A. Pennacchietti and M. Tosco (eds.), *Semitica: Serta Philologica Constantino Tsereteli Dicata* (Turin: Silvio Zamorani, 1993) pp. 273–287.

Sabar, Yona, 'From Tel-Kēpe in Iraqi Kurdistan to Providence, Rhode Island: The Story of a Chaldean Immigrant to the United States of America in 1927', *JAOS* 98/4 (1978): pp. 410-415.

———. 'A Folktale and Folk Songs in the Christian Neo-Aramaic Dialect of Tel-Kēpe (Northern Iraq)', in R. Contini, F.A.

Pennacchietti and M. Tosco (eds.), *Semitica: Serta Philologica Constantino Tsereteli Dicata* (Turin: Silvio Zamorani, 1993) pp. 289-297.

Sachau, Edward, *Skizze des Fellichi-Dialekt von Mosul* (Königlich-Preussischen Akademie der Wissenschaften zu Berlin, Berlin: Georg Reimer, 1895).

Sara, Solomon, *A Description of Modern Chaldean* (Janua Linguarum, Series Practica, 213, The Hague: Mouton, 1974).

———. 'Feminine Gender in Modern Chaldean: Form and Function', in W. Heinrichs (ed.), *Studies in Neo-Aramaic* (HSS, 36, Atlanta: Scholars Press, 1990) pp. 45–52.

———. 'Marked Gender in Modern Chaldean [ta/θa] Suffix', in R. Contini, F.A. Pennacchietti and M. Tosco (eds.), *Semitica: Serta Philologica Constantino Tsereteli Dicata* (Turin: Silvio Zamorani, 1993) pp. 229-308.

Socin, Albert, *Die Neu-aramäischen Dialekte von Urmia bis Mosul. Text und Übersetzung* (Tübingen: Laupp, 1882).

Tsereteli, K., 'The Aramaic Dialects of Iraq', *AION* 22 (1972), pp. 245–250.

Milton Keynes UK
Ingram Content Group UK Ltd.
UKHW021431021224
3319UKWH00007B/126

9 781463 24583